White Magic

The Age of Paper

Lothar Müller

Translated by Jessica Spengler

polity

First published in German as *Weiße Magie* © Carl Hanser Verlag München 2012

This English edition © Polity Press, 2014

The translation of this work was funded by Geisteswissenschaften International – Translation Funding for Humanities and Social Sciences from Germany, a joint initiative of the Fritz Thyssen Foundation, the German Federal Foreign Office, the collecting society VG WORT and the Börsenverein des Deutschen Buchhandels (German Publishers & Booksellers Association).

Polity Press
65 Bridge Street
Cambridge CB2 1UR, UK

Polity Press
350 Main Street
Malden, MA 02148, USA

ISBN-13: 978-0-7456-7253-3

A catalogue record for this book is available from the British Library.

Library of Congress Cataloging-in-Publication Data

Müller, Lothar, 1954-
  [Weisse Magie. English]
  White magic : the age of paper / Lothar Müller.
    pages cm
  ISBN 978-0-7456-7253-3 (jacketed hardback : alk. paper) 1. Paper–History.
2. Papermaking–History. 3. Paper industry–History. 4. Printing–History. I. Title.
  TS1090.M8513 2014
  676–dc23
                              2014019958

Typeset in 10.5 on 12 pt Sabon
by Toppan Best-set Premedia Limited
Printed and bound in the United Kingdom by Clays Ltd, St Ives PLC

For further information on Polity, visit our website: politybooks.com

Contents

〜

Thanks

Paper is accommodating, and that's what makes it such a wide field. It's not a field you can till on your own. I would like to thank Martin Bauer for his continual reading of the text, and his suggestions and objections right from the start; Henning Ritter for discoveries, feedback, and encouragement; Eberhard Sens for extensive supporting work on the basic scaffolding and bibliography; Philippe Despoix for Canadian commentary and the insight into Harold Innis's literary estate; Justus Fetscher—as always—for opening up side doors in the universal library; and Dirk Liebenow for papers from collections in Lower Saxony.

Fortunately, print media are not only made of paper; they are also conversational media. Thank you to my *Süddeutsche Zeitung* colleagues Jens Bisky in Berlin for ideas shared in passing and Thomas Steinfeld in Munich for his parallel commentary and editing.

In every field there are proven experts, and some of them are open to visitors from the neighborhood. I would like to thank Frieder Schmidt, head of the Cultural and Historical Paper Collections in the Museum of Books and Writing of the German National Library in Leipzig, for his enlightening discussions and patient/critical review of the manuscript.

The idea for this book first took shape during a three-month stay at the Institute for Advanced Study in Berlin from October to December 2008. For their suggestions during this hiatus I would like to thank the rector Luca Giuliani, all of the employees, my co-Fellows and, above all, the librarians working for Gesine Bottomley and her successor Sonja Grund.

PROLOGUE

The Microbe Experiment

∽

On November 16, 1932, the French writer Paul Valéry gave a lecture at the Université des Annales in Paris entitled "La politique de l'esprit." In this lecture, he described the present day as a state of chaos which made it impossible to foresee the future. We live, he said, in a civilization based on a kind of trusteeship. Just as banks can only survive as long as all of their account holders do not try to withdraw their deposits at once, civilization can only exist as long as the imaginary resources sustaining it are not suddenly revoked. To illustrate civilization's "*structure fiduciaire*," its dependency on the interplay between trust and credit, Valéry proposed a thought experiment. It was not his idea, he said, but one borrowed from a review he had read long ago of a book by some English or American author whose name he had forgotten. Imagine, Valéry suggested, that a mysterious microbe attacked and swiftly annihilated all of the paper in the world. "No defense, no remedy; it is impossible to find any means of exterminating the microbe or of countering the physiochemical phenomenon attacking the cellulose. The unknown destroyer penetrates drawers and chests, reduces to dust the contents of our pocketbooks and our libraries; every written thing vanishes."[1]

At the time, Valéry knew nothing of the rapid deterioration of paper made from groundwood pulp. The purpose of his thought experiment was to draw attention not to the actual decay of paper but to the fact that paper is omnipresent and indispensable in modern civilization. He needed an image to illustrate a crisis in the ongoing self-preservation of civilization as a whole, not just of literature or the arts. This is why he referred to pocketbooks and libraries in the same breath. He described the civilization around him as having paper coursing through its veins, with social institutions and routines dependent on paper. Imagine a world with no more paper, he said, with no more banknotes, bonds, files, laws, poems, or newspapers.

When Valéry gave his lecture, radio and gramophone technologies were still young and people had just begun to experiment with television. Even cinema, the telegraph, and the telephone had failed to replace paper as the key medium for storing and circulating words, images, and numbers. The tremendous destructive force of Valéry's hypothetical microbe highlighted the ubiquity and universality of paper in modern civilization. His thought experiment revealed all of the places that paper could be found.

The philosopher Jacques Derrida may have been familiar with Paul Valéry's lecture. In a long and very personal interview with the journal *Cahiers de Médiologie* at the end of the last century, in 1997, Derrida stripped the elements of fantasy from Valéry's microbe vision of the year 1932 and transformed the notion of paper's swift, sudden disintegration into a prediction that paper would gradually retreat from the universality that Valéry had in mind. Derrida said we are currently experiencing the kind of shrinkage that Balzac envisioned in his novel *La peau de chagrin*: just as the magical parchment inscribed with Arabic letters retracts in the novel, paper is shrinking and contracting in our world.[2]

Derrida was clever. He did not talk about the end, much less the "death," of paper. He expected paper to continue to have a massive presence in modern civilization even after the explosion of digital media. He only said that the age of paper's structural hegemony as a medium for images and symbols was drawing to a close—and when he spoke of the *"retraite"* or retreat of paper, he did not mean a retreat across the board, but a retreat from key positions.

Derrida had spent his whole life thinking about the written word. In the interview, he described how his writing hand would glide over a sheet of white paper; he talked about writing on a manual typewriter, then on an electric one, and finally on a computer; and he said that the overlapping transitions between these writing routines were a defining experience of his generation. But to both Derrida and Valéry, paper was more than just a writing surface. Derrida, too, talked about the merging of paper, money, and banking—about *"monnaie fiduciaire,"* or paper money, and how it came to be replaced by credit cards and plastic. And he talked about the conflation of legal persons and "papers" in modern society and the problem of the *"sans-papiers,"* the undocumented immigrants in France; in the eyes of the state, I am whatever "my papers" identify me as, even if those papers are actually made of plastic.

This book picks up on Valéry's thought experiment, where the microbe acts as a detector revealing the universality of paper. At the same time, it follows up on Derrida's suggestion that we should contemplate the age of paper's expansion and structural hegemony from the perspective of its retreat.

When we talk about books, letters, and newspapers, we think we understand our world of origin; it exists in our general consciousness as the "Gutenberg era." But decisions go into the establishment of terms like this, and the decision behind the term "Gutenberg era" was to make the printing press, and thus the printed book, into the perspectival anchor of modern media theory. The Canadian media theorist Marshall McLuhan played a key role in popularizing this decision with best sellers such as *The Gutenberg Galaxy* (1962) and *Understanding Media* (1964). Both books portray the printing press as the mother of the modern world and the model for all "media revolutions." For all that historians have vigorously critiqued McLuhan's interpretation of printing and typography in recent decades, his ideas persist in our everyday understanding of the "Gutenberg world." For this reason, several passages in the book at hand analyze the "paper age" in the context of McLuhan's media theory.

Paper is older than the printing press, and its history encompasses far more than just the history of printed paper. Above all, paper is not merely inert matter or a passive object upon which the intellect expresses itself in the form of letters. "Paper, you know," Paul Valéry said in his lecture, "plays the part of a storage battery and a conductor; it conducts not only from one man to another but from one time to another, carrying a highly variable charge of authenticity or credibility."[3] It was not from the world of books that Valéry, the advocate for the mind, borrowed terminology for his incidental media theory of paper. By describing paper as an "*accumulateur*" (storage battery) and "*conducteur*" (conductor), he charged it with energy. This metaphorical electrification moved paper into the realm of batteries and circuits. The book at hand also takes the view that paper is a dynamically energized medium for storage and circulation.

Paper can be folded and creased, crumpled and cut, torn and burnt, covered with numbers, letters, and lines, filed away and pulled out again, mailed or concealed. It comes in a variety of formats and qualities, from notes to folios, from packing paper to decorative paper. The following account cannot compete with Valéry's microbe, which tracks down paper everywhere, in all of its forms. Instead, it attempts to bring together three different ways of looking at paper. The first focuses on paper in its physical, material form, as a product of civilization, something which does not occur naturally in the world but instead requires a technology to produce it. This cursory history of paper technology is largely limited to a European-American perspective; it encompasses Arab paper as the direct precursor to European paper but only looks at Asian papermaking from afar. Every episode in the history of paper technology comes back to the question of how paper became a basic element of Western civilization and how it came to occupy such a key position in the world we think of as the "Gutenberg era."

This leads to the second way of looking at paper, namely, the way it appeared to Paul Valéry: as a storage battery and conductor. This book explores the cultural techniques, infrastructures, and routines in which paper functions as a medium for storing and circulating words, images, and numbers. The printing press is given its due as the single most significant entity in the paper age, but printed and unprinted paper are fundamentally placed on an equal footing. Writing paper appears throughout this book, and glances are thrown in the direction of the postal system which supplied the infrastructure necessary for circulating it. Just as Valéry mentioned libraries and pocketbooks in the same breath, this book looks not only at the blank sheets of authors and scholars but also at the correspondence and accounting techniques of merchants.

The third approach to paper involves looking at the paper age from the inside. Has this age developed an awareness of itself, and, if so, what characteristics does it attribute to paper when it turns its interpretive gaze inward? Paper is more than just a practical basic material; it is a metaphorical resource, a fact that can be seen in our everyday language when we refer to someone as a blank page, when we consider obligations to be honored on paper alone, or when we attempt to turn over a new leaf. Paper metaphors can be found throughout the history of science and ideas, from John Locke's comparison of the human mind with white paper to Saussure's description of the dual nature of linguistic signs as being like two sides of the same piece of paper. It goes without saying that this book can only touch on paper's long history as a material for reflection.

The avenues of exploration have been determined by this author's profession. As a literary scholar and newspaper journalist interested in cultural studies, I have focused in particular on the question of what modern European literature knows about the material from which it is made, as well as on the links between the history of paper technology and the emergence of periodicals. In doing so, I have relied on the fact that, apart from its many other charms, modern literature has the advantage of being an exemplary chronicler of paper. The history of paper therefore goes hand in hand with the history of literature in this book. Art historians would have a different focus; their sights would be set on paper in the graphic arts since Albrecht Dürer and the use of paper in the collages of twentieth-century visual art. Social or economic historians, in turn, would describe the paper production landscapes of Italy, France, and central Europe and the paper trade in more detail; they would hone in on the trade relations and internal social structures of the old paper mills and the economy of eighteenth-century factories and industrial paper plants. Historians of everyday life could not recount the history of paper production without going into an equally detailed history of papermaking at home, in prisons, in factories and plants, and the diffusion of paper in the form of sacks and bags, envelopes and accounting books, and festival and party supplies.

The examples used in this book to illustrate the universality of paper—at least rudimentarily—were not chosen at random. The approach was driven by the author's overriding interest in paper as a medium for words and images, and it coalesces in a general thesis which states that by embedding our media origins in the paper age, we can better understand both the "Gutenberg era" from which we have come and the transitional period we now find ourselves in, as digital paper begins to compete with analog paper. The idea that the "age of books" and the "age of the internet" are in rigid opposition to each other—a view promulgated in talk shows and media debates throughout the first decade of the twenty-first century—is a product of our common understanding of the "Gutenberg era." The book at hand was written to counter the fixation on this supposed opposition, which prevents us from recognizing that the paper-based routines and cultural technologies which have shaped our infrastructures of knowledge, economics, leadership, the arts, and modern public life since the early modern era are antecedents to our digital storage and circulation media. Electronic media and our rapidly expanding digital infrastructure are transforming not just the "Gutenberg world" but the entire paper age. Paper is a virtuoso of substitution. By insinuating itself into existing patterns and routines, it was able to take over key roles in modern civilization, in banks and libraries, post offices and press agencies. It faced no serious competition until the age of the telephone and telegraph. But we have lived for some time now in a world where paper-based routines and cultural technologies, such as written communication over long distances, are being supplanted, supplemented, or transformed by their digital successors. Electronic paper is getting better and better at mimicking its analog counterpart. Newsprint and book paper have accounted for a declining proportion of total paper production since the end of the twentieth century, and elegiac predictions concerning the future role of conventional paper are certainly not in short supply. At the same time, we generally have only a vague awareness of paper's history to date. But since origin stories sometimes tell us more about the future than predictions do, this book only turns its attention to electronic paper after recounting the tale of the analog paper age.

PART ONE

The Diffusion of Paper in Europe

1

Leaves from Samarkand

⟨⟩

1.1. The Arab Intermediate Realm

Paper is a protean substance. It not only refuses to be restricted to a single purpose, it also eludes any attempt to reliably pinpoint its origins. Its roots undoubtedly lie in China, but unlike the European printing press, it is not an invention that can be precisely dated. There is, of course, Ts'ai Lun, the high-ranking court official who, with the support of the emperor, introduced paper on a large scale as a less expensive writing material for administration in 105 AD. But the new material he presented was not an invention plucked from thin air; it was the result of improvements to an older production technique. Modern historians trying to trace the gradual, long-term development of papermaking have uncovered a kind of "proto-paper," derived from plant fibers, which was produced by imitating the methods used to make felt, as well as silk or cotton wadding—but this was still a long way from writing paper. Once a process has become established in the world, it can seem obvious in retrospect. In actuality, though, it must evolve step by step.[4]

Basic Chinese papermaking can be described as follows: "The raw material generally used by Chinese papermakers was the bast fiber of the paper mulberry, which was soaked in water with wood ash and then mechanically processed until the individual fibers separated. To make sheets of paper, screens were employed consisting of cotton or hemp fabric stretched on a wooden frame. The screen floated in water and the fibers were poured onto it from above and distributed evenly by hand. The screen was then lifted out of the water and set

蕩料入簾

Paper production in China. Woodcut by Sung Ying-Hsing, 1634

out to dry with the sheet of paper on it. Only afterwards could it be used for another pass. The daily output of a Chinese papermaker was therefore limited to just a few dozen sheets."[5]

Ts'ai Lun's primary improvement lay in the expansion of the resource base for paper production. According to a chronicle from 450 AD, it was Ts'ai Lun who had the idea to use pieces of hemp, textile scraps, and the remains of fishing nets in papermaking. Essentially, however, paper manufacture arose anonymously and gradually. As it proliferated in China, productivity increased with the introduction of flexible bamboo screens and a wide variety of applications for paper emerged. "It was not just a writing surface, it was used to make windows and doors, lanterns, paper flowers, fans and umbrellas. Toilet paper was produced on a massive scale as early as the ninth century, while paper money was a generally accepted means of payment in the tenth century."[6]

An old tale based on Arab sources describes the first movement of paper from the East to the West. The story says that during a battle in the year 751 between the Arabs and Turkish troops, who fought with Chinese reinforcements, Chinese papermakers were taken prisoner by the Arabs. According to this account, the prisoners were brought from Taraz in Tashkent, the site of the battle, to Samarkand, where they were forced to reveal the secrets of their art. From that point on, paper was produced in and around Samarkand, which the Arabs had conquered in the early eighth century—paper that was in no way inferior to that of the Chinese.

What modern narratives of the history of paper take from this tale is that military conflicts in Central Asia may have accelerated a transfer that had probably begun centuries earlier. The acceleration and violent conquest of secret knowledge from the East as recounted in military history took place against the backdrop of the long-term east-to-west movement chronicled in the history of commerce. The Silk Road was pivotal to the transfer of paper. It was via the routes of the Silk Road that paper had reached Central Asia as a commodity long before Chinese prisoners of war could be forced to give up the secrets of its production. The Silk Road was also a paper road. From this perspective, papermaking was not so much a technology adopted on a specific date as it was a cultural technique that slowly seeped into the Arab world. The inclusion of Chinese paper in long-distance trade triggered the double step that generally takes place when exclusive knowledge is transferred in the form of goods: first a product is imported, then the ability to produce it. The high cost of importing goods over lengthy distances made this kind of double step attractive.

Arab papermakers may have initially continued to use floating screens until the "pour method" was gradually replaced by the dip method. But regardless of the specific modifications made to the technique for creating sheets of paper, Arab papermakers had to adapt the production process to the climatic conditions in their world: they had to keep water consumption to a minimum and find a replacement for the main raw material in Chinese paper, the inner bark of the paper mulberry. It was, above all, this pressure to adapt that pushed the rags, used textiles, and cordage which had at most played a supporting role in China to the center of Arab paper production.

This was the birth of a proto-model for the type of recycling in which a material—such as metal—is not just reclaimed from waste in a different form, but a new, structurally different material is created instead. Paper was henceforth a man-made substance constructed from raw materials that were, for their part, a product of civilization. Granted, even the paper mulberry trees of the Chinese and the papyrus reeds of the Egyptians were not purely "products of nature" since the energies of the civilization around them flowed into their cultivation. But rag paper was free of the natural limits imposed on the propagation of both the paper mulberry native to subtropical southern China and the papyrus of Egypt. Its raw materials could be found wherever people lived, wore suitable clothing, and engaged in trade. Thanks to this freedom from natural, locally bound resources, paper was essentially in a position to spread universally. It took the nomadic nature it already possessed as a long-distance trade product and absorbed it into its material structure, offering little opposition to the surmounting of local production restrictions. As early as the eighth century, paper mills were built in Baghdad, then on the Arabian Peninsula, in Cairo, and in Syria, where paper was produced in Damascus, Tripoli (now in Lebanon), and Hama from the tenth century, and soon began to be exported as well. A Persian traveler in the eleventh century reported that traders in Cairo wrapped their wares in paper, and even in the tenth century, Syria was exporting not just paper to North Africa but also the art of papermaking.[7]

Though papermaking gradually lost its ties to natural raw materials as production shifted to raw materials that were themselves products of civilization, this certainly did not mean that its resource base was boundless. Its raw materials were obtained from cities and villages, not fields and forests, so from the Arab civilization of the Middle Ages until well into the nineteenth century, paper production remained closely linked to factors such as population development and textile production and, on account of its association with ropes and rigging, to the evolution of trade and seafaring.

The history of paper's arrival in Samarkand and its diffusion through the Arab empire was not traced in detail until the late nineteenth century. Joseph von Karabacek, an orientalist and director of the Imperial Library in Vienna, played a major role in this. His essay *Arab Paper* (1887) was based on the study of over 20,000 paper fragments, discovered in the winter of 1877–78 near the Middle Egyptian city of Al-Fayyum and in Hermopolis, which had entered the papyrus collection of Austrian Archduke Rainer. Karabacek translated the fragments dating from the eighth to the fourteenth century and described the wide variety of scripts, colors, and paper formats employed for administration. He mentioned as well the extraordinarily thin "bird paper" that was used for "pigeon post" correspondence and was also popular for love letters. Karabacek published his own translation of the *Umdat al-kuttab*, the only surviving eleventh-century Arabic treatise on papermaking. Finally, he presented a selection of the papers to the public in an exhibition and assembled a catalog which documented paper's wide range of uses and geographic distribution.[8]

At the same time, the botanist Julius Wiesner was researching the material composition of Arab paper using microscopic methods developed for studying plant physiology. He published his findings parallel to Karabacek. The two worked independently of each other, but they followed the same hypothesis—namely, that the Arab world was not just a transit station on paper's journey from China to Western Europe, but that Arab civilization permanently changed the technique for making paper and, in doing so, made a substantial contribution to the upsurge in European paper mills from the thirteenth century onward. With polemical verve, Karabacek pursued his goal of demonstrating that Arab civilization was the source of "rag paper" made from linen scraps and hemp fibers and was therefore the model for European paper production. This parallel historical-antiquarian and scientific-microscopic analysis of Arab paper in Vienna received a few welcome critical responses from the experts, but it barely made an impression on the general consciousness of Europeans. In part, this was because Karabacek and Wiesner were not so much filling a gap in knowledge as they were breaking down an old transmission paradigm.

When Joseph von Karabacek called his essay on Arab paper a "historical and antiquarian enquiry," there was a programmatic accent on this subtitle. What he meant was that his work described Arab paper with the kind of methodological diligence and attention to detail that had previously been reserved for Greek and Roman antiquity. By placing Arab paper in the position of origin with respect to European paper—a position occupied by Chinese paper in Arab culture itself—Karabacek drew attention to a divide that had barely been perceived as such in Europe: the divide separating the European paper of the modern era from the papyrus of the ancient world.

In his commentary on the depiction of papyrus production in Book 13 of Pliny the Elder's *Natural History*, the American paper historian Dard Hunter highlighted the differences between the two writing materials. Papyrus used for writing is made by pasting together thin strips peeled from the core of the plant's stalk and laminating them to create a smooth writing surface, a process most comparable to very fine carpentry. Sheets of paper, on the other hand, are formed when the fibers of the raw material are disintegrated in water and the resulting suspension is scooped out to achieve the desired consistency.[9]

Since the name for paper is derived from the word papyrus (in English and other languages) and, conversely, papyrus was often referred to as "Nile paper," it stood to reason that the European paper which flourished during the Renaissance and in humanism would be perceived as a direct descendant of the papyrus of ancient Greece and Rome and the two materials would be associated as a single unit. In translations of Pliny, the term papyrus was frequently used only in connection with the plant itself, while the product made from it was called paper. The parchment that was so bound up with Christianity and monastic culture, in turn, was the bridge between the papyrus of the ancient world and the paper of the modern one. This left merely a supporting role for Arab paper. Even well into the twentieth century, overviews of the history of paper reduced the centuries-long story of Arab paper to brief formulaic statements: "Knowledge of papermaking reached the West via the Arabs."[10]

When orientalists such as Joseph von Karabacek studied the source materials compiled in Europe in the eighteenth and nineteenth centuries following trips to the Orient and the archaeology boom, and when they began to look beyond Arab paper's function as an intermediary between China and Europe, it emerged that Europe was not the first place paper had taken hold despite strong competition. Paper faced two rivals in its role as a writing material and, in particular, as a medium for calligraphy when it arrived in the Arab world: papyrus and parchment. Parchment could coexist with the newcomer because it became a comparatively exclusive medium of transmission. But the arrival of paper heralded a continuous decline in papyrus production. The attempt to establish a papyrus industry in Baghdad decades after the construction of the first paper mills quickly ran aground. The ties to the Nile Valley that had spawned the Egyptian papyrus monopoly and made it so successful became a barrier in the face of nomadic paper, the quality of which continually improved as its popularity grew. Papyrus production ceased in Egypt in the eleventh century due in no small part to the economic advantages of paper, even though there was initially only a slight price difference and paper itself was also a costly commodity. Paper was able to achieve its first major victory over a rival writing material because the raw materials used to make it were no longer linked to natural growth cycles.[11]

The displacement of papyrus by paper was an early example of the pattern underlying paper's rise to prominence. Paper stepped in as a substitute in established economic and cultural functions and then stimulated further demand for itself by proving its capabilities. It was not responsible for the invention of the letter or of writing, for the creation of viziers or for calligraphy. Instead, it slipped into the gaps in communication systems, transmission media, and governance techniques by combining a nomadic existence in the geographic

Paper production in Egypt. Trading card from the Liebig Fleisch-Extrakt company, 1905

realm with a non-specific attachment to a variety of uses in the social realm. Its proponents in the Arab caliphates were also administrators, just as the high-ranking official Ts'ai Lun had been.

Under the Umayyad dynasty (661–750), which had conquered the Sasanian Empire of ancient Persia, the Arab domain stretched from the borders of China and India to North Africa and Spain. After the Abbasids came to power in 750, they moved the empire's capital east from Damascus to Baghdad, which was founded in 762. The young Islamic empire adopted administrative techniques from the conquered culture of Persia, and it inherited the legacy of ancient Greek science and philosophy from Byzantium.[12] The fledgling medium of paper was ideal for copying this Greek legacy into Arabic, and it was also attractive to the bureaucrats and state administrators of the Abbasid Caliphate. The historian and politician Ibn Khaldun (1332–1406) dated the administrative shift from parchment to paper to the rule of Caliph Harun al-Rashid between 786 and 809. Paper was an appealing option for administration, the legal system, and trade, not least because it was less susceptible to forgery than papyrus, where the writing could be wiped off, or parchment, where it could be scratched out.[13]

Ibn Khaldun considered the diffusion of paper to be an effect of the growing textualization of bureaucracy and the boom in intellectual output in the Abbasid Caliphate. He also viewed it as a motivator for the emergence of chanceries and the evolution of literature and science. Nineteenth-century orientalists such as Joseph von Karabacek and Alfred von Kremer—the latter in his book *The Orient under the Caliphs* (1875)—adopted Ibn Khaldun's interpretation.[14] Current American research on Arab paper also picks up on this interpretation. It sheds light on the Arabic and Ottoman world, which was long assumed to have rejected the rapid adoption of the printing press, only reluctantly accepting it in the eighteenth century. Instead of studying the effects of the absence of the printing press, researchers are increasingly tracing the history of "paper before print"[15] in Arab culture.

1.2. Calligraphy and the Cairo Wastepaper Basket

Written words and numbers have never been tied exclusively to a single writing material in any civilization. Paper brought a swift demise to its rival papyrus in the Arab world, but as a medium for calligraphy it coexisted not only with parchment but also with flat stones, wood and bark, palm fronds and silk, brass and gold leaf, and other materials such as camel bones. It was additionally used to store sketches and drafts of designs that were later transferred to metal or other materials.[16] Above all, however, it was quickly accepted as a medium for copying the Koran. Papyrus and parchment are the only writing materials mentioned in the text of the Koran, but from the tenth century paper became the most important medium for disseminating the book itself in the Islamic world. It was ideal for the cursive scripts developed in the early tenth century by the secretary and calligrapher Ibn Muqla, who standardized the letterforms for various large writing surfaces using a geometric system of proportions.[17] Copying the Koran was considered a pious activity, like praying, and the ease of writing in cursive, where each letter is connected to the next, was kept in check by the rigors of calligraphy in order to prevent careless haste. Like parchment before it, the paper used for especially precious copies of the Koran was colored and finely decorated with gold. This decorated paper testified to the power of the Koran. The artistic recitation of the Koran was a sister art to calligraphy. In this union between the oral and written transmission of the prophet's words, recitation was a kind of acoustic calligraphy.[18]

People today usually encounter ancient Arab paper in the form of precious illuminated Koran manuscripts in museums and exhibitions on medieval Islamic art. It is therefore associated primarily with calligraphy and book art. The decorative side of Arab paper generally overshadows its role in administration, law, commerce, and everyday life. An extensive corpus of such pragmatic writing was discovered in the late nineteenth century in Cairo in the ruins of the Ben Ezra Synagogue of ancient Fustat. Large parts of this collection found their way into various Western libraries in subsequent decades. From the 1960s the Jewish Arabist and historian Shelomo Dov Goitein systematically surveyed these materials in a monumental five-volume study which introduced them to the English-speaking world as the "Geniza documents."[19]

The documents consist of tens of thousands of pages and fragments, the majority stemming from between the tenth century and the second half of the thirteenth century. Nearly all of the documents are written on paper in the Arabic language but using Hebrew letters. The Jews of medieval Cairo did not live in a ghetto, so they interacted with Muslims on a daily basis and spoke the lingua franca of their world: Arabic. The word of God plays only a minor role in the Geniza documents, but the papers were preserved because Jews believed that Hebrew was the language of God and the holiness of the language extended to its characters. The paper was respected for the characters written on it, regardless of the content. The documents were saved not because they were intended to be passed on but because of an inhibition against destroying them.

The Geniza—a Hebrew word literally meaning "hidden," which referred to the windowless room in a synagogue for depositing papers retired from everyday use—was not an archive, as archives involve registries as well as criteria for exclusion. And though the documents included fragments of books, book catalogs with and without price lists, and lending slips, the Geniza was even less of a book depot or a library than it was an archive. If anything, it was more like a giant wastepaper basket where papers that had once belonged together were taken out of context and thrown into a chaos of miscellaneous sheets sharing only one abstract, general characteristic: they were covered with Hebrew characters. Just like a wastepaper basket, the Geniza was not a sealed, inaccessible space from which nothing returned; it was a place of interaction between the papers stored there and the passing generations. If necessary, papers which still had writing space on them could be retrieved and used again. Long-fulfilled contracts covering only one side of a page could be torn into pieces and turned into notes.

In the catalogs of older libraries in the West, these fragments were often classified as "business letters, and therefore valueless."

But Goitein was not fixated solely on the fragments of valuable manuscripts or books. Even when Joseph von Karabacek was pursuing his historical inquiry into the intermediate realm of Arab paper, his essays and exhibition included not only talismans inscribed with suras, pen and ink drawings of riders, or fragments of astrology books, but also receipts, land registries, and excerpts from tax records. Two generations later, Goitein employed cultural anthropology methods to reconstruct the world in which medieval Arab paper circulated.

Shelomo Dov Goitein was born under the name Fritz Goitein in 1900 in Bavaria. He came from a rabbinic family and was trained in the Talmud from an early age. Goitein studied Arabic and Islam under Joseph Horovitz in Frankfurt, and in 1923 he sailed on the same ship as Gershom Scholem from Trieste to Palestine, where he helped establish the Hebrew University in Jerusalem.[20] He first encountered the Geniza documents in 1948, and they became the focus of his research after he moved to the United States in 1957. After 1957 he lived in Princeton and socialized with the cultural anthropologist Clifford Geertz, who had written about both Balinese cockfighting and the economic system of the bazaar in Suq. In the epilogue to his great work *A Mediterranean Society: The Jewish Communities of the Arab World as Portrayed in the Documents of the Cairo Geniza* (1967–88), Goitein stressed the proximity of his "interpretative sociography" to the "interpretive anthropology" of Geertz.

Goitein viewed and analyzed the paper chaos of the Jewish Geniza as a source of information on the life of the Jews in Cairo and the wider society in which they lived. He pored over the wastepaper basket as if it were a centuries-spanning newspaper filled with reports from distant lands, local interest stories, and miscellany: "Almost every conceivable human relationship is represented in these records, and they often read like local news told by a gifted reporter."[21] From these marriage contracts and wills, waivers and court orders, business and private correspondence, and letters from people giving and receiving charity, Goitein pieced together the image of an urban civilization with a dense internal network of written communication and far-reaching external trade relations. In doing so, he revealed the multiplicity of inconspicuous and indispensable functions fulfilled by paper beyond the realm of calligraphy and book culture in medieval Arab society. He described paper formats and proved that merchants with business relations in India considered paper valuable enough to give as a gift, and that pilgrims to Jerusalem would record the stations of their pilgrimage on thin, strong, large-format paper with which they then covered themselves at night as protection against evil—a testament to the belief in the magical power of paper.

Goitein occasionally noted that paper was made by a number of small enterprises as well as some larger ones in the Arab empire, but his reconstruction of everyday life in medieval Cairo did not include a history of Arab paper production. In passing, however, he illustrated the diffusion of paper technology to the western provinces of Tunisia, Spain, and Sicily, so his reconstruction signposts the routes by which Arab paper arrived in Europe.

1.3. In Scheherazade's World

The collection of tales now known as *The Thousand and One Nights* can be traced back to a core of pre-Islamic, Persian-Indian stories entitled "The Thousand Nights" (*Alf Layla*). The earliest reference to its later title, *Alf Layla wa-Layla*, comes from the Cairo Geniza. Goitein found this reference in the Bodleian Library in Oxford, in the notebook of a Jewish doctor who had also been a book dealer and notary. Around 1150, the doctor recorded the name of the person to whom he had lent *Alf Layla wa-Layla*.[22] No one with even a passing knowledge of the world of *The Thousand and One Nights* would be surprised to hear that these popular tales left their mark in the Geniza of ancient Cairo. The city of Cairo—a western counterpart to Baghdad, and even to far-off China—is one of the most prominent topographies in *The Thousand and One Nights*. Jewish doctors and Christian brokers alike can be found in both the Geniza and the tales of Scheherazade.

Caliph Harun al-Rashid was the link between these two spheres. As a historical figure he promoted the diffusion of paper—the medium of the Geniza fragments—and as a fictional figure he was immortalized on paper himself in *The Thousand and One Nights*.

The Jewish doctor wrote his lending note in the twelfth century, but other evidence indicates that Scheherazade's tales were committed to paper even earlier. The Oriental Institute of the University of Chicago has a fragment of a ninth-century codex, one of the oldest Arab papers in any international archive or library. When the fragment was written upon in 879, the book from which it was taken had already become wastepaper. A scribe by the name of Ahmad Ibn Mahfuz used it as scratch paper to practice writing phrases for notarizing legal documents. These marginalia on the fragile brownish fragment surround the title and first page of a manuscript of *Alf Layla* ("The Thousand Nights").[23] Experts reckon that the fragmentary book is at least half a century older than the legal scribe's notes, meaning that it was written around the time of Harun al-Rashid's reign (786–809). This finding by paper experts fits with the hypothesis of literary historians who believe that the new writing material encouraged the spread of both the Koran and secular, popular Arab prose.[24]

The transcription and expansion of the narrative cosmos of *The Thousand and One Nights* took place over the course of centuries and ran parallel to the diffusion of paper from Samarkand to Baghdad, Damascus, Cairo, and beyond. As a medium for reproduction, paper promoted the circulation of the Koran. But in the case of *The Thousand and One Nights*, paper was a medium for the successive production of the text itself. It accommodated both the Arabization of the original Persian-Indian material and the continual addition of new tales to the corpus. Since the stories in *The Thousand and One Nights* have no identifiable author, collector, or editor—unlike the German fairy tales compiled by the Brothers Grimm, for example—the text corpus was always in flux. Just like old papers were pulled out of the Geniza and overwritten, old stories were pulled out and overwritten in *The Thousand and One Nights*. The Frenchman Antoine Galland introduced Europeans to *The Thousand and One Nights* in the early eighteenth century, but his source manuscript had not been written until the second half of the fifteenth century.

Considering that the diffusion of paper in Arab culture and the development of the narrative cosmos of *The Thousand and One Nights* ran parallel to each other for so long, it seems reasonable to ask whether paper transcended its role as a transmission medium to become a literary subject and motif in Scheherazade's tales. After all, many episodes in *The Thousand and One Nights* are a mythic-poetic monument to the blossoming literary culture of Baghdad under Caliph Harun al-Rashid, and books and writing are often associated with magic in the tales. In Scheherazade's stories, the Abbasid Caliph appears as a legendary ruler who wanders through Baghdad at night and experiences numerous adventures. He is also a man of books and letters, however.[25] In one of the tales, he visits a library in Baghdad, takes a book at random, starts to read, bursts into laughter and tears, and then banishes his faithful vizier Ja'afar from his sight, prompting the distraught Ja'afar to flee to Damascus. After encountering many adventures there, Ja'afar returns to Baghdad, where the Caliph leads him to the library and hands him the book that had originally provoked his sorrow and mirth. In this book, Ja'afar finds a detailed account of his own adventure in Damascus. What the Caliph read in Baghdad thus becomes a self-fulfilling prophecy. The culture of writing repeatedly appears in this form and others in the tales.

The East-West axis between China and Samarkand which brought paper to the Arab world shapes the poetic space of the tales from *The Thousand and One Nights* right from the start. The frame story is set in the era when Persia was still ruled by the Sasanian dynasty. Shahrayar, the eldest of the two kings mentioned in the story, is lord over "the remotest corners" of "India and Indochina."[26] He gives his younger brother the land of Samarkand to rule as a sultan. The tale of the brothers' unfaithful wives wanders like merchandise on the Silk Road, traveling back and forth along the East-West axis before finally returning to Shahrayar's kingdom, where Scheherazade's own story emerges. From the viewpoint of Damascus or even Baghdad, the story is set in distant Eastern lands which would later take shape for Europeans in *The Thousand and One Nights*. In the poetic cosmos of Scheherazade, where mythical and real geography overlap, Cairo lies in the far reaches of the West. But the storyteller, like the space she inhabits and describes, is a hybrid. She has always been viewed as the apotheosis of oral storytelling, and for good reason. After all, her task is to pass the time during the night, so she has to tell her stories in the dark—and you can't read aloud in the dark. But from her very first appearance, she is saturated with writing through and through. She has read philosophical, literary, and medical books, she knows many poems by heart, she has a predilection for historical works, and she is a living compendium of famous quotes and sayings from wise kings and judges.

This accomplished, well-versed reader gives rise to the nightly storyteller. Scheherazade therefore evades the conflict between orality and textuality. She represents a culture of writing in which one of the noblest jobs of a book is to serve as a template for recitation or a prop for narration. Professional storytellers in the cities often worked on the basis of written texts, just like reciters of the Koran. Anyone who reads *The Thousand and One Nights* will quickly stumble across one of the set phrases—usually uttered by a ruler—by means of which an especially exciting story is ennobled by being committed to writing: "This story ... should be recorded in the books, even in letters of gold."[27]

The interplay between calligraphy and the text-based recitation of the Koran is a recurring motif in Scheherazade's stories. Characters are always returning home from ceremonial readings of the Koran, and it is not uncommon to find a handsome young man sitting on a carpet before an open Koran and loudly chanting from the book. In one tale, a mendicant who has been transformed into an ape and robbed of human speech by a demon known as an ifrit is delivered from his curse when he wins a calligraphy competition. The mendicant is actually the learned son of a king who has mastered the cursive scripts developed by the Abbasid calligrapher and secretary Ibn Muqla in the tenth century. The king's son covers a large roll of paper with a hymn to pen and ink, the progeny of Allah which make it possible for people to extend the chain of transmission beyond the bounds of death. The pen becomes the tongue and the inkwell becomes the mouth by means of which the words recorded by the writer are delivered into the hands of time for safekeeping long after the writer's death. The king's son invokes the counterspell of calligraphy to combat the evil forces that turned him into an ape. When considering the ape who uses calligraphy to escape enchantment, modern readers cannot help but recognize Thoth, the Egyptian god of writing. The prince in the form of an ape praises the beauty and, above all, the power of writing: "Yet even the Nile, which destroys the earth / Cannot its ink use with such mighty hand."[28]

Paper is part of the fabric of the world in Scheherazade's stories. It is always present, as inconspicuous as it is indispensable, as a medium for storing and circulating documents, letters and notes. Claudia Ott, the German translator of *The Thousand and One Nights*, has noted that there is an entire semantic field surrounding the main terms for paper—*kagad* and *waraq*—found in the collection of tales. There are special words for a sheet of paper and a slip of a paper, for a bag and for wrapping paper. Here, as in the Geniza, the many practical applications for writing in the fields of law, commerce, and administration stand alongside magical writing and calligraphy.

Take the story of the two viziers, Nur al-Din from Egypt and Badr al-Din from Basra, for example. It is like a poetic reflection of the cosmopolitan, urban, paper-based world of contracts, wills, and business correspondence that Shelomo Dov Goitein found in the Cairo Geniza. The two viziers are brothers, sons of a father who was himself a vizier adept at drafting documents. In this story, paper helps to bridge physical distances and verify identities. At the beginning of the tale, both brothers live in Cairo. When they decide to marry, they agree that if one has a son and the other a daughter, these children should marry each other. But they quarrel over the marriage agreement, and the younger brother angrily moves to distant Basra, where he becomes the stepson and successor to the vizier there. The tale subsequently strives to resolve the fraternal strife and close the resulting spatial distance between the families by means of the protagonists' knowledge of writing. Written paper helps bring the families together as well as maintain and ultimately reveal the carefully disguised identities of the characters. On his trip to Cairo, the son of the vizier from Basra carries his father's life story with him on a piece of paper, sewn into the lining of his turban like an amulet. The content of the sealed scroll confirms the identity of its carrier, and the lettering which the vizier from Cairo recognizes as his brother's handwriting confirms the identity of the author.[29]

In a plethora of such supporting roles, paper was a part of everyday life in medieval Arab culture. In his commentary on bonds and other financial documents, Goitein spoke of the "paper economy" of Cairo, by which he meant both cashless payment transactions, or the orders of payment known as *ruq'a* (meaning a piece of paper), as well as purchases made on credit.[30] Numerous examples of both can be found in *The Thousand and One Nights*. In the story of the viziers from Cairo and Basra, two pieces of paper work hand in hand to lead the son of the vizier from Basra into the arms of the woman for whom he is destined. One piece of paper is a contract with a Jew concerning the speculative sale of a cargo shipment that has not yet arrived. The other piece of paper, the amulet, contains the life story which ensures that the money acquired through the contract is allocated to the correct genealogical line. As is so often the case in *The Thousand and One Nights*, paper retrospectively reveals what has happened, and the Sultan of Cairo himself orders "that these events be dated and recorded."[31]

But that's not the end of the story. In a world in which the jinn, or evil spirits, like to move characters from one location to another, the ability to confirm the identity of places as well as people is also a common motif. Before the vizier from Basra sets off on his journey to Cairo, he takes pen and ink and records precisely where the furniture in his house is placed. This written verification of the identity of a physical location ultimately confirms the rightful identity of the bridegroom. In this and other ways, paper proves to be a convenient medium for making and upholding laws, even in a world of poetical adventures. But its loveliest task is to serve as a poetic metaphor in the form of fine calligraphy paper. A twelfth-century poem harks back to the oldest Arab center of paper by comparing a snowy landscape with the workshop of a papermaker in Samarkand. And in *The Thousand and One Nights*, seafarers report that "the sea lay before us like a smooth sheet."[32]

1.4. Timur and Suleika

In his "Notes and Essays for a Better Understanding of the *West-East Divan*," Goethe portrays himself as an author in the middle of a grand reference library, surrounded by excerpts from the books of

English, French, and German travelers and scholars. From Jean Chardin's *Voyages en Perse* (1711), he noted down "Dried fruit / Bokhara-granted / Silken leaf of Samarkand."[33] Chardin, who had traveled through Persia and neighboring countries between 1664 and 1677, wrote an account of the culture of correspondence in the Persian court, in which he recorded the customs surrounding the choice of letter paper and the use of seals. Goethe excerpted a passage referring to the circulation and origins of goods.

The names of important cities reverberate with both the merchandise that made them famous and the rulers who resided in them. Samarkand, for instance, brings to mind not only the oldest stratum of paper's history in the Arab world but also the figure of Tamerlane (1336–1405), the Mongolian ruler who built his imperial residence in the city. In Goethe's *West-East Divan*, this double reverberation is apparent in the tension between "The Book of Timur" (Timur is a version of the name Tamerlane) and the "Book of Suleika" which immediately follows it. In "The Book of Timur," winter employs "frost-pointed" storms and "fatal" cold to bring a halt to Timur's campaign in China shortly before the conqueror's death. In "The Book of Suleika," the world of tyranny and war to which "myriad worthy men" have fallen victim stands in contrast to the blithe taunt with which Hatem, the poet, provokes the mighty conqueror. The poet's imagination subjugates Timur's realms, appropriates the tribute that cities must pay to the ruler, and delivers the treasures to his lover as gifts in the language of poetry.

> I in the tavern sit serene;
> Serene at home, content, confined;
> But soon I think of *you*—my dream
> Filling my broadened, conqu'ring mind!
>
> The empire-wealth of Tamerlane
> Should serve you, his commanders hear:
> Rubies from Badakshán you'd gain,
> Caspian turquoise rare and dear,
>
> Dried fruit, and honey-sweet, for you,
> Bokhara-granted, sunny land,
> And myriad loving lyrics, too,
> On silken leaf of Samarkand.
>
> And you elatedly would read
> What I from mighty Hórmuz write,
> How all my global trade, indeed,
> Shuttles and moves for your delight.[34]

The poet jousts with the warlord in the language of merchants and travelers. On the pages of the poems he sends to his lover, he records the inventory of his gifts. In the poetic order of things, fine paper from Samarkand stands side by side with precious gems and fruits. The "silken leaf" is the soil from which the highest form of writing—calligraphy—grows. It is omnipresent in the poems of the *Divan*. When Suleika mischievously asks Hatem whether he has composed many poems, she is thinking of gold-edged pages "prettily written," "every stroke and point complete," pledges of love made from paper. Even in the short romantic riddle entitled "Exchanging Flowers and Symbols" that Goethe includes in his notes on the *Divan* as a play on oriental charades and logograms, paper acts as a code in the dialogue between lovers. The sequence of terms that precede and follow it swathe it in a dense network of associations encompassing figs, the sweetness of passion, stillness, and the uninhibited desire for words:

Figs	Keep still—no jigs.
Gold	I'm kind though bold.
Leather	Write with a feather.
Paper sheet	I'm yours, my sweet.
Ox-eye daisy	Write me, lazy.[35]

This section of wordplay can be read as an erotic mini-romance and account of the lovers emerging from secrecy. Love apparently has to be worth its weight in gold if it is to be put into writing. Inspired by gold-leaf calligraphy on parchment (leather), the poet reaches for his quill. As in *The Roman Elegies*, the act of love here becomes a medium for poetry, and the properties of paper—smoothness, pliability, ease of inscription—are attributed to the lovers and also enlisted for the purposes of poetically depicting flirtation without limits: "Write me."

When he composed his short romantic charade in 1815, Goethe had in mind the Arab manuscripts that he had woven into the emphasis on writing found in the *Divan*. In February 1814, when he was director of the ducal library in Weimar, Goethe had been offered a bundle of Arabic manuscripts which included an anthology of poems by Hafiz. While Goethe poetically reflected himself in the figure of Hafiz in the *Divan*, he used the manuscripts themselves for an act of profane writing magic: he tried to familiarize himself with writing Arabic characters. His immersion in the spirit of oriental calligraphy was disconnected from actually understanding the verses he copied. But the copyist wanted to absorb the combination of the spirit, word, and script: "I'm so close to learning Arabic. I want to at least practice the lettering enough to be able to copy the amulets, talismans, Abraxas and seals in the original script. In no other language are spirit, word and letter embodied in such a primal way."[36]

When the orientalist and manuscript collector Heinrich Friedrich von Diez sent his translation of a small volume *On the Cultivation of Tulips and Narcissus in Turkey* to Goethe in April 1815, Goethe wrote a poem of thanks on "a sheet of silky paper" and had it "adorned with a splendid golden floral design."[37] His everyday correspondence therefore incorporated calligraphic pages such as those exchanged as gifts by Suleika and Hatem. At the same time, in the poetic emulation of amulets and talismans, paper took its place alongside precious gems and fruits as a supporting character in the "Orient" of the *Divan*, which was assembled from Turkish, Persian, and Arabic elements. The impetus for this came from Joseph von Hammer-Purgstall, who had translated Hafiz into German. From Hammer-Purgstall's essay "On the Talismans of the Muslims," Goethe learned of the Arabic papers and engraved gems that he collectively referred to as "blessing pledges" in "The Book of the Singer": talismans, amulets, inscriptions, Abraxas and seal rings.

Hammer-Purgstall wrote about the Persian and Arabic talismans, "small cylinders or hemispheres with engraved figures threaded lengthwise on a cord," upon which the eastern fashions of women in Europe's capital cities—especially Vienna and St. Petersburg—were modeled in the early nineteenth century: "The Arabs referred to such suspended stones, or the written sheets that were used in place of stones, as a *hamalet* or pendant, a word which has entered all European languages as 'amulet.' Today, the difference between talismans and amulets is that the inscription is written on stone in the case of the former and on paper in the latter, and that the former is largely worn only by women at their belt or bosom, while the latter is worn by men, usually soldiers, as a scapular or *en baudrier*."[38] This passage is the basis of the verse in which Goethe compares paper amulets, which provide more space for writing, with the stone talismans that enforce brevity:

For an amulet divine
On a paper write a sign.
Gems confine in narrow frame;
Here a wider space you'll claim.
Souls may write with piety
Longer verses and more free.
Shoulder-hanging, some prefer—
Making them a scapular.[39]

In the disguise of poetry, Goethe's *Divan* heralded the exploration of the Arab intermediate realm in the late nineteenth century. The Viennese orientalist Joseph von Karabacek was a (more philologically rigorous) successor to Goethe's source of information, Joseph von Hammer-Purgstall. In Karabacek's "historical and antiquarian enquiry" and his public display of Arab papers from Archduke Rainer's collection, the amulets, stones, and inscriptions were a prime example of the link between paper and the magical writing of the East.

2

The Rustling Grows Louder

2.1. The European Paper Mill Boom

The art of papermaking traveled via North Africa to Spain, where production sites were established in Cordoba—Islam's most important cultural center in the West—along with Cadiz, Seville, Toledo, and Xàtiva near Valencia. As had been the case when paper migrated from the Far East to Samarkand, first the product began to circulate in Europe, then the knowledge of how to produce it. The paper used for a papal bull in the ninth century would have come from Arab papermakers in North Africa, Egypt, or Spain.

It was no coincidence that the first European paper mills were built around 1235 in Fabriano in the province of Ancona in Italy. The profession of the blacksmith (*il fabbro*) is echoed in the name of the town, and both metalwork and weaving were common throughout the region. It was during the expansion of the caliphate that the Arabs had modified and developed the technology they adopted from the Chinese. Europe, in turn, imported paper technology from the Arab world during the "technical and commercial revolution of the late Middle Ages."[40] European paper production quickly diverged from that of the Arab world. In Fabriano, all three phases of production—preparing the raw materials, forming the sheets, and processing the paper (drying, pressing, sizing)—underwent permanent changes. Rag stampers mechanized and intensified the raw materials preparation phase. Camshafts translated the water-driven rotation of the trough beam into the up-and-down motion of the hammers. By adopting mill technology and hammer mills from the textile and metalworking industries, European papermakers could pulp macerated rags with much more power than their Arab counterparts. During the sheet formation phase, the process of scooping the "stuff" (the fiber suspension made from the rags) out of the vat became a specialized step that was carried out using screens or molds consisting of fine metal wires stretched on wooden frames. The Chinese had used bamboo screens and the Arabs had made screens from reeds, both of which were flexible. The use of stiff metal screens was the most important European innovation at the heart of the papermaking process. Paper mills therefore benefited from the metalworking industry both indirectly, through stamp mill technology, and directly, through the use of wire-pulling techniques to make the dip molds. While rag stampers intensified the pulping process, both the degree of fiber mingling and the speed of the dipping procedure increased during the sheet formation phase. The vatman would vertically tilt the mold with the water-logged sheet to drain, and before the coucher transferred or "couched" the sheet to a felt blanket to dry, he would pass the vatman another empty mold. Scooping the pulp from the vat with double molds like this was very challenging, and this step largely determined the uniform structure and strength of the final product. Although the procedure was manual, the movements made here approached a mechanical regularity. The couching, pressing, and laying of the untreated paper were all specialized steps, as was the hanging of the partially dried sheets in the mill's drying loft.

For the third and final phase, when the still highly absorbent raw product was treated so that it could be written on, European paper mills replaced the plant-based sizing substances of the Arabs with a size made from sheep's hooves, deer feet, bones, and hides which facilitated the absorption process. Each sheet had to be immersed in the size individually or in a stack.

The European paper mill was a self-contained space for specialized phases of production, from the cellar where the noisy stamping gear was housed to the drying loft under the raised roof. Sites near cities were advantageous for paper producers, as this facilitated a steady flow of raw materials from ragpickers and ensured that the final product would be close to the market. Additionally, it was best to build mills where there was an abundance of clear, swift-flowing water. Mills needed water for power and for transforming their raw materials. Pre-industrial paper was created by water flowing through rags. In the topos of the mill and the valley, the rushing stream and rustling forest—themes found in poetry even before Joseph von Eichendorff turned "rustling" into a buzzword of the Romantic era—there was no room for the "proto-factory" of the paper mill.[41] Mills emitted a

Interior view of a paper mill. Woodcut, circa 1600

stench when they boiled down animal remains for sizing, and they polluted the water they needed for macerating the rags and scooping pulp from the vats. Their connection to the landscape and the rhythm of the seasons actually posed a risk for the mills. Ice and cold temperatures, or water shortages during heat waves, could bring the stamping mechanisms to a standstill or affect the rag preparation process, and wet weather would leave less time for drying the paper.

Paper mills were also a risky enterprise on account of the large amount of capital required to construct or convert a building, prefinance the raw materials, and pay the workers. In addition, mills needed a distribution network to successfully market their finished product.

A good, meticulously researched example of this is the mill that the businessman Ulman Stromer purchased and converted into a paper mill in June 1390 in Nuremberg. The mill was located outside the Wöhrder Gate on the southern arm of the Pegnitz River before it flowed into the city. Picturing this mill from the perspective of Google Earth is the best way to get an impression of the metropolitan area it bordered and to see how Nuremberg became a city of paper, a northern European counterpart to ancient Samarkand. Here, as in Samarkand, long-distance trade was crucial to the birth of papermaking. Ulman Stromer, a powerful patrician councilman, presided over a trading house active along the north-south and east-west axes of a

European system of coordinates. His business connections stretched from the Black Sea to the Atlantic and from the Mediterranean to the North and Baltic Seas. The ore smelting and metalworking industries of the Upper Palatinate region and the production of cut and thrust weapons and firearms in Nuremberg contributed to his company's strong position in the arms business. Stromer's involvement in the supply of coinage metal enabled him to foster connections with the worlds of high finance and politics, and his extensive warehouses, stables, and wine cellars in Nuremberg were based on a business model geared toward appropriating technological as well as commercial and financial innovations.

Ulman Stromer bought the mill outside the city gates not because he wanted to be a miller himself but because, as a wholesaler whose territory included northern Italy and Genoa, he realized he could expand his trading house by incorporating this lucratively promising industry. Stromer hired papermakers and signed the first paper mill lease agreement with his master papermaker Jörg Tiemann in 1394. The product he manufactured was not dependent on the local market.

Paper mill in Nuremberg from Schedel's *Nuremberg Chronicle*, 1493

Instead, it could be fed into Stromer's long-distance international distribution channels.

Nuremberg, Ravensburg, Augsburg, and Basel were among the early papermaking centers in southern and southwestern Germany. All these cities were situated on important long-distance trade routes. In France, too, in the Poitou-Charentes region around Angoulême and the Champagne region around Troyes, merchants played a key role in the establishment of paper mills. A paper mill with one dipping vat was capable of producing up to 3,000 sheets in a single day. It would thus have had a yearly output of nearly one million sheets, far exceeding the demand of local markets in the fifteenth century. Since paper was frequently produced in one place but used elsewhere, its to-and-fro flow—like that of the rags used to make it—shaped the history of the paper regions that emerged in Europe from the late Middle Ages. Behind every paper mill was a story of market demand and trade. From the perspective of world history, this close connection between paper technology and trade route infrastructure led the Arab world to experience a reversal of the old Samarkand effect, where the paper boom and long-distance trade mutually influenced each other. European paper mills quickly posed overwhelming competition to Arab papermaking, not only in Spain but even in their countries of origin.

European paper inherited its nomadic nature and its connection to trade routes from its predecessors in the Asian and Arab worlds. From the mid-fourteenth century, it became an increasingly successful export to the Islamic world. It soon popped up in the chanceries of North Africa and penetrated the centers of Arab papermaking. By the early fifteenth century at the latest, the fate of the paper industry in Egypt and Syria had been sealed.[42]

2.2. Paper, Scholars, and Playing Cards

Paper before the invention of the printing press may appear to have been an inert material waiting to be kissed awake by technology—but only at first glance. Its history unfolded in the form of an unrelenting, irresistible incursion into a variety of cultural practices instead of a sudden, striking explosion. But even in paper's relatively inconspicuous diffusion, there were signs of what the printing press would later become known for, namely, eliminating exclusivity by supporting reproduction technologies.

In their definitive work on *The Coming of the Book*, historians Henri-Jean Martin and Lucien Febvre described the development of

European paper technology from the thirteenth century onward as a prerequisite for the spread of printing with movable type.[43] It was in the context of reproducing manuscripts by hand that paper eclipsed parchment as a writing material in the scriptoria and universities of the late Middle Ages—and as was so often the case, the replacement of an older medium went hand in hand with an overall increase in the reproduction activity. Book historians disagree as to whether the availability of paper produced in northern Italy and, eventually, north of the Alps was responsible for the rise in manuscript production in the late fourteenth and early fifteenth centuries, or whether paper merely gave impetus to a writing boom that was already underway with the spread of literacy. The decisive factor is that paper was there when it was needed. One symptom of the need that it fulfilled could be seen in the lettering on parchment manuscripts, which had become more and more cramped. If you wanted to write more without using up more writing material, you had to make more thrifty use of the material you had. As a result, lines of writing moved closer together in the late Middle Ages, line height decreased, writing density increased, and the number of characters per page grew. The arrival of paper helped loosen these constraints. It gave texts a more reader-friendly breathing space.[44]

This greater legibility was a benefit to readers, whose numbers were growing—not only among the monks and nuns in cloisters, but also where the urban world of notaries, city scribes, and professors (in the guise of secular clerics) crossed over into the world of religious institutions. Both the priesthood and the expanding base of clerics in minor orders faced intensified literacy pressure from the fourteenth century onward.

At the same time, paper profited from the growing demand for manuscripts at universities. In addition to making a general contribution to textualization, these educational institutions supported the process that placed utilitarian books on a par with holy books. Paper quickly found its way into the "pecia" system that had emerged in Italian universities around the year 1200.[45] The pecia method was an effective way of dealing with the costly reproduction of textbooks by dividing up the original manuscript. A university-authorized exemplar of the original text would be split into smaller pieces (*peciae*) by book dealers or stationers, who would rent out the pieces to students. These sub-sections would then be copied by the students themselves or by scribes who worked not for a heavenly wage, like monks, but to earn a living. This system resulted in cheaper duplicates of practical books which could be produced more quickly since the sections of the original manuscript were copied synchronously. The University of Paris played a role in the establishment of the paper industry in nearby Champagne in the fourteenth century. To free itself from dependence on paper dealers from Lombardy, the university success-fully petitioned the king in 1354 for the right to run paper mills in Troyes and Essonne operated by *papetiers jurés* who had the status of university employees.[46]

Looking at its arrival in cloisters, urban scriptoria, and universi-ties, paper seems to have been fulfilling its most important purpose, namely, to facilitate written routines, store and universalize knowl-edge, and prepare the ground for the printing press. In today's ter-minology, we would say it was contributing to the emergence of the information society. But early papermakers could not live from such noble purposes alone. Supplying writing paper to cities, cloisters, or universities was just one possible economic foundation for a paper mill. Even in Germany's larger imperial cities in the fourteenth century, chanceries rarely needed more than a few reams of 500 sheets each. Ulman Stromer's mill survived not only, or even primarily, by making writing paper, but by making the commercial paper used by manufacturers in Nuremberg to package their needles, grommets, and so on. The paper mills of the fifteenth century also found another major sales opportunity in Europe's rampant passion for a new pastime: card games.[47] Playing cards were made from layers of paper glued together, and the gambling craze consumed far more paper than chanceries and town councils.

This strand of paper's history prior to the printing press is note-worthy not least because it led paper out of the world of cloisters, universities, and chanceries and into the world of the illiterate general population and early entertainment media. The beneficiaries of the playing card rage included the print colorists who were always found alongside papermakers in the so-called books of trades from the early modern period. These craftsmen colored in profane playing cards using the same techniques they applied to the colorization of popular devotional images of saints. Together with papermakers and early woodcutters, print colorists formed a triangle for the mass produc-tion of playing cards.

In the eighteenth century, the Leipzig music publisher Johann Gottlob Immanuel Breitkopf (1719–94), son of the publishing house founder Bernhard Christoph Breitkopf, drew on his ample library in an attempt to illustrate this triangle. His *Inquiry into the Origin of Playing Cards, Paper Made of Linen, and Wood Engravings in Europe* (1784) remained fragmentary, however. Only the first part, "covering playing cards and paper made of linen," was published by Breitkopf's own publishing house.[48] This work drew on a wide range of sources to tell the story of the emergence of a modern, paper-based entertainment medium. It is a perfect example of an analysis of media alliances. As a child of the bookish city of Leipzig and a typography historian, Breitkopf knew that printed books had become an important domain for woodcut illustrations not long after the printing press was invented. But he also knew that woodcutting was older than book printing, and he approached his subject matter by separating the two crafts which, as he said, had been "naturally confused due to the similarity of their products" and were assumed to be more closely related than they originally were.

Breitkopf exchanged letters with Gotthold Ephraim Lessing, the librarian in Wolfenbüttel, concerning the dating of old Bibles. In September 1779 he had offered to send Lessing his manuscript on the history of book printing, remarking that "Gutenberg's intention was clearly none other than to unite those existing individual inventions which resembled our printing so that new processes would bring about greater beauty, speed, affordability, and availability."[49]

This insight led Breitkopf to dispute any direct line of technological development from the woodcut to Gutenberg's invention. Breitkopf held up fourteenth-century German playing cards as the first product of the art of woodcut. In the first part of his work he investigated the migration of card games from the Orient to Europe, and in the second part he looked at the introduction of their physical medium, namely, paper made of linen. This incomplete second part would have culminated in a section on the fusion of paper and woodcut. This had been the point of Breitkopf's study right from the start—to demonstrate the link between the medium of paper and the reproduction technology of woodcuts in the creation of playing cards: "The prevalence and proliferation of these card games lead us to investigate the material from which the cards were fabricated and the invention that allowed them to be easily duplicated, thus making them less costly for the common man."[50] In short, the apex of Breitkopf's card/paper/woodcut triangle pointed to the common man.

The fusion of the physical medium and the reproduction technology did, in fact, turn playing cards into a mass-produced product, one which depended not on the literacy of its consumers but on their addiction to gambling. These gambling addicts included many people who preferred more challenging card games to simple dice games. The rapid increase in the production of playing cards in the fourteenth and fifteenth centuries was accompanied by card game bans enacted by cities out of a fear that their citizens would be unable to pay their taxes. It is no accident that Breitkopf's treatise mentions burghers as well as the illiterate characters who are often overlooked in historical accounts that are fixated on the symbiosis of the printing press and the written word: "a mass of poor and dissolute folk" from the fourteenth and early fifteenth centuries, including soldiers whose undemanding card games were "no great invention" and could therefore sit easily alongside dice games.

Breitkopf contrasted the soldiers' playing cards with a sumptuous, unique deck of painted cards for which Duke Visconti of Milan paid "fifteen-hundred gold scudi." This duke primarily played the role of a foil for Breitkopf. The arts were assigned to a social index in Breitkopf's triangle, and the existence of the Duke of Milan meant that playing cards could still be painted at great expense even after the emergence of woodcut printing. This gave rise to a modern configuration in which "cards were painted for nobles but printed for the common man."[51] When Breitkopf mentioned printing here, he did not mean the art of book printing in the Gutenberg sense but rather low-quality, mass-marketed woodcuts on glued paper. In this context, woodcuts—like the paper they were associated with—became a medium for breaking down social barriers long before they found their way, via block books, into published books and later into the pamphlets and broadsheets of the Reformation.

When Breitkopf researched woodcuts and playing cards as examples of paper-based reproduction media before Gutenberg, he employed a methodological premise which made him a pioneer in the historical analysis of media alliances: "The origins of such arts, which are connected to many others and emerge as new arts from the attempted combination of various existing ones, are—if those existing arts themselves are not considered the origins of the new ones—generally so overlooked that if the newly perfected art is of noticeable value and benefit, the chronicler will, at most, note only its sudden appearance and not its gradual development."[52] There is no doubt that printing was precisely this kind of suddenly emergent art "of noticeable value and benefit" which overshadowed the unassuming succession of media couplings that had preceded it. Breitkopf's account of the fusion of paper and woodcuts in the production of playing cards is a prototypical example of the circulation of a medium through mass reproduction which antedates printing. More recent woodcut historians have expanded on Breitkopf's account—which primarily offers a historical explanation for the adaptability of paper and the migration of playing cards from the East—by holding up colored textile printing as a precursor to woodcuts.[53] This does not detract from Breitkopf's core insight, however.

Card games had made their way from Egypt to Italy, where they experienced their first major European success. Clear evidence of this migration can be found in both the figures depicted on European cards and the history of paper terminology. The Italians named their imported card game *naibbe*, after the Mamluk governors who were the main characters on the Egyptian cards. The cards themselves, the first mass-produced paper goods to be circulated, were named after their carrier medium: *cartae*. This word thus acquired a double meaning, as it could refer to either a sheet of paper or a playing card. It was in the latter incarnation that the term migrated through Europe.[54] Nuremberg—where the nuns of St. Catherine's convent were expert textile printers, and where Ulman Stromer's paper mill probably profited from the gambling craze as well—became a center for the mass production of playing cards north of the Alps. The awareness of paper's proximity was preserved for all time in popular figures of speech and anecdotes. In the seventeenth century, Abraham a Sancta Clara wrote of a great altercation between parchment and paper. In this fable, paper boasts of its ancient lineage but prides itself above all on not serving the purposes of bloody battle—unlike parchment, which is stretched on drums—and instead being associated with a peaceful life. In its riposte, parchment counters paper's pomposity by sneering that paper actually comes from rags, and it goes so far as to accuse its rival of causing "most of the quarrels and squabbles" in the world: "'What are playing cards besides paper which the Latin scholars call *charta*? And what provokes more discord, strife and blows, what causes more evil and frivolity, than cards?' At that, paper had to shut its trap."[55]

2.3. The Rise of the File: Paper Kings, Chanceries, and Secretaries

When the titular hero of Goethe's tragedy *Egmont* returns home in the play's second act, he is met by his impatient secretary who does not want to miss an evening rendezvous: "Still he comes not! And I have been waiting already full two hours, pen in hand, the papers before me."[56] Three couriers wait with the secretary. Egmont is expected to respond rapidly to the correspondence informing him of unrest in the Ghent region, the difficulties his emissary has had collecting debts and, finally, the warnings of a Spanish nobleman who is worried about Egmont's safety following loose talk during a convivial bout of drinking. When he arrives, Egmont criticizes the ceremony of the Spanish court ("My blood rebels against the Spanish mode of life, nor have I the least inclination to regulate my movements by the new and cautious measures of the court") and delegates the unpleasant task of writing letters and issuing instructions to his secretary: "Of all detestable things, writing is to me the most detestable. You imitate my hand so admirably, do you write in my name." The concerns of his secretary, who wants his lord to carefully think out each response, stand no chance against Egmont's haste: "Collect your papers."[57] The secretary and couriers will write down and disseminate their lord's political intentions and interventions without his involvement. In the play's third act, the cautious precision with which Margaret of Parma—regent of the Netherlands, daughter of Charles V, and half-sister to Philip II—mulls over the letters and instructions she receives from Spain stands in stark contrast to Egmont's lax approach to correspondence. In the regent's discussion with her advisor, whom Goethe names Mechiavel, the dispatch of the Duke of Alba and the troop movements associated with it appear to be a result of the correspondence from Philip II and his secretary of state. The hard line personified by Alba will override the conciliatory policies of the regent Margaret. But she knows how to rule and analyzes her brother's attempt to undermine her power as follows: "He will bring his instructions.—I am old enough in state affairs to understand how people can be supplanted without being actually deprived of office.—First he will produce a commission, couched in terms somewhat obscure and equivocal; he will stretch his authority, for the power is in his hands; if I complain, he will hint at secret instructions; if I desire to see them, he will answer evasively; if I insist, he will produce a paper of totally different import; and if this fail to satisfy me, he will go on precisely as if I had never interfered.—Meanwhile he will have accomplished what I dread, and have frustrated my most cherished schemes."[58]

In the play's depiction of the conflict between the humane and gallant Egmont, a man of the people, and the absolutist court intrigue to which he is subject, in its organological view of the state and, above all, in its language, this eighteenth-century tragedy brings the Netherlands' secession from Spain two hundred years earlier into Goethe's own world. But it is the historical figure of Philip II who looms large in the regent Margaret's internal drama. Unlike his northern-born father Charles V, Philip II rarely traveled through his realm and instead attempted to rule it from its center in Spain by evaluating information flows and issuing writs. Even among his contemporaries he was known as a *rey papelero*, a paper king.

Modern historians have painted a detailed portrait of this type of ruler. It depicts Philip II in the midst of papers circulating near and far, all the way to distant overseas provinces in South America. When Philip II assumed the throne from his abdicated father in 1556, the archive that Charles V had founded in 1540 in Simancas for his ministerial records became the central state archive. The king preceded every decision with an extensive review of these records. He was surrounded by ministers and secretaries who themselves composed, studied, and appended urgent notes to documents. For decades he often had to write his signature several hundred times a day, until the 1580s when he started using a stamp to sign routine correspondence. In March of the year 1571 he personally dealt with more than forty petitions per day, or over 1,250 in the entire month. He indulged his passion for beautiful gardens and hunting, but from the late 1580s he had to wear reading glasses. He was convinced that "these devils, my papers" made him prone to repeated fits of coughing.[59] The instructions spoken of in Goethe's *Egmont* were only one aspect of the papers flowing to and from his court. They were accompanied by the paper instruments that the court used to systematically accumulate hegemonic knowledge throughout the realm. The secretary at Egmont's side was a many-headed creature in the court of the paper king. He was a key figure of the early modern age.

The media of modern bureaucracy can be traced back to Spain under Philip II. Questionnaires, forms, and tables were sent to officials in overseas provinces. Map-based indices were developed to synoptically display incoming information so that an overview could be maintained as the volume of paper grew. At the same time, correspondents were urged to keep their writing short and systematic. The paper king ruled according to the principle that every single one of his subjects should be able to send him a letter. He continued to hold audiences and listen to reports from his secretaries, but the paper king's inclination to favor written petitions over oral audiences touches on an important element of absolute rule—namely, access to the ruler. Carl Schmitt described this sphere of access as a "corridor," an "antechamber of indirect influence and force" leading to the ear of the ruler.[60]

In the theater of early modern Europe, this was a whisper-filled corridor thick with intrigue and opportunities to acquire power simply by being physically present. The value of being present declined in the realm of the paper king, however. You were just as likely to gain prospects for power by having the eye of the sovereign as by having his ear. The Venetian ambassador Francesco Morosini remarked in 1581 that Philip II preferred written petitions and consultations in part because they gave him more time to respond. The noisy forecourt of power was therefore joined by a paper corridor, and the delaying, blockading, and expediting tactics that were cultivated in this corridor affected those present at the court as well as those who appealed to the sovereign from afar rather than attempting to tip the scales in their favor through their physical presence.[61]

Even when the paper king did grant petitioners an audience, he subjected them to the pressure of the papers in circulation around them. We know that Philip II sometimes took papers with him to audiences just so that he could hold them demonstratively as he spoke. This gesture signaled to the petitioner that the king knew more about his situation than he was saying. Playing the role of a mute participant in the audience, paper symbolized the potentially infinite background knowledge that Philip II could potentially bring into play—even if the papers he held had no actual bearing on the case in question. Papers "are like another person in the room. They don't identify themselves, but they are on the side of the powerful and have already shared their observations with him. Paper represents the unknown denouncer who has not only given his 'voice' to the authorities but has also transferred responsibility for the executive consequences."[62] Even in the world of Philip II, paper—in its dual role as a bearer of secrets and barrier to physical access to the sovereign—had a hand in shifting the center of power to the sphere of invisibility which would influence the modernization of administration in the early modern state.

The technological roots of the circulation and functional revaluation of administrative papers in Philip II's empire reached back to the thirteenth century. When James I of Aragon conquered Valencia and established a kingdom there in 1238, he used the Arab paper mills on the east coast of Spain for his administrative correspondence. James I left behind an extensive archive when he died in 1276. His son Peter III conquered Sicily for the Kingdom of Aragon in 1282. Since Peter III had married Constance, daughter of Manfred of Sicily, in 1262, he was considered the heir and successor to the Hohenstaufen dynasty. Two generations earlier, administrative practices with Roman-canonical and Byzantine origins had merged with Arab paper in the Sicilian chancery of Frederick II, resulting in a prototype of modern, file-based leadership. Frederick II had issued a legal code in 1231 which stipulated that all deeds (*instrumenta publica* and *cautiones*) were to be written only on parchment to protect their evidentiary value against age-related deterioration. Though this sounds as if parchment had been given precedence over paper, it was actually a regulatory statute governing the division of labor between parchment and paper, the latter of which was supplied to Frederick II's chancery by Arab merchants. Sicily under the Hohenstaufens, like the caliphate of Harun al-Rashid, had discovered that paper was an attractive medium for administration because it was cheaper. In both cases, however, paper competed with parchment not solely on the basis of its economic advantages or greater resistance to forgery; it was also the ideal writing material for all documents that had to be quickly composed, easy to read, and available only for a limited time. In light of these requirements, the combination of paper and cursive script which had proven successful in the Arab world could also be advantageous here, even taking into account the disadvantage that paper deteriorated faster. This certainly applied to the registers that were first used for administrative purposes in Europe in the chancery of Frederick II. These registers or regesta were, as their name (*res gestae*) implies, sequential records of bureaucratic dealings and correspondence: expenses incurred, orders placed, and taxes levied. They could also include proceedings which previously would not have been worthy of note. In Frederick II's chancery, even the king's interest in falconry was documented in the form of extensive correspondence on the topic.[63]

The last surviving files from Frederick II's *cancellaria*, fragmentary as they were, were destroyed by German soldiers in 1943. But in Cornelia Vismann's history of files in Europe, the exemplary character of these records was vividly illustrated based on older research. The dual use of parchment and paper was linked to the difference between documents and records. Medieval documents demanded a writing medium with a long lifespan, as their purpose was to record legislation effective for all time. The location of these documents was secondary to the information they preserved. The expressions of eternal validity (*ad perpetuam rei memoriam*, etc.) found on such documents were consistent with the representative visual design of the documents, which were produced by highly specialized writing workshops. The authority of the issuer had to be expressed in the appearance of the script, even at the expense of legibility. Like seals and signatures, the arrangement and size of the letters and other ornamental details on a document served the purposes of authentication.

The papers in a register, by contrast, were designed and stored in accordance with the economy of time imposed by a temporary working memory. Administrative procedures determined both the arrangement of text on the page and the economy of writing. Identical letters sent to multiple recipients were formulistically registered (as *similes*) but not copied multiple times. The content of mandates was summarized in keywords, and salutations and greetings were left out. Because paper's material value was less than that of parchment, each month could start with a new sheet even if the previous month's sheet was not full. One decisive element of a register was that each individual sheet was dated. A margin was reserved especially for this, introducing a top-to-bottom organizational grid alongside the left-to-right reading direction. Whereas documents had been a symbolic embodiment of metaphysical eternity, the serial entries in a register reflected the ever-changing nature of administrative activities. Eternity was temporalized in the endlessness of the register: "With this specific form of writing, which combines a content-based entry with a date in the margin, registers link acts and time: *actum et datum*. ... Generally speaking, this registering technology removed power from the realm of eternity and subjected it to time."[64]

Certificates written on parchment were, for a long time, the preferred source texts for diplomacy, both as legal documents and as representative depictions of authority. When this fixation finally ended, registers and files—along with their dominant writing material, paper—emerged from the shadow of documents and parchment as objects of historiography from the late Middle Ages and early modern period. This revealed how, from the second half of the fourteenth century, paper contributed to the transition from document-based rule to file-based administration on an imperial, curial, territorial, and municipal level. As always, however, paper was not the source of the practices it encouraged.

In both their name and substance, files can be traced back to Roman law and the administrative texts of Roman magistrates, praetors, emperors, and provincial governors (edicts, instructions, reports, etc.). Their roots go deeper than the history of paper, and they connect the dawn of the age of files, by way of the age of documents, to the Roman practice of coupling authority to administration. But these connections to antiquity are less important than the lines leading to the future of the modern state.

Files in their broader sense—as bundles of written documents relating to a single business transaction, with officially registered incoming, outgoing, and internal texts—may not have existed yet in the fourteenth century. In general, written documentation was an option in territorial states, not the norm. But chanceries dealt with a range of time spans that paper accommodated very well. Along with the *registrum perpetuum*, which brought together enfeoffments, endowments, privileges, pacts, and peace treaties, there was the *registrum temporale*, with liens, loans, income orders, and other texts of limited temporal validity. As the volume of correspondence grew between the monarchy and imperial princes, and between cities and city alliances, it was always paper that contributed to the surge in writing. Most official administrative books were written on paper from the second half of the fourteenth century, as were the registers and surviving fragments of the imperial administrators of Charles IV and of the Elector—and later German king—Rupert of the Palatinate (1352–1410).[65] Rupert and the administrative techniques of the Palatinate territory were part of the political and cultural environment surrounding the first German paper mills.

Ulman Stromer, founder of the Nuremberg paper mill and a powerful patrician of his city, was a key figure in the strained relationship between the king, the princes, and the cities. In the great Rhenish-Swabian League of Cities—which Nuremberg had joined in 1384, partially at his urging—Stromer made a pact with King Wenceslaus. But when the king was deposed, Stromer did not hesitate to help his opponent Rupert of the Palatinate ascend to the throne in 1400 by engaging in encrypted correspondence. From his activities as a Nuremberg magistrate and his insight into territorial and imperial politics, Stromer must have known when he established his mill in 1390 that the importance of paper in administration was growing.[66] Paper historians have been able to prove that paper from his mill was used in Rupert's chancery. Paper's genealogy as a medium for the growth of administrative documentation, from the municipal all the way to the imperial level, can be traced back to the earliest paper mills in the Old Kingdom. As the ideal vehicle for objectifying sovereignty in the form of administration and as an everyday medium, paper was suffused with the spirit of the laws whose bureaucratic consequences it recorded.

In the age of modern bureaucracy, when you find one sheet of paper you are bound to find more. Harbingers of this tendency toward plurality can be found in phrases such as the one with which the secretary in Goethe's *Egmont* describes himself: "Pen in hand, the papers before me." This plural—"the papers"—had a bright future ahead of it.

2.4. The Merchant of Genoa and His Silent Partner

Among his other activities, Ulman Stromer—merchant, politician, financier, and founder of the first paper mill in Germany—maintained trade relations with Genoa, which had quickly become a long-distance trading hub for Arab paper. Two main factors helped Genoa evolve into one of the most important regions for European paper production. First, the commercial seaport benefited from the migration of experts who disseminated the knowledge that had originated in the oldest European paper mills in Fabriano. And second, the boom in local paper production was abetted by the success of Genoese merchants and financial specialists who, from the sixteenth century onward, played a key role in north-south European trade and the movement of goods and gold between the New World and the markets of Europe. In his monumental work *The Mediterranean and the Mediterranean World in the Age of Philip II*, Fernand Braudel explained how Genoa developed into a "fulcrum of international finance" in the second half of the sixteenth and first third of the seventeenth century.[67]

Genoa's paper mills, which had clustered west of the city in Voltri, along the waterways in the mountains near the coast, owed their fame above all to the fine writing paper they produced. In 1544 there were already twenty-nine mills producing white paper in the valleys around Voltri; in 1588 there were forty, and by 1612 their number had risen to sixty-two. The resulting production landscape comprised an entire village of paper mills, complete with a piazza, a small palazzo, and a church. This village, named San Bartolomeo delle Fabbriche, was embedded in the infrastructure of the international trading center whose port facilitated the large-scale import of rags and export of the end product. Paper factories boomed thanks to the growing demand for paper among municipal administrators, merchants, and the Genoese world of finance, as well as to the fact that high-quality paper—like wool and silk before it—was an increasingly attractive commodity, one which merchants wanted not only to market but also to produce themselves. So they invested in paper.

The Genoese merchant Giovanni Domenico Peri (1590–1666) depicted the paper landscape of Voltri in a chapter entitled "Fabrica della carta da scrivere" in the third volume of his work *Il Negotiante*, which was published from 1639. It is clear from his writing that he was proud of these factories. He describes their favorable location in a landscape with streams which had enough of a gradient to force-fully drive the stampers, and with northerly and westerly winds that were good for drying paper. Peri provides a detailed overview of the structure and size of the factories, their technical equipment, the number of waterwheels and vats they had, and the position of the rooms in which the rags were sorted and macerated. When he describes the production process—from shredding the rags to pressing and sizing the paper—he gives precise information regarding the quality of the tools used and the amount of material processed. The result is an in-depth depiction of a multi-story facility where rags of various qualities were beaten into a pulp in marble troughs with large stampers. The water required for this was cleaned by a sophisticated filtration system. In one room, vatmen scooped pulp from several masonry vats, next to which stood a wooden press about eight feet (or 2.5 meters) tall, which was anchored to the ground with iron bolts. Another room held copper boilers where the size was made.[68]

Unlike *A Papermaker's Instructions to His Sons Concerning This Art* (1766) by the German Georg Christoph Keferstein, Peri's text was not written by an authority in the art of papermaking. And unlike *The Art of Papermaking* (1761), written in France by Jérôme Lalande, it was not a treatise on paper mills from a state inspector. Instead, it was written for a trans-regional audience by an experienced representative of the commercial and financial capital of Genoa; he presented a model enterprise in his hometown, where they used advanced technology to produce papers that were absolutely perfect (*"perfettisimi"*). His depiction of the mills in Voltri reads like a promotional brochure for potential investors. It includes data on the number of workers in the mills, their working hours and annual output, as well as a special section with detailed information on the annual agreements between the merchants who financed the paper mills and the masters who, in the role of temporary employees, processed the rags that were supplied on the account of the owners. The merchants had to provide everything needed for production, while the masters had to hand back the production facilities at the end of the year in the state in which they had taken them over. Peri, who was clearly familiar with this system, warns readers about the evasive tricks employed by the masters, who were obliged to sell any surplus goods exclusively to the mill's owner at a set price.

Peri portrays the paper mills as a lucrative object of investment. But the Genoese businessman also analyzes the origin and physical properties of the material from Voltri that he dealt with every day— when handling his correspondence, keeping his accounts, or issuing bills of exchange. Paper is therefore omnipresent in his work long before he describes the *"fabrica della carta da scrivere"* in the third volume. The genre to which *Il Negotiante* belongs, the merchant's treatise, can be viewed as a literary counterpart to the portraits of merchants painted by European artists. Such portraits—like that of the Danzig-born Hanseatic merchant Georg Giese, who was painted by Hans Holbein the Younger in London with a half-opened letter in his hand—prominently depict papers of various types as well as writing instruments and seals. The merchants' treatises, like self-portraits in prose, are no different.

Giovanni Domenico Peri was a highly educated man. The qualifications demanded in his profession included a knowledge of Latin. *Il Negotiante* is saturated with quotations from Roman writers like Pliny and Cicero. But even in the preface to his book, he distances himself from the cultivated style of the *letterati*. His book is written in the language of merchants—not of scholarship or of art, but of practical experience. Though he portrays himself as a "*scrittore*," he means not an author but rather a writer in the literal sense, one who describes his tools and his technique: the position of his body and fingers, the shape of the letters poised between forced rotundity and prim rigidity, the form and quality of the pen and how he puts it to the paper, and the balance between legibility, beauty, and the speed of writing. The merchant's writing technique proves to be a compromise between the speed demanded of him by his economy of time and the need to maintain legibility and produce a well-proportioned script which would contribute to his business success. Peri's words back up the findings of historians: "For the cleric, the purpose of the writing process was to create documents and theological or scientific books which were destined to be preserved. For the merchant, writing was a liability which was necessary to generate assets for the business."[69]

In three separate chapters—"Dello scrivere," "Del modo di scrivere lettere, ordini, e commissioni," and "Della Scrittura Mercantile"— Peri outlines the written techniques for storing and circulating information that the ideal merchant was expected to master. The quality of the paper was considered just as important as the quality of the pen. In his chapter on the composition of letters, instructions, and orders, Peri praises the invention of paper ("*inventione della carta*") as a medium for written correspondence over long distances. His praise is directed above all at paper's lightness and foldability which, when combined with seals, made it possible for documents to circulate freely and be addressed to privileged recipients. Merchants and lovers alike benefited from this kind of long-distance communication ("*consolatione grande delle persone che s'amano, ma commodità grandissima della Mercatura*").

When he starts to describe the mills of Voltri, Peri extends his praise from the private sphere to the realm of world history. He portrays paper as an invention through which humanity imitates the omnipotence of God. Peri says paper encourages virtue by transmitting tales of heroism and, because it is a convenient way to connect different eras and different peoples, it stimulates all of the arts and sciences, from architecture and navigation to philosophy and rhetoric. This passage sounds as though it were lifted from a paean to printing, but references to printing and book dealers are remarkably rare in Peri's account. Genoa certainly had its printers, booksellers, and publishers; one of them published the first edition of *Il Negotiante*. But later editions and reprints of the work were published in the book capital of Venice, a fact that accentuates the constellation of factors which gave rise to Peri's treatise. The union of printing and paper production in Venice and its environs stood in contrast to the union of paper production, trade, and banking in Genoa.

Il Negotiante views paper not from the perspective of the library but from the perspective of the office. When Peri talks of *"libro," "scrittura,"* and *"carta,"* this humanist triangle of books, writing, and paper is embedded in the context of his daily life as a merchant. For Peri, *"il libro"* is a ledger, *"scrittura"* is not writing in general but accounting, and *"la carta"* is not only used for wide-ranging business correspondence—Peri includes numerous sample letters in *Il Negotiante*—but is also the medium through which merchants issue bills of exchange and handle credit transactions. The crux of the Genoese constellation was that the trading and finance capital invested money in paper mills which had been earned through business practices dependent on paper as a medium for storage and circulation.

In Fernand Braudel's observations on "The Age of the Genoese," Giovanni Domenico Peri acts as an informant concerning the dominance of Genoese merchants in the network of Mediterranean trading centers and its complicated system of exchange rates. Braudel's depiction of this configuration—as demonstrated by the critically important market of Piacenza—confirms that paper acquired a dual significance on account of its capacity to unite the circulation of correspondence with the circulation of money: "The entire fortune of the Genoese depended upon a subtle mechanism, subtly operated. Their reign was the reign of paper, as the Fuggers' agent in Spain ill-temperedly said, accusing them in 1577 'of having more paper than hard cash.' ... The coming of the age of paper, its extension if not its first appearance, in fact marked the beginning of a new economic structure, an extra dimension that had now to be reckoned with."[70]

Braudel was no longer talking about the physical product of paper mills here but about paper as the symbol and embodiment of modern banking. Like paper technology in the stricter sense, this aspect of paper—which it acquired in its role as a silent partner in financial transactions—was also a legacy of Arab culture.

The spatial dimensions of trade in the Abbasid Caliphate had led to the creation of bills of exchange and exchange laws, allowing payments to be sent from one place to another while avoiding the risks of sending actual money. Even in the Arab world, the same term had been used for both the financial transaction itself and the document with which it was carried out.[71] In its logical structure, this transaction was not tied to a specific medium. Historically and practically, however, the development of bills of exchange and paper technology had already merged in the Arab world.

Familiarity with the Arab model is apparent in the dual origin of European bills of exchange, namely, in Aragon and the trading republics of Italy after the Crusades. Peri, who described the ideal merchant in the early seventeenth century as a spider in a web of maritime navigation and paper-based correspondence and credit transactions, could already look back on a centuries-old tradition of using media to separate the merchant from the traveler. Just as bills of exchange prevented the need to transport money physically, paper documents (waybills, agreements, orders) set merchandise into circulation without the merchant himself having to circulate. The merchant's office was the navigation center from which he monitored the flow of goods and money. In the fourteenth century, the Tuscan merchant Datini advised his agent to wear shoes of lead, to be bound to his desk, his books, his pen.[72]

Just as the flat surfaces of the sea and paper are metaphorically reflected in each other in *The Thousand and One Nights*, the sea in European long-distance trade became a surface which could be traversed via short, straight routes—routes which could be planned and calculated on the surface of a sheet of paper. Shakespeare's *Merchant of Venice* bears witness to both the hardships of credit and the hazards that distance and transportation posed for merchants.

The title of the fourth chapter of *Il Negotiante* is "Dell' Abbaco." By including arithmetic in the educational program of the merchant, thus completing the triad of "*libro*," "*scrittura*," and "*carta*," Peri was paying his respects to an Arab legacy. The fusion of arithmetic and economics was given a lasting boost in Europe when Hindu-Arabic numerals were imported to Italy. In the twelfth century, the representative of a Pisan trading house in the port city of Béjaïa in North Africa made sure that his son studied the numerals and calculation techniques used by his trading partners on lengthy trips between Provence and Syria. This son, Leonardo Pisano, published his *Liber abaci* in 1202. The book contained far more than just the multiplication tables associated with the word *abbaco* in Italian; it introduced basic arithmetic operations, fractions, root extraction, and the use of the most important achievement in the Hindu-Arabic numeral system, the number zero. Pisano's work was geared toward coupling numbers and words in a cohesive notation system consisting of columns of letters and figures.[73] Abacus schools, whose "*libri dell' Abbaco*" included problems and sample calculations oriented on everyday commercial transactions (unlike the arithmetic curricula of most monastic schools), were part of a merchant's education from the early fourteenth century.

Numbers, lines and columns, or instructions for converting coin denominations were abstract, paper-based equivalents to the physical space in which a merchant moved. In order to depict movements in space and monitor the amount, presence, or absence of goods, it was critical to combine data storage with "updates" which involved over-writing and amending existing data. To depict a process which took place over a period of time—in a diagram, for instance—merchants ideally needed a technique which enabled amended data to continue to be stored instead of being deleted. This is precisely why the material properties of paper made it so attractive. Unlike the dust abacus of the Persian mathematician al-Khwarizmi, paper was not just a buffer where the numbers needed for a calculation disappeared when the final result was presented. Data recorded on paper could be crossed out or carried forward, but these procedures did not necessarily result in the physical deletion of the data. The prerequisite for using this updating technique—which "stored each deletion as a movement" but took up a great deal of space on the page—was an ample amount of paper.[74]

The third book of *Il Negotiante*, into which Peri seamlessly weaves his depiction of the paper mills, bears a title—"I frutti d'Albaro"—which indicates that it was the product of the leisure time its author spent in the sophisticated villa suburb of Albaro. The gardens of the rich merchants who lived there rivaled those of Genoa's old aristocracy. But while Peri invokes the villas of Pliny and Cicero and plays on associations with Tusculum, the phrase "fruits of Albaro" has a double meaning which does not fit with the "*procul negotiis*" or the idyll outside the world of business. In *Il Negotiante*, the metaphor of "bearing fruit" always relates to current debates in the business world. Even in the second volume of his book, Peri had rejected the platitude that money was by its nature sterile. He did so by comparing agriculture to modern mercantilism, saying that dormant money left to its own devices was unfruitful, like grain in a sack, but that circulation stimulated the fertility inherent in it. One central motif in the third volume of *Il Negotiante* is Peri's defense of bill transactions at exchange fairs, and of credit systems in general, which were viewed skeptically even by his educated contemporaries on account of old edicts against usury.

Peri had come up against this skepticism after publishing the second volume of *Il Negotiante*. In the third volume, he makes a case for fruitfully coupling "*Scrittura doppia*,"[75] or double-entry book-keeping, with a mastery of navigation and the use of exchanges and protests. It is a case for the "new economic structure" which Fernand Braudel mentions in relation to Genoa. In the early twentieth century, the German sociologist Werner Sombart defined "modern capitalism" as a triad of a legal entity, an accounting entity, and a credit entity. He closely linked the term "capital" to double-entry bookkeeping, and he insisted that "prior to double-entry bookkeeping, capital was not a category that existed in the world, and without it, it would still not exist. One could almost define capital as assets recorded by means of double-entry bookkeeping."[76]

This assertion was based on the view that "modern capitalism" was an element of occidental rationalism as a whole, where double-entry bookkeeping stood alongside the likes of quantitative science, the discovery of the circulatory system, the theory of gravity. The proposed link between an economically exploitable cultural technology and the big concepts of twentieth-century modernization theory or the "spirit of capitalism" was critiqued by later historians who had studied late medieval accounting books. Their micro-historical revision resulted in remarkable hypotheses regarding the role of paper in the development of double-entry bookkeeping.

The criticism leveled at Sombart largely revolved around his definition of double-entry bookkeeping as a balancing function. This was Sombart's key evidence for tracing bookkeeping back to the advance of "economic rationality." According to his critics, however, the Italian merchants of the late Middle Ages were not primarily concerned with gaining fast, reliable information about profits and losses—in other words, generating a company balance sheet—in their everyday accounting. And even in the business enterprises of the Renaissance, full-fledged double-entry bookkeeping was not as widespread as Sombart's theory would lead one to expect. Instead, for a long time it was just one of many methods used for keeping books of account. These account books were, in turn, merely a pragmatic way of storing data concerning a merchant's current business. They were used more for their mnemonic function than for their balancing function.

Such memory aids were needed to maintain an overview of the credits and debits, or open and settled invoices, in a web of heavily staggered, unplanned transactions by various individuals over the course of time. If we view this web not from the perspective of an overarching, abstract organizational principle like "economic rationality" but in terms of the methods employed to fulfill this mnemonic function, then bookkeeping techniques no longer appear to emerge from the "spirit of capitalism" but rather from the practical interplay between the mnemonic function of accounting—which led to increased writing—and the storage medium which was best suited to this. Historian Franz-Josef Arlinghaus illustrated this interplay in his nuanced critical analysis of the account books—nearly all of which have survived—of the Florentine merchant Francesco Datini, who had a company in Avignon between 1367 and 1373.[77]

The fear of data loss and the need to continually regroup data in the course of day-to-day business resulted in a trio of records which is characteristic of accounting: the *ricordanze, memoriale,* and *libro grande. Ricordanze* were used to record business transactions, such as purchases and sales, as they took place. As this data accumulated, however, merchants could quickly lose track of which customers had made purchases when and how often, or who had paid or not paid a bill. For this reason, the same data was copied and reorganized in the *memoriale* in accordance with specific search criteria, so that transactions associated with a single customer could be provisionally grouped together, for example. The presorted data was then collated in an internally structured customer account in the *libro grande.* This tripartite structure was an established aspect of bookkeeping in general. Within this basic framework of data preservation and networking, double-entry bookkeeping evolved due to the special attention paid to the debit and credit columns. These took on larger dimensions for urban merchants than they did for monasteries, which kept more straightforward accounts of their dealings with tenants, benefactors, and so on.

The unrelenting flow of data was the decisive element in this configuration. Double-entry bookkeeping emerged from attempts to control this flow of data, but it was not a sudden, superior invention of the Renaissance; it was an evolutionary effect of trial and error, of pragmatic data tinkering within the boundaries of late-medieval models of writing. The pressure to process a steadily growing volume of data revealed the limits of pen and ink as recording media. Looking at the *ricordanze, memoriale,* and *libro grande* from the perspective of electronic data processing, the tripartite structure proves to be an effect of the "inflexibility" of paper, where the only way to regroup data or create searchable data units is to copy and reformat the data to a second paper buffer. This is why Arlinghaus asserts that the "internal momentum of textualization"[78] played a key role in the development of double-entry bookkeeping.

But even for Arlinghaus, paper remained a silent partner. It accepted and ratified the transactions of merchants without being in a position to dictate the laws that they followed. But it also became indispensible to the activities of the market. The increased functional importance of paper was not identical to its increased physical presence in everyday early modern life, however. The physical demand for paper arising from the *ricordanze, memoriale,* and *libro grande* did have an impact on the production of writing paper, but paper's growing functional significance was a result of the role it played as a storage medium in world-changing contexts. This is why Peri's *Il Negotiante* is an enlightening source of information—not only on account of its depiction of the mills of Voltri, but also because this depiction was embedded in the self-portrait of a successful merchant who participated in the emergence of modern paper-based capitalism.

2.5. Ragpickers, Writers, and the Pulpit

Pre-industrial paper mills were the site of a qualification divide that was also a social divide. At the heart of the mill, where the molds were dipped in the vats and the sheets of paper were couched and pressed until dry, papermaking was more than just a craft to the papermakers: it was an art. This was one reason papermakers never organized themselves in guilds like craftsmen. In the neighboring rooms, however, where the rags were presorted and cleaned—because their color and quality would determine those characteristics of the paper, and because fine white paper could only really be made from white linen—and in the drying loft, too, there might be women and children working. This divide extended to the procurement of the raw materials. In contrast to grain mills, the raw materials processed in paper mills were not delivered by customers; they were obtained either from the surrounding area or from afar if necessary. Because of this, ragpickers soon became a publicly visible counterpart to the papermakers who guarded the secrets of their art deep inside the mill.

Ragpickers were hunters as much as they were gatherers. Their ideal territory was the city, and they remained part of its cast of characters for centuries. Little did they know when they first appeared in the late Middle Ages that in the waning days of their existence, in the nineteenth century, they would experience an aesthetic apotheosis in the poetry of Baudelaire, the paintings of Edouard Manet, and the writing of Charles Dickens. Ragpickers were conspicuous figures because they had to attract attention. Their cries of "Rags! Rags!" and their whistling were long a part of the acoustic fabric of European cities and villages. A considerable number of women practiced this disdained trade as well. Like the paper mills, the ragpickers were soon surrounded by a dense network of social relationships and legal regulations. Rag dealers acted as middlemen between the ragpickers and the papermakers; the ragpickers' licenses and the boundaries of their collection areas were determined by regional rag collection privileges which were granted to the mills; and state bans on the export of rags regulated the large-scale circulation of their wares.

Though even wholesalers could get rich on the back of their efforts, the ragpickers themselves were menial laborers in the early modern age, embodiments of the concept of "dirty work." The German word *Haderlump*—derived from *Hadern* and *Lumpen*, two words for rags—soon became a term of abuse, one which was frequently also applied to Jews who were well represented among the ragpickers. In the late eighteenth century, the German doctor Johann Christian Gottlieb Ackermann adapted and translated *De Morbis Artificum Diatriba* (Diseases of Workers), a treatise by his Italian colleague Bernardino Ramazzini. In this treatise, ragpickers are mentioned in a chapter entitled "On the Diseases of the Jews." The houses in which Jews spread out the rotting rags they had collected are emphatically described as a source of disease by Ackermann. " 'Tis not credible what an ugly Stench" arose to envelope the occupants and permeate their bodies. "By this Means they become subject to Coughs, difficulty of Breathing, loathing of Food and Vertigos; for what can be imagined more vasty and abominable than a joynt heap of all the Filth that comes from Men, and Women, and Dead Corps? So that 'tis a piteous as well as a horrible Spectacle, to see Carts loaded with these remains of Poverty and humane Misery."[79]

The connection between pre-industrial papermaking and rags meant that paper mills formed relationships with ragpickers as well as the world of weavers. The menial ragpickers stood in contrast to the highly qualified vatmen in the mills, while in the wider world they stood in contrast to the most important consumers of finished paper, namely, writers and scholars.

In *Des Knaben Wunderhorn* (The Boy's Magic Horn [1806–8]), a collection of German folk songs compiled by the Romantic writers Achim von Arnim and Clemens Brentano, we find what amounts to a poetic book of trades of the late Middle Ages and early modern period rendered in the language of Romanticism. In many of these songs, the tailors and millers, smithies and farmers, hunters and weavers speak on behalf of themselves. "The Dignity of Writers" is one such song. The first verses are as follows:

It is the nature of paper to rustle,
And it can rustle a great deal.
You can easily overhear it,
Because it always wants to rustle.

It rustles everywhere
A sheet of it can be found,
So even the scholars rustle
Without any deceit.

Rags are used to make
The noble writer's stuff.
You may laugh at that,
But I tell you no lie.[80]

Modern readers may well discern a mocking tone in this song about writers; "murmuring in the press" is all too familiar as a metaphor criticizing the fleeting stir generated by accomplished blowhards among an audience primed for agitation. But the song is actually about writerly self-assurance, and it draws on a very old secondary meaning of rustling, namely, as an expression of an untamable, elementary force. As dictionaries will attest, this force may be love or the Holy Spirit "which stirs wildly within."[81] The implication here is that it is in paper's nature to have a strong impact. This impact is not tied to the amount of paper used; it can be felt in the chambers of scholars who use a great deal of paper, but it is equally present when a single leaflet circulates in an otherwise largely paperless sphere, or when paper bears an order which everyone must follow. The writer knows that his association with chanceries and the authorities makes him an object of mockery in popular song, with irate fellows writing coarse replies in painful letters like welts across his back. But because he is in league with the rustling of paper, his song can end with a self-confident challenge to the heroes whose pride is based solely on their physical strength:

Many a proud hero
Must bow before the writer
And huddle in a corner
Even though it displeases him.[82]

The self-praising writers of the early modern era were far removed from the servile scribes and wily secretaries of eighteenth-century literature. They knew they belonged to an ambitious new educated class which was distinguished by its knowledge of writing and its familiarity with Latin and the scholarly world. If they were mocked in the same breath as these scholars, they could reply with ease, for they had at their disposal a rich reservoir of metaphors in praise of writing, one which had been nurtured by medieval scholarly culture. This arsenal included comparisons between the pen and the sword

as well as between the pen and the plow, such as that found in a book
inscription from 1690:

> The paper is my field,
> That is why I am so stalwart,
> The pen is my plow,
> That is why I am so clever.
> The ink is my seed
> With which I write my name.[83]

In *Des Knaben Wunderhorn*, the song about the dignity of writers
has a counterpart in "The Weaver's Song." This song praises weaving
for the bed sheets, tablecloths, and napkins it produces, then for the
battlefields upon which war heroes pitch their canvas tents and
ensigns wave their heraldic banners. The last verse transforms the
technological connection between the textile industry and paper mills
into a metaphysical alliance. When woven products die, they are
resurrected in a new form to join in the rustling of paper:

> And if the canvas becomes worthless
> Or if the flag is lost,
> Then its true value is realized:
> Paper rustles in the ears,
> One prints the word of God on it
> and writes on it with ink.
> The weaver's work endures forever,
> No one can fathom it.[84]

The rustling of paper resonates with a promise of eternal life for
the weaver's work. This is the view from a post-Gutenberg world,
where printers have taken their place alongside writers. Weaving thus
becomes a partner in paper's potency. Though there is an intermediate
stage to its metamorphosis, when the textile products descend into
the realm of rags, the word "rags" itself is avoided. But reading
between the lines, it can still be found. The fact that paper mills made
paper from rags was basic knowledge which circulated in folk songs
and figures of speech long before paper technology and its history
was discussed in detail in the encyclopedias, academic treatises, mon-
ographs, and essays of the eighteenth century. Papermakers were
loath to divulge the secrets of their art, but their resource base was
advertised by the ragpickers who traveled through the cities and
villages.

The contrast between paper's base origins and its lofty calling is
a common motif in the texts accompanying visual depictions of

papermakers and paper mills in early modern books of trades. The
*True Description of All Ranks on Earth, High and Low, Spiritual and
Secular, of All Arts, Crafts and Trades* from 1568, with woodcuts by
Jost Amman, who was a writing master as well as an illustrator and
engraver, and verses by Hans Sachs, shows the interior of a contemporary paper mill, where a vatman lifts a mold out of the vat as his
assistant carries away a stack of sheets laid on felt to dry. The press
and stampers are visible in the background, and the mill's two water-
wheels can be seen through the window. The poem by Hans Sachs
acts as an intermediary between the rags that readers would have seen
for themselves and the papermaker's own description of his work:

> My need is rags for my good mill
> The wheel with water shreds them still
> Next press the pulp into a sheet
> On frame to place and dry to beat
> Then high I hang it, paper white
> And smooth, a joy to printer's sight.

Fine, smooth, white paper was highly prized as writing paper. The
transformation of a base, contemptible material into a snowy white
writing surface fit comfortably with the religious schema of the purification and conversion of humanity's corrupted nature. In Christoph
Weigel's *Depiction of the Main Public Trades from the Regents and
the Servants Assigned to Them in Times of Peace and War to All
Artists and Craftsmen* (1698), the chapter on papermakers can be
found in the section covering "Trades Which Are Very Useful for
Promoting Study."[85] It follows the chapters on book dealers, type
founders, book printers, and bookbinders. The brief history of writing
materials culminates in a hymn of praise to paper as "a means of
learning and propagating all notable sciences and arts." The engraving shows a papermaker holding a mold over a vat while three laborers work a drying press in the background. The water wheel which
drives the stampers can be seen through the open door of the mill,
while women and children sort rags nearby. The accompanying poem
draws a moral/metaphysical conclusion from the production process
depicted:

> Through hard work, old rags
> Are given new life, beautiful and white;
> Shall you remain contemptible, my heart?
> Emerge from the old state of sin,
> New and pure, that God's hand
> May write His will on thee.[86]

Even in the book of trades by Hans Sachs and Jost Amman, the papermaker was surrounded by the type founder, illustrator, woodblock cutter, book printer, and bookbinder—a host of servants to the dark art. In this post-Gutenberg context, paper's base origin in rags could be canceled out by the virginal white sheet and the black of the printing ink.

In his book *Something for Everyone* (1699), the preacher Abraham a Sancta Clara bridged the gap between the pulpit and the Baroque book of trades. In both oral sermons and illustrated books, the production of paper was associated with the concept of the resurrection of corrupt material. The fact that the textile and papermaking industries were technologically related made it easy to metaphorically interpret paper as a garment for the soul. Just as papermakers transformed discarded material and turned shredded, pounded, decomposed rags into snow-white paper, God would clothe the wretched and discarded *Haderlumpen* after their temporal death "in the snow-white mantle of eternal salvation."

3

The Universal Substance

3.1. Marshall McLuhan and the Pantagruelion of Rabelais

In *Gargantua and Pantagruel* by François Rabelais, the title characters and their names are the product of a virtuosic parody of mythological creation stories, historical chronicles, and Old Testament
genealogies. The giants' education covers the entire genealogy of
humanist knowledge, upon which Rabelais draws and whose bawdy
praises he sings. The introduction of printing marks a decisive break
in these educational histories: it separates Gargantua's world of origin
from that of his son, Pantagruel. In his first unsuccessful attempt at
an education, the young Gargantua is taught by the sophist Master
Holofernes, the epitome of dry bookishness, who introduces him to
the art of writing the "Gothick" script but fails to open the door to
true knowledge. This doctor of theology, who drills ABCs into his
pupil, is a writing machine and memory automaton in one, an ossified
latter-day product of scholasticism, a monster of the blind idolization
of writing. His writing desk weighs seven thousand hundredweight,
and his quill is the size of a pillar in a gothic cathedral because "he
copied out all his books by hand, since the art of printing was not
yet in use."[87] A second teacher is needed to induct Gargantua into
the world of true knowledge. Later on, Gargantua's son Pantagruel,
who is studying in Paris, receives a letter from his father. In this now-
famous passage, Gargantua looks back on his own education and
celebrates the world his son is growing into:

I never had an abundance of such tutors as you have. The times were still dark, redolent of the disaster and calamity of the Goths, who had brought all sound learning to destruction; but, by the goodness of God, light and dignity have been restored to literature during my lifetime: ... Now all disciplines have been brought back; languages have been restored: Greek—without which it is a disgrace that any man should call himself a scholar—Hebrew, Chaldean, Latin; elegant and accurate books are now in use, printing having been invented in my lifetime through divine inspiration just as artillery, on the contrary, was invented through the prompting of the devil. The whole world is now full of erudite persons, full of very learned teachers and of the most ample libraries, such indeed that I hold that it was not as easy to study in the days of Plato, Cicero nor Papinian as it is now.[88]

Much has been written of Rabelais' close connections with the printers in Lyon, the third major center of the printing industry in Europe after Paris and Venice. Lyon was a flourishing commercial hub; the silk industry was firmly established there, and the city attracted merchants and capital from all over Europe. The Medici family from Florence had opened a bank branch there in 1461, and trade connections stretched to Antwerp, Augsburg, and Nuremberg as well as Barcelona, Valencia, and Genoa. International capital flowed into the city and reached the peninsula at the confluence of the Rhône and Saône where the printing industry had put down roots. In 1515 there were sixty printers there, twenty-nine booksellers, numerous lead casters, bookbinders, engravers—and several paper mills. Unlike Paris, however, Lyon had no university and no parliament. The printing industry in Lyon had not emerged from the manuscript copying culture of academia, the scriptoria of bishops and monasteries, or large private libraries. Instead, like the paper industry of Genoa, it was a profitable branch of trade for a commercial city, and the new technology blossomed rapidly in part because it met with no stubborn resistance from manuscript writers and book illustrators.[89]

It was just a few steps from the Hôtel Dieu, where Rabelais the doctor was employed, to the printers with whom Rabelais the author worked. Rabelais was an early example of a publishing strategist; he released his vernacular works under the burlesque anagrammatic pseudonym of Alcofribas Nasier, and he knew which printers had experience with the new small-format books and which sold large runs of octavos. Allusions to the world of books can be found throughout his series of novels about the giants Gargantua and Pantagruel. In his letters, Rabelais partook of the humanist rhetoric that celebrated printing as a light-bearer which would drive away the

"Cimbrian darkness of the Gothic age."[90] And when Gargantua, in the famous letter to his son, characterizes printing as a gift from God, he is also speaking on behalf of his author.

Marshall McLuhan frequently held up Rabelais and the letter-writing Gargantua as star witnesses in his media theory, particularly in his bestseller *The Gutenberg Galaxy* (1962). Rooted in the oral world of manuscript culture but already a virtuoso of the typographic era, Rabelais is a key literary figure in McLuhan's Gutenberg galaxy, a counterpart to James Joyce, who stood at the threshold of the waning typographic world and introduced the techniques of electronic media to literature.

McLuhan's interpretation of Rabelais incorporated ideas from a chapter entitled "The World in Pantagruel's Mouth" in Erich Auerbach's book *Mimesis* (1946), as well as from the book *Ramus, Method and the Decay of Dialogue* (1958) by Walter J. Ong. McLuhan picked up on Auerbach's views concerning the utopian slant of the motif of the journey into the mouth of the giant (which was taken from medieval chapbooks), the references to the discovery of new worlds, and the mingling of styles and continually shifting viewpoints. According to Auerbach, Rabelais was like a late medieval preacher who mixed informal erudition with crude folksiness. But Rabelais' book—by virtue of being a book—was aimed not at the common folk but at the educated humanist elite to which he himself belonged: "The preachers addressed the people; their vivid sermons were intended for direct delivery. Rabelais' work was meant to be printed, in other words to be read."[91]

This reference to the break between sermons directed at the ear and books as objects to be read brings into play the polarity of sound and sight which McLuhan took from *Ramus, Method and the Decay of Dialogue* (1958) by his student Walter J. Ong. Ong explained Petrus Ramus' ideas on logic and method by highlighting the contrast between aural dialogic learning and visual learning in view of the type area of printed textbooks. As soon as Rabelais appears in McLuhan's "Gutenberg galaxy," he is placed alongside Ong's Ramus as an interface between the oral and visual worlds. Rabelais the storyteller is depicted as "a collective rout of oral schoolmen and glossators suddenly debouched into a visual world."[92]

The world into which Rabelais tumbles is the world of Marshall McLuhan's media theory with its dramatic epochal ruptures. In this world, the introduction of the phonetic alphabet led ancient oral cultures to be replaced by a manuscript culture which reached into the Middle Ages. After the invention of the printing press, "alphabetic man" was shaped into the "typographic man" of the Gutenberg galaxy, a creature whose feelings and thoughts were entirely informed by the linearity of the page and the way it translated all content into an abstract ribbon of black lines. For McLuhan, technologies and media are agents affecting the plasticity of the human mind. They stunt our senses, isolate them or drive them to hypertrophy, separate them from one other or extend them. His media theory is also a type of speculative historical anthropology, according to which—following the theories of Milman Parry, Albert B. Lord, and, above all, Walter J. Ong concerning the relationship between "orality" and "literacy"—medieval manuscript culture related to the ear while typography privileges the sense of sight. Ramus' method of spatially segmenting and displaying knowledge on the page led to the use of diagrams, branching charts, and tables which could not be read aloud. Ong described the printing press as the ideal tool for visualizing knowledge in the way advocated by Ramus. Typography, according to McLuhan, silenced the dialogic clamor of voices surrounding books that had previously been handwritten and read aloud. It granted typographic man the powers of "detachment and noninvolvement"[93] which were essential to his determination to drive the advancement of medicine, the natural sciences, and technology. Additionally, the eye—an organ of distance which evolved at the expense of our most social sense, hearing—fostered the emergence of modern individualism.

In old triadic models of the philosophy of history, the collapse of an original order was followed by an age of consummate wickedness, from which the original order reemerged on a higher level. As McLuhan saw it, the spell of typography was cast over the entire culture, only to be broken by the electric revolution. In the electric age, culminating in the invention of the computer, this reciprocal permeation of man and technology reached all the way to our central nervous system. The end of the book age, which was shaped by mechanization and individualism, brought about an opportunity for a culture of non-linear thought and art; the clamor of voices returned on a higher technical level and became universal; and a "social consciousness electrically ordered" began to coalesce in the "global village."[94]

The metaphor at the heart of McLuhan's interpretation of Rabelais is the superimposition of the printing press and the wine press. It illustrates the toxic effect of new media as well as the intoxication and exuberance they are capable of invoking. "Rabelais is concerned with the democratization of knowledge by the abundance of wines from the printing press. For the press is named from the technology it borrowed from the wine-press."[95] It is true that in Rabelais' poetic universe, books strive to take the form of bottles, and from the outset the narrator eagerly assumes the role of the cupbearer who addresses his readers as though they were revelers. With their giant mouths, Gargantua and Pantagruel are both sots and gluttons, and time and again Rabelais lets the language of reading, knowledge, and scholarship slip into enthusiastic poetic inebriation. Don't the long lists of absurd book titles—a parody of library catalogues—and the terminological genealogies snarled in a mess of quotes from classic authors sound like the gibberish muttered by a boozer? Isn't there something of a drinking ritual about the high-proof Latinate mumbo-jumbo that a dimwitted student spouts as a type of linguistic calling card in order to play up his university connections? Aren't the scatological digressions that intersperse Rabelais' work like disquisitions which have deliriously stumbled into the toilet? And isn't his novel as a whole—that beast of unbridled stylistic promiscuity—something like an attempt to heavily doctor the waters of sober scholasticism and humanist knowledge with the wine of the grotesque and of folk culture?

Rabelais is a master at transforming all humanist knowledge and knowledge technologies into hallucinogenic drugs and aphrodisiacs.

His strangest invention, the fantastical herb known as pantagruelion, is situated somewhere between hemp and flax in the plant kingdom. The "Third Book of Pantagruel" ends with a eulogy to this miracle plant. The eulogy is delivered in the form of a long literary digression just as Pantagruel and Panurge are about to embark on an Atlantic voyage from Thalassa near Saint-Malo. This is a risky moment for the characters because the sea is dangerous. Pantagruel takes the plant on board as a talisman in both its raw green state as well as dressed and preserved. The powers that Rabelais, a trained doctor, ascribe to the miracle plant surpass those of any magical universal medicine. Generations of readers and philologists have been stumped by the unsolvable riddle that is Rabelais' eulogy to pantagruelion, a delirium of ambiguous description and denomination. Allegorical or symbolic interpretations can be found for nearly all of the plant's uses: as medicine or clothing, as a means of revealing and capturing invisible creatures, as a way of propelling ships around the world and from pole to pole, and possibly even taking humans to the moon in the future. Pantagruelion gives us a glimpse of the universal library in Rabelais' mind and the folk traditions and realities of his social and political world; references to its properties of protection against fire and water can be read as an allusion to the age of religious wars and the repressions with which the orthodoxy persecuted heretics.

Marshall McLuhan resolutely interprets the miracle plant as a symbol of the revolutionary power of typography. He says there can be no doubt "about Rabelais' insistence on *pantagruelion* as the symbol and image of printing from movable types. For this is the name of the hemp plant from which rope was made. From the teasing and shredding and weaving of this plant there came the lineal cords and bonds of greatest social enterprises."[96] For McLuhan, pantagruelion is a magical representation of linearity, which is the magic word in his own media theory. "Typographic man" was not spawned by the mass circulation of identical, mechanically generated products as such. As a dominant force in the visual realm, the linearity of typography was the decisive factor in the standardization, uniformity, and "homogenization of men." Printing was the model which "taught men how to organize all other activities on a systematic lineal basis."[97]

But what role did paper play in all of this? In McLuhan's media theory, paper was one of the "earlier technological achievements" which were regrouped and revolutionized by printing. Once the printing press appeared on the scene, paper merged with it.

Though Gutenberg continued to print some of his Bibles on parchment, his invention had an epochal impact only because paper was available as a more economical but also higher-quality medium for images and text, one which increasingly supplemented and replaced parchment wherever the mass reproduction of a book was more important than its elaborate design. This shift clearly did not start back in 1450; it only emerged during the Reformation, when Bibles and pamphlets began to be sold in many different formats. If we look more closely at the center of printing technology, where the printing press met the paper, we can see that there was an innovation gap—and Gutenberg's hand mold for casting type was situated at the pole of innovation. This tool made it possible to reproduce identical letters any number of times, making it the most important device in Gutenberg's "machine for producing calligraphy without a reed, stylus or quill."[98] Hand-cast letters, the metallic embodiment of the relatively small phonetic Latin alphabet, helped typography take off in the West; in China, by contrast, the large number and pictographic nature of Chinese characters hampered the rapid adoption of printing technology. McLuhan's theory of printing is an exaltation of the hand mold because it is, above all, a theory of the standardization and mechanization which allowed print shops to produce books in which any word—if not in actuality, then at least according to the regulative idea—could look exactly the same on the first page as it did on the last. Since this innovation at the heart of the print workshop was made of metal, printing found itself in league with a material which contained the seeds of the modern industrial age. The hand mold was an object of mechanical precision which was kept secret from all potential competitors.

This was not true of paper. It was one of the non-innovative elements of the printing process—much more obviously than the wooden press, though even this was not taken from the world of viticulture without further ado. The American paper historian Dard Hunter mentions the seemingly trivial fact that Gutenberg could not have commissioned special paper for his press without giving papermakers a good look at his invention, thereby lessening its exclusivity. He therefore had to develop his new technology based on the range of writing paper already available.[99] Paper could be the non-innovative element in this context because it was the product of nearly two hundred years of prior innovation. It was no longer the comparably fragile substance that had arrived in Europe via the Arab world. Instead, it was a material which could withstand the pressure of the metal type without being perforated and which was opaque enough to be printed on both sides—assuming, of course, that the pressure exerted during the pressing process had been adjusted to suit the nature of the paper, and that the interaction between the wooden press and the metal type had been finely tuned. The screw shaft and the bar that turned it had to act on the printing plate in such a way that the screw's movement was not transferred to the platen which pressed against the paper. In addition, a printing ink was needed which, unlike other inks available at the time, would produce precise and permanent characters when the metal type met the page.[100] The type, in turn, had to be made from the only material that was guaranteed to create this effect on paper: lead.

A network of interrelationships between typography and papermaking coalesced around this technological nucleus. Both quantitatively and qualitatively, the development of paper production was heavily stimulated by demand from the printing press. It was no coincidence that the Nuremberg-based printer and book dealer Anton Koberger had several of his own paper mills in the late fifteenth century. Papermakers soon stood side by side with printers in the books of trades. In Basel, documents from the incunabula age show that well-funded papermakers would come to the aid of printers looking to pre-finance complex projects if the printers guaranteed to purchase their paper in return. In other cases, printers would ensure a steady supply of paper by putting either their future publications or other valuables in pledge to papermakers.[101] In this spectrum of relationships, printers and papermakers were like twins who often argued but were inseparable nonetheless.

We have seen how paper flowed along the East-West axis of migration of cultural technology before Gutenberg, how it engulfed his invention and continued on along a number of different channels: in the imperial chancery of Frederick II of Hohenstaufen in Sicily; in Nuremberg, where playing cards were imported from Egypt; in the paper mills of Genoa, where money circulated from the financial world, which had adopted the Arab practice of using bills of exchange; and in the offices of merchants, where paper contributed to the rise of double-entry bookkeeping. For all that paper was metaphysically elevated by preachers who cocooned it in metaphors of purification and sublimation, it could always be put to baser uses as well. Woodcut allied itself early on with paper for the purposes of mass reproduction, and though woodcutting subsequently developed into a sophisticated artistic genre, paper itself never relinquished its ties to the entertainment industry. Paper's most important function was as a means of conveying signs and symbols, but it was not strictly defined by this role, and its fusion with the printing press did not force it to forfeit its technological independence or its autonomy as a medium.

Paper also had its own ties to pantagruelion, the miracle plant of Rabelais. Restricting pantagruelion to a symbol of typography and linearity does not do justice to its universality. Pantagruelion is an ambisexual natural substance, one which is sown and harvested as a crop and can only be described by trotting out a host of mythologems from around the world and comparisons with its supposed relatives in the plant kingdom. Like any magical plant, its power is only released when it is prepared according to rules known exclusively by the initiated. Pantagruel is one of the initiated: "*Pantagruelion* is dressed over the autumn equinox in various ways, depending upon people's ingenuity and local conditions. The first directions which Pantagruel gave were: to strip the stalk of its leaves and seeds; to macerate it in stagnant—not running—water for five days if the weather is dry and the water warm, or for some nine or twelve if the weather is cloudy and the water cold; then to dry it in the sun, stripping off the outer layer in the shade and separating the fibers (in which, as we said, consist its excellence and its value) from the woody parts, which are useless except for producing a bright blaze, or as tinder, or, by children at play, for blowing up their pig's bladders. ... Some Pantagruelists nowadays avoid the manual labor involved in separating the plants by using certain contunding machines (constructed in the shape made by ferocious Juno when she interlocked her fingers, heckle-shaped, to impede the birth of Hercules from Alcmene his mother) by means of which they break and heckle out the woody part, setting it aside as useless but keeping the fibers."[102]

This description of the proper way to prepare pantagruelion is similar to a passage in which Pliny, in the thirteenth book of his *Natural History*, discusses how papyrus for writing is made using the papyrus plant in Egypt. It stands to reason that Rabelais—whose laudation of pantagruelion is generally meant as a parody and mimicry of Pliny's *Natural History*—would make reference to the passages where Pliny describes how papyrus stems were split into thin, long strips: "The quality of the papyrus is best at the center of the plant and decreases progressively towards the outsides."[103] But the "contunding machine," which, according to Rabelais, is used as a defibration technology by modern Pantagruelists, takes us out of Egypt and brings to mind the stampers and shredders in paper mills. This association is made all the stronger because Rabelais explicitly distinguishes between two methods of breaking down pantagruelion. The first method entails simply smashing the woody part of the plant in order to get to the fibers used by rope makers—the same rope makers to whom McLuhan referred when he said that pantagruelion promoted linearity. Rabelais presents the second method without further comment: "Those who desire more evidently to increase its value do what we are told to be the pastime of the three Fatal Sisters, the nightly diversion of noble Circe and the long-maintained pretext of Penelope to her fond suitors during the absence of her husband Ulysses."[104] The Fates spin, Circe and Penelope weave, and Penelope also represents the undoing of what is woven. This is where the textile industry, a neighbor to the printers and papermakers of Lyon, enters the picture. Rabelais mentions the fine tablecloths, bed sheets, and coarse sacks made out of pantagruelion—in other words, the raw materials of paper which are produced through the Penelopean activity of undoing woven material. Pantagruelion supplies the material for the printing press, but it is not the printing press itself: "Without it the miller could bring no corn to the mill and take home no flour. Without it, how would lawyers bring their bundles into court? Without it, how could we carry plaster into the workshop? Without it, how would we draw water from the well? Without it, how could notaries-public, clerks, secretaries and scriveners manage? Would not all legal deeds and rent-agreements perish? Would not the noble art of printing perish?"[105]

The poetic pantagruelion should not be interpreted as the symbol of an actual substance in the physical world, and certainly not a single substance. It is neither the hemp that intoxicates nor the hemp used to make ropes for navigating and exploring the world—neither typography alone nor paper. But through its association with the world of weaving, spinning, and contusive defibration, pantagruelion acquires one of the many guises ascribed to it by Rabelais—namely, as a fantastical cross between papyrus and paper. The thrust of Rabelais' parodic natural history of this "hallowed" herb, however, is not that the plant is similar to one thing or another, but that it is universal. Pantagruelion owes its name to this universality, something which Rabelais rationalizes with conspicuous rhetorical effort. It acquired the name primarily on account of its resemblance to Pantagruel, with the Greek root *pan* ("all") signaling the diverse talents of its namesake. This diversity is carried over to pantagruelion itself, so the titular hero of the book is reflected in the plant. This observation leads to the most surprising and, for our purposes, very welcome interpretation of the miracle plant. The interpretation proposes that pantagruelion represents the very book in which it appears—that is, the book as both a physical object and a product of its author's intellect. Pantagruelion would thus symbolize medicine, which Rabelais summons up in the form of the book to counteract the burns from the ordeals by fire and water of the orthodoxy and of Parisian professors; it would symbolize the printed letters and paper which make up the book; and it would symbolize the rhetorical and literary skill with which its author brought the book into being.[106] This interpretation easily answers the question of why Rabelais' natural history of this miraculous universal plant ends with a digression on the non-combustible "asbestine" pantagruelion: because it epitomizes the intellectual and fantastic poetical substance that Rabelais poured into the book about Pantagruel. The intellect can't be burned.

Marshall McLuhan elaborated his theory of typographic man in a demonstratively non-linear book and visualized it as a galaxy, though he conceptualized this galaxy as a system of planets revolving around the printing press. But the world of pantagruelion is non-linear. It resists being assimilated into McLuhan's central-perspective space, just as paper does.

3.2. Harold Innis, the Postal System, and Mephisto's Scrap

Some versions of the story of Cadmus, the mythological founder of Thebes, credit him with bringing the Phoenician alphabet to Greece. It is easy to draw a connection between this element of the story and Cadmus' most important deed: slaying a sacred dragon. Following the advice of Athena, Cadmus sowed the dragon's teeth, and a host of armed men sprang from the earth, among them the future Theban patriarchs. A stanza in Charles Fontaine's "Ode de l'antiquité et excellence de la ville de Lyon" (1557) praises the millions of "black teeth" which populate the city even when there are no book fairs being held: "*En mille maisons, au dedans, / Un grand million de dents noires, / Un million de noires dents / Travaille en foires et hors foires.*"[107] These black teeth, which clearly represent ink-stained lead type, update the old metaphorical connection between teeth and letters. McLuhan frequently cited the Cadmus myth as proof that even ancient "typographic man" was aware of the power of the medium that had shaped him. His interpretation of the myth references Elias Canetti, who analyzed the aggressive act of baring one's teeth in his book *Crowds and Power*. In the mythology of the Gutenberg galaxy, letters became the successors to the dragon's teeth of Cadmus, powerful tools of "aggressive order and precision."[108] Even in the Greek alphabet we find forerunners of the linear battle formation of typography, in which letters are turned into metal type.

The mythical power attributed to the alphabet in McLuhan's media theory is an example of the basic principle of the Toronto School of communication taken to the extreme. The name of the Toronto School was bestowed in retrospect by Jack Goody. *The Consequences of Literacy* (1963), which Goody co-authored with Ian Watt, and *Preface to Plato* (1963), a genealogy of the phonetic alphabet by Eric A. Havelock, were immediate neighbors to the *Gutenberg Galaxy*. The discipline of classical studies, which began to focus on the relationship between orality and literacy in Greek culture in view of Homer's epics and Plato's critique of writing, anchored the Toronto School in the field of philology. Philology had a counterpart, however, in the media theory of the Canadian Harold Innis, who developed his theory in his later writings from around 1950 based on his work in economic history. Innis had published a dissertation entitled "A History of the Canadian Pacific Railway" in 1923, and he earned a reputation as one of Canada's leading economic historians through books on the succession of staple industries in Canada. It was by way of the history of fur trading and cod fishing that he arrived at the history of the Canadian wood and paper industry which, from the nineteenth century, had contributed to the rise of the American press. His research into the connection between paper production and the development of America's economic and cultural dominance flowed into later essays on media theory and the books *Empire and Communication* (1950) and *The Bias of Communication* (1951). The interdependency of the paper industry and the modern popular press led Innis to formulate his thesis that communication media play the role of key industries in the modern industrial age. Referring all the way back to the great empires of antiquity and to Arnold Toynbee's universal history, he elaborated his basic argument that the infrastructure of communication is a historical constant and directional factor in both economic and political history.

McLuhan once remarked that *The Gutenberg Galaxy* was merely an explanatory footnote to Harold Innis's work. And indeed, McLuhan's trademark phrase "The medium is the message" echoes a comparatively cautious formulation by Innis: "We can perhaps assume that the use of a medium of communication over a long period will to some extent determine the character of knowledge to be communicated."[109] But while McLuhan explored the effects of the phonetic alphabet, medieval manuscript culture, and typography as a speculative historical anthropologist of media-generated man, Innis examined the material media of communication, particularly with respect to the options they open up for exploiting and controlling space and time. By taking this approach, Innis the economic historian became Innis the paper historiographer and media theorist. One of his sources of information, the English literary historian Henry Hallam, had called paper a "universal substance" in light of the "paper revolution" of the late Middle Ages. Innis picked up on this phrase and ascribed to paper a key function in the communication structures of the modern era.[110]

According to Innis, stone, clay tablets, and parchment are "heavy" media which enable a civilization to anchor itself in the past and eternalize itself. They promote temporally wide-ranging, diachronic communication and transmission, and their storage function trumps their circulation function; the only way for an inscribed obelisk to circulate is as loot. "Light" media, by contrast—like papyrus and paper—encourage spatially wide-ranging, horizontal communication. They make it possible to control large territories, and their circulation function trumps their storage function. Innis developed this hypothesis within a concept of balance which has obvious origins in the classic aesthetic of the mean and moderation. He depicts the rise and fall of empires as a series of successful and failed attempts to maintain an equilibrium between time- and space-biased communication media. With the mistrust of a former Baptist, Innis claimed that the association between priestly castes and time-biased media threatened this balance because it led to the formation of monopolies of knowledge. He generally viewed religion as being in league with the media of duration: stone in Egypt, parchment in the Christian Middle Ages. The rise of empires depended on light media such as papyrus and, later, paper, which made it possible to exploit and control territories. The conquest of Egypt facilitated the emergence of written administration and bureaucracy in the Roman Empire because it opened up unimpeded access to papyrus. In Egypt itself, the scribes' monopoly of knowledge and their affiliation with the ruling classes and religious institutions limited the circulation potential of papyrus and hindered the development of an Egyptian empire.

In his memoir of Innis, Eric A. Havelock pointed out the ambiguity of Innis's concept of space, which oscillates between the political space of the empire, or the territory to be controlled, and the space of Western civilization, where messengers and letters, scholars and merchants, circulate without being subject exclusively to the logic of political power. It is within this space of Western civilization, incorporating the political sphere, the economic realm, and the living environment alike, that paper-based cultural technologies took off. In view of this space, the basic idea behind Innis's media theory—which coupled the term "communication medium" to the old definition of communication as "conveyance," or the infrastructure of transportation—can be applied to the historiography of paper.[111]

From a modern perspective, paper appears to be the lightest medium of the old industrial world, one which could guarantee storage as well as circulation. It was the last precursor to digital data streams and their network infrastructure, which has been decoupled from traditional transportation routes. Paper is a relatively light medium, but it is still a physical object which must move through space, so it remained bound to the transportation infrastructure in which travelers moved as well. It was only by aligning itself with this infrastructure that paper could circulate and set off on its Arabian adventures, or become indispensible to the merchants and financiers of Genoa, or make it big in the court of the paper kings, or profit from the invention of the printing press. In its easy alliances and ability to embed itself in a variety of routines, paper challenged the storage metaphor of the closed container that readily sprang to mind particularly in reference to books.

We get a deceptive impression of the link between paper technology and spatial development if we simply subsume it under the rise of the printing press, as McLuhan does in *Understanding Media*: "With the moving of information in printed form, the wheel and the road came into play again after having been in abeyance for a thousand years. In England, pressure from the press brought about hard-surface roads in the eighteenth century, with all the population and industrial rearrangement that entailed."[112] The connection to the Roman *cursus publicus*—the ancient model upon which the early modern information and transportation network was based—was

not an effect of the printing press, and it had far-reaching consequences even earlier than the eighteenth century. In fact, as Wolfgang
Behringer showed in his history of the central European postal system
entitled *Im Zeichen des Merkur* (Under the Sign of Mercury), projects
aimed at establishing a modern successor to the Roman *cursus publicus* far predated printing. They were prompted not so much by a
recourse to the wheel/road combination as by the revival of the
mounted courier service.[113] Postal historians have found evidence of
the first instance of such a revival in the Duchy of Milan in the late
fourteenth century. It was here, in the center of early capitalist banking
and the textile and arms industries, that we find the first "time sheets"
used by mounted messengers—who had to be able to read and
write—to record the stages of their journey.[114] So as European paper
technology was taking off, a form of linearity different to that of the
printing press was emerging at the same time: a fixed network of
transcontinental postal routes.

The evolution of this central European communications infrastructure forces us to reconsider the idea of an essentially static pre-
modern age which was not gripped by an acceleration imperative
until the so-called *Sattelzeit* (saddle period) of the eighteenth century.
Unlike the Roman *cursus publicus*, the central European postal
system was not an institution of "empire," to use Innis's word.
Although the postal service of the Holy Roman Empire—the
Reichspost, which legally existed between 1597 and 1806—had been
authorized by imperial right, it was in fact a private company which
was essentially forced to grant access to everyone, if only to recoup
its costs. If we view this communications network not from the perspective of modern media since the telegraph, but instead from the
perspective of the late Middle Ages, then we can see that it achieved
a remarkable increase in the speed and frequency at which both messages and people circulated.

As paper became the dominant medium of written communication,
paper and the postal system formed an alliance which was just as
epochal as that between paper and the printing press. The effects of
these two alliances overlapped, but they sprang from autonomous
sources which could not be traced back to each other. This becomes
apparent as soon as we relinquish our fixation on typography and
put unprinted paper on an equal footing with printed paper. The
alliance of paper and the postal system transcended the polarity
between printed and handwritten materials because it was as closely
tied to one pole as it was to the other. Countless letters were printed,
but this was always just a small subset of all the unprinted papers
which circulated and then disappeared.

It is hard to overstate the importance of the connection between paper and the postal system. The *epistola docta* or "treatise letters" sent between scholars in the seventeenth century were predecessors to the journals of the eighteenth century.[115] The to-and-fro of letters contributed to both the dissemination of knowledge and its production. The most prominent characteristic of the postal system was its periodicity: people and messages circulated at increasingly frequent cycles in an increasingly reliable system at a specific place and a specific time. Paper's association with the periodicity of the postal system was momentous, just as its acceleration of reproduction on the printing press was long-lasting.

A defining element of the modern world crystallized here: "Mail delivery day" became a recurring interlude in the temporal continuum of everyday life not to mention a cardinal motif in literature. Long before the railway age it gave rise to timetables and, eventually, to the medium that made it possible to experience the present as the present and turn spatially dispersed individuals into contemporaries—namely, newspapers. Newspapers came into being in the early seventeenth century, not as direct descendants of the printing technology that had been introduced a good 150 years earlier but as products of the interplay between handwritten correspondence on paper, news reports printed for German trade fairs, and the postal system.[116]

The stable, continuous circulation of news was essential to the rise of the periodical press. This prerequisite had not yet been met during the age of the *Newen Zeitungen*, the early sixteenth-century German newspapers—similar to illustrated ballads—which reported on catastrophes and comets, murders and witch burnings. Conditions were not right until around 1600 when the Reichspost was established, spawning an infrastructure that benefited early periodicals like the Strasbourg *Relation* of 1605 and the Wolfenbüttel *Aviso* of 1609. Newspaper and postal historians have shown that the core of the new medium coalesced when the paper-based handwritten correspondence which had been circulating in the Fuggers' far-flung communication network encountered the infrastructure of the Reichspost. The next step in the development of the new paper-based medium was the shift from handwritten to typographic reproduction, initially in small print runs of between 100 and 300 copies. This was a step that could always be reversed, as we will see in the eighteenth century when handwritten newspapers from modern publishers began to circulate widely for a wealthy audience.

The importance of the first newspapers grew rapidly during the Thirty Years' War on the Continent and the ongoing conflict between

King and Parliament in England. These newspapers were heralds of a future cultural superpower: topicality.

In the polarity of space- and time-biased media, the ease with which paper circulates through space seems to come at the expense of longevity. This was certainly the suspicion when books printed on paper began to grow in popularity in the second half of the fifteenth century. In his work *De laude scriptorum* (1494), Johannes Trithemius, the famous abbot of Sponheim, warned against the ephemerality of the new books printed on paper and recommended that they be copied to parchment to ensure their survival. Trithemius is occasionally held up on the internet as the prototype of a deluded Luddite, an example of the absurd beliefs held by someone who has not realized for whom the media bell is tolling. But the abbot, who was one of the most important bibliographers of his time, was primarily interested in taking advantage of a future technology to preserve the achievements of medieval penmanship. He certainly did not ignore the media situation created by the printing press, and he actively dealt with the print shop of Peter von Friedberg in Mainz, to whom he sent many of his manuscripts—including *De laude scriptorum*—so that they could be distributed as widely as possible, as quickly as possible. He simply made a point of ensuring that his manuscript was printed on parchment as well as on paper.[117] In short, the abbot did not blindly extol handwritten copies on parchment; he was just clever enough to take the polarity of time and space into account well before any modern media theorist. It suited him fine to have large numbers of his printed works in circulation. But when it came to anchoring manuscripts in time, it seemed safer to make base copies on an older medium designed for duration instead of entrusting them to a medium whose long-term reliability was as difficult for him to estimate as that of digital formats is for us.

Trithemius' paper skepticism was informed by a concept of "the book" that was older than printed books, and even older than the medieval combination of codex and parchment. This concept stretched back to antiquity and the world of papyrus scrolls. The Roman poet Horace captured the book's claim to endurance in verse: *Exegi monumentum aere perennius.* The Egyptologist Jan Assmann has uncovered the Egyptian roots of this locus classicus, whereby a literary work ensures that the name of its author survives not only longer than bronze monuments, but even longer than the pyramids. According to Assmann, epitaphs inscribed in stone were the inspiration for the literature of Egypt. In Egypt, self-immortalization in a book took over from the immortality of the tomb, so a communication medium was able to assume and even surpass the cultural functions of stone without being made of stone itself. Horace's monumental claim was inspired not by the material qualities of the papyrus on which he wrote but by the writing itself, which would be passed on to an ever more distant posterity in future copies of his work. Pliny could therefore attribute immortality to the use of papyrus long before papyrus was pitted against the even more durable medium of parchment.[118]

Books printed on paper adopted this model so successfully that they quickly became guarantors of immortality in the rhetoric of humanism. Because printed books could be reproduced rapidly in large quantities, it was difficult to take the arguments that had been made against papyrus in favor of parchment and apply them to paper as well. Trithemius had estimated that a parchment manuscript would last about a thousand years while a paper book would last two hundred at most.[119] But he underestimated both the longevity of paper and the possibility that books printed on paper could offer the same perpetuity as the old media of duration, from parchment all the way down to stone.

The intervention of the abbot of Sponheim shows that throughout the history of storage and circulation media, the guarantee that a text will be passed on has always been viewed in relation to the apparent durability of the medium on which it is written. The time-space axis along which Harold Innis placed communication media is therefore not a rigid polarity based solely on the physical heaviness or lightness of a medium; it is a continuum embedded in the time-space concepts of actual cultures. Jan Assmann provides an enlightening example of this in his analysis of the "digraphia" of Egyptian culture. According to Assmann, Egyptian culture was characterized by a dichotomy between the media of eternity and the media of the present. Achievements endured immutably in the one, while various events flowed through cycles of celestially governed time in the other. Monumental stone architecture was the medium of time as duration, while clay buildings were the medium of the continuous renewal of all that was transient. The polarity of stone and clay in architecture had a communicative counterpart in Egypt's digraphia, the parallel use of two different writing systems.[120] Hieroglyphics, like stone architecture, related to the eternal, while cursive writing, like clay architecture, related to the present and the rhythm of events associated with pragmatic functions. The inscriptions captured in the rigid situational context of stone monuments stood in contrast to the fluid manuscripts on portable papyrus which evaded fixation in space or time.

Assmann's illustration of digraphia in Egyptian culture can be combined with Innis's space-time polarity in a way that contributes to the media theory of paper. Even in the modern world, writing is coupled with heavy media in the form of inscriptions on tombstones and the façades of museums and theaters. But the differentiation of paper-based cultural technologies since the late Middle Ages has brought something new into the mix. The time-space polarity which had applied to different media, like papyrus and stone, in ancient cultures evolved in the modern age into a polarity between different formats of a single medium: paper. This becomes apparent as soon as we stop hastily associating paper with the printed book and instead look at the entire spectrum of printed and unprinted paper. Within this spectrum, paper is suitable as a medium for circulating data of a limited range and longevity as well as for combining wide-ranging circulation and long-term storage. This diversification of the scope and spatial range of transmission took place outside of the printing press, around it, through it, and along temporal axes of various lengths. The alliance that paper, as a light medium, formed with carrier pigeons in the ancient Arab world persisted through World War II. Paper could be incorporated into folios that were heavier than stone, but it could also be used as a short-term storage and circulation medium for all kinds of ephemera. It saturated immediate everyday life in the form of pamphlets, letters, leaflets, and notes—which were joined by the telegraph in the electric age—while also serving as a physical carrier for long-distance communication in time and space.

Faust lived in the world of books. Around 1800, Goethe placed him in a study where he soliloquized on his disillusionment with book learning. In his conversation with Mephistopheles, he nearly flies off the handle when Mephisto demands "a line or two in writing" to seal the deal instead of settling for a handshake and "man's word": "A formal deed, with seal and signature, / A specter this from which all shrink afraid. / The word resigns its essence in the pen, / Leather and wax usurp the mast'ry then." There is an irony in the fact that Faust ends his philippic against the world of documents by making an offer which implies he has every writing surface and writing instrument since antiquity right there in his study: "Spirit of evil! what dost thou require? / Brass, marble, parchment, paper? Shall I use / Style, pen or graver? Name which you desire." This grandiloquent tirade falls flat because Mephisto is too modern to be held up by a recap of writing materials and their respective implements. He tacitly assumes that paper is a suitable medium for a document and slips into the role of a spry secretary, pulling from his bag a prepared contract which merely needs to be signed: "With passion why so hotly burn, / And thus your eloquence inflame? / The merest scrap will serve our turn, / And with a drop of blood you'll sign your name."[121]

Mephisto is in tune with the times. He brings the turbulence associated with bills, credit, and speculation into the old ritual of the pact with the devil. The lurid, grotesquely archaic signature in blood ratifies a diminutive piece of paper—a "scrap"—which is readily to hand yet also capable of outlasting the lifespan of a man of books who is obsessed with the present. Mephisto's scrap returns in the second part of *Faust*, in a world in which paper has left bronze, stone, and parchment far behind and devoted itself entirely to banking in the form of money. In brief, paper in the modern era shared the legacy of the old transmission media oriented on time as duration—going all the way back to stone—while also associating itself with the accelerating circulation of people, goods, and money. It was a precursor to digital media in the analog world. When communication media became more diversified after the invention of the printing press, paper served the purposes of enduring transmission in time as well as ever-expanding circulation in space. The book and the page—mentioned in the same breath by Faust's famulus Wagner, because Wagner acknowledges nothing less than the book—thus went their separate ways. But before examining the polarity between the page and the book, we have to look more closely at the page itself.

3.3. The World in a Page: Watermarks, Formats, Colors

Neither the printing press nor the book is an appropriate starting point for contemplating paper. If we want to avoid defining paper from the outset in terms of the alliances it forms, the only fixed point available to us is the sheet of paper as it is scooped out to form a page. This is the basic unit of paper, and in the pre-industrialized world this basic element emerged from a vat. It determines how paper is measured: one quire is twenty-four sheets of writing paper or twenty-five sheets of printing paper, twenty quires form a ream, ten reams form a bale. The sheet and the page are the origin of all other forms of paper's existence—bound or unbound, printed or unprinted, used for short- or long-term information storage. The sheet, like the book, is an abstraction which corresponds to a number of very different formats in reality. It was scooped from a vat and subsequently processed in a variety of sizes and qualities which continually expanded the range of available paper types. Its degree of sizing regulated its ability to absorb writing and printing inks so that they would not run or quickly fade. Its pliability and foldability, its tear resistance and weight, its lacerability and shearability, its combustibility, and its sensitivity to fire and, above all, to the element to which it owed its existence—water—established the conditions for its diffusion. They made paper an attractive option for use in various cultural technologies involving the storage, circulation, and even deletion of data.

Sheets of paper were turned into bags and medicine capsules in the paper processing industry; they were used to line clothing, shoes, and headwear; they found their way into the middle-class homes and palaces of Europe in the form of wallpaper; and they were an everyday companion in a multiplicity of other guises. The book at hand focuses on paper's function as a storage and circulation medium, so it is most interested in examining the sheet of paper as a carrier of symbols, be they words or images. But to analyze paper as a medium for words and images, we would do well not to start with the written or illustrated page. The historiography of pre-industrial paper arose from the study and cataloging of watermarks. The impulse to peer through a piece of paper held up to a light did not come from academia. It came instead from a desire for historical affirmation on the part of papermakers themselves who, in the era of industrialization, began to look back to the origins of their craft. Geneva-born Charles-Moise Briquet systematized the study of watermarks in the late nineteenth century. He had been a publisher and paper merchant before dedicating himself to copying around 40,000 watermarks on paper made between 1282 and 1600 which he had found in European archives.

Watermarks were artifacts of the sheet formation process. A rigid wire mold in a wooden frame was required to make them, so they only made inroads when paper began to be produced in Europe. Watermarks were formed by copper wire which was fixed to the mold and left a permanent imprint in the fibers that were scooped from the vat. Paper manufacturers used them as trademarks and certification marks, and their shapes may have been inspired by the heraldic symbols and emblems used by rulers to certify their signatures. In any case, many watermarks were visually related to the crests based on the seals of cities or royal families. They depicted the orb and the crown, the eagle and the scepter, the symbols of piety and the fabulous beasts of mythology; they depicted weapons, ships and anchors, the fool's cap and the staff, the human face and the oath hand, animals or parts of animals such as the ox head; they depicted letters and numbers, and in the eighteenth century they even depicted the liberty tree of the French Revolution. In brief, they were a visual atlas of the early modern world.[122]

At the same time, watermarks were indelible traces of the dipping process and thus witnesses to both the birth and the circulation of paper. Whether they were restricted to a pragmatic identification function or intended to be read symbolically, they always imbued pre-industrial paper with a genealogical element. Watermarks tell origin stories and anchor paper in a system of time and space coordinates. In this respect, it is not just their religious or heraldic content that makes them so informative. Economic historians can use them to trace the route that a piece of paper took from Ravensburg across the Rhine, the Danube region, or the Hanse area, while philologists, art historians, and musicologists can use them as a means of dating a book with an incorrect publication date, a page attributed to the wrong work, a drawing, or a handwritten music score. Every mystery fan knows that even detectives such as Sherlock Holmes—a modern relative of the philologist and a passionate clue hunter—have tried to elicit the secret of a piece of paper's origins. But watermarks are reluctant to reveal information about the geographic provenance and date of the papers in which they are found. A subtle methodological apparatus is required which takes account of the fact that watermarks can usually be traced back not to one but rather to a pair of dip molds which were not necessarily perfectly identical and may have also had differing lifespans. It is also important to consider the timeline along which a piece of paper might have traveled from its production to its sale, storage, and use.

The central metaphor in the study of watermarks likens the sheet formation process to an act of birth, whereby a watermark is imprinted on the paper like a birthmark. This organic metaphor makes sense because watermarks in paper—unlike the symbols stamped on a coin, the hallmarks of a goldsmith or silversmith, or a mason's mark on a keystone—are not added to the material after the fact but are actually generated during its production. The birth comparison is also apt because, in pre-industrial papermaking, every single sheet of paper manually scooped out of a vat was an "individual" in its material structure, and this individual was an artifact long before anything was written on it. The watermark that a sheet acquired as it took shape in the dip mold marked the start of a continual cultural, social, economic, and political impregnation of its physical materiality. Each handmade piece of paper was an original, but it was also subject to standardization and formatting. Even in the sixteenth century, watermarks were no longer just marks of origin or trademarks; they also indicated the quality and format of the paper.

The individuality of paper was balanced out by this formatting. The history of formatting was older than the craft of wire-pulling

Cylinder mold with watermark

which inspired European watermark technology. Formatting harked back to Arab culture and the Chinese origins of paper, and it had equivalents in ancient Greece, Rome, and Egypt. Even sheets made of papyrus had no "natural" size; they were formatted, too. After the Romans conquered Egypt, they changed the papyrus formats used in administration. Joseph von Karabacek and, more recently, Helen Loveday have shown how the diffusion of paper went hand in hand with a differentiation of formats in the age of Harun al-Rashid. Between packaging paper and calligraphy paper there arose a graded assortment of papers whose sheet size and quality were related to their social and cultural functions, and whose types were frequently named after high-ranking officials or the governors of local production sites.

Size and quality were often connected to each other. Paper in the largest format—sheets of 109.9 × 73.3 cm which were used for the caliph's documents and contracts—was also of a high quality. The very small "bird paper" (9.1 × 6.1 cm), which was used for communicating via carrier pigeon, was the lightest paper.[123] The use of the most common Arab paper formats was determined by the social position of the writer and the political rank of the addressee. Rules stipulated which paper was to be used to write to a caliph and which formats could be used by secretaries and merchants. These formats were the same in Egypt and Syria; they standardized the paper that circulated between Cairo and Damascus, and their relative sizes were calculated for their ease of manageability in administration and business. The three most widespread formats were 29 × 42 cm, 42 × 58 cm, and 58 × 84 cm. The length of the smaller paper was identical to the width of the next largest paper, so the different formats could be easily adapted by folding the sheets. Arab paper was sold in units known as a *rizmah*, which comprised five "hands" of twenty sheets each. European paper inherited the term "ream" from Arab paper, along with the tradition of imbuing formats with social significance. The oldest European formats were recorded in Bologna in 1389 and inscribed on a stone: *inperialle* (50 × 74 cm), *realle* (45 × 62 cm), *meçane* (35 × 52 cm), and *reçute* (32 × 45 cm). These formats were used for most manuscripts and archived paper documents, as well as the first printed books, from the early fourteenth into the sixteenth century. Modern book historians have tried to correlate the folio, quarto, octavo, duodecimo, and sextodecimo book formats with the paper formats used for printing.[124]

Format sizes clearly could not expand indefinitely in pre-industrial papermaking because they were constrained by the size of the dip mold and its manageability at the vat as well as by the human arm span. Furthermore, production difficulty increased as you moved up the format scale. The rule of thumb was that the smaller the piece of pre-industrial paper, the easier it was to make. The larger the sheet, the harder it was to produce an even white surface of uniform consistency and strength. This had to be taken into account when considering which paper formats to use when, so the large imperial format played only a minor role in the diversification of paper types and in archives and libraries. Chancery paper, by contrast, had evolved from the reçute format and experienced a meteoric rise with the development of civil administration in the seventeenth century, playing an important role as paper became ubiquitous in everyday life. The eighteenth century saw a wide range of papers, from lightly sized printing paper and fine writing and post paper, through the coarser, greyish draft paper, all the way to the thin "bogus paper" made from leftover material and used for sacks and packaging. There were also special formats such as music paper, which had to be especially heavy so that the ink would not bleed through when the musical notes were colored in. Post paper is a good example of the diffusion of watermark technology and standardization. It branched off from writing paper to become its own format in the late sixteenth century as the infrastructure of the Reichspost was being established, and its watermark consisted of a post horn underneath the name of the paper mill that produced it.[125]

Watermarks linked standardization to the network of paper mills, while formats were closely associated with the institutions and bureaucracy of the early modern state.

The old combination of paper and administration gave rise to stamped paper, the model for all papers subject to fees, which bore the emblem of the state. Stamped paper was the product of a public competition held in Holland in the early seventeenth century to find an easy way for the state to bring in additional revenues. It experienced its heyday in Germany after the Thirty Years' War. Stamped paper guaranteed the legal validity of the contracts and documents printed on it, but it was disliked by the general public and also met with resistance from papermakers who were reluctant to submit to the regulations of the authorities when it came to the formats and quality of their paper.

The standardization of pre-industrial paper should not be thought of as an uninterrupted triumphal march of normalization over large distances and areas; after all, the standards in Prussia were not necessarily the same as those in Hanover. Instead, the history of pre-industrial paper formats reflects the topography of Europe's territorial states between the late Middle Ages and the French Revolution. It encompasses the contrast between the centralism of France and the patchwork of the Holy Roman Empire as well as the rebellion of the States-General of the Netherlands against Spain. Above all, however, the paper formats of early modernity delineate the internal structure of absolutism and a hierarchical society. As papers circulated, so too did a knowledge of the social and political significance of each format. In place of the human secretaries we encountered in the court of Philip II, there were books with the word "secretary" in their title. Their purpose was to instruct clerks and private citizens alike in the ways of written communication with their authorities and superiors. Comprehensive books appeared such as Georg Philipp Harsdörffer's *The German Secretary. That is: The useful and almost necessary book of titles and form letters for all chanceries, studies and offices, now in its third edition* (1655–59) and Kaspar Stieler's *The Prepared Secretary. Or: Instructions on how any half-learned person can compose a pleasing and appropriate letter in the current style for princes / lords / authorities and special occasions* (1673–74). These books taught the rhetoric of compliments and salutations and provided examples of the kinds of lettering and letter sizes to be used for different audiences and for the design of title pages and dedications. They also always gave detailed instructions on the appropriate types and formats of paper to use.

In the world of the baroque letter, paper quality was equivalent to the clothing one wore when appearing before a ruler at court. A gold edge was like a stripe of rank, and paper could be powdered or perfumed as well. In the hierarchical society of Europe during the age of absolutism and in the Arab caliphate, paper formats were tied to the respective ranks of the writer and the addressee. Correspondence with royalty or other persons of high rank called for large folio; letters to ministers and officials were to be written on small folio; and the relationship between one's own rank and that of the addressee determined whether large quarto or small quarto should be used for correspondence with councilors, women, or one's peers.

According to these secretaries in book form, rank was reflected not only in the script and paper format but also in the white space between the lines. The rationing of writing space thus became a social gesture. Like the depth of a bow, the distance between the salutation and first line of a letter was a *spatium honoris* which made the social distance between the writer and addressee visible at a glance. Fixed rules determined the distance to be maintained between people of higher and lower ranks, both within physical space and within this white space on the page. A letter to the high nobility demanded a *spatium honoris* two fingers wide, one to the lower nobility required a finger's width, and, if you were writing to a peer, it was enough to write the addressee's title on its own line. When the letter was finished and had been signed in accordance with the secretary's rules, the paper was imbued with another layer of social significance in the way it was folded for a particular addressee.[126]

Every single physical, material element of paper could carry some sort of meaning. The blue paper on which death sentences were issued in Syria and Egypt signified grief; court petitions were often written on red paper; and pure white was considered to be a challenge to the eye in Arab culture, so white paper was covered with as much writing as possible.[127] In Europe, the blue paper mentioned in the statute of the city of Bologna in 1389 remained the only colored paper for a long time. Even Albrecht Dürer used this *carta azzura* for his drawings on his second trip to Italy in 1506–7. At roughly the same time, the leading humanist printer Aldus Manutius was producing special editions of books on blue or blue-grey paper in Venice. At the other end of the quality scale, the blue wrapping paper which resembled the paper used for file folders and packaging became the hallmark of the popular *Bibliothèque bleue* in seventeenth-century France, with its astrological almanacs, ghost stories, chivalric tales, and poems.

The production of colored paper—which involved mixing in rags of different colors, a technique that spread through Europe from the eighteenth century onward—and the wider range of paper qualities opened up new opportunities for social and aesthetic distinction in written correspondence and book design alike.

A major turning point in this regard took place when the English printer John Baskerville collaborated with the papermaker James Whatman to develop wove paper, or velin, which Baskerville first used for his edition of Virgil in 1757. Their technique eliminated the traces left by the laid lines and chain lines in the wire grid of the hand mold. To make wove paper, the wire grid was overlaid with a fine, very closely woven wire mesh so that no ribbing would be visible in the final sheet of paper.[128] This smooth, unribbed paper recalled older writing papers made of parchment, so it was an innovation with a classy retro design. Friedrich Schiller—a thrifty but ambitious consumer of paper in his private correspondence, and an author who was well versed in the use of different types of paper for books— informed his Leipzig publisher Siegfried Lebrecht Crusius on December 6, 1799, of the materials he desired for his new volume of poetry: "You would do well to arrange for a large number of good copies on both post paper and velin; in my experience with the five almanacs I have published, there is always strong demand for editions of this kind."[129] Wove paper created options for further social and aesthetic distinction, and from the second half of the eighteenth century it permeated both private correspondence and the trade fair catalogs published by book dealers to announce special editions of books from prominent authors. It also happened to reveal how the technology for forming sheets, which evolved along with changes in paper usage, could have unexpected side effects. When we look at the industrialization of paper production later on, we will see that the method for making high-quality wove paper was the bridge that enabled inventors around 1800 to start mechanizing sheet formation by building the first paper machines.

PART TWO

Behind the Type Area

∽

1

The Printed and the Unprinted

1.1. The Pitfalls of a Formula: "From Script to Print"

In 1945 Henry John Chaytor, a medievalist teaching in Cambridge, published his book *From Script to Print*, an introduction to the study of vernacular medieval literature. In the book's first pages, the scholar warned readers not to apply the reading habits they had learned from the modern printed book to the writing of the Middle Ages: "The breadth of the gulf which separates the age of manuscript from the age of print is not always, nor fully, realized by those who begin to read and criticize medieval literature."[130] Marshall McLuhan said that it was Chaytor who gave him the basic idea for *The Gutenberg Galaxy*. The contrast between the "age of manuscript" and the "age of print" thus became more than just a propaedeutic warning against the unhistorical reading of medieval literature, and "from script to print" became a formula marking a revolutionary epochal upheaval, a master key to the Middle Ages, as "from mythos to logos" was thought to be for antiquity. This revolutionary upheaval came to be viewed as a longer-term process by more recent book historians, and the equals sign that McLuhan placed between typography and the advance of uniformity, standardization, and rationalization became a question mark. The printed book was no longer viewed as a rigid container, and the printer's workshop became the setting for a rivalry between the imperative of standardization and the everyday partisans of variability and instability.

What Chaytor meant by the phrase "from script to print" was the evolution from handwritten to printed books. But modern book

studies was no longer concerned with the book alone; it looked at
the full spectrum of printed material and took ephemera just as seri-
ously as the Bible. It also grew very conservative in its estimate of
the reach of the new technology's social and cultural effects between
the fifteenth and eighteenth centuries: "Until early in the Goethe era,
printing remained a branch of production for the noble and bourgeois
elite. With the exception of a few truly popular printed materials such
as Luther's House Postils or Catechisms, the vast majority of the
European population—if they came into contact with the written
word at all—dealt almost exclusively with handwritten documents
(namely, files and letters)."[131]

By viewing the "media revolution" as a diversified transitional
period—when the printing press extended to books but only selec-
tively to documents and letters, and when medieval copyists were
dying out but clerks and secretaries were becoming more important—
then the "Gutenberg era" can be more easily embedded in the paper
age. This transitional period in which printed paper was on the
advance has not been adequately described. Paper appeared in a web
of aggregate states here, and the "script to print" concept encounters
resistance and limitations within it. This web was a product of all
the possible combinations of the opposing states of printed/unprinted
and bound/unbound paper. Paper appeared in a printed/bound combination in books, in an unbound/unprinted combination in most
letters and documents, and in a printed/unbound combination in
pamphlets and flyers. The bound/unprinted combination applied to
files as well as to the broad field of notebooks which merchants used
for jotting down fleeting comments and dates, diarists for writing
their entries, and authors for recording ideas. By viewing paper-based
media and cultural technologies as an ensemble of aggregate states
for the basic unit of the sheet, the "script to print" formula can be
untethered from a diachronic temporal axis. This makes it less of a
one-way street and turns historical progression into synchronous
polarity.

The parallel use of handwriting and print was part of Luther's
publication strategy. He praised printing as a gift given to the
Reformers by God himself so that they could free the Holy Scripture.
This praise and the virtuosity with which he and his followers used
the new technology have often been described as catalysts for the
cultural acceptance of typography. But Luther's resolute adoption of
the printing press did not lead him to abandon or devalue handwriting. When Luther offered a printed catechism or "lay Bible" for the
faithful to consult daily, from childhood onward, so that Bible reading
would become a regular practice, he integrated handwriting into his

program as a way of learning, absorbing, and memorizing the printed text. And when he discussed the duties of the authorities and expounded on just leadership, he always kept both forms of written media in mind—the manuscript as well as the printed book, the chancery scribes, judges, and notaries as well as the learned *doctores*. In the form of book excerpts or handwritten sermon notes, both types of written media were also associated with speech and the words spoken from the pulpit. The notes taken during Luther's sermons, lectures, and disputations by his pupils, colleagues, and associates fill more than twenty volumes.

In view of this web of aggregate states, "from script to print" no longer brings to mind the notion of a general cultural shift after Gutenberg, but it does describe the context in which the modern concept of authorship emerged. Medieval manuscripts were often collections of writings from different authors, with only loose associations between names and texts. As has been demonstrated many times over, the printing press led to the emergence of the modern author and to the legal and symbolic bond of ownership between texts and individual writers.

One does not become an author simply by writing a manuscript, after all. In the dictionaries of the seventeenth century at the latest, the definition of an "author" was strictly associated with being printed. But "from script to print" relates not only to the historical emergence of modern authorship but also—synchronously—to every single act of printing, because the printing press gave rise to a new type of manuscript culture.

It was beyond this interface that printed paper entered the space in which its many cultural relationships developed, and it was behind the print-ready manuscript that the space of its origin opened up, the space of the modern handwritten script. This reveals a fundamental feature of the constellation formed by the printing press: its reproduction function was freed from the sphere of the manuscript that had given rise to specialized copyists in the Middle Ages. Copying technology and writing technology diverged at the printing press, but readers of printed books and authors remained tied to handwriting until well into the nineteenth century, and even copying by hand did not die out. In the constellation of modern authorship, authors were authenticated by the printing press even though their work was still produced in the realm of handwriting and unbound paper. The zeal with which humanists hunted for ancient manuscripts was countered by the widespread tendency of authors between the fifteenth and eighteenth centuries to destroy their own written manuscripts after they had been printed. But the figure of the modern author and the advance of literacy transformed the space of the manuscript into a heavily staggered production area with its own internal logic.

The printing process involves more than just reformatting a manuscript with the goal of generating a large number of copies to circulate through time and space. It also encompasses a text's transition into a sphere of error correction and heightened claims to truth. Printing involves press proofs, preliminary corrections, and thorough reviews. The inevitability of printing errors is not eliminated by the ability to print an improved, revised edition of a book, but it is kept in check. Picking up on the theories of Elizabeth L. Eisenstein, Niklas Luhmann has interpreted the privileging of the most recent version of a text to be printing's contribution to the valorization of the new.[132] He argues that the number of errors tended to grow as manuscripts were copied in medieval scriptoria, so the text at the end of a chain of copying was the one most likely to have been corrupted. Printing, by contrast, encouraged readers to assume that the latest edition of a work was the best. It also upended the notion that the "original" was a text written long ago and that the manuscript copies were merely—often dubious—derivatives. This freed up the term "original" to be applied to something that had not previously existed. It lost its function as an index of the past and instead became a container for something new.

Luhmann emphasized that it was in the nature of the printed book to be the product of, and a setting for, continual revision. There is a counterpart to this in the world of the manuscript. Modern authors are their own editors even before they approve their manuscripts for publication. When Erasmus of Rotterdam described the printed book as an object which permitted, and demanded, a theoretically endless sequence of corrections and revisions, he was not referring to printing alone. Correcting misprints is the job of the printer and typesetter, but factual errors or imperfect verses are corrected in the manuscript itself. In other words, this is the job of the author. In a letter from 1651, Guez de Balzac wrote that in the course of abridging, editing, and reworking a single satire he had used up *"une demy rame de papier,"*[133] or half a ream. Taken literally, this would have been 250 sheets of paper. The amount may have been exaggerated, but it highlights a characteristic of modern manuscript culture: the volume of writing paper that goes into the fair copy of a text is not apparent on the printed page.

The inconspicuous roots of this connection between authorship and paper usage reach back to the late fifteenth century and the functional manuscripts produced by scholars associated with universities. Tilo Brandis has described this type of manuscript as "a volume of glosses and collectanea with an individual character, ... a work-book and notebook, a collection of copies of texts and glossed older manuscripts and prints which have been personally produced and assembled." This type of manuscript contained brief commentaries and excerpts, compilations, tables, and indices "exclusively in quarto or octavo format paper; the script is cursive with no effort put into the arrangement of the writing on the pages or decoration."[134] These beginnings led to the ensemble of the sketch and outline, excerpt and working copy, draft and fair copy, the "small tools" that became fixtures in the individual routines of scholars and authors. They may have been physically destroyed after a manuscript was printed, but instead of disappearing without a trace, they were absorbed into the reservoir of materials and motifs reflecting the modern concept of authorship, within which the figure of the author moved further and further from that of the "writer." At first glance, the phrase "from script to print" would seem to herald the subsumation of unprinted paper under the logic of the printing press. A second look, however, reveals that at its heart is the *a priori* tension between script and print in modern literature.

1.2. The White Page

The German word *Blatt* (leaf, sheet, page) appears more than 3,000 times in the works of Goethe, and more than three-fourths of that time it refers to a sheet of paper.[135] *Blatt* can mean a letter, a drawing, a leaf in a manuscript, or the page of a book, a broadsheet, or a newspaper, a playing card, a form, an index card, or a deed. The term *Blatt* is surrounded by a dense lexical field which includes the diminutive *Blättchen*, used to denote both the piece of paper that seals Faust's fate and the paper money that appears in *Faust II*. Both the *Goethe Dictionary* and the dictionary of the Brothers Grimm document how the leaves of plants and trees were joined by man-made leaves of paper in the modern era. Just as a single organic leaf stands out from foliage, the single pliant page stands out from the book when a reader leafs through it. "Leaf" brings to mind the image of an open book, with the verso and recto facing each other. It accentuates the idea of movement in the fixed form of the codex. Though the word *Blatt* encompasses both the printed and unprinted page, it gravitates toward the world of loose, unbound sheets in the guise of public papers, or newspapers. In its singular form, *Blatt* can refer to a letter, a note, or an enclosure to a letter, while in the plural it often refers to a multi-page letter.

The vast lexical field around *Blatt* encompasses compounds ranging from *Ahornblatt* (maple leaf) to *Zifferblatt* (clock face). In the midst of this, the *weißes Blatt*—or white page—plays a special role. Nothing can be read from such a page. It waits to be covered with words, numbers, or images, and it is the symbolic form at the heart of modern authorship. As authors—the originators of a text—began to be trailed by copyists and compilers who might be suspected of plagiarism, the white page extended beyond its function as a neutral, physical writing medium and took on symbolic significance. It became the visual representation of originality, the setting for the act of writing, the symbolic birthplace of authorship. As such, it entered into competition with the central metaphor of philosophical empiricism. When John Locke compared the human mind to "white paper, void of all characters" to explain how ideas came from "impressions" and "sensations," the ancient wax tablet analogy was the most essential aspect to join the concept of the passive, virginal sheet of paper.[136] In terms of modern authorship, however, the white page was more than just the setting for the act of production; it was an organic component of it.

Archives and libraries are filled with thousands of books from the sixteenth century and later which are interleaved with white pages. It was not very difficult for bookbinders to insert white sheets between printed pages, and this was apparently an attractive option for many of their clients. It provided a personal writing space within an enhanced printed book and brought the blank sheet of the manuscript face to face with the printed page. Johann Gottfried Zeidler's bookbinding manual, *Buchbinder-Philosophie oder Einleitung in die Buchbinderkunst* (1708), explicitly stated that sized writing paper was to be used for these blank pages instead of more lightly sized printing paper.[137] Just as writing paper was folded lengthwise to create columns for corrections and comments in the fair copies of administrative books from the sixteenth century, interleaving opened up the apparently closed reading space of the book and left room for intervening in the text by means of comments or revisions. For authors, interleaved copies of their own works were the ideal medium for editing their writing with an eye to future editions of a book. But the opportunity to use printed materials for both reading and writing was not reserved for scholars alone. The printed *Schreibkalender* (writing calendars) which began to appear in the sixteenth century consisted of a calendar for the year, market dates, and weather lore surrounded by a writing space for the owner to keep a rudimentary journal.

As the value of imagination grew in the eighteenth century, the white page became the author's mute imperative to write. Johann Peter Eckermann wrote in the spring of 1831: "I asked about 'Faust,' and what progress he had made with it. 'That,' said Goethe, 'will not again let me loose. I daily think and invent more and more of it. I have now had the whole manuscript of the second part stitched together, that it may lie a palpable mass before me. The place of the yet wanting fourth act I have filled with white paper; and, undoubtedly, what is finished will allure and urge me to complete what has yet to be done. There is more than people think in these matters of sense, and we must aid the spiritual with all manner of devices.'"[138] Books interleaved with or consisting solely of white pages were part of the trappings of authorship, and white became the color that signaled production. An excerpt from Jean Paul reads: "Leibniz: travels with a book of white. Paper through the world: soon you will have a good library."[139] And in one of Georg Christoph Lichtenberg's "waste books," we find: "A white sheet of paper commands more respect than the most beautiful sheet of wastepaper. It fills one with a desire to animate it."[140] The connection between white paper and productive writing continued to apply even when production had come to a standstill: "They have books bound with white paper so they can get off to a good start, and then they write little or nothing in them."[141]

Loaded as it is with writing options and mute productivity imperatives, the white page is the barrier between writing and not-writing that must be surmounted anew each day. This barrier aspect is the source of the mythic "fear of the white page." "The first page," Jean Paul wrote, "is not a playground or pleasure garden for the author, it is a drill ground and arena; and because he wants to start off with only the best ideas, it is also the execution site for the many thoughts he strikes out."[142] Despite its barrier function, it would be a mistake to view the white page above all as a symbol of inhibited production—because a production inhibition is not the same thing as a writing inhibition. Guez de Balzac's complaint about his paper consumption from the year 1651 shows that a production inhibition can be just as easily associated with the over-production of text as with not writing at all.

The "Second Roman Visit" in Goethe's *Italian Journey* includes an account of Goethe resuming his interrupted work on *Faust* in March 1788: "To finish the piece now will be a different matter than it would have been fifteen years ago, but I do not think it will lose by the delay, for I believe I have found the thread again. I am also confident about its general tone. I have already written one more

scene, which, if I were to scorch the page a little, would be indistin-
guishable from the others. A long period of peace and solitude has
given me back myself and I am surprised to find how much I resemble
my old self and how little my newer self has been touched by all that
has happened to me during the years. It gives me an odd feeling
sometimes when I see the old manuscript lying before me. It is still
the untouched first version in which I flung off the principle scenes
without making any preliminary draft, so that it really looks like the
fragment of some old codex. Instead of transporting myself by
thought and intuition into a remote past, as I did then, I must now
transport myself into a past in which I once lived myself."[143]

The "codex" to which Goethe refers is the lost manuscript of the
Urfaust which has only survived as a copy made by Luise von
Göchhausen. The idea of scorching the pages of the new scenes
written in 1788 to materially certify that they were stylistically indis-
tinguishable from the old fragment is a notion which springs from
the modern author's awareness that, as a single creative entity, he can
unify all fragments and erase all traces of stagnated production in the
finished work. But the act of bringing the new manuscript into line
with the old "codex" actually emphasizes what it is meant to obscure,
namely, the discontinuous chronology of writing within the production space of the white page, which has since yellowed.

This discontinuity stands in contrast to the temporal compression
of the writing process as depicted in the printed book, where the first
and last pages are close chronological neighbors. Adding new pages
to a stack of papers set aside years earlier is not the only form of
discontinuous manuscript production; particularly in the pre-industrial era, when a sheet of paper was not a throwaway product, phases
of production would be superimposed on a single page like geological
layers. By crossing out, deleting, or inserting text in the blank spaces
on a page, temporal discontinuity could be combined with non-linear
writing techniques in the modern manuscript, so that scribbles and
scrawls competed with the steady flow of writing, and lines of text
dissolved into scattered clusters of characters. In brief, a sheet of
paper could be the medium for stuttering, spasmodic production, or
it could be a document of how isolated lines of writing unraveled
across the white expanse of the page. It could mimic the page of a
book, but it could also be a non-linear, non-uniform counterpart to
the typographically structured page. Modern manuscript culture
evolved from the process of exhausting the options for covering a
blank page with writing. This culture has brought forth "brain
workers," who primarily use the page to write down thoughts they
have mentally pre-formulated, and "paper workers," who make mul-

tiple written passes in order to produce a text. And, as genetic philology and modern manuscript research have impressively demonstrated in recent decades, it has brought forth a whole spectrum of combinations of the two types.[144]

Upon closer inspection, the page was not a self-contained storage medium. As the setting for the written word, it was a room filled with other manuscripts, letters, excerpts, open books, and pictures. This room did not have to be a writing room, a scholar's study, or a library. The medieval scriptorium had been left far behind. The books bound with white paper that Lichtenberg mentioned became ambulatory. We will run into them again in the chapter on excerpts. With the boom in travel literature, open-air reading was joined by open-air writing. It was hard to write in a coach, but it was easy enough to write in an inn during a walk. In the wealth of options it offered, in the palpability of what it lacked, in its good relations with bound and printed paper, and in its willingness to follow an author wherever he or she went, the white page became a mirror reflecting the form of the modern author.

1.3. "Found among the Papers ... "

It sounds trivial to say that the printing press brought both printed material and unprinted material into the world. However, this realization is important for understanding the fusion of paper technology and the printing press, because unprinted material encompassed more than just the ancient writings and medieval manuscripts that were fed into the printing press. To get an impression of how much time the educated functional elite of the seventeenth century spent dealing with a whole network of bound and unbound, printed and unprinted papers, it is worth reading the diary of Samuel Pepys, which was written during the Restoration between 1660 and 1669. Pepys, a leading administrator in the Admiralty of the British Royal Navy, had his own stationer, paper dealer, bookseller, and bookbinder. He took great care to ensure that the books in his library all had identical attractive bindings, but at the same time he was flooded with unbound papers both in his work and in his household bookkeeping in the evening. The worlds of finance, politics, and news jostle against each other in his writing. Pepys was a member of one of the first generations of newspaper readers, and he made it into the news himself by accompanying Charles II on his return from exile in the Netherlands. Paper probably served as a navigational aid on this voyage, because while large master nautical charts were made of parchment, working copies for the helmsmen were often drawn on paper. Pepys had a private music teacher, and he needed staff paper in order to compose music, an act which would involve copying by hand far into the future, even beyond Jean-Jacques Rousseau and the "Poor Musician" of Franz Grillparzer. In the end, Samuel Pepys would have his diary— which was only discovered in his library after his death—bound exactly like all of his printed books. But the carefully designed bindings held handwritten pages, unique specimens making up a fair copy of his daily diary entries.

Within this spectrum of paper's aggregate states, a synchronous tension arose between what was printed and what was not. The printing press represented the optional horizon for the modern manuscript, but the space of the manuscript did not funnel directly toward it because this space always contained more than what was put into it. Many manuscripts, concepts, and notes were destroyed instead of being passed down, and much of what was passed down was never printed. This asymmetry between printed and unprinted materials could be described as a phenomenon of selection and censorship. By making authorship conditional on being printed, the manuscript was given priority over unpublished papers; the state, for its part, preserved its *arcana imperii* by sealing the papers of high-ranking officials, and it distributed its documents—*acta publica* and *acta inedita*—among libraries and archives. But as the growth of literacy and textualization resulted in biographies being saturated with all sorts of "papers" ranging from letters to IOUs, unprinted materials acquired a strangely paradoxical function. This becomes apparent when we try to establish the position of unprinted papers in the polarity between orality and textuality which was inherited from ancient cultures. At first glance there seems to be no question that unprinted papers are situated at the pole of textualization and abstraction, the counter-pole to live speech and physicality. However, a closer look reveals that the modern opposition between printed and unprinted materials is inherent in these papers, even at the pole of textualization. Ever since the invention of typography and the printed page, handwriting has been more closely associated with the body. Viewing handwriting from the perspective of live speech emphasizes its written nature, but viewing it from the perspective of the printed page highlights the fact that it is the trace left by a living hand. The opposition between the esoteric and the exoteric was linked to the opposition between oral speech and writing in the ancient world. But in the modern era, the textualization process itself opened up a polarity between the esoteric and exoteric, one which was connected to the opposition between printed and unprinted materials. As the printed word became the core of modern public life, unbound and unprinted paper assumed a symbolic position analogous to that of the oral and the esoteric. At the same time, the realm of unprinted material became a reservoir for the assiduous completion of a modern author's body of work beyond the author's death.

One indication of this emerging constellation was the appearance of the word "papers" in the titles of printed books and periodical articles. A title such as *Pensées de Mr. Pascal sur la religion, et sur quelques autres sujets, Qui ont esté trouvées aprés sa mort parmy ses papiers, A Amsterdam, Chez Abraham Wolfganck 1677* not only emphasized that the origins of the printed text lay in unprinted papers, it also told a story in which the editor was the protagonist. In a title such as this, the deceased author was a second, equally reliable main character. By searching through the papers left behind by an author and selecting texts to be published, the editor broke down the boundaries of authorship. The author could only write as long as he was alive—but his authorship did not end with his death. The *Pensées* went on to become one of Pascal's key works for posterity. *Papiers inédits* were usually presented as selections from a reservoir which had not yet been exhausted, implying that the kind of authorship rooted in unprinted papers was, in principle, temporally open-ended.

This background world of unprinted papers, which grew even as printed papers continued their triumphal march, could harbor not only an author's main work but also a political or historical truth. By the time newspapers emerged in the early seventeenth century, the reservoir of unprinted papers already rivaled the published news and opinions of the periodical press as well as historical literature. Among the modern, politically engaged public, the truth was not negotiated solely through the clashing of rival voices. The *papiers inédits* that were still hidden in the private sphere were just as likely to be a source of truth as public discourse. A title such as *The history of the most unfortunate Prince, King Edward II with choice political observations on him and his unhappy favourites, Gaveston & Spencer: containing several rare passages of those times, not found in other historians / found among the papers, and (supposed to be) writ by the right honourable Henry Viscount Faulkland, London 1680* acknowledged the uncertain authorship of the papers in question without weakening the assurance that the printed truths had been examined and were complete. Once the symbolic order of unprinted materials had been established as a source of truth, the printing press tended to ratify the existing authority of unpublished papers rather than bestow authority upon them through printing.

Bringing *papiers inédits* into the realm of printed paper was an act which sanctioned the authority of the unprinted while simultaneously neutralizing its aggregate state. The fusion of unprinted papers with their opposite left a residue—namely, these "papers" began to be mentioned in the titles of books. Gotthold Ephraim Lessing's publication strategy in the *Fragmentenstreit* (fragments controversy) is a prominent example of this. The title of Lessing's first volume in the controversy—*Von Duldung der Deisten: Fragment eines Ungenannten* (On the Toleration of Deists: Fragment from an Unnamed Writer [1774])—established an authorial figure who was joined in the second volume by the background world which Lessing the editor was drawing from: *Ein Mehreres aus den Papieren des Ungenannten, die Offenbarung betreffend* (Sundry Fragments from the Papers of the Unnamed Writer Concerning the Revelation [1777]).[145] This title was ideal for adding fuel to the fire that had been lit by the question of the Bible's truth. In both his first and second appearance, the unnamed writer pointedly remained an anonymous figure who, even posthumously, had to be protected from the explosiveness of his own writings. This unnamed writer was the authorial figure who represented the boundaries of public discourse. He was a published author, yet he remained in the realm of unprinted paper. His public voice was paradoxical in that it said something which it was not thought possible to say in the realm of the printed word. As the advocate and editor of this paradoxical voice, Lessing landed himself a publication ban that brought an end to the fragments controversy.

In expressions such as "found among the papers," "trouvés parmiles papiers de," and "aus den Papieren," the key elements are the prepositions—*among, parmi, aus*. Within them is an unspoken promise, or a threat: "to be continued." After the Thermidorian Reaction in the French Revolution, Edme-Bonaventure Courtois published the truth about Robespierre and his clique under the title of *Rapport fait au nom de la commission chargée de l'examen des papiers trouvés chez Robespierre et ses complices dans la séance du 16 nivôse, an III. De la République francaise, Paris Impr. Nat. Des lois, l'an III* (1795). However, this official committee report was bound to trigger a response invoking the authority of the papers that Courtois had omitted: *Papiers inédits trouvés chez Robespierre, Saint-Just, Payan etc., supprimés ou omis par Courtois; Précédés du Rapport de ce député à la Convention Nationale, avec un grand nombre de facsimile et les signatures de principaux personnages de la Revolution. Paris Baudouin Frères* (1828). Facsimiled manuscripts and autographs such as those mentioned explicitly in this title grew in popularity in the early nineteenth century thanks to lithography.

This is when the production of facsimiles became a technique for acknowledging the authority of unprinted material by means of printed material. The phrase "found among the papers" benefited from the rise of "hidden" truth both as a resource for the kind of public life that was emerging in the medium of print and as a weapon in the fight between political camps and religious denominations. To emphasize its transparency effects, the expression was often woven into a dense web of intimated secrets: *The Legation Secretary, or the Cabals of Secret Catholics and Jesuits in Germany. A Most Peculiar Royal Conversion Story from the Year 1825, Wherein the Catholic Conversion of the Duke and Duchess of Anhalt-Köthen, the Russian Conspiracy, etc. Were Prophesied by a Jesuit / Found Among the Papers of the Secret Legation Secretary R*** Who Was Poisoned in Paris. With Commentary Concerning the Religious and Political Machinations of Catholics in Germany* (1828).

The "found among the papers" formula originated in the historical and political publications of the seventeenth century. It indicated that a hidden historical, political, or biographical truth was emerging from the shadows of the ancient *arcana imperii* or modern secret societies. At the same time, it found its way into the realm of sensitive philosophical and theological literary remains, fragments of which were published anonymously. In this way, the opposition between the private and the public, secrecy and transparency, became linked to the opposition between unprinted and printed paper. The resulting background world, the reservoir of unprinted material—material which skirted the pole of oral and esoteric secrets but was also fixed in writing and had the option of being printed—grew in importance in the eighteenth century as the *arcana imperii* were joined by the *arcana personae*, an equally deeply layered world of "confidentiality" and "secrets." When we look at the epistolary novel of the eighteenth century, we will see the abundant literary fruits borne of this constellation. "Unpublished papers" also increasingly found their way into the titles of journal articles in the eighteenth century, an indication that this category of material was becoming routine. The papers did not always contain revelations; sometimes they simply completed what was already known by supplying something previously unknown. But even fragments from the literary remains of prominent authors benefited from the opposition upon which they were based: "Unpublished Letter by Mr. Voltaire."[146] We will have to look more closely at literary estates in the nineteenth century, as this is when the all-powerful philologists and autograph hunters fell on unprinted papers with an intensity never seen before.

2

Adventurers and Paper

⟨∾⟩

2.1. Don Quixote, the Print Shop, and the Pen

Early on in *Don Quixote*, we find a priest and a barber examining the hero's library so that they can root out and burn the "enchanting" books suspected of having contributed to their owner's madness. The library contains over 100 beautifully bound volumes ranging from classic chivalric romance, such as *Amadis of Gaul* and its imitators, to the new releases of the year 1591.[147] This date certifies the claim in the first sentence of the novel—which was published in 1604–5— that the gentleman in question "lived not long ago." Don Quixote, forefather of the bookish heroes of modern literature, is a product of the age of Philip II, the paper king. His stubborn, anachronistic loyalty to chivalric romance acquires a historical dimension in its contrast to the growth in administration and bureaucracy; the adventures of the "governor" Sancho Panza attest to this growth most remarkably because Sancho can neither read nor write. But merely disposing of the chivalric novels is not enough to exorcize the demons of literature, as can be seen in the aplomb with which Don Quixote parries the priest's and barber's idea to wall up the library after the condemned books have been burned: He immediately attributes the disappearance of his room full of books to the "arts and learning" of an enchanter who is his arch enemy.[148] At first glance, Cervantes seems to be concerned with quashing the belief in the demonic power of books. In fact, however, he does everything he can to continually complicate the relationship between the readers of *Don Quixote* and the novel's protagonist. At the start of the book's second volume, which appeared in the autumn of 1615, Don Quixote and Sancho Panza are informed by Bachelor Carrasco, who has just returned from studying in Salamanca, that the first volume of the book has been tremendously successful—twelve thousands copies sold! But Cervantes goes even further in the second part of the book, depicting the readers of the first part as being not entirely satisfied with the adventures recounted there. Just as Don Quixote continues to live out a chivalric tale, these readers perpetuate the tale of *Don Quixote* and, as soon as the self-proclaimed knight errant crosses their path, they devise all manner of schemes and deceptions to entangle him in new adventures. They have accomplices in the novel, underlings who assist them. But their most important accomplice is the author Cervantes. He put just as much effort into complicating his own role in the novel as he did into constructing the hall of mirrors in which the hero meets his audience. In *Don Quixote*, the unfathomable apotheosis of the modern reader merges with the equally unfathomable self-reflection of modern authorship.

This starts shortly after the purging of Don Quixote's library, which is followed by the famous adventure of the windmills. The windmills appear to Don Quixote to be giants who, as he makes a point of mentioning, must have been transformed by the same enchanter "who stole my room and my books."[149] Enchanters are also suspected of having turned an abducted princess, whom Don Quixote wants to rescue, into a Basque woman traveling to Seville to sail with her husband to America. But just as Don Quixote falls on her Basque attendant with his sword drawn, an editor emerges from behind the narrator, as if from behind a curtain, and announces that the account found by the author ends here. "Which author?" readers will find themselves asking—and the answer is the "second author" who refused to accept that Don Quixote's tale ended at this point and successfully set out in search of its conclusion.

Interrupting the action to increase the tension was an established narrative strategy in chivalric romance. But it is worth taking a closer look at what Cervantes does with this literary device. He first points out how unlikely it seems "that the great minds of La Mancha possessed so little interest that they did not have in their archives or writing tables a few pages that dealt with this famous knight." Then he hands the story back to the "second author" who, at the start of the tale's continuation, explains how he found what he was looking for not in the writing tables or archives of the Spanish authors of La Mancha but, by chance, on a street in Toledo:

One day when I was in the Alcaná market in Toledo, a boy came by
to sell some notebooks and old papers to a silk merchant; as I am very
fond of reading, even torn papers in the streets, I was moved by my
natural inclinations to pick up one of the volumes the boy was selling,
and I saw that it was written in characters I knew to be Arabic. And
since I recognized but could not read it, I looked around to see if some
Morisco who knew Castilian, and could read it for me, was in the
vicinity, and it was not very difficult to find this kind of interpreter,
for even if I had sought a speaker of a better and older language, I
would have found him. In short, fortune provided me with one, and
when I told him what I wanted and placed the book in his hands, he
opened it in the middle, read for a short while, and began to laugh.

I asked him why he was laughing, and he replied that it was
because of something written in the margin of the book as an annotation. I told him to tell me what it was, and he, still laughing, said:
"As I have said, here in the margin is written: 'This Dulcinea of
Toboso, referred to so often in this history, they say had the best hand
for salting pork of any woman in all of La Mancha.'"[150]
As soon as this name is spoken, the "second author" knows that
he must make a move. He buys all of the boy's papers and notebooks,
quickly finds translators in the city (which is known for its translation
schools), and has all of the notebooks relating to Don Quixote rendered in Spanish "in a little more than a month and a half."
Fortune steps in right before the copy of the tale—or is it the
original?—disappears forever; the silk merchants on the Toledo
market street, which is populated by converted Jews and Moriscos,
would have used the old paper to wrap up their wares. The familiar
motif of the discovered manuscript is not treated superficially by
Cervantes. The papers being sold by the boy include a manuscript
with commentary in the margins. This manuscript therefore contains
not only the continuation of the story but also the traces left behind
by unknown readers. Their knowledge of Dulcinea of Toboso clearly
comes not from the writing desks and archives of La Mancha but
from hearsay, so they recall the silk merchants of Toledo whom Don
Quixote encounters in one of his first adventures in the novel.
Early on, Cervantes spreads a net of cross-references over every
element in his novel, including a character whose name appears in
the subtitle of the manuscript found in Toledo: "*History of Don
Quixote of La Mancha. Written by Cide Hamete Benengeli, an Arab
Historian.*"
The novels of chivalry read by the hero stand in contrast to *Don
Quixote* as a "history." This brings into play the truth claims that
are explicitly affirmed by the "second author" after he has found the

original manuscript. Since the author of the manuscript is an Arab but "the people of that nation are very prone to telling falsehoods," there is a conflict between the adjective and the subject in the manuscript's byline: "Arab Historian." With a good degree of pathos, the "second author" attempts to allay any doubts cast on the work on account of its Arab author by means of a quote from Cicero which educated readers may have recognized:

> Historians must and ought to be exact, truthful, and absolutely free of passions, for neither interest, fear, rancor, nor affection should make them deviate from the path of the truth, whose mother is history, the rival of time, repository of great deeds, witness to the past, example and adviser to the present, and forewarning to the future. In this account I know there will be found everything that could be rightly desired in the most pleasant history, and if something of value is missing from it, in my opinion the fault lies with the dog who was its author rather than with any defect in its subject.[151]

Once he has been introduced, the Arab historian Cide Hamete Benengeli accompanies the characters until the end of the novel. His importance grows in the final passages of the second volume for reasons which lie beyond the boundaries of the novel itself. In the summer of 1614, an as yet unidentified author writing under the pseudonym of Alonso Fernández de Avellaneda published a continuation of *Don Quixote* in Tarragona before Cervantes had finished his own second part of the tale. Cervantes took a look at this novel, which had appropriated his characters, and responded to the challenge with a series of well-considered maneuvers in both the plot and emphasis of his own text.[152] For example, in chapter 59 of Cervantes' second part, Don Quixote and Sancho Panza stop at an inn and overhear two aristocratic travelers in a neighboring room mocking the other *Don Quixote* and deriding it as an unenjoyable absurdity compared to the first part. The travelers even show the book to Don Quixote, who leafs through it and then briefly maligns his doppelgänger before launching into a dialogue illuminating the merits of the true Sancho Panza as compared to the false one.

Don Quixote has a doppelgänger only because his author has a doppelgänger: the plagiarist who kidnapped his characters. Even Rabelais had seen how a book's success could threaten the author's control over that book. His heroes' adventures had been paralleled by his own adventures in publishing. A tumultuous novel could be written about Rabelais' relationship with the printers of Lyon. Rabelais stopped using the facetiously scholarly pseudonym of Alcofribas Nasier and started releasing books under his own name when he published the *Tiers Livre* (1546) of his Gargantua and Pantagruel cycle, partially in response to the reprints that had appeared of *Pantagruel*.[153] The close connection between authorial awareness and plagiarism awareness was palpable here; the process of fending off plagiarists strengthened the bond of ownership between the author and the text. Rabelais responded to unauthorized reprints of his first two books by publishing new editions of them with an added *avis au lecteur* which assured readers "*que les derniere feuilles de son oeuvres plagiare ne sont correspondantes á celles du vray original que nous avons eu de l'autheur.*"[154] In *Don Quixote*, the fight against plagiarism moved from the foreword of the novel into the narrative itself—taking the readers of the rival novel as well as its characters along with it.

When Cervantes' Don Quixote finds out that his doppelgänger traveled to Zaragoza in Avellaneda's book to take part in the annual jousts there, he changes his travel plans and goes to Barcelona instead, a move intended to "proclaim the lies of this modern historian to the world." Wittily, Cervantes has his Don Quixote visit a print shop in Barcelona. This is where the protagonist elucidates his translation theory and reveals a remarkably pragmatic grasp of sales figures and an astute knowledge of the accounting practices of printers and the arrangements they made among themselves. He also discovers that one of the books currently being corrected is the *Second Part of the Ingenious Gentleman Don Quixote of La Mancha* by "somebody from Tordesillas"—in other words, Avellaneda. Don Quixote is a witness to the duplication of his doppelgänger, so it comes as no surprise that he leaves the print shop "showing some signs of displeasure."[155]

In *Don Quixote*, the print shop in Barcelona—a city in a region filled with bandits and thieves—is the polar opposite of the market in Toledo where the "second author" acquires the manuscript of Cide Hamete Benengeli. Because Don Quixote and Sancho Panza interact with their readers, they know that their "first author" is Cide Hamete Benengeli. When asserting themselves against the book by "somebody from Tordesillas" in the second part of the novel, they frequently invoke their Arab historian, who represents the link between the "true" printed novel and its unprinted manuscript. Cervantes masterfully incorporates this genealogical perspective into the hall of mirrors that is his *Don Quixote*, as can be seen in the final twist he gives to his inclusion of the rival novel in his own text. This twist brings the readers into play, but also—in an act of plagiaristic revenge—an Avellaneda character in the form of Álvaro Tarfe from Granada, a nobleman of Moorish descent. Don Quixote encounters

Don Álvaro at an inn and asks him to officially declare to the village magistrate "that he did not know Don Quixote of La Mancha, also present, and that he, Don Quixote, was not the one who had appeared in a history entitled *Second Part of Don Quixote of La Mancha*, written by someone named Avellaneda, a native of Tordesillas." This attestation is as paradoxical as a Cretan saying that all Cretans are liars, because the authority to testify to the truth of the real Don Quixote has been given to a character from the fake *Don Quixote*.

This official written statement is not the last word that the novel has to say about itself, however—nor is the account of its hero's death. The last word is given to Cide Hamete Benengeli, who addresses his feather quill, which he will leave hanging on a hook "down through the ages" to prevent all attempts to resurrect Don Quixote and force him into new adventures in a third volume. In this grandiose closing speech, the author's pen finally takes its place alongside the knight's sword while simultaneously asserting its rights vis-à-vis the authority of the print shop in Barcelona. Sovereign authority lies solely with the author, who has the hero's death at his command: "For me alone was Don Quixote born, and I for him; he knew how to act, and I to write; the two of us alone are one, despite and regardless of the false Tordesillan writer who dared, or will dare, to write with a coarse and badly designed ostrich feather about the exploits of my valorous knight, for it is not a burden for his shoulders or a subject for his cold creativity."[156]

Michel Foucault once said of Don Quixote: "He is himself like a sign, a long, thin graphism, a letter that has just escaped from the open pages of a book. His whole being is nothing but language, text, printed pages, stories that have already been written down."[157] But Don Quixote's life as the hero of a novel emerges not only from the printed page but from the tension between the poles of typography/press/book and manuscript/pen/paper. The editorial fiction so ingeniously employed by Cervantes had a glittering future ahead of it in the poetics of the European novel. Entire libraries of novels which let the reader peek behind their type area owe their existence to the old papers sold by the boy in the Alcaná market of Toledo.

2.2. Picaresque Paper: Simplicius Simplicissimus and the *Schermesser*

Unlike Don Quixote, the heroes of the picaresque novels of the seventeenth century whom Fortune shepherds through the world tell their stories themselves. First-person narrative is the weatherproof

clothing in which they appear before their audience. Hans Jakob
Christoffel von Grimmelshausen's Simplicius Simplicissimus is no
exception, at least not in the first five books of the novel *The
Adventurous Simplicissimus*, which were published in 1668 and
ended with the word "end." A final part, or *Continuatio*, appeared
the following year, however: the *Continuation of the Adventurous
Simplicissimus, or the Conclusion of the Same. By German Schleifheim
von Sulsfort, Mompelgart, published by Johann Fillion*. In this
Continuatio, the Thirty Years' War is over and Lucifer fears that the
peace treaty will be detrimental to his infernal kingdom, even though
avarice and wastefulness show that vice is still alive and well.
Simplicius sticks with his first-person narrative in his new adventures,
which see him shipwrecked with a carpenter on an uninhabited island
in the Indian Ocean where, following the death of his comrade, he
decides to live out his life in solitude as a hermit. But how do his
adventures come to be written down and ultimately printed? There
is no paper on the isolated island, and hence no spiritual books, so
Simplicius consoles himself by reading the island itself as a "great
book" in which every natural thing refers to a Bible story. He ultimately compensates for the lack of paper and ink with palm leaves
and a mixture of brazil wood juice and lemon juice, which he uses
to write "regular prayers" as well as his entire life story. Simplicius
is his own Cide Hamete Benengeli. He is not an oral storyteller, but
the author of a book made from palm leaves which he leaves to
posterity. In order for this book to be reformatted so that it can reach
future readers, there is an abrupt break at the start of chapter 24 of
the *Continuatio*. Simplicius' voice falls silent at this point and is
replaced by the "Narrative of Jean Cornelissen of Harlem, a Dutch
sea captain, to German Schleiffheim von Sulsfort, his friend, about
Simplicissimus." In the report addressed to German Schleiffheim—
the anagrammatic pseudonym under which Grimmelshausen published the *Continuatio*—the Dutch captain recommends the palm-leaf
book as "the greatest rarity" for Schleiffheim's art chamber. The
captain tells the story of how he found the book and its author, whom
his sailors initially thought to be either a criminal put ashore as pun-
ishment or a "fool." As it transpires, he is "not a fool, but ... an
ingenious poet" who has carved Bible verses and other sayings into
all of the smooth-barked trees, along with warnings against the
magical power of certain fruits.[158] This annotation of the island,
which takes places before Simplicius writes his life story, brings an
end to a thematic strand that has followed Simplicius since his childhood and youth. He may be a figure of folly, but in the Simplician
world, folly does not preclude an acquaintance with pen and ink,

books and writing. The *Continuatio* in particular leaves no doubt that Simplicissimus—despite being partial to the carnal, the physical, to all of the baser pleasures—is also familiar with writing. To thank the hosts who, on account of his oddity, take him in during his journey through Switzerland to Savoy and then to Italy, he dishes up tales of monsters and natural wonders taken from "old writers and poets" ranging from Phylarchus and Apollonides to Hesigonus and Pliny as if they were his own travel experiences.

One of the characters in *Simplicius Simplicissimus* first appears in the *Continuatio*, and from the moment he shows up the writing climate of the entire book intensifies, as indicated by the fact that the character himself is a literary quotation. Grimmelshausen borrowed the character with the descriptive name of "Baldanders" ("Soonchanged" in German) from a poem by Hans Sachs. Baldanders represents ceaseless metamorphosis, fundamental vicissitude, the transformation of the unliving into the living and vice versa. He has taught Hans Sachs how to converse with a ducat and a horse hide, and he teaches Simplicius how to talk to objects and how to create an impression of magical writing and word sorcery using certain cipher techniques. Simplicius, who learned to read in the first section of the novel and then took this experience to the next level by learning to decipher secret codes, quickly picks up Baldanders' method of hiding German sentences in what appear to be foreign words: "Without wanting to brag, I am rather good at breaking codes; it was one of my lesser arts to write a letter on a thread (or even a hair) which nobody could decode."[159] Simplicissimus is thus affiliated with an occupational category that could be found in one of Grimmelshausen's main sources, the encyclopedic book of trades known as *La piazza universale di tutti le professioni del mondo* (1585) by Tommaso Garzoni, in the twenty-eighth "discourse": "Of the writers and scribes, papermakers, pen cutters, cipherers, hieroglyphists and orthographists."[160] The cipherer's inks and encryption techniques which Garzoni describes as convenient tools for modern correspondence are, for Simplicissimus, the original models for a living dialogue with mute things; in principle, all writing is magical writing.

Baldanders sparks a desire in Simplicissimus to speak with mute objects, and it was an ingenious idea on Grimmelshausen's part to have his hero fulfill this desire using a European counterpart to the palm leaves found on the island in the Indian Ocean. A dialogue with a piece of paper—"Simplicius' strange conversation with the toilet paper"—begins in the eleventh chapter and continues to the end of the twelfth chapter. In keeping with the picaresque novel's low register, the conversation takes place in a privy where Simplicissimus relieves himself. Employing a conceit which would have made the master Rabelais proud—after all, the thirteenth chapter of *Gargantua* concerns the hero's disquisition on the best method for wiping one's rear—Grimmelshausen goes off on a scatological paper digression which superimposes the crapper on the chancery, the chamber pot on the court chamber.

It is worth noting that paper does not pipe up out of the blue in the concluding section of *Simplicius Simplicissimus* to tell its life story. It is a silent background presence right from the start of the novel. It appears in the first chapter of the first book when the hero describes his origins; Simplicius says that the windows in his house were made of oiled paper instead of glass, and he even refers to the fact that hemp and flax seed were used in its production. Its absence is felt in the forest of Gelnhausen, where a hermit teaches the young Simplicius to read and write using tree bark instead of paper, fore-shadowing the palm-leaf book. Soon after it turns up in the form of a map from China, and then in the office of a servile secretary who demonstrates an art which prefigures that of the "cipherers." Like the Baroque books with word "secretary" in the title, this secretary knows all of the ways to address princes, counts, and other high-born individuals, and he calls ink the "*spiritus papyri.*" Simplicius employs a bodily weapon here to counter the subservient spirit of paper: He contaminates the secretary's office with a powerful fart that presages the superimposition of the crapper and the chancery framing the dialogue with paper in the *Continuatio*. In the fourth book of the novel, Simplicissimus lists paper in the inventory of essentials he needs to become a quack doctor. A short time later, he imagines paying doctors to write a testimonial advertising his health springs which he would have engraved and printed.

Going back to the octavo paper in the crapper-chancery, which complains about having to wipe the backside of a tramp instead of the king of France, it is notable that this toilet paper refers to itself as a *Schermesser* (shearing blade). A number of explanations have been suggested for this, the most reasonable being that this is the toll taken by the upside-down logic of the picaresque novel. The face shaved by the shearing blade is the obverse of the rear wiped by the paper; the two come together in the compound noun "buttface."[161] In its asso-ciation with the body, with filth and with a low register, the *Schermesser* is related to the protagonists in the picaresque novels of the age. The toilet paper's life story is a counterpart in miniature to the book in which the story is found. It revolves around how the *Schermesser/* paper has been maltreated, pounded, tortured, and a witness to the world's vices. Grimmelshausen based paper's origin story and journey on the paper production process that he would have seen illustrated in the *Piazza* of Tommaso Garzoni. The *Schermesser*—who clearly knows his Pliny—explains how his journey started as a hemp seed in the earth, which had to molder in dung before it grew into a hemp stalk and then, once it had become a plant, how it was crushed, beaten, rubbed, and finally hackled, sold in barrels at the market, spun into yarn, and woven on a loom to make Dutch cloth. It becomes apparent here that the *Schermesser* is subject to the law of ceaseless metamorphosis which is embodied in the novel by the character of Baldanders. The *Schermesser* sees a weaver steal some of the yarn he is working with; in the form of a shirt, the *Schermesser* witnesses a chambermaid consorting with both a nobleman and his secretary; the shirt gets worn out and finally, after serving as a diaper to the maid's bastard child, it decays into rags which are taken off to the paper mill. There it is made into a fine sheet of writing paper, then bound up in a quire, a ream, and a bale, before being purchased by a merchant from Zurich "who took us home and sold the ream I was in to a manager or bookkeeper, who made a large book or accounting journal out of me. Till that had happened, I had passed through the hands of about thirty-six people since I'd been a rag."[162]

In the story of the palm-leaf book, the fictitious authorship of Grimmelshausen's hero, who turns out to be a "poet," is tethered to a natural writing material which suits the paradisiacal traits of what is—from a European point of view—an extraterritorial island. In the *Schermesser* episode, European paper mutates from a mute thing into a picaro. Like a picaro, it recounts its adventures in the first person, thus becoming a counterpart to the novel's hero, who converses with it—and then seals its fate by relinquishing it to an earthly hell: the toilet. When it took the form of fine octavo writing paper—before becoming wastepaper, packing paper, and, finally, toilet paper—it had not been associated with poetry. It had been a servant of the law, bureaucracy, and economics.

The "large book or accounting journal" into which it was bound is something we encountered in the world of Giovanni Domenico Peri: it is the *liber grande*, the ledger of the merchant, the heart of double-entry bookkeeping. Even without going so far as to say that Grimmelshausen oriented his tight poetic management of time on bookkeeping techniques, we can view paper's metamorphosis here as evidence of the modernity of *Simplicius Simplicissimus*. In a strikingly extended passage, the novel expresses the realization that, for *Homo oeconomicus*, such a ledger balances out an entire scholarly library of classic authors, or even the Bible:

This book (in which I, as an honest sheet, took the part of two leaves) was loved by the bookkeeper as much as Alexander the Great had loved Homer. I was his Virgil, in which Augustus had so diligently studied; I was his *Oppianus*, in which Antonius, the son of Emperor Severus, had so busily read—and his *Commentarii Plinii Junioris*, which Largius Licinius had valued so much; I was his *Tertullianus*, which Cyprianus always held in his hands, and his *Paedia Cyri*, which Scipio knew so well; I was his *Philolaus Pythagoricus*, which pleased Plato so much, and his *Speusippus*, which Aristotle loved so well; and I was his *Cornelius Tacitus*, which had brought such pleasure to Emperor Tacitus, and his *Comminaeus*, which was valued above all else by Carolus Quintus. To sum it up, this book was the Bible he studied night and day. But not so that the account would be honest and just—but because he wanted to hide his thievery, cover up his disloyalty and roguishness, and arrange everything so that his books would seem to be in order.[163]

Mind you, this library catalog, which is supposed to put the importance of bookkeeping into perspective, was compiled not by the deceitful bookkeeper but by Simplicius in his dialogue with the sheet of paper. In order to be a rogue and an adventurer in the Baroque world, you had to be a vagabond and soldier, but you also had to position yourself in relation to the world of paper—both so that your adventures would be written down and so that no adventures would be left out.

2.3. Robinson's Journal, Ink, and Time

How do you keep time on a deserted island where there are no clocks? In the robinsonade that is the culmination of Grimmelshausen's *Simplicius Simplicissimus*—as if the picaresque novel were ushering its successor into the affections of the European public—the castaway hero and his companion erect three crosses on their island in the Indian Ocean to ward off the Devil and show God how penitent they are. This is the start of a new way of calculating time: "From then on we began to live somewhat more piously than we had done before. In order to be able to honor and celebrate the Sabbath without a calendar, I cut a notch in a pole every week-day and a cross on Sunday, when we sat down together and talked about holy and divine things. I had to do it that way because I had not yet thought of anything I could use instead of paper and ink to write things down."[164]

Daniel Defoe's Robinson Crusoe does not know that he will have to spend twenty-eight years, two months, and nineteen days on the island upon which he has been shipwrecked. But he quickly grasps that time and the ocean have something in common, that fixed points of reference can be lost just as easily in the uniform passage of the days as on the high seas. He is not on the island long before he begins to fear that he could lose the ability to tell time "for want of books and pen and ink."[165] Like Simplicius, he starts to record and delineate time calendrically by means of notches. He erects a square post on the spot he first came ashore and cuts a notch into it every day; he marks Sunday with a doubly long notch and the start of each month with a notch double the length of Sunday's. The starting point for all of the notches is the date he arrived on the island, which is carved in capital letters on the post: "I came on shore here on the 30th of September 1659." Robinson's calendar links religion and economics, the reckoning of the Christian year and the reckoning of the working day. Year after year, Robinson will observe a day of remembrance on the anniversary of the start of his calendar, his landing date, an act which some scholars have interpreted as the seed of a national holiday. The birth-of-a-nation aspect of this date is fitting in as much as September 30—in one of the many coincidences pondered by Defoe's protagonist—is also Robinson's birthday, "so that my wicked life and my solitary life began both on a day."[166] The novel follows two lines leading away from this calendar post: the story of the island is written down along one line, while the other line is Robinson's lifeline. There . is not enough space to write this on the calendar post, and notches are an inconvenient method of inscription anyway. For this reason, Defoe gives his hero the ideal medium for joining the two lines leading from the calendar post: a journal as a place for reporting, recording, and continually balancing the accounts of a castaway life. The shipwreck off the shore of the island is the narrative prerequisite for this. It plays a substantial role in Robinson's story, to the extent that this is a story of stockpiles, supplies, and surrogates for that which has been lost. The trips Robinson takes to recover the remains of the shipment from the wreck comprise some of his first adventures on the island. Among these remainders, which represent the last tenuous links to civilization in far-off England, are paper and ink, which Robinson takes ashore along with compasses, mathematical instruments, telescopes, nautical charts, and navigation books as well as several other books, including "three very good Bibles." These allow him to record "the state of [his] affairs in writing," to keep an account of his life, which he begins to do by comparing his debits and credits, the advantages and disadvantages of his island existence. This gives rise to the idiosyncratic overlapping of the journal and the novel which shapes Robinson's early accounts of his island life. Like Simplicius, Robinson is a first-person narrator, but he doubles himself—he is the author of the journal he keeps during his first years on the island, and he is also the author of the retrospective report he writes based on his journal after he is rescued.

When Robinson first observes the anniversary of his arrival date, his ritual consists of fasting, religious exercises, and prayers in which he thanks God "with the most serious humiliation." At this point he finally does what he had resolved to do at the beginning and cuts a longer notch for Sunday in his calendar post. Prior to this, he had "observed no Sabbath day, for as at first I had no sense of religion on my mind." Robinson Crusoe cannot be expected to explain the strange coincidence that gives September 30 its dual significance and connects the date commemorating the shipwreck to a puritanical conversion narrative. This makes it all the more pressing to ask the question of Daniel Defoe. Why does he place so much importance in dating his hero's adventure? Why does he give Robinson a recording medium which dissects the first years of his island existence in such a tight data grid? Because by means of his fictitious editor and fictitious journal, Defoe was attempting to authenticate the subtitle of his novel about Robinson the castaway: "written by himself."

Defoe wanted to form an association between the "novel" and "news," and because he was a newspaper man himself, an early journalist, he knew that in the world of newspapers, part of what made something a news item was that it could be dated. The date is the most basic connection between a newspaper and the world. It is more than just a chronological marker indicating the newspaper's day of publication; it is part of the newspaper's promise of truth, part of what links its news stories to an identifiable place and an identifiable time. In a culture where newspapers were becoming commonplace and the novel was booming as an art form, the date of a shipwreck could serve two purposes: it could become a news story, such as the story of the shipwrecked Alexander Selkirk which Daniel Defoe used as a source, and it could also contribute to the fiction that the story in a novel had the status of a news story. This is because the flip side of saying that "a news story has to be dated" is that dated stories are associated with news. Crusoe's journal not only obeys the formal law of puritanically accounting for one's life, it also reflects the distant past much like a newspaper reflects events in the empirical world. For all that Robinson skirts close to the genre of the puritanical journal in his moments of contrition, it is Defoe's intention that the diary also be a kind of "newspaper," with Robinson Crusoe acting as an island reporter whom readers trust to directly chronicle "the truth." But only something newsworthy can take the form of a news story, and Defoe took this into account. "December 25—Rain all day"—entries such as this make the journal more believable, but an accumulation of them would cause readers to lose interest in the novel. Robinson Crusoe lacks the resource that supplied the great diarists of seventeenth-century France and England with their material: the world of the court of Versailles or the world of the metropolis of London, where Samuel Pepys wrote between 1660 and 1669—the years that Robinson spent on his island. The castaway is deprived of such social subject matter, and the resulting vacuum is filled with dense descriptions of the activities that sustain his existence, such as the "strange multitude of little things" that must come together to create something as seemingly simple as a loaf of bread. A journal is the ideal medium for this. For the entire first third of the novel, it is the perfect gateway drug for habituating readers to the detail-soaked realism for which Defoe is now famous.

But in the long run, a journal is not a convenient way of telling a story which takes place over twenty-eight years in a setting where one day is much like the next and noteworthy events are a rarity. Therefore, Defoe could only leverage the journal's credibility in the novel by making sure he was able to ditch the journal eventually. He solved this problem by grouping together paper and ink with the supplies which, like food, would run out but which, unlike bread or clothing, could not be substituted with something else. Even in the entry on the first anniversary of his landing day, Robinson notes that his ink is running low, a problem which becomes terminal by the end of the fourth year: "My ink, as I observed, had been gone for some time, all but a very little, which I eked out with water, a little and a little, till it was so pale it scarce left any appearance of black upon the paper. As long as it lasted, I made use of it to minute down the days of the month on which any remarkable thing happened to me."[167] Once the journal has successfully saturated the novel with a suggestion of factuality, Defoe lets it gradually disappear in a fading trace of ink. The story of its disappearance helps anchor the novel to the "found among the papers" model and gives it a genealogy which links the island report to the calendar post erected on the island. It not only incorporates paper and ink in the novel's reservoir of materials, but also makes the depletion of this resource into a formative power—one which is all the more meaningful because Robinson will spend decades on the island. Daniel Defoe rejected the *Simplicius Simplicissimus* option of bringing paper surrogates into play. He could not allow Robinson to stumble upon the obvious idea of continuing his journal on palm leaves with ink made from lemons or other fruits. The shortage of paper and ink in *Robinson Crusoe* is the source of the novel's narrative economy.

3

Transparent Typography

∽

3.1. The Epistolary Novel's Mimicry of Letter Paper

The coupling of the communication medium of paper and the infrastructure of the postal system encouraged private correspondence to flourish from the late seventeenth century. As literacy spread and postal traffic grew more stable, private letters became a critical medium for textualizing everyday life. Letters concerning family matters and affairs of the heart had been exchanged prior to this, of course, but they were secondary to commercial, political, diplomatic, and scholarly correspondence. This was because the more effort it took to cover a physical distance, the more significant the content had to be to justify the effort. In order for more people to write more letters about more mundane things, it was necessary to increase postal traffic between cities and introduce innovations such as the Penny Post, which was established in London in 1680. This made the frequent to-and-fro of letters economically tenable for the first time, so correspondence could take the form of a discussion in which the physical distance between the interlocutors was bridged through the medium of writing. The rise of electronic correspondence may have something to do with the fact that, in recent decades, greater emphasis has been placed on the material aspect of the letter-writing culture of the past. In modern letter theories, the decisive factor is "that the recipient not only reads something but actually holds something in his hands."[168] Such theories conceive of the letter as a medium for writing as well as a physical object which is capable of transporting a wealth of extralinguistic messages. Though the rules to be observed in official correspondence retreated into the background in private letters, and though the language of the chancery gave way to the ideal of a naturalistic style in Germany from the time of Christian Fürchtegott Gellert's *Praktischer Abhandlung von dem guten Geschmacke in Briefen* (Practical Guide to Good Taste in Letters [1751]), the production of letters was still governed by certain principles even as forms of address dwindled. And production began not with the act of writing but with the selection and preparation of the writing paper.

The Germanist Ulrich Joost has described this process in detail using the example of the author and experimental physicist Georg Christoph Lichtenberg from Göttingen. Lichtenberg wrote on particularly fine Dutch paper from Cornelis & Jan Honig, a company whose watermark was a beehive with a post horn. On special occasions he made use of paper with gilt edging, and he apologized when he wrote letters of condolence on pages without a black border. It would have been impolite not to trim the writing paper, which was usually purchased uncut. Folding a sheet of paper in manuscript folio format, which was somewhat smaller than a chancery sheet, resulted in a bifolium with four pages, providing three pages of writing space to be filled if possible. The address was written on the fourth page after the sheet had been folded. Envelopes were not yet in widespread use in the eighteenth century, so letter-writing guides provided instructions on how to fold paper artfully so that it was impossible to see the written pages without damaging the seal. The color of this seal could indicate the witty (blue/yellow) or sorrowful (black) content of a letter, while a crest or monogram could identify the sender who, unlike the addressee, was not named on the outside of the letter.[169]

As a self-contained object to be unsealed and unfolded, the private letter became a medium of sentimentality in the eighteenth century. It was marked not just with ink but with tears—real or fake—and it was held to the heart. When the lips were pressed against it, they might feel small grains if the ink had been dried not with blotting paper but with blotting sand. The handwriting—the "beloved features"—could be a surrogate for the person who had written it, but so could the letter as a whole, a physical object that could be read as well as touched, tasted, and smelled, a product of the hand and pen, ink and paper, as well as the heart, mind, and soul.

Even in the ancient world, the letter had been viewed as a way to continue or take the place of a conversation hindered by the physical separation of the participants. Sentimental letter culture looked to this topos when it adopted its axioms of naturalness and suggested the use of an effortless, orally oriented style. But the concept of a halved dialogue obscures the fundamental paradox of the letter: it is a form of communication whose dialogic intention is realized by means of a monologue. Even when the addressee is imagined to be in the writer's presence, as a character who speaks and responds to the author and whose reactions to what has just been written are anticipated by that author, the letter's approximation of a dialogue remains bound to the apriority of the monologic form. For all of the extreme grammatical and stylistic orientation on friends, lovers, fathers whose hearts are to be softened, or confidants who have proven to be traitors, the absence of the addressee remains an inescapable premise of the letter. When you write a letter—even in the company of others—you are alone. You are not engaging in conversation; you are writing on a blank piece of paper and cannot be interrupted by your virtual addressee. The sentimental letter acquired its intensity and the tension between its poles of existence—as a form of notification and a medium for its author's self-reflection—as much from distance itself as from its bridging of that distance. Through the apriority of its monologic nature, letter paper became a stage for modeling and verbalizing intimacy and interiority. But beyond everything that connected the letters of the eighteenth century, in their style and self-interpretation, to the letters of antiquity, what was most important were the new options that opened up with the development of the postal system. It was through the postal system that the letter was reinvented as a medium; in the surge of correspondence and the statistical success curve of the epistolary novel, there was a heady moment comparable to the delirium attested to by the work of Rabelais in the age of the printing press.

Letter paper became a member of the family in everyday middle-class life. The entry for *Brief* (letter) in Zedler's German *Universal-Lexicon* of 1743 explicitly mentions the "convenience of writing letters on paper as compared to ancient writing materials."[170]

As it became more popular and less socially exclusive, letter writing lapped against the threshold of authorship. Private letters were frequently copied, circulated, and printed, often without their author's knowledge. But this did not eliminate the distance that the internal logic of the letter placed between letter writing, letter paper, and the printing press. This was true in two respects: First, the naturalistic ideal demanded that writers remain focused on the present—not on posterity, printing, or authorship—because they would otherwise compromise the energies of self-disclosure and openness toward the addressee which were the hallmarks of a "real" letter. And second, a letter could only cross the media threshold between manuscript and print by abandoning all the communicative elements associated with its existence as a physical object. This made the letter fundamentally different from a manuscript. The fair copy of a manuscript strove for self-sublation in typography and for transformation into a generally accessible text addressed to the public. In a fair copy of this kind, handwriting was an incidental feature which could be relinquished at no loss and which was often destroyed. In a letter, however, the handwriting was not incidental; it was the seal of authenticity which the writer impressed upon the letter and which was intended to reach the individual addressee intact. If you broke the seal of a letter not addressed to you, you were breaching the privacy of correspondence. But because printed letters were addressed to an anonymous public, they abolished the exclusivity of the individual addressee. The letter therefore became an editorial problem in the field of modern philology, which described letters as physical objects and, in doing so, emphasized characteristics that eluded printing. It was for this reason that facsimiles came into increased use.[171]

The insurmountable tension between the internal logic of the unprinted letter and its printed version was not discovered by advanced philological study. It was discovered by the authors who, in the eighteenth century, made the epistolary novel into a resonance chamber for the swelling volume of private correspondence and placed it side by side with those other collections of imaginary letters, the letter-writing guides. The authors of epistolary novels, who always portrayed themselves as the editors of the letters they were publishing, faced the same problem as modern edition philologists—namely, they presented their bundle of letters using the medium of typography, but within this medium they had to create an impression of the handwritten originals, the fictitious physical objects upon which their novels were based. This held true even when the public saw through the editorial fiction. As the most thoroughgoing literary embodiment of the "found among the papers of X" model, the epistolary novel relied on the virtual bundle of handwritten letters not solely for documentary authentication, but also—and above all—for aesthetic authentication. It is still fascinating to see the imaginative ways in which this task was tackled by eighteenth-century authors. Leading the way was the key figure of the epistolary novel, the English author Samuel Richardson, who was also a printer and who used his considerable typographic knowledge to make the printed page of the book into a surrogate for the virtual letter paper it represented. Take, for example, the third edition of Richardson's massive, multi-perspective epistolary novel *Clarissa*, which was first published in 1747–48. The title of the third edition from 1751 is a prime example of how to imply that the editor has drawn on a reservoir of handwritten letters to create the novel. It even promises to surpass the original version: CLARISSA. OR, THE HISTORY OF A YOUNG LADY: *Comprehending the most* IMPORTANT CONCERNS *of* PRIVATE LIFE. *In* EIGHT VOLUMES. *To Each of which is added* A TABLE OF CONTENTS. THE THIRD EDITION. *In which many Passages and some Letters are restored from the Original Manuscripts. And to which is added, An ample Collection of such of the Moral and Instructive* SENTIMENTS *interspersed through the* Work, *as may be presumed to be of general Use and Service.*

Richardson's epistolary novels were the product of his intimate acquaintance with the language and style of "familiar letters" as well as his knowledge of the formalities of postal traffic, the accouterments of writing, and the physical characteristics of folded letters. Even the heroine of his first novel, *Pamela, or Virtue Rewarded* (1740), was a kindred spirit to the young women found in his collection of sample letters, published under the title *Familiar Letters on Important Occasions* (1741), who wrote from London to their sisters in the provinces to report on how they had fended off the advances of pushy suitors or seducers. The heroine of *Clarissa*—who refuses to enter into a marriage arranged by her family and instead flees to London, where she is held captive by her seducer Lovelace—is ensnared in a dense web of other letter writers. To get an impression of this flurry of letters from which the characters emerge, it is worth comparing Richardson's *Clarissa* with the epistolary novel *Julie ou la Nouvelle Héloïse* (1761) written by his admirer Rousseau. The 263 letters exchanged by the protagonists in Rousseau's book cover a period of thirteen years, while the 537 letters in Richardson's novel are exchanged in the space of just one year. Without London's Penny Post, which had receiving offices throughout the city and made deliveries up to twelve times a day, this back-and-forth of letters—many of which were dated not just with the day, but with the time of day or even the hour they were composed—would not have been possible.

At the same time, drifts of paper piled up in *Clarissa* because, as would later be the case with Rousseau and the *Liaisons dangereuses* (1782) of Choderlos de Laclos, letter writing was not a product of the correspondents' physical separation. In many cases, the writers were close enough to each other that they could have conversed. The fact that they wrote letters instead was often a result not of the physical impossibility of dialogue but of the psychological necessity of shifting communication to an area unencumbered by the physical presence of one's conversational partner. Letter paper was enveloped by a space in which things that could not be said could be written instead.

This was especially true of declarations of love. In *Liaisons dangereuses*, Madame de Tourvel would have had to interrupt Valmont had he spoken the words he writes to her instead. But she can read his letter to the end, no matter how furtively. Harlowe Place, the family home of the heroine of *Clarissa* and the main setting of the novel early on, is entirely subject to the law that places internal separation above external separation. It is a world of closed doors, doors half-opened, and conversations that break off when Clarissa enters the room. As a result of the quarrel with her family, she corresponds with her relatives in writing even though they all live under the same roof. After she has been confined to her room and the key to the house has been taken from her, all she can do is write letters in her "closet," which is simultaneously a place of retreat and a place for the development of her self. The letters ceaselessly flowing from and circulating through her "closet," and later through the locked rooms in London where she falls victim to Lovelace, almost become characters themselves in *Clarissa*. This is because Richardson, like a modern edition philologist, depicts the letters not merely as texts but as physical objects. Letter paper reaches its apotheosis in his novel. The book tells a story in letters, but also about letters, and what the characters write is always embedded in the situation in which they write it. How often does Anna Howe add an exhausted "I have written all night" as a postscript to her letters to Clarissa? How often do the characters write about the pens they must lay down, or cannot even bear pick up, because of their welling emotions? How often do they reflect on the way their confusion, fear, or haste is expressed in the very appearance of the letters they write? And how often are letters transcribed and added to other letters, enclosed within them, so that they mutually annotate one another in the closest of quarters? Clarissa Harlowe casts an eagle eye over a note conveying accusatory words from her mother, searching for signs to confirm her suspicion that her mother had been reluctant to use such a harsh tone. She finds these signs in the traces of tears that she discovers: "This answer I received in an open slip of paper, but it was wet in one place. I kissed the place; for I am sure it was blistered, as I may say, with a mother's tear!—The dear lady must (I *hope* she must) have [written] it reluctantly."[172] Clarissa's letter to her confidant Anna Howe, in which she encloses this and other evidence of the rift with her family, was used by Samuel Richardson for one of his most complex attempts at employing typography to make the published novel approximate the original manuscripts upon which the book was supposedly based. To this assortment of letters he added an "Ode to Wisdom" on a fold-out sheet of music said to have been composed by Clarissa herself, an ambitious harpsichord player. The text of the ode is presented to readers as a copy made by Clarissa. This was a complex undertaking, not only because of the special size of the sheet music but also because a unique font had to be created for the engraved handwriting. Richardson accepted the effort and expense in order to give readers a suggestive representation of Clarissa's handwriting early on, the charms of which are frequently mentioned in the novel even after the heroine's death.

Using typographic tricks alone, Richardson could not achieve the same degree of illusionistic realism found in the *trompes l'oeil* and pictorial quodlibets of the eighteenth century, which brought to life folded and unfolded letters, invoices, wills, and newspapers. But he went to great lengths to rob the novel—which was set in the Caslon Pica Roman typeface—of its typographic uniformity by employing italics and dashes which are sometimes scattered across the page like pustules. He frequently invoked the physical characteristics of letter paper, the appearance of handwriting and how it spread across the page, as in this account from Anna Howe after Clarissa's death: "I met with a most affecting memorandum; which, being written on the extreme edge of the paper, with a fine pen, and in the dear creature's smallest hand, I saw not before."[173]

At the cusp of the novel, after the heroine has been raped, Richardson exploits typography to perform a virtual autopsy on the original manuscripts. The tenth and last of the "mad papers" that Clarissa writes, tears into pieces, and scatters under the table as if in a trance is presented to readers in fragments. The reader has to turn the book to read the snippets of writing, printed vertically and at different angles on the page, which reveal that the heroine has lost her own voice and can only lament her fate through quotes from Otway's *Venice Preserved*, Dryden's *Oedipus*, and Shakespeare's *Hamlet*. Richardson puts typography into the service of the aesthetic strategy of the epistolary novel, which allows readers to look through the page of the book and see the letter paper of the non-existent original manuscripts attested in the book's title. A short time later, Clarissa composes the preamble to her will, which is not written in ink but is instead stitched with black silk on a separate sheet of paper. In doing this, she gives a final dramatic twist to a central motif of eighteenth-century letter-writing culture: the genre picture of the writing woman, who is as skilled with a pen as she is with a needle, becomes an embroidered epitaph.

3.2. Laurence Sterne, the Straight Line, and the Marbled Page

It is a particular joy, when reading *Tristram Shandy*, to trace the battle between two lines. One of the author's pet passions is to harp on about the difference between a straight line and one that is curved, broken, bent, or in any case not straight. In one instance the curved line takes the form of Corporal Trim who, as he reads aloud from a book of sermons, falls just within the limits of William Hogarth's line of beauty; in another, the author claims to have borrowed a ruler from a writing master to draw the straight line that has been set on the page of his book by a printer. He is not speaking pro domo when he quotes the divines who declare the straight line to be the path that Christians should walk, or Cicero who said it was the "emblem of moral rectitude." Even before the sixth volume of the book, when he uses woodcuts to illustrate the jagged, looping, and curling lines which "I moved in through my first, second, third, and fourth volumes," it is clear that, all down the line, this author has dedicated himself to deviating from a straight line—aesthetically, philosophically, morally, and typographically. Back in the first book, he had claimed it was a moral impossibility for a historian to drive his history before him like a mule-driver would drive a mule—"straight forward": "For, if he is a man of the least spirit, he will have fifty deviations from a straight line to make with this or that party as he goes along, which he can no ways avoid."[174] Tristram Shandy adheres to this maxim right from the start. He is an author of digressions and interruptions, of meandering asides and a refusal to proceed from A to B by the shortest route possible. And as the hero's birth is delayed by one digression after another, it begins to dawn on the reader why this tale of siring and birth can only be told by continually deviating from a straight line: because, as in the original interpretation of Horace's *"mors ultima linea rerum,"* a straight line means death.

Like Samuel Richardson, Laurence Sterne used typography to support his narrative strategy. But while Richardson was interested in making absent letter paper virtually visible in the printed book, Sterne wanted to cover up the absence of the author in the printed book. He was not content with merely interspersing scenes in which pens are sharpened and dipped, or blots of ink are spattered about the room, or with having Tristram Shandy chat to readers in an ostentatiously conversational way. Sterne also scrupulously supervised the printing of the book to ensure that not a single short or long dash, italicized word or line—straight or curved—was left out.

By shattering typographic linearity and uniformity in this way, *Tristram Shandy* broke ranks with other printed books, both in its aesthetic strategy and as a physical object.

Sterne himself positioned his book in the sphere of earlier experiments at the new intersection of storytelling and typography, and he even has Tristram Shandy call upon "the ashes of my dear Rabelais, and dearer Cervantes!" But in his clever coupling of aesthetic and typographic non-linearity, he was very much a child of his time. He took advantage of every printing option available to him, including inserting special pages in the printed book. And he could rest assured that his audience would have learned—from reading Jonathan Swift, Samuel Richardson, or Henry Fielding—to pay attention to the visual design of his printed novel, a form still in its infancy.

Tristram Shandy contains a black page as an epitaph for Yorick, a white page for drawing a portrait of Widow Wadman, and the famous marbled page which Tristram Shandy (parenthetically) declares to be nothing short of the "motley emblem of my work." All three of these pages break the flow of the text. The first was saturated with printer's ink, the second was pointedly left unprinted, and the third was marbled on both sides using a complex method. These pages are not meant to be read; they are meant to be looked at. They do not just interrupt the text; they surpass it. There are two mentions of the three words which make up the brief "epitaph and elegy" inscribed on the plain marble slab over the grave of the deceased Yorick: "Alas, poor Yorick." In the first instance the words are typographically framed as if they were an inscription, and in the second instance—at the climax and end of the chapter—they are sighed by people passing Yorick's grave on the path through the churchyard. This is followed by the black page, where it seems as though the black border of a letter announcing a death has spread over the entire sheet. It recalls a gravestone, and this is what makes its lack of an inscription all the more striking: it is not mute, but silent. In this way, Sterne returns his Yorick to the sphere of Shakespeare's *Hamlet* from whence he was taken: "The rest is silence."

The black page used up many times the amount of printer's ink it would have taken to print a normal page which said nothing. With the white page, Sterne achieved a similar effect with less effort. He inserted the page at the point where readers are encouraged to imagine Widow Wadman, around whom Uncle Toby's love story revolves, as the most desirable woman in the world: "To conceive this right,—call for pen and ink—here's paper ready to your hand.—Sit down, Sir, paint her to your own mind—as like your mistress as you can—as unlike your wife as your conscience will let you—'tis all one to me—

please but your own fancy in it." Just as the black page surpasses all the words of an epitaph—and thus the text of the novel—the white page surpasses the book's illustrations. Sterne was able to get Simon François Ravenet, a leading book illustrator and engraver, to engrave the frontispiece of his book based on a drawing by William Hogarth. But in this passage, visual art as a whole—not to mention portraiture in words—is declared incapable of accurately portraying the Widow Wadman for readers. Sterne probably knew that Samuel Richardson had rejected two of Hogarth's drawings for his book *Pamela*, declaring that a reader had written to him and said he so jealously guarded his inner image of Pamela that he dreaded any illustration which claimed to resemble her. And he certainly knew of the suggestive potential of the blank sheet and the practice of interleaving books with white pages. The Earl of Orrery had sent a finely bound book with blank pages to Jonathan Swift for his birthday on November 30, 1732, along with a poem in which he referenced John Locke's famous metaphor and called upon Swift to fill this *"rasa tabula"* with satires castigating their era. But Swift did not take up this challenge to compose on demand and instead announced that he would leave the pages blank. Sterne would have known that, like Swift, his readers would reject the pen and ink he placed in their hands. The blank space he offered them was not a precursor to "interactive" literature. It was not waiting to actually be written on or illustrated; it was merely an invitation to readers to accept the challenges of the novel with imagination and understanding.

The white and black pages interrupt the text, but they remain true to its aesthetic principle—namely, to pose riddles. The page of marbled paper is a much more emphatic and elaborate riddle than the white or black page. It appears in the text suddenly, just as the summary of Tristram's father's collection of treatises on noses is interrupted by the question of who "Tickletoby's mare" was. Even readers who did not know that "Tickletoby" was a term for the male member in popular parlance, or that Sterne's digression about the mare was a reference to a bawdy passage from Rabelais' *Gargantua*, could guess that the novel was indulging in its passion for double-entendres here. The riddle posed by Tickletoby's mare was just the run-up to the riddle of the marbled page, however: "Read, read, read, read, my unlearned reader! read,—or by the knowledge of the great saint *Paraleipomenon*—I tell you before-hand, you had better throw down the book at once; for without *much reading*, by which your reverence knows, I mean *much knowledge*, you will no more be able to penetrate the moral of the next marbled page (motley emblem of my work!) than the world with all its sagacity has been able to unravel the many opinions, transactions and truths which still lie mystically hid under the dark veil of the black one."[175]

Nowhere else in the novel does Sterne challenge his readers' wit as cryptically as he does here. In passing he alludes to Yorick's gravestone, which we know is the black page, and intimates to the reader that it may not be a representation of silence and the limits of speech in the face of death, but instead merely a curtain covering the incessant overproduction of text. And for a moment it seems as though he is saying that the marbled page is the same type of riddle as the black page. But even if readers honestly thought they could come to grips with the black page through knowledge alone, it was clear at a glance that the marbled page simply deflected the imperative to "read, read, read, read, unlearned reader." In an even more fundamental way, it is just as unreadable as the black or white page. With this marbled page, the novel is interrupted—like Richardson's *Clarissa* is interrupted by the fold-out sheet music for the "Ode to Wisdom"— by an element from another world. Or, to put it more precisely, by an element that would not normally be found in the place it appears in *Tristram Shandy*. Marbled paper was a decorative paper used for book covers and endpapers. Readers would buy unbound books and have them bound according to their tastes, so marbled paper belonged to the world of the bookbinder, not that of the author, or the external world of the text, or the text itself. Considerable effort was needed to free this paper from its traditional place of residence: "To create this unique page, a blank sheet has to be folded, dipped into a 'Turkish-style' dye bath, dried, then marbled on the other side, then dried again, stamped with a page number, and manually sewn or glued to the edge of a page that has been cut from the body of the book."[176]

Sterne gave his readers a dual challenge when he encouraged them to view the marbled page set intentionally in the middle of the text as an emblem of the entire work. For one thing, it was puzzling as to how a finely veined, brindled construction of colors could be emblematic of the novel as a construction of words. For another thing, the question arose as to what this striking page could mean when viewed in the context of the already striking typographical concept of the novel as a physical object. With respect to this second question, the marbled page was a distinctive way of disrupting the uniformity and seriality of the printed book. It turned each of the 4,000 copies of the first edition of *Tristram Shandy* printed in 1763 into a unique specimen. Sterne's exhortation to view the marbled page as a "motley emblem" of the whole work was therefore paradoxical, as there would have been 4,000 different emblems of a single novel which, aside from the marbled page, was identical in its text and physical design. The emblematic aspect lay solely in the characteristic that all marbled paper shared *as* marbled paper. This shared characteristic, which related to the aesthetic principle behind the novel, was found not in a particular color or distribution of flecks and spots, but in the production process that was used to create all marbled paper. The aesthetic principle behind marbled paper was the blossoming of color at the expense of the line. The year 1759 saw both the publication of the first volume of *Tristram Shandy* and the appearance of the first "blot" drawings by the painter Alexander Cozens. These blots—abstract colored daubs and shapes—were the starting point for a new method of composing landscapes with trees, clouds, and mountains. Cozens's formula for these blots, "a production of chance, with a small degree of design," could also be applied to marbled paper.[177] It did not start with an outline drawn by a draftsman's hand, and the key concept in all classical art theory—the contour—was overridden by the lightly controlled, haphazard flow of colors. Diderot and d'Alembert's *Encyclopédie* corroborates this in its entry for "marbled paper," which describes how the dispersion of colors and the uniform movement of the comb creates the "*nuages*" and "*ondulations*" which give marbled paper its unique beauty.

From a modern viewpoint, it is almost impossible not to view marbled paper as a precursor to abstract painting. But such an art form did not yet exist for Sterne's audience. Sterne's readers will have viewed the marbled page above all as a nobilitation of the endpaper, a colorful disruption among the black-and-white printed pages, a page which refused to acknowledge the type area and rejected typographic linearity, thus turning the delight in digression and deviation and the denial of the straight line into a denial of authorship itself. At least one reader took exception to Sterne's and Shandy's denial of writing in favor of an unsolvable puzzle. When he read the "New Edition" of *Tristram Shandy* which appeared in 1768, the year that Sterne died, this reader left an indignant comment in the margin of the marbled page: "Mr. Tristram Shandy might much better imploy himself in wrighting than sending a Marble Paper Leave in to the World."[178]

3.3. The Fragmentation of the Printed Page: Jean Paul, Lichtenberg, and Excerpts

Novelists seldom got involved in the complex game of playing with the physical design of their books. Such experiments reached their zenith in the eighteenth century, in the decades between Samuel Richardson and Laurence Sterne, as if their main purpose had been to use all means available to convince readers of the many possibilities and diverse charms of the nascent novel. But in the texts themselves, the tension between handwriting and print—which had been identified as an aesthetic resource early on—was put to use in ever more inventive ways. The "found among the papers" formula had been put to the test with real papers in the historical and political sphere, and it subsequently became one of the most popular title conventions for works of fiction. In Friedrich Heinrich Jacobi's *Aus Eduard Allwills Papieren* (From the Papers of Eduard Allwill [1776]) or Schiller's *Geisterseher. Aus den Papieren des Grafen von O*** (The Apparitionist. From the Papers of the Count of O** [1787–98]), there was still a suggestion that these novels were based on actual papers. This was no longer the case with Jean Paul's satire *Auswahl aus des Teufels Papieren* (Selections from the Devil's Papers [1789]). But Jean Paul showed that the material for the masques of editorial fiction was not produced by the imagination alone; it was the result of the real development of literature itself and its ally, the advance of literacy. As everyday life grew saturated with unbound paper, more options arose for someone to write something, in some way, for some reason, on some piece of paper, and have it printed—or not.

It would be paradoxical to say that the line leading from Rabelais through Cervantes and Sterne to Jean Paul was a straight one. But this line existed, and it branched off into genealogies in which the printed text could trace its origins back to the world of manuscripts. The writing scenes to which these manuscripts owed their creation acquired a spatial depth and were embellished with more and more details and accouterments springing from the evolution of the literary market. In Jean Paul's *Leben Fibels, des Verfassers der Bienrodischen Fibel* (Life of Fibel, Author of the Bienrodian Primer [1811]), a baptized Jew takes on the role of the Morisco boy who sells the Cide Hamete Benengeli manuscript in *Don Quixote*. The market street in Toledo has become an extensive trading network for manuscripts, empty book covers, and fragmented chunks of pulped books, where some buyers are interested in "costly marbled volumes" while others, the "material peddlers," are only interested in "the content (the paper)." Among the empty husks of books whose content has been chopped up for use in paper windows, scarecrows, and toilets, the narrator finally strikes it rich: He finds the title pages and remaining sheets of Fibel's printed biography, the first volume of which—in a nod to Tristram Shandy—"covers the fate of the selfsame individual in the womb."[179] Based on this "wreckage of historical sources," he searches his hero's village of birth for the remaining handwritten "biographical paper scraps" and finds them in the form of "coffee sacks," "herring papers," "fidibuses," "chair covers," "paper dragons and other flying leaves." From these fragments piled up in "a bio-graphical scrap heap of paper clippings," the narrator pieces together not only Fibel's life story but also the story of the creation and pub-lication of the manuscript. As is so often the case with Jean Paul, the "found among the papers" formula refers not to letters and diaries but to parodies of scholarly biographies. In *Leben Fibels*, Jean Paul turns a key medium of literacy (*Fibel* means "reading primer" in German) into an authorial figure whose work is used to compile extensive bibliographies. In *Leben des Quintus Fixlein, aus funfzehn Zettelkästen gezogen; nebst einem Mußteil und einigen Jus de Tablette* (Life of Quintus Fixlein, as Drawn from Fifteen Boxes of Paper Slips; Along with a Widow's Share and a Few Bouillon Cubes [1795–96]), the title alone leaves no doubt that the practices of scholars play a key role here.

The Classical and Romantic period of German literature has become famous for ushering in the concept of the *Originalgenie* (original genius), but this period emerged from the fusion of poetry and knowledge. What it contains—in magnificent abundance in the case of Jean Paul—is a poeticized inventory of cultural technologies for knowledge production in the paper age. This includes the box of paper slips which, in *Quintus Fixlein*, appears in the book's subtitle and as a heading in each chapter. The hero himself, who, like his author, rates literary history "some ells higher than Universal or Imperial History," has divided the story of his life into boxes of paper slips or "letter-boxes," starting with his childhood as related to him by his mother: "This perspective sketch of his early Past, he committed to certain little leaves, which merit our undivided attention. For such leaves exclusively, containing scenes, acts, plays of his childhood, he used chronologically to file and arrange in separate drawers in a little child's-desk of his; and thus to divide his Biography, as Moser did his Publicistic Materials, into separate letter-boxes."[180]

In the work *Vortheile vor Canzleyverwandte und Gelehrte in Absicht auf Akten-Verzeichnisse, Auszüge und Register, desgleichen auf Sammlungen zu künfftigen Schriften* (Advantages for Chancery Staff and Scholars with Regard to File Indexes, Excerpts, Registers, and Collections for Future Writings [1773]), the jurist Johann Jacob Moser explained in detail the methods he used to manage his "paper slip box." This was part of a long tradition of works which proved that the reverse of the formula "from script to print" was also true:

printed and bound materials were continually being turned back into unprinted and frequently unbound paper, a transformation which describes the process of excerpting from books.

Just as certain aspects of paper-based letter culture only become apparent when viewed from the perspective of email and text messaging, and just as there is an advantage to exploring double-entry bookkeeping from the perspective of digital data processing, we get a better insight into the routines and technologies of excerption by comparing them with their digital descendants, namely, the technologies of downloading. But in all of these cases, the benefit arises not from drawing a direct analogy but from highlighting the differences. A famous *bon mot* by Georg Christoph Lichtenberg, a master of witticism and an excerption skeptic, illustrates this: "He continually wrote down excerpts, so everything he read went from one book *past his head* straight into another."[181] Here, the excerpter is just the interface who triggers the reformatting of a data set which passes through him, leaving no trace behind. It is much easier to bypass the mind when downloading and saving data which will probably never be read than when writing down excerpts, a process in which it is difficult for the mind to separate itself from the ensemble of the eye, hand, and head. This is because even after the basic decision has been made to excerpt from a particular book or journal, the excerpter needs to continue making selection decisions. Excerpting is not the same as copying, as it entails the production of "extracts." Lichtenberg was skeptical of the hoarding impulse prompted by hypertrophic erudition—leading to the "excerpt-book savings box"—and of the autonomization and proliferation of reception routines, as contrasted with the productive coupling of the imagination and the intellect: "For most people, compilation and the collection of excerpts is an activity that fuses one's entire mental capacity."[182]

But it is not enough to describe the art of excerpting merely as a receptive mnemonic technique for filling mental savings boxes in unproductive minds. The writings of Johann Jacob Moser and even the definition of "excerption" in Zedler's *Universal-Lexicon*, which revolves entirely around mnemonics, illustrate that excerption techniques reversed the polarity of the data streams being processed and turned them into production energies: "Excerption is the scholarly practice of abstracting from that which has been read in order to remember it so that it may be found and used again when the time is right." It is no coincidence that this dictionary definition is immediately followed by a description of a suitable method for finding the information again when the time is right: "Some have sheets of paper inserted into a book in which they want to collect things, familiarize themselves with the organization of the book, and then note down within it what they find in other books."[183]

As the excerpt books of important authors have been studied in recent decades, the catalysis function of excerpting has come to the fore. Excerpting is not limited to transforming knowledge into data sets and information; it can contribute to an author's linguistic, stylistic, and conceptual innovation. The familiar form of the expression *"edle Einfalt und stille Größe"* (noble simplicity and quiet grandeur) can be traced back to Johann Joachim Winckelmann's extensive excerpts, the product of his accentuation, refinement, and Germanization of the conceptual apparatus absorbed from English and French Classicism.[184]

On account of its catalysis function, excerption was accompanied from the outset by the question of which tools were best suited to organizing and storing the excerpts. This question arose for scholars just as it had for merchants during the emergence of double-entry bookkeeping. In both cases, a growing stream of data had to be stored and organized along an access grid without consuming more paper than necessary. And in both cases, there was no way to avoid having to regroup or copy the data that had initially been recorded. As skeptical as Lichtenberg was of excessive excerpting, he used double-entry bookkeeping as a model for organizing the thoughts and observations he noted in his "waste books." "Merchants have a waste-book (*Sudelbuch, Klitterbuch*, I think it is in German) in which they enter from day to day everything they have bought and sold, all mixed up together in disorder; from this it is transferred to the journal, in which everything is arranged more systematically; and finally it arrives in the ledger, in double entry after the Italian manner of book-keeping. [In the ledger, each man is accounted for separately, first as a debtor and then as a creditor.] This deserves to be imitated by the scholar. First a book in which I inscribe everything just as I see it or as my thoughts prompt me, then this can be transferred to another where the materials are more ordered and segregated."[185]

Excerpt books or notebooks could either be written chronologically and then indexed, or divided into sections in advance and only then filled with extracts. At the same time, ever since the appearance of the *Bibliotheca universalis* (1545–48) by the Swiss polymath and naturalist Konrad Gesner, attempts had been made to keep excerpts flexible, regroupable, and only temporarily fixed instead of permanently locked in a stable organizational framework. Even if the excerpts were eventually to end up in another handwritten book, the purpose of these attempts was to create an alternative to the book. Their focus was on the slip of paper. In Gesner's case, such slips were the product of working with scissors, which he used to cut up high-quality sheets of paper upon which noteworthy items had been written in a random order. For Gesner and his correspondents, using scissors as an excerpting tool also meant cutting up letters and books. But this fragmentation of loose papers, which were only temporarily fixed with pins or soluble glue, had a counter-pole in the props used for their permanent storage and preservation once an organizational structure had been found. The treatise *De Arte Excerpendi: Vom gelehrten Buchhalten* (The Art of Excerpting: On Scholarly Bookkeeping [1689]) by Vincentus Placcius, a scholar from Hamburg, includes an image of a large excerpt cabinet where slips of paper could be hung from pins for permanent storage.[186] The polarity between the closed book and the unbound slip of paper became apparent here, and also later on in the furniture that surrounded scholars and authors. The rigid bookshelves of the library stood in contrast to the many movable elements in the cabinets, desks, and, especially, "secretaries" which—like the books with this word in their title—were used by the individuals of the same name. Even today, drawers are the preferred place for storing loose papers.[187] And—in the realm of things, beyond the scholar's study—every attempt from the eighteenth century onward to develop a library catalog which did not take the form of a book ultimately ended in a chest of drawers. Here, too, the loose slip of paper was experimental ground.

It is no coincidence that our old friend from the fourteenth-century world of paper—one which had little to do with scholarship at the time—should crop up again as a tool for organizing books: the playing card. When, in 1775, Abbé Rozier took on the task of cataloging everything published by the Académie Royale des Sciences from its foundation in 1666 to the year 1770 in a general register, he recorded the titles of the publications on the unprinted backs of playing cards. He used cards not only because they came in a standardized format but also because the multiple layers of glue on the cards made them very stable. Like in the catalog of the Imperial Library of Vienna, which was started in 1780, these cards were a precursor to index cards.[188]

Jean Paul played with the concept of paper boxes in his literary work and elevated the ability to move and regroup loose sheets of paper to an aesthetic principle in his narrative poetics. But his own collection of excerpts, which he started as a student and which eventually amounted to 110 sequentially numbered volumes, was designed as a handwritten library. This took the place of a normal library for him. In his "Leaflets" of 1816–17, he wrote: "As an author and old man, I now benefit more from reading my excerpts than unfamiliar books."[189] This comment is not just about reading; it is also about writing. There was a good reason for Jean Paul to say that he would not have given up this excerpt library "for a library with 200,000 volumes." For him, the excerpt library was not a Baroque cabinet of curiosities filled with desiccated collectanea; it was a powerhouse of his work, the terrain in which printed material rotated with unprinted material. This rotation was characterized by a very modern kind of paradox resulting from the fact that Jean Paul was, and wanted to be, a published author, but his writing was powered by his continuous rebellion against the definitive nature of the published work. The realm of excerpts and manuscripts was a realm of options, and their openness and open-endedness had to be saved—virtually, anyway—from the realm of the definitive printed page.

When excerpt libraries were valued more highly than libraries full of printed books, it heralded the emergence of a type of author who would act as a partisan for the realm of the optional in the world of the printed. The act of compiling indexes and copying excerpts in contexts which erased the bibliographic links to their original source produced handwritten books which Jean Paul read over and over again; this was an enormous reservoir he could draw on when he placed the art of comparison and the surprising analogy at the heart of his paradoxical authorship.

Jean Paul quoted extensively from the *Introduction to Bibliology* (1777) by Michael Denis, author of the *Systematic Index of Butterflies in the Vienna Region* (1776) and custodian of the Imperial Library in Vienna when it was being cataloged.[190] Denis was one of the countless sources of the knowledge concerning the physical design of books that flowed into Jean Paul's literary work. A small book of excerpts relating to paper ("Booksellers bring prohibited books into the country, often passing them off as paper," "600 centners of rags produce 3,000 reams of paper") could be compiled from his excerpt library. In 1782, when Johann Immanuel Breitkopf's book on the origins of linen paper was published, he noted: "Playing cards were the predecessors to the art of printing."[191]

But Jean Paul would not have been Jean Paul had he not looked at playing cards more closely and seen in them—as the *Life of Quintus Fixlein* shows—a metaphor for life itself: "For, in morning and evening, and much more in youth and age (life's morn and eve) man raises his earthy head, full of dreams and strong fancies, to the

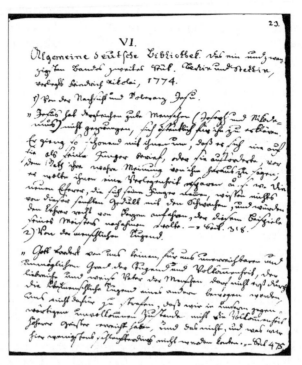

Jean Paul, *Excerpt Books*, Hof 1780 ("Miscellanea from the Latest Writings," Vol. 6)

tranquil heavens, and gazes at them fixedly and longs—and longs! whilst on the contrary, in the hot middle of life and of the day, his sweat-dropping brow bends towards the earth and towards her tubercules and truffles. Just as the middle strata of a playing-card is formed but of *macule*, whilst the two extremes are of fine paper. ..."[192]

PART THREE

The Great Expansion

1

The Demons of the Paper Machine

1.1. The Mechanization of Sheet-Making

Louis-Jacques Goussier spent six weeks in the Langlée paper mill near Montargis, a good hundred kilometers south of Paris, to research his "Papéterie" article for Diderot and d'Alembert's *Encyclopédie*. This was just one of many trips he took to the production sites of the mechanical arts. Goussier, an illustrator and engraver, was the most important contributor to the many volumes of illustrations that accompanied the text of Diderot's encyclopedia. The articles that he occasionally produced in addition to his engravings contained detailed descriptions of machines and processes, and they were interspersed with copious references to the engraved plates. It was almost pointless to read them without looking at the engravings at the same time. This was true for his "Pompe" article, for which he had visited the lead mine in Pont-Péan in Brittany, and it was true for the "Papéterie" article which was published in 1765. Verbal description and illustration were closely linked in both articles following the concept that Diderot had outlined in the prospectus for his encyclopedia.[193]

Goussier's approach had something journalistic about it, an element of illustrated reportage. Goussier had studied physical mathematics, but he was not an expert in either paper production or pump mechanics. He was, however, an expert at describing them. The text of his article gave readers an overview of the paper production process, from collecting and sorting the rags to drying, sizing, and storing the sheets. The accompanying engravings, in turn, took readers on a kind of imaginary tour of the paper mill of Montargis, a tour which was far more detailed than the depictions of papermaking found in early modern books of trades. The virtual tour also took in the women and children who pre-sorted and cut up the rags in Montargis. Goussier was able to focus on this precise description because he had been absolved of the duty to recount the history of paper production in China, Egypt, and Europe, or to discuss different types of paper, from packing paper to marbled paper. This was covered in the separate entry for "Papier" which consisted of articles penned by the Chevalier de Jaucourt, a member of the editorial board and one of the main contributors to the *Encyclopédie*.[194]

The articles were portioned out in this way in response to both the growing body of knowledge about paper in the eighteenth century and the prevailing trends for organizing and presenting this knowledge. The dissection and technological description of contemporary paper production increasingly spun off from the historical and philological reconstruction of the history of paper. Prior to the *Encyclopédie*—a non-governmental, privately financed undertaking supported by the new modern intellectual—the government had been responsible for inspecting and documenting the *arts mécaniques* since the late seventeenth century. This had been one of the main tasks of the Académie Royale des Sciences founded in 1666 on the initiative of Jean-Baptiste Colbert. Information gathered by the academy from all parts of the country was incorporated into the treatise *Art de faire le papier* (The Art of Papermaking [1761]) by the astronomer and academy member Joseph-Jerôme Lalande, which had appeared four years ahead of Goussier's encyclopedia article. Here, too, the production process was described in detail, the mill in Langlée near Montargis played a key role, and the engravings were an indispensable part of the work. But while Goussier would take a close-up view in his article, Lalande pulled back for a more generalized look at how scientific knowledge had penetrated the production process. Lalande explained why particular methods were used, he positioned individual mills such as the one in Montargis in the overall spectrum of French paper production, and, above all, he understood them to be economic enterprises: he listed their expenses (raw materials, tools, labor costs, etc.) and sales revenues, and he explained why properly managed paper mills could be a lucrative business.

The technological traditionalism of many papermakers and their tendency to keep secrets meant that paper mills were long surrounded by an atmosphere of hostility toward innovation. This cordon finally loosened in the eighteenth century. The Hollander beater, which took its name from its country of origin, had replaced the old stamping gear in the seventeenth century as a superior machine for processing paper's raw materials. This machine was widely discussed in the age of paper manufactories. In his treatise on paper, Lalande said that technological modernization combined with the optimal use of labor was the key prerequisite for ensuring that a mill could make a profit through a high sales volume instead of a high price for its goods: "Upon investigating the sequence of tasks carried out to finally produce paper, one sees that a sheet must pass through the hands of the workers more than thirty times, and through the presses approximately ten times. On account of the speed of each operation and the assistance of the necessary machines, paper has now become a rather common ware."[195]

Lalande's treatise indicates that paper was becoming an increasingly "common ware" in the eighteenth century, at least within the limits set on it as a mass product in the pre-industrial era. Paper's object of comparison, the needle, sat very close to it in the *Descriptions des Arts et Métiers, faites ou approuvées par Messieurs de l'Académie Royale des Sciences*, a large series of volumes published between 1707 and 1781.

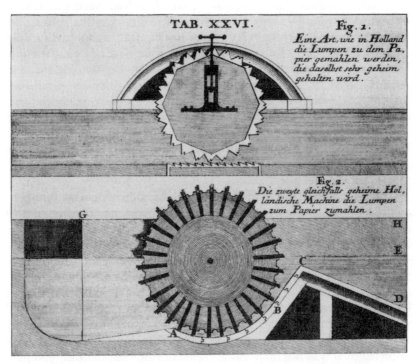

Hollander beater. From: *Complete Mill Construction, 1718*

In the preface to Lalande's treatise, the academy went to great lengths to justify the disclosure of French manufacturing knowledge, opposing the view "that it would be to the advantage of the state not to make the study of these arts public knowledge so as not to share them with outsiders." The Montargis mill was also considered a model enterprise because its owner had rejected "jealous apprehension" and "self-serving zeal" in order to shine "the light of natural history and the spirit of investigation" on the world of the mechanical arts, which had long been characterized by "misplaced secrecy."[196] The academy also propagated its ideal of transparency by criticizing its competitors in Holland whose treatises on paper included illustrations of their own advanced machines for shredding rags and preparing suspensions—illustrations which could not, however, have been used to actually build a functioning machine.

When the French academy invoked the illumination metaphor of the Enlightenment in its plea for the free circulation of papermaking knowledge, it did so in its own interest. French paper mills were attempting to counter the strong position of their Dutch competitors by studying and adapting Dutch production methods. In 1768, not long after Lalande's and Goussier's treatises had been published, inspector Nicolas Desmarest received financing from the Bureau de Commerce—the central governmental institution for monitoring factories—to travel to Holland for the first time to study not just the Dutch machines but the entire paper production chain. He made a second trip in 1777. His findings were published in two memoranda for the Académie Royale des Sciences, and they also influenced the modernization of the important paper mills in Annonay owned by the Montgolfier brothers. These mills would soon be famous when Étienne Montgolfier, a passionate patron of the first hot-air balloons, used paper from his mill to make the magnificent outer envelopes of this symbol of the age.[197]

The Enlightenment entailed not just the philosophical self-enlightenment of the mind but also a comprehensive stocktaking of the mechanical arts. Compendia and hymns of praise were written to the division of labor even before Adam Smith theoretically nobilitated it. And through figures such as inspector Nicolas Demarest, who opposed the meticulous state regulation of French paper factories and argued that they should be oriented on the needs of market participants following the Dutch model, economic liberalism quickly gained ground within the infrastructures of mercantilism. Translation, like travel, was an important medium for the international circulation of paper knowledge. It was not on account of its thoroughness and empiricism alone that Lalande's *Art de faire le papier* (1761) already appeared in German in 1762. The *Schauplatz der Künste und Handwerke, oder vollständige Beschreibung derselben, verfertiget oder gebilliget von denen Herren der Academie der Wissenschaften zu Paris*, a compilation of German translations of the *Descriptions des Arts et Métiers* which included Lalande's treatise in its first volume, was intended to make the work of the French academy accessible to a German audience. The publisher, translator, and editor was the cameralist Johann Heinrich Gottlieb von Justi. The title of his *Schauplatz* (stage) harked back to Baroque compendia such as Garzoni's *Piazza universale* and Jacob Leupold's *Theatrum machinarum* (1724–27). But every bit of theatricality had been driven out of his depiction of technology. Justi translated and annotated extracts from the monumental French work on the mechanical arts while completing another project at the same time, his main cameralist work entitled *Die Grundfeste zu der Macht und Glückseligkeit der Staaten oder ausführliche Vorstellung der gesamten Policey-Wissenschaft* (The Foundations of the Power and Happiness of States, or a Detailed Introduction to the Study of Policy [1760–61]). Both works were published in Berlin and were addressed to the Prussian government, from whom Justi was hoping for a position. In the title of Johann Beckmann's *Anleitung zur Technologie* (Guide to Technology [1777]), the type of knowledge to which Justi was contributing with his translation of Lalande was finally given a name. In this foundational work on technology as a scientific discipline, which was continually revised and reprinted in the following decades, papermaking was no longer associated with the book industry, as it had been in early modern books of trades. It now brushed up against weaving and wool dyeing on one side and beer brewing on the other. The history of paper was covered in a brief footnote.

Mercantilism and cameralism led to a boom in technological literature which contributed to the exponential growth of writing about papermaking in the eighteenth century. The bibliography of German-language "Works Concerning Papermaking in Chronological Order," which was published anonymously in the *Technologisches Magazin* in 1790, listed a total of just seven titles from the sixteenth and seventeenth centuries but over eighty titles from between 1703 and 1789. This surge in technological knowledge left a lasting impression on Diderot and d'Alembert's encyclopedia. In its articles and engravings covering "Gravure," "Imprimerie," "Papeterie," "Papier," "Plume," and "Reliure," the encyclopedia described the media and technologies to which it owed its own material existence and form. In doing so, it familiarized the general public not only with the ideas of the Enlightenment but with the craft of knowledge production. But the encyclopedia and the knowledge it contained did not start to spread through Europe with the first folio-format editions of the work.

This diffusion only became possible when high numbers of smaller quarto and octavo editions were published between 1777 and 1782. Robert Darnton researched the publishing history of these editions in the files of the Société Typographique de Neuchâtel and revealed the key role that paper procurement played in this:

> Printers made calculations based not on the number of book copies in a press run but on the number of printed sheets per press run, according to which they determined the cost of the paper and presswork. To print an initial run of 4,000 copies of the first volume of the quarto edition in Neuchâtel, the printer would have needed 10,000 reams of paper. But to print all thirty-six text volumes of the quarto edition in a total press run of around 8,500 copies, the printers in Lyon, Geneva, and Neuchâtel would have required 72,000 reams or thirty-six million sheets of paper of a specific quality, or 13,000 centners of paper made from textiles.[198]

The major project for producing the quarto and octavo encyclopedias at the end of the pre-industrial era of paper was a worthy counterpoint to Gutenberg's Bible project, which posed challenges of a similar dimension for paper mills at the dawn of the age of printing. Paper was the main cost factor in printing in the eighteenth century. It accounted for at least half, and often up to two-thirds, of the entire budget. Unlike typesetting costs, which remained the same regardless of the size of the press run, printing costs and paper costs rose along with the number of copies produced. But paper costs rose more quickly than printing costs because paper itself became more expensive. Robert Darnton describes how the agents working for the Lyonnaise bookseller Joseph Duplain, head of the consortium overseeing the publication of the encyclopedia, roamed the paper mills of France and Switzerland to find fine paper, as well as the tricks used by the consortium to counter the tricks used by the paper manufacturers. The huge project for publishing small-format encyclopedias pushed pre-industrial paper production to its limits—but in the end, it rose to the challenge. The text and engravings of the *Encyclopédie* and its successor, the *Encyclopédie méthodique*, captured an image of pre-industrial paper production which had not changed fundamentally since the thirteenth century.

Its modernization began under the Ancien Régime. Plans were made to increase production by improving traditional technologies and establishing new production sites. Treatises on paper, such as the one by Lalande, were essentially advertisements and instructions for how to set up and run a paper factory. Technology writers and educated representatives of the publishing industry alike, such as Johann Immanuel Breitkopf, called upon the state to fund paper mills.

In his work *Über die Geschichte der Erfindung der Buchdruckerkunst* (On the History of the Invention of Printing [1779]), Breitkopf included a four-page petition addressed to the Saxon cabinet minister Friedrich Ludwig von Wurmb which stated: "Few of the state's manufactures are as distinctive and useful as the paper manufacture; the flax crop—after varied applications in diverse factories, after long economic usage, even in the form of discarded remnants—is the basic material that brings forth this manufacture, which in addition to new employment for a large number of laborers can be a mother to many other factories and a treasure chest for all human wisdom, science, and knowledge."

The propaganda for the funding of paper mills had a flip side in both Germany and France: the fear that the supply of raw materials would not be able to keep up with rising production capacity. The vision of modernized paper production in the eighteenth century revolved not around a revolution in sheet formation but a revolution in its resource base. Whole swathes of papermaking literature were dedicated to accounts of the search for a replacement for rags. René-Antoine de Réaumur, a member of the Académie Royale des Sciences and editor of the *Descriptions des Arts et Métiers, faites ou approuvées par Messieurs de l'Académie Royale des Sciences* until his death in 1757, had suggested as early as 1719 that much like wasps used wood fiber to build paper-like nests, wood could be used to make paper. Jakob Christian Schaeffer attracted attention even outside of Germany with his *Experiments and Examples of Making Paper Using No Rags or Only a Small Proportion of Them* (1765) and, in particular, his three-volume *New Experiments and Examples of Making Economic Use of the Plant Kingdom to Make Paper and Other Things* (1765–67). But these plant experiments never progressed to the point that they could offer an alternative to traditional manufacturing methods. Much the same happened with ideas for recycling wastepaper to create an inexhaustible source of raw materials. A short booklet by the law professor Justus Claproth from Göttingen concerning *An Invention for Making New Paper from Printed Paper by Entirely Washing Out the Printing Ink* (1774) recounted the attempts by a papermaker named Schmidt in the village of Lengden near Göttingen to implement the idea mentioned in the title. Claproth had provided him with "three folios which had been completely printed in blackletter on poor-quality writing paper." The inspiration for this may have come from his experiences as a factory magistrate, but it was also the product of a widespread contemporary scholarly dream: to dispose of surplus or worthless books in a profitable way. Claproth apparently won over the Göttingen bookseller Johann Christian Dieterich. Another of Claproth's Göttingen colleagues, Georg Christoph Lichtenberg, noted in one of his waste books that "Dieterich is collecting waste paper in his garden."[199] For his part, Lichtenberg distanced himself from the epidemic of complaints about the flood of books by humorously defending maculature as fertilizer for the literary world.

The actual revolution in papermaking came not from these rampant fantasies of innovation but from the opposing interests of the factory owners and the vatmen which had been characteristic of European paper mills right from the start. In 1798, Louis-Nicolas Robert developed the basic idea for a paper machine which mechanized the sheet formation process. Identifying himself as a "mécanicien à Essonnes," he applied for a patent in January 1799. Robert, a Parisian by birth, had been posted with an artillery regiment from Grenoble to Santo Domingo in 1781, where he fought in the American War of

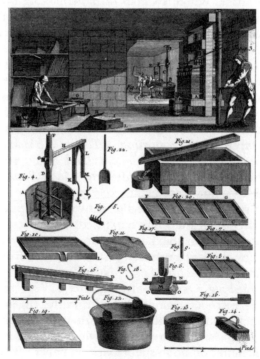

From the *Encyclopédie*: Illustration for the article on papermaking

Independence. Upon returning to France at the start of the Revolution in 1789, he worked in the printing office of Pierre-François Didot in Paris. Robert was eventually transferred to a paper factory in Essonnes managed by Didot's son, Saint-Léger Didot. Saint-Léger Didot helped Robert develop his idea by supplying him with material and workers. Like all paper factory reformers—including, first and foremost, the Montgolfier brothers in Annonay—he aimed to make his actual production space match the illustrations which accompanied the paper-making articles in Lalande's *Art de faire le papier* and the *Encyclopédie*. These engravings depicted the paper mill of Montargis in its Sunday best, devoid of all filth and production obstacles, where the workers at the vats and presses were seamlessly integrated into the rhythm of production. In reality, however, these workers—like the heat and cold of the changing seasons which caused the water to ice over or dry up—were frequently the cause of disruptions to continuous production. Unlike the women and children who prepared the rags, the vatmen and couchers were highly qualified itinerant laborers who circulated through France and Europe and were well aware of how indispensable and irreplaceable they were. At first, the circulation of technological knowledge did not threaten their artisanal monopoly. Factory owners could not really prevent the strikes that the workers habitually staged to have their wage demands met. The acceleration of production was an effect of the paper machine developed by Louis-Nicolas Robert, but it was not the primary motive behind the machine's invention. The primary motive was to bring an end to the permanent conflict with the well-organized labor force by breaking its monopoly of practical knowledge. This was true for Saint-Léger Didot, it was true for the Montgolfier brothers in Annonay, and it was no less true for the owners of English paper factories.[200] Mechanization ensured continuous movement.

A screen which moved forward horizontally and mechanically emulated the vatman's dipping and shaking motions offered the promise of uninterrupted production, a prospect questioned by the workers themselves. For the prototype of his continuous screen which circulated on rollers, Robert had used the fine, flexible wire mesh which ensured a smooth, unribbed surface for velin paper. Instead of the rigid mold and dipping motions of the skilled vatman, Robert's machine involved a hand crank and an endless belt of woven wire cloth. A simple hand movement, for which a skilled worker was no longer necessary, could now set complicated machinery in motion.

In retrospect, the development of Robert's idea and introduction of the first machines shows that technological innovations could take root transnationally even in times of confrontation between nations.[201]

From the *Encyclopédie*: Illustration for the article on papermaking

John Gamble, who acquired a patent in London in 1801 to use Robert's machine in England, was Saint-Léger Didot's brother-in-law. Gamble was a member of British Army who had been sent to Paris to negotiate an exchange of prisoners of war, and he used his assignment as an opportunity to have Robert's machine transported to London. At the same time, he convinced the Fourdrinier brothers, who ran a wholesale stationery business in the British capital, to back the project. The project took a lasting toll on its investors. But when it migrated from Paris to London, the machine invented by Robert— who quickly disappeared from the history of its evolution—was integrated into the infrastructure of the Industrial Revolution in England. This revolution had already brought mechanized looms to eighteenth-century textile factories, the old sister enterprises to the paper mills. Now the French invention was united with advanced English mechanical engineering in the form of Bryan Donkin. Donkin, an engineer, widened the paper web and also mechanized the crank handle and improved both the screen-shaking and couching mechanisms. The bankruptcies that had to be overcome in the course of perfecting the machine, and the parliamentary licenses that had to be applied for and renewed, do not need to be described in detail here.

However, it is important to take note of the model followed by the English when they eagerly imported and then technically perfected the paper machine. What this model did for sheet formation—the heart of the papermaking process—in the early nineteenth century was a repeat of what the remarkably rapid adoption of Dutch innovations had done for raw material processing in the mid-eighteenth century. England had, for a long time, primarily produced packing paper and brown paper while importing fine paper, but it began to free itself of this dependence on imports in the late eighteenth century.[202] The political and military conflict with revolutionary and Napoleonic France led to import disruptions which encouraged English manufacturers to expand their position in the domestic market. At the same time, the emerging English paper industry benefited from a development pattern which the Russian-American economic historian Gerschenkron has called "the advantages of backwardness." England was "backwards" in terms of papermaking, but as pre-industrial papermaking reached its zenith and approached its demise as a handicraft, the country came up from behind and rapidly advanced to become the leading paper nation. The first paper

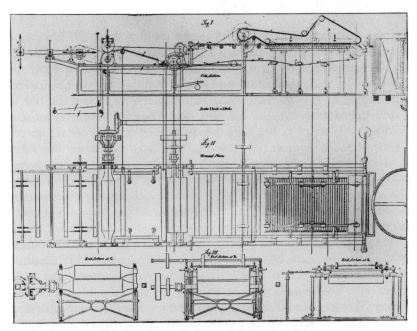

Fourdrinier machine by Donkin, 1807

machines went into operation in England in 1806, and they were exported to France from 1811 and to Germany not long after. In 1818, the first German patent for operating an English machine from the Donkin company was granted in Berlin.

Though the paper machine spread rapidly from the 1820s, paper production did not reach industrial dimensions until the late nineteenth century. But the first step in this direction had been taken. This represented a striking break with the eighteenth century, largely because the cumulative effects of mechanization amplified each other in the first third of the nineteenth century. The cylinder printing press invented by Friedrich Koenig in Germany (and brought to maturity in England) rapidly increased the speed of printing, while stereotypes made it possible to quickly produce new editions of works while lowering typesetting costs at the same time. In this context, the paper machine contributed to a rise in the number of printed books, a rise in the number of editions, and a reduction in the cost of printed works. The diffusion of the paper machine affected the history of technology as well as the history of literature.

1.2. The Loom of Time, the French Revolution, and Credit

The mechanization of the English textile industry from the late eighteenth century prepared the ground for the diffusion of the paper machine. Productivity in this industry grew more quickly than the population, making cotton and linen clothing more affordable. The supply of raw materials was able to keep pace with the rise in paper production because clothing was changed more frequently. Additionally, when paper mills began to use chlorine bleach in the 1880s, a wider range of rags could be processed for paper. All of this kept rag prices stable despite growing demand. The English paper production curve rose more sharply than the curve of imports from the international rag market. Most of these imports had traditionally come from Germany, where Hamburg was the largest shipment center.[203]

One of the printers and publishers who was asked about the effects of the paper machine by the Fourdrinier Committee in 1837 reported that it had given birth to a new class of cheap publications that could never have been produced otherwise. These newcomers included the *Penny Magazine* founded by the Society for the Diffusion of Useful Knowledge in 1832, which soon reached a circulation of 200,000 copies sold each week. Its success indicated that the technological modernization of printing and paper production would go hand in hand with far-reaching changes in the literary market and publishing industry.[204] The most important change was that the market shifted its focus to periodicals from the 1820s on account of their economic appeal. The new magazines founded between 1812 and 1832— including *Blackwoods Magazine, The London Magazine, Colburn's New Monthly Magazine*, and *Fraser's Magazine*—began to assume positions that had been occupied in the early nineteenth century by volumes of poems from Shelley and Keats, Byron and Walter Scott. Today we automatically associate poetry with small print runs, but a good 20,000 copies of blockbusters such as Scott's *Lady of the Lake* (1810) could have been sold quickly in different formats and editions. Byron addressed a verse along these lines to his publisher John Murray: "As the opinion goes, Verse hath a better sale than prose."[205]

The paper machine was partially responsible for reversing the relationship between poetry and prose. Paper became more expensive when imports were interrupted during the decade of the French Revolution and the Napoleonic Wars, making small volumes of poetry an attractive option for English publishers. But when the price of paper fell again, prose began its triumphal march, with periodicals playing a key role in this. Aristocrats and the affluent middle-class had helped make expensive volumes of poetry a success, often for their prestige value. When the literary market expanded, however, the lower classes became a significant audience.

The rapid development of periodicals caused essays and short-form prose to grow in popularity at the expense of volumes of poetry. Periodicals also prompted the first serious predictions concerning the mechanization and commercialization of literature. In his essay "Signs of the Times," published in the *Edinburgh Review* in 1829, the Scottish writer Thomas Carlyle critiqued the modern age in view of the conflict between mechanics and living dynamics, an opposition he had borrowed from Kant and Romantic German natural philosophy:

> Were we required to characterise this age of ours by any single epithet, we should be tempted to call it, not an Heroical, Devotional, Philosophical, or Moral Age, but, above all others, the Mechanical Age. It is the Age of Machinery, in every outward and inward sense of that word; the age which, with its whole undivided might, forwards, teaches and practises the great art of adapting means to ends.

For Carlyle, mechanization was not merely an element of modern technology, it had become a universal principal of the world order as a whole: "There is no end to machinery." In Carlyle's depiction of the mechanical age, the periodical press had taken on the mantle of a secularized religion: "The true Church of England, at this moment, lies in the Editors of its Newspapers. These preach to the people daily, weekly; admonishing kings themselves; advising peace or war, with an authority which only the first Reformers, and a long-past class of Popes, were possessed of; inflicting moral censure; imparting moral encouragement, consolation, edification; in all ways diligently 'administering the Discipline of the Church.' "[206]

In England in the 1820s, the steeply rising curve of mechanically produced paper left the ever-declining curve of handmade paper far behind it. When he expressed his unease with the periodical press, Thomas Carlyle did not overlook the growing mountains of rags, which subsequently found their way into one of the oddest novels of the nineteenth century, *Sartor Resartus: The Life and Opinions of Herr Teufelsdröckh* (1834–35). The title references *The Life and Opinions of Tristram Shandy*, but it is no accident that Herr Teufelsdröckh is German, as the novel owes as much to Jean Paul as it does to Laurence Sterne. Carlyle had made a name for himself in England as a translator and editor of German literature; he was as familiar with Jean Paul as he was with Goethe, whose *Wilhelm Meister* he had translated, and with Schiller, whose biography he had written. In *Sartor Resartus*, which was first published as a serial in *Fraser's Magazine*, he depicts himself as the translator, editor, and reviewer of a work by the German professor Diogenes Teufelsdröckh. He also introduces Hofrath Heuschrecke, a friend of Teufelsdröckh, who sends him the professor's main work as well as "six considerable paper-bags" filled with "fragments of all sorts; scraps of regular Memoir, College Exercises, Programs, Professional Testimoniums, Milkscores, torn Billets, sometimes to appearance of an amatory cast; all blown together as if by merest chance, henceforth [to] bewilder the sane Historian." Diogenes Teufelsdröckh's main philosophical work—*Clothes, Their Origin and Influence*, supposedly published in 1831 in Weissnichtwo ("Don't-know-where")—is therefore surrounded by a mass of unbound scraps of paper, covered with outlines and incoherent ideas written in a "scarce legible *cursiv-schrift*."

Like Jean Paul's biography of Quintus Fixlein, the biography of Teufelsdröckh is pieced together from fragments, and, like the protagonist of *The Life of Fibel*, Carlyle's protagonist is surrounded by manuscripts and wastepaper. Teufelsdröckh, who makes full use of speculative license in his role as a representative of German philosophy, speaks solely through papers in Carlyle's novel. However, as the "paper-bag documents" also include "detached thoughts on the steam engine" and their author is clearly familiar with the current theories of the Saint-Simonists in Paris, Teufelsdröckh reveals himself to be a critical contemporary essayist and thus a potential contributor to the English magazine. When he writes "the Journalists are now the true Kings and Clergy," it sounds as though he were quoting from an essay by Carlyle. But the essayistic contemporary criticism found in *Sartor Resartus* is conveyed by means of poetic demonology. The re-tailored (or newly tailored) tailor of the novel's scholarly Latin title is clothed in prose, but his philosophy was inspired by the verses of the Earth Spirit in Goethe's *Faust*: " 'Tis thus at the roaring Loom of Time I ply / And weave for God the garment thou seest him by."[207]

Teufelsdröckh is not a constructive natural force, however; he is a witness to the modern forces that have diabolically drawn the spirit down into the world of rags. When Teufelsdröckh visits the old-clothes market on Monmouth Street in London—"under that ink-sea of vapor, black, thick, and multifarious as Spartan broth"— he finds himself in a world where Goethe's roaring loom of time has become the mechanical loom of Richard Arkwright, a pioneer in the industrialization of textile factories who plays a major role in Carlyle's essay. This layer of contemporary clothing philosophy, which includes an interpretation of English dandyism, also encompasses Teufelsdröckh's reflections on the connection between the proliferation of typography and the piles of rags. In a strange way this, too, relates to the work of Jean Paul, who noted in his excerpt books: "The cooks in France therefore often printed on aprons made of paper or waste paper. Gets in the food." This excerpt found its way into *Quintus Fixlein*, in the depiction of the protagonist's passion for wastepaper books: "It was also this respect for all waste-paper that inspired him with such esteem for the aprons of French cooks, which it is well known consist of printed paper; and he often wished some German would translate these aprons; indeed I am willing to believe that a good version of more than one of such paper aprons might contribute to elevate our Literature (this Muse *à belles fesses*), and serve her in place of drivel-bib."[208] Carlyle's Teufelsdröckh, who had probably read Jean Paul, makes a very similar argument for counting recycled wastepaper as modern literature: "I consider those printed Paper Aprons, worn by the Parisian Cooks, as a new vent, though a slight one, for Typography; therefore as an encouragement to modern Literature, and deserving of approval." In both cases, the purpose of the thought experiment was to associate modern literature with wastepaper and to ridicule the exponential growth of the literary market. Teufelsdröckh goes on to say:

If such supply of printed Paper should rise so far as to choke up the highways and public thoroughfares, new means must of necessity be had recourse to. In a world existing by Industry, we grudge to employ Fire as a destroying element, and not as a creating one. However, Heaven is omnipotent, and will find us an outlet. In the meanwhile, is it not beautiful to see five million quintals of Rags picked annually from the Laystall; and annually, after being macerated, hot-pressed, printed on, and sold,– returned thither; filling so many hungry mouths by the way? Thus is the Laystall, especially with its Rags or Clothes-rubbish, the grand Electric Battery, and Fountain-of-Motion, from which and to which the Social Activities (like vitreous and resinous Electricities) circulate, in larger or smaller circles, through the mighty, billowy, stormtost Chaos of Life, which they keep alive![209]

In the preface to his *Lyrical Ballads* (1801), Wordsworth had written with pride that given two equally skillful descriptions of passions, manners, or characters, one in poetry and one in prose, the prose description would be read once while the verse would be read a hundred times. Teufelsdröckh's vision of paper rising up from rags to become a source of energy for modern society in its printed form before sinking back into the realm of rags once again heralded the future of the periodical: after being read once, it was wastepaper.

Book two of the first volume of Carlyle's next great work, *The French Revolution: A History* (1837), is entitled "The Paper Age." It describes the decade prior to the outbreak of the French Revolution as an apparently uneventful period of baseless hopes and illusions; of masquerades and a thirst for the theatrical as the state's finances lay in ruins; of quiet internal decay:

Time of sunniest Stillness—shall we call it, what all men call it, what all men thought it, the new Age of Gold? Call it at least, of Paper; which in many ways is the succedaneum of Gold. Bank-paper, wherewith you can still buy when there is no gold left; Book paper, splendent with Theories, Philosophies, Sensibilities—beautiful art, not only revealing Thought, but also so beautifully hiding from us the want of Thought! Paper is made from the *rags* of things that did once exist; there are endless excellences in Paper.[210]

Carlyle's account of the Revolution is not historiography, it is a prose poem which should be read like Milton's *Paradise Lost* and which, when it descends into the Reign of Terror and the excesses of the guillotine in its third part, rivals Dante's *Inferno*. The dual inflation of unsecured money and unsecured thought in this decade of calm before the storm was reflected, according to Carlyle, in the "paper-dome" that the Montgolfier brothers filled with the smoke of burned wool and set aloft in June 1783 near their paper mill in Annonay in the Vivarais, becoming the sensation of Paris. The balloon that had been applauded by the French aristocracy in the Tuileries was, for Carlyle, a "windbag" soaring above the chaos, hunger, and uncertainty, filled with the illusions and false hopes of the final decade before the Revolution. It had been brought to Paris by Jean-Baptiste Réveillon, the Montgolfiers' business partner and owner of the city's largest paper business, which specialized in colored paper and wallpaper. Readers of Carlyle's book are reminded of this a few chapters later when, in the first sparks of revolution prior to the storming of the Bastille, it is not a Montgolfier balloon but rather a hungry mob from the suburbs that rises up in a bloodily suppressed revolt and attacks Réveillon's paper warehouse on the Rue Saint-Antoine.

In essays such as "Signs of the Times," Carlyle characterized the French Revolution as the origin and catalyst of the mechanical era. In his diagnosis of the times, references such as these came into play even when he mocked the age in which he lived by saying that "every little sect" had to have its own periodical press. In *The French Revolution*, the "Paper Age" extends beyond the pre-revolutionary decade to encompass the relationship between revolution and journalism in general. "New printers, new journals"—Carlyle's essay is shot through with inked pamphlets, revolutionary and royalist newspapers, the *Ami-du-Peuple* and *Ami-du-Roi*, all of them energized batteries, as Teufelsdröckh would describe them. It was through these publications that the clash between the Jacobins and the Girondists, which Carlyle depicts as a dramatic break preceding the plunge into the Reign of Terror, was taken out of the National Convention and into the streets of Paris: "One Sansculottic bough that cannot fail to flourish is Journalism."[211] When Carlyle introduces his English audience to *La Sentinelle*, the *journal-affiche* or "placard journal" by the Girondist Jean-Baptiste Louvet de Couvray, which was printed in large letters on pink paper and pasted on the walls of Paris, and when he says that this new type of journalism, which was hawked, pasted, and proclaimed, could preserve for only one day what might be preserved in a book for decades, he makes repeated reference to Louis-Sébastien Mercier's *Le Nouveau Paris* (1799).

We should stay a while with Mercier's depiction of revolutionary Paris and the first years of the Directory—which was one of Carlyle's main sources for *The French Revolution*—because in both its form and content, it is a key witness to the emergence of modern topicality, of experiencing the present *as* the present, in paper-based media.

Mercier had achieved European success with his multi-volume *Tableau de Paris*, an exemplary depiction of urban life which was published in pre-revolutionary France from 1781 to 1788. It is telling that the word *Tableau* was absent from the title of his *Nouveau Paris*, however. Mercier the author had become Mercier the journalist, someone who wanted to keep pace with the cascade of events, with the new gestures and idioms of everyday revolutionary life, whose ears took in the neologisms and whose eyes noted the "fleeting and shifting nuances"—who, ultimately, wrote *"sur la Révolution actuelle,"* and not just in his article of November 22, 1789. Many of the articles he had written as a contributor to the *Annales patriotiques et littéraires* and the *Journal de Paris* were incorporated into *Le Nouveau Paris*. Mercier portrays the Revolution as a visual and acoustic explosion of journalism triggered by the sudden freedom of the press. He dedicates an entire chapter to the "Cris Nouveaux" of the newsboys who would shout out the news of victories and intrigues, battles and revolts, the death of a general or the arrival of an ambassador, for those who could not read. He includes a profile of *Le Patriot Français*, a daily newspaper by the Girondist Brissot, with whom he sympathized, and he damns Jean-Paul Marat and the newspapers of the Jacobins, which he believed plagiarized, misinterpreted, and exploited the pre-revolutionary philosophic writings of Voltaire, Helvetius, Diderot, and Rousseau. To illustrate the mercurial nature of the *"esprit publique,"* Mercier took inspiration from the title of the Girondist newspaper *Le thermomètre du Jour* and exhorted journalists not to be distracted by the cacophony of voices but to take the temperature of the *"esprit publique."*

Even in his *Tableau de Paris*, Mercier had commented on the amount of paper used by printers in the capital city of the Ancien Régime, a fact that did not escape Jean Paul's excerpts in 1788: "They use 160,000 reams of paper for printing in Paris each year."[212] In Mercier's *Le Nouveau Paris*, the acceleration of the great political machine (*"la grande machine politique"*) and the rising temperature of everyday life caught up in the Revolution have led to an increase in the consumption of paper, to which Mercier dedicates another whole chapter. His prevailing tone is one of grievance regarding the dangers posed by the Revolution on account of the license it granted: "The evils that paper caused in various phases of the Revolution are such that one might wish it had never been invented."[213] Unrestricted freedom of the press had resulted in the calumnies of libelers which endangered the public; the declaration of human rights had brought about such extensive freedom of petition that the mass of data could barely be kept in order; the townhouses which had been emptied of clerics and emigrant nobles had become offices which devoured mountains of paper for printing bills of indictment; day after day, millions of blue, purple, green, and red placards had turned the walls of the city into public platforms where no one was prevented from inciting murder or looting; and thousands of printed copies of the laws circulated throughout Paris and all of France. Added to this were the countless paper bills that moved through the countryside and the capital. Printers and booksellers multiplied endlessly, papers and offices multiplied endlessly, and pens flew off the shelves thanks to the expansion of bureaucracy by the Directory. Mercier's *Nouveau Paris* is a city flooded with paper.

This depiction was not based on statistical research. Paper production had not yet been mechanized. But when Mercier described the climate of day-to-day events, he illustrated an innovation which, following the invention of the paper machine and the cylinder press, would go from being a mirror of the Revolution to an element of everyday middle-class life in the nineteenth century. The same applies to the chapter dedicated to the most striking paper-based medium of the revolutionary years: the placards or "*affiches sur le mur.*" Though he castigated their outgrowths—the offers from profiteers, the public slander—Mercier also viewed them as a medium reflecting the character of Paris as a major city, a self-portrait of the revolutionary metropolis. Previously, he wrote, placards only announced the sale of a country estate, the death of a cardinal or the departure of a ship setting off for India. But they had become a basic introduction to the morals, politics, and literature of the present day. Instructions in the art of dominating people stood next to the golden promises of life insurers; the services of artists, craftsmen, and master bakers could be seen at a glance; a brief analysis of the sample texts enabled you to pass judgment on every possible scientific discipline; and on every street corner, you were ensnared in a silent discussion about your own health or your own assets. Gastronomy and finance, physics and diplomacy—everything was covered. If you had to take a trip tomorrow, you could find a carriage today. If you were looking for peace and quiet, you could find an apartment vacated by the recently deceased. Mercier's panorama of the "talking walls" that magnetically attracted the public and turned passers-by into lingering readers is drenched in sarcasm At the same time, he was fascinated by the affiches and produced a masterful essay on the encroachment of vertical writing and pictorial advertising in the modern urban space. When he contemplated reclaiming the affiche walls from the charlatans and turning them into a tool of public instruction, he imagined taking advantage of the special media status of this regularly updated "*bibliothèque instructive*": to use the walls, you needed neither a bookseller nor a book nor a podium on which to set the book.[214]

The paper machine, with which Mercier was not yet acquainted, permanently boosted the number of placards and posters by both speeding up the paper production process and eliminating the restrictions on formats. Continuous paper made it possible to produce affiches in sizes that Réveillon's paper shop could only achieve by pasting sheets together. When Mercier envisioned a *"Paris-Affiche"* where every wall, every pillar, and every doorway was covered by a poster either large or small, wide or narrow, he was anticipating the developments of the early nineteenth century. Vertical script and posters began to shape the face of big cities. As Thomas Carlyle was writing *The French Revolution*, London was filled with walls and wooden boards thickly plastered with posters, a sight vividly captured in John Orlando Parry's painting "A London Street Scene" (1835). Describing Paris during the same era, Walter Benjamin said: "Le Charivari of 1836 has an illustration showing a poster that covers half a housefront. The windows are left uncovered, except for one, it seems. Out of that a man is leaning while cutting away the obstructing piece of paper."[215]

Mercier's observations on the growing use of paper in revolutionary Paris encompassed the assignats that had circulated as paper money from December 1789. But for Mercier, these bills played a secondary role to the press, politics, and bureaucracy. Carlyle's "Paper Age," by contrast, coupled the inflation of the intellect to the inflation of money and the decline in literary values to the decline in economic value. In the chapter covering the decade prior to the Revolution, when Carlyle introduces the phrase "Paper Age," the threat of national bankruptcy hangs like a cloud over the parties and masquerades. Carlyle refers back to this at the start of the book's main section when, after the Revolution has become a key player following the storming of the Bastille, the assignats make their striking entrance. The National Assembly's decision to print paper money and issue it as bonds secured against confiscated church property had been born of the need to reduce the national debt. But this financial operation became a striking image of the "Paper Age" only when Carlyle interpreted it as "the first of a long series of like financial performances, which shall astonish mankind. So that now, while old rags last, there shall be no lack of circulating medium: whether of commodities to circulate thereon, is another question."

This question of the relationship between the circulation of ragborn money and the circulation of commodities harbored a suspicion, namely, that paper money would not prevent bankruptcy but was actually the form that bankruptcy had taken. Carlyle came up with a very arresting image for this suspicion. Earlier, when describing the lavishly decorated, paper-covered Montgolfier balloons rising into the sky, he had highlighted the fact that they could not be steered. Here, he depicts the assignats falling over revolutionary Paris like a gentle snow which conceals its catastrophic nature:

> But, after all, does not this Assignat business speak volumes for modern science? Bankruptcy, we may say, was come, as the *end* of all Delusions needs must come: yet how gently, in softening diffusion, in mild succession, was it hereby made to fall;—like no all-destroying avalanche; like gentle showers of a powdery impalpable snow, shower after shower, till all was indeed buried, and yet little was destroyed that could not be replaced, be dispensed with! To such length has modern machinery reached. Bankruptcy, we said, was great; but indeed Money itself is a standing miracle.[216]

The image of bankruptcy being alleviated by paper money only applied to the early years of the Revolution in France. The assignats that were printed by Didot for the second major issue in September 1790 had a nominal value of fifty to two thousand livres, but five-livre bills were printed from May 1791 and even ten-sous bills appeared in December of the same year. Carlyle's snow imagery was a reference to this wide range of values, which led the assignats to circulate in all strata of society and caused paper consumption to multiply. To ensure that the notes could be issued quickly, the facilities for drying paper were expanded and more printing presses were set up. By 1793 the assignats had lost half of their nominal value. They collapsed to zero in 1796, and in February 1797 the paper money—which ultimately even beggars refused to accept—was done away with. The paper money of the French attracted a great deal of attention among the general public in Europe. The assignats became a leitmotif in anti-revolutionary publications. In Edmund Burke's *Reflections on the Revolution in France* (1790), which was quickly translated into German by Friedrich Gentz, Burke referred to them as "paper amulets" and excoriated the speakers in the National Assembly for taking it as an unproven article of faith "that there is no difference in value between metallic money and their assignats." In commenting on the assignats of the Revolution, Burke and others recalled the memory of the gambler and speculator John Law who, after the death of Louis XIV, had convinced the regent Philippe d'Orléans that issuing paper currency in combination with property mortgages and joint stock companies would prevent state bankruptcy. In Goethe's *Faust II*, published in 1832 after the author's death, Mephisto's paper currency project is modeled on Law's speculations, and the recovery of the exhausted state coffers and illusory delight of the public hark back to the assignats. Carlyle had translated the Helena scene back in 1828, so as he was writing *The French Revolution* he would have been familiar with the words that the emperor uses to ratify Mephisto's paper money: "To whom it may concern: Whoever owns / This note is owed a thousand crowns. / For its sure guarantee and certain bond / Untold wealth's buried in the imperial land."[217]

Carlyle's "Paper Age" formulation placed him in the sphere of contemporary political, poetic, and journalistic reactions to the French assignats. But when he described the paper bills as snowflakes or depicted the Montgolfiers' balloon as a "windbag," he was drawing on an older reservoir of metaphorical connections between paper, air, wind, and credit. This reservoir had been created in the financial satires of the early eighteenth century, which included a number of "Publick Credit" allegories following the establishment of the Bank of England in 1694. Poetic verse and the prose of the flourishing periodical press still worked hand in hand here. In *The Spectator* in 1711, Joseph Addison envisioned a virgin on a golden throne in the Great Hall of the Bank of England. This allegory of public credit falls victim to tyranny and anarchy, bigotry and atheism, and upon her death it is revealed that only a tenth of the money bags piled behind her throne are actually filled with money—others hold absolutely nothing. They "had been blown up with Air, and called into my Memory the Bags full of Wind, which Homer tells us his Hero received as a Present from Aeolus."[218] In Homer's *Odyssey*, the leather bag given to Odysseus by Aeolus contains the howling storm winds which, when unleashed, blow the ship astray. When Addison's allegory was published, the joint-stock South Sea Company had just been founded and England was experiencing its first major stock market frenzy. When the South Sea Bubble collapsed in 1720, the response from writers was fierce, in part because many of them— including Alexander Pope, Jonathan Swift, and John Gay—had themselves lost money on speculation. This sharpened their tongues. In *A Panegyrical Epistle to Mr. Thomas Snow* (1721), Gay drew a connection between the millions in imaginary gold that the subscribers had hoped for and the image of a child's paper kite, while in the brilliant satire *Epistle to Bathurst* (1732), the Classicist Pope picked up on Addison's metaphorical connection between credit and wind:

> Blest Paper-credit! last and best supply!
> That lends Corruption lighter wings to fly!
> Gold imp'd by thee, can compass hardest things,
> Can pocket States, can fetch or carry Kings;

A single leaf shall waft an Army o'er,
Or ship off Senates to a distant Shore;
A leaf, like Sybil's, scatter to and fro
Our fates and fortunes, as the winds do blow:
Pregnant with thousands flits the Scrap unseen,
And silent sells a King or buys a Queen.[219]

The mythology of paper money arose not from its function as a means of paying for goods but from its function as a medium of credit. This is why the concept of wind—along with bubbles and bloating—not only influenced the term "inflation" which emerged in the mid-nineteenth century but also became associated with modern money as a whole. Paper money acquired this modernity when the British Parliament gave in to pressure from Prime Minister Pitt in February 1797—just as the assignats were failing in France—and relieved the Bank of England of its obligation to convert paper notes into coinage. When this guarantee of redemption was suspended, the credit function for which paper money had initially laid the ground-work suddenly applied to every single banknote in a way. Mephisto had fended off any misgivings about his project by advertising the many ways in which the paper money could be redeemed for its nominal value:

Should you want metal, the exchange will do a deal;
Or if not, you must dig a while.
You auction off a torque or precious pot,
This paper then, amortized on the spot,
Shames the doubter who had dared to mock.
Accustomed now, we don't want the old way back.
Throughout the imperial lands henceforth there'll be
Jewellry, gold and paper in plenty.[220]

From the nineteenth century, Mephisto's assumption—that there would always be someone willing to exchange paper money for metal—no longer held true. Instead, money could only circulate smoothly as long as there was no pressure to have to redeem it. The modern banknote thus fulfilled its role as the "unification of the characteristics and functions of a credit instrument and a means of payment in a single note."[221]

There had been very few attempts to counterfeit bank notes in England in the eighteenth century. But in the two decades between 1797 and 1817, no fewer than 870 cases of counterfeiting were pros-ecuted and 300 convicted counterfeiters were put to death. The Bank of England alone had seventy employees whose job it was to track down counterfeited bank notes. At this point, paper proved to be an ideal medium for circulating money not only on account of its light weight, its strength, and its foldability, but on account of a dowry it had inherited from pre-industrial production techniques: watermarks. Watermarks had already been used in the eighteenth century to protect against forgery, and with the introduction of the paper machine—with its continuous paper which initially bore no watermarks—they became a key technology in the production of banknotes.

Carlyle's depiction of the assignats as being like snowflakes of bankruptcy ended with the sentence "Money itself is a standing miracle." This was a hint that the phrase the "Paper Age" referred not to an episode in the French Revolution but to the entire nine-teenth-century world in which he was writing. The first attempts to probe the mysterious relationship between money and credit in the context of economic theory had no impact on Carlyle's writing. But this was not unusual, because the European mythology of paper money remained largely untouched by modern theories of credit and financial management. The memory of Homer's bag of evil winds was never forgotten, not even when "security papers" lost their mate-rial substrate of paper. Even today, speculation and speculators are pursued at every turn by the adjective "breezy," a sign that old European credit metaphors live on in current attempts to keep the real economy separate from the speculative financial economy. And Addison's credit allegory, where bags apparently filled with gold turned out to be sacks of paper, remains alive and well, too. Entire swathes of nineteenth-century literature, from Gottfried Keller's *Martin Salander* to the French stock-market novels of the late nine-teenth century, were influenced by the tension between gold—the old money that recalled the coin shortages of the Middle Ages, money that came from the earth and was allied with property and land—and the volatile, airy paper money that was always in illusory abundance. At the same time, the hunt for hidden treasure in the form of old precious metals and coins became an obsession of the age. Treasure seekers and gold rushes were so appealing during the "Paper Age" because money was no longer ruled over by Plutus, the god of wealth, but by Aeolus, the god of the winds.

1.3. Balzac, Journalism, and the Paper Scheme in *Lost Illusions*

The first full French translation of Goethe's *Faust I* by Frederic-Albert Stapfer appeared in 1823 in the *Œuvres dramatiques de J. W. Goethe*

(1821–25). The third edition, which was published in 1828, included seventeen lithographs and a Goethe portrait by Eugene Délacroix. These lithographs drew the work and its author into the realms of the fantastic and demonic, they bridged the gap between the *Faust* of the Germans and the dark romanticism of the French, and they contributed to the proliferation of witches and devilish characters, sorcerers and magicians in French culture, a culture which had previously been dominated by the mythological figures of Classicism.

One of the readers of *Faust* was the young Balzac, who was not even thirty years old. He had not yet published a single novel under his own name, and all of his entrepreneurial activities in the book industry had failed: the publishing company that he had hoped would earn money with Molière and other classics, the print shop with a book shop attached, and finally the type foundry he had acquired in 1827. In 1828, these enterprises finally bankrupted him.[222] His debts and unwillingness to limit his spending drove him back to authorship, to a dual existence as a novelist and journalist who, after the death of his father in June 1829, claimed a nobiliary particle for his name and from then on published books as Honoré de Balzac. *La peau de chagrin* (1831) was a product of the tension between his two poles of existence. It appeared in the wake of the scandal and success of *Physiologie du mariage* (1829), which was his breakthrough as a novelist. With its allusions to Goethe's *Faust*, *La peau de chagrin* updated the pact with the Devil and moved it to France under the newly established July Monarchy. In *La peau de chagrin*, too, a scholar gambles with his life, a common girl falls in love with him but cannot free him from the pact, and though the protagonist's name is not Faust, it sounds like a character from *Faust*. Balzac's scholar is named Raphael de Valentin, and he is a young, impoverished aristocrat, the descendent of an old family from the Auvergne. In a cheap garret in Paris, a study dedicated purely to ideas in the immediate vicinity of one of Rousseau's houses, Valentin has written a comedy and a theory of the will, for which he studied oriental languages, anatomy, and physiology. His obsessive and hopeless love for a sophisticated countess, the sellout of his scholarly existence on the literary market, his debts and, ultimately, his total financial ruin in a gaming room in the Palais Royal drive him from a state of world-weariness to thoughts of suicide. But on his way to the Seine, he enters an antiquities shop and, among the chaotic collection of relics from all ages and cultures in this cabinet of curiosities, he discovers a piece of shagreen. It bears the Seal of Solomon on its back, while its front is encrusted with Arabic characters spelling out the pact into which whoever buys the skin will enter. The leather can fulfill all of its owner's desires, but it shrinks with each granted wish, as does the life span of the person making the wish. The narrator compares the kaleidoscope of impressions in the antiquities shop with Faust's experience of the witches' Sabbath on the Brocken. The shagreen is to the orientalist Valentin what the book by Nostradamus, with its sign of the macrocosm, is to Faust. It is the everlasting, impenetrable counterpart to Mephisto's scrap of paper. The owner of the cabinet of curiosities, a gaunt old man in a black velvet robe, is said to have a face that a painter could have altered with a few brushstrokes from "a fine painting of God the Father" to "the sly mask of Mephistopheles."[223]

Balzac's pact with the Devil, which exchanges the protagonist's quick suicide for a prolonged one, is incorporated into a precisely dated and localized contemporary social novel which Goethe (though somewhat disconcerted by its audacity) saw as proof of undeniable talent. The protagonist acquires the shagreen in Paris in 1830, just a few months after the July Revolution. He lives in a world of operas and cafés, libraries and theater foyers, journalists' offices and salons, restaurants and brothels. Just as he leaves the antiquities shop, Valentin encounters friends from the journalism scene who are in the process of founding a newspaper—with Valentin as its editor-in-chief—using money from a millionaire who owes his fortune to a crime. The newspaper is expected to ward off any discontent by appearing to be a tool of the opposition while actually working secretly on behalf of the government. The immutable characters of the old magic embodied in the shagreen thus come up against the modern demonic possession of the periodical press, where words have little weight. In France, as in England, many newspapers were founded in the 1820s, and just as Carlyle had done in his essays, Balzac depicted the periodical press in *La peau de chagrin* as having taken the place of religion, with journalists instead of priests and subscribers instead of believers. " 'Journalism, you see, is the religion of modern society, and we are making progress.' 'What do you mean?' 'Their high priests don't have to believe what they say, nor the people either.' "[224] In exchanges such as this, Balzac portrays journalism as the religion of the godless, so the Mephistopheles role in his novel is played not only by the representative of old magic, the enticer from the antiquities shop, but also by the journalists who say: "We, the true members of the sect of the god Mephistopheles, have taken it upon ourselves to whitewash public opinion."[225]

Between the great success of *Physiologie du mariage* (1829) and the publication of *La peau de chagrin*, Balzac had worked almost exclusively as a journalist for a good year and a half, writing for periodicals such as *Le Voleur, Le Feuilleton des Journeaux Politiques, La Silhouette,* and *La Mode,* sometimes without signing his articles. Balzac philologists have described this phase around the revolutionary year 1830 as a turning point in his authorship, one in which he resorted to writing articles in part because it guaranteed quicker payment than the slower moving, more uncertain book market. *La peau de chagrin* was his return to the novel and to a dual existence as a journalist and an author. He continued to be active in both fields, but while books and newspapers may have complemented each other within his authorship from a sociological and economic point of view, from an aesthetic point of view his *Comédie humaine* capitalized on the relentless confrontation between literature and journalism. The combination of a pact with the Devil, suicide, and journalism found in *La peau de chagrin* established a basic motif which Balzac fully developed in the centerpiece to his *Comédie humaine,* the trilogy *Illusions perdues* (1837–43). The protagonist here, Lucien de Rubempré, is a poet who moves to Paris from the countryside, falls victim to journalism, and returns home defeated, then sets out into the world again and, finally, in *Splendeurs et misères des courtisanes* (1838–47), commits suicide.

Lucien de Rubempré is a successor to Raphael de Valentin. He, too, enters into a deadly pact with demonic forces, and Balzac does not hold back on comparisons between the Paris of the journalists and the Inferno of Dante. At the same time, his protagonist's journey to Hell is embedded in a panoramic view of the rise of the periodical press which is beyond compare in terms of economic, technological, and sociological reification in the literature of the nineteenth century. "At the time when this story begins, the Stanhope press and inking-rollers were not yet in use in small provincial printing-offices. Angoulême, although its paper-making industry kept it in contact with Parisian printing, was still using those wooden presses from which the now obsolete metaphor 'making the presses groan' originated."[226] In this opening passage, an expert acquainted with the state-of-the-art technology of the big city casts an eye over the print shop of the old Jérôme-Nicolas Séchard and sees an inventory of backwardness: the leather balls still used to ink the press, the stone printing plates to which the paper was applied, and, above all, the owner, who can neither read nor write and who is not a printer in the strictest sense of the word but merely a "pressman," someone who inherited the printing office when its owner died in the revolutionary year 1793 and hired a nobleman who had gone into hiding to print decrees for him during the Reign of Terror. Balzac portrays the old Séchard as a figure of monstrous avarice and drunkenness. The old printer is given a descriptive name ("soaker") in the style of Laurence Sterne, and his satirical profile is an homage to the oft-cited Rabelais. The avarice of this obsessive hoarder leads him to completely reject all innovation, and with the distrustfulness of a narrow-minded provincial he views the modern Stanhope press as a perfidious trick by the British to secure a market for their iron industry. Old Séchard travels backward along the route that Rabelais' characters had taken into the future: he swaps the printing press for the wine press. His son has to finance his own training with the famous Didot in Paris, where he ultimately becomes a scholar. When the son returns to the provinces, he brings with him the technological knowledge and intellectual skills needed to live up to the principle of modernity, namely, permanent innovation. David Séchard takes over his father's outdated printing office, carefully modernizes it, and becomes an inventor in the field for which Angoulême had been renowned for centuries: paper production. For Balzac—who had formerly owned a type foundry, was familiar with the literature of the eighteenth century, and had read both the *Encyclopédie* and Mercier's *Tableau de Paris*—"*imprimerie*" and "*papeterie*" were inseparable from one another. Balzac was aware of the mechanical printing presses made of iron, and he knew about the paper machines that had been making inroads in France since the 1820s. When, in 1833, he began to pursue his project for selling large numbers of novels on a subscription basis, he traveled to Angoulême and sought out the single paper factory among a total of more than thirty in the region which already had a paper machine.[227]

"Les deux Poètes," or "The Two Poets," is the title of the first part of *Illusions perdues*. In this part, David Séchard and Lucien de Rubempré—who initially still goes by his austere middle-class name Lucien Chardon ("thistle")—are linked together by a deliberate chiasmus. The printer's son has had a poetic and philosophical nature since childhood, but he remains true to his origins out of a sense of responsibility and passionately devotes himself to the exact sciences. Lucien, the mathematically and scientifically gifted son of a former surgeon in the Republican army, becomes addicted to literary ambition, and the beauty he has inherited from his mother feeds the poetic aura with which he surrounds himself. His father, who died prematurely, had been passionate about chemistry and worked as a pharmacist in Angoulême after being wounded in the army. Lucien tells his school friend David about his father's experiments, which included searching for plant-based raw materials for making paper. In return, David supports his friend's literary career. Technology and poetry, paper and printing, authors and inventors are firmly bound together in this chiastic construct.

The novel leaves no doubt that the social topography of Angoulême, and of its industrial suburb L'Houmeau, has preserved hierarchies which have been long drained of substance. The satirical depiction of the provincial, vacuous aristocracy and the clergy who look down on the world of craftsmen and merchants is contrasted with the portrait of the quiet, determined, profound inventor David Séchard. This literary elevation of the inventor was a deliberate choice on Balzac's part. Balzac had never been an avowed follower of the Saint-Simonian movement, and in *L'illustre Gaudissart* he mocked its phraseology. But he was very familiar with the world of the Saint-Simonians through his work on the journal *Le Feuilleton des journeaux Politiques*. The phrase he uses to characterize the ingenuity of Lucien's father could have been taken from a Saint-Simonian: "the application of science to industry." Just as the Saint-Simonian view of society inverted the traditional hierarchy and put inventors on its highest rungs in place of the devalued clergy and aristocrats, David Séchard embodies the spirit of productivity in Balzac's trilogy. He is not a narrow-minded tinkerer, but a philosophical inventor whose project grows out of his understanding of the laws of motion governing society itself. David Séchard demonstrates this in one of the strangest declarations of love to be found in nineteenth-century literature. It takes place on a long beam under the wheels of a paper mill, where the educated young printer tells his future wife, Eve, Lucien's sister, the secret of the invention upon which their marital fortune depends— by giving her what amounts to a lecture on the history of papermaking as it moved from China through Asia Minor to Europe. David Séchard does not neglect to mention playing cards, and he describes the fusion of paper production and typography in the fifteenth century and the connection between the dimensions of printing paper and the dimensions of the press stone, along with such a detailed list of old paper types ("Raisin, Jésus, Colombier, Pot, Ecu, Coquille ...") it seems as though he wants to compete with Homer's list of ships in the *Iliad*.

The fixed point of perspective in this historical lecture is the problematic disparity between the growing demand for paper and the limits placed on production by the lack of high-quality rags. David Séchard notes that since the end of the Empire, cheaper cotton clothing had replaced the more durable but also more expensive linen among both the poor and the middle class. He views this as a symptom of the law of development governing modern civilization. Civilization's material culture, he believes, will lose its weight, size, solidity, and permanence: "We are nearing the time when, as fortunes are equalized and so diminished, poverty will be wide-spread; we shall require cheap linen-wear and cheap books, just as people are beginning to require small pictures for lack of space in which to hang big ones. Neither the shirts nor the books will last, that's all. Sound products are disappearing everywhere. So then the problem facing us is of the highest importance for literature, the sciences and politics."[228]

His response to this problem is inspired by the debates he participated in during his apprenticeship at the center of advanced typography in Paris. These discussions revolved around the question of whether it was possible to use modern techniques to return to the Chinese method of producing paper using plant materials. Séchard the inventor recalls that Comte de Saint-Simon—who was working as a proofreader at the time, as Fourier and Pierre Leroux would later on—had proved to be a very well-informed adviser.

Balzac turns the derivation of his inventor's idea into a model anecdote illustrating the fusion of technology and science. Scholars from the Institute (formerly the Royal Academy of Sciences) get involved, and the librarian of the Arsenal provides decisive evidence in the form of an illustrated Chinese encyclopedia of papermaking. In brief, Séchard's basic idea is to replace the bamboo fibers pulped by the Chinese with a type of domestic reed, and to combine the Chinese model with European technology for macerating the stuff and mechanizing the sheet formation process. It is no accident that Balzac associates this idea with social reformers such as Saint-Simon, Fourier, and Leroux. David Séchard's idea is an exemplary response to modern civilization's apparent tendency to favor things which are lighter, smaller, and less durable. It aims to give paper a future as a medium for storage and circulation which maintains the balance between space and time constraints. As a successor to the dwindling but durable linen paper and the prevalent but short-lived cotton paper, the philosophical inventor wants to create a modern type of "Chinese paper" which is very thin, very light, very fine, and yet opaque enough to be printed on both sides—and durable at the same time. David Séchard's vision anticipates the twentieth-century utopias of lightness. "If we succeeded in producing cheap paper of the Chinese quality we should reduce the weight and thickness of books by more than one half. A bound edition of Voltaire which, when printed on our vellum paper, weighs more than two hundred and fifty pounds, would not weigh fifty pounds on Chinese paper. And that would certainly be an achievement. Finding much-needed shelf-space in libraries will become a more and more difficult problem in a period when a general reduction in size—both things and men—is affecting everything, even human habitations. The great mansions and suites of rooms in Paris will sooner or later be demolished, for soon private fortunes will be no longer be able to keep up the constructions of our forefathers. What a shame it is that our era cannot make books which will last!"[229]

Balzac the narrator justifies his inventor's digression by saying that it was not out of place "in a work which owes its very existence as much to paper as to the printing-press." He was aiming for a kind of material self-reflection on the part of literature which was distinct from the self-reflection on its aesthetic strategies that had been found in European writing since *Don Quixote*. With this form of reflection, the question of what literature was made from was placed on an equal footing with the poetological question of how it was made.

Both the inventor and the poet go through a narratively richly orchestrated process of disillusionment. Lucien fails in his aspirations to write a book, David in his aspirations to acquire a *brevet* or patent. Balzac linked these two processes of disillusionment with great artistic judgment. The literary self-reflection woven into the story of the inventor David Séchard is combined with a meticulous analysis of the structure of the literary market.

The middle section of the trilogy, "A Great Provincial in Paris" (1839), starts with a dramatic slump in all the values upon which Lucien de Rubempré had based his project of becoming a poet of national significance in the capital. The sheen of his aristocratic benefactress is dulled in the salons of Paris, he himself is reduced to a figure of ridicule, and money circulates in the metropolis so much faster that the resources which would have lasted for years in the provinces are depleted soon after he arrives in the city. Above all, however, the value of his authorship declines. Just as he thinks he can stabilize his situation by selling the manuscripts that had earned him the reputation of a poet with a great future in Angoulême, the booksellers teach him a lesson. He has to learn that the poet is not a higher being, but merely a participant in the market, and literature is a commodity like anything else. This lesson was modeled on the analyses of the crisis in the book trade and publishing industry that Balzac had outlined in his newspaper articles after the July Revolution. Lucien encounters the hyenas of intermediary trade, the book dealers working on commission who profited from short-term price fluctuations and market turbulence. He also encounters a new type of publisher, uneducated and uninterested in the content of books, which had emerged since the French Revolution. You no longer needed a license and skills to become a publisher; you just needed capital. A number of publishers with no equity to speak of released books financed on credit which had to turn a quick profit so as not to jeopardize the loan constructions and redemption periods of their bills of exchange. Books by established authors, which were very low risk in terms of sales, as well as advice books and light fiction, were all very popular. What made a manuscript attractive to this type of publisher was the probability of being able to cash in on short-term profit expectations. Lucien's sonnet collection *Les Marguerites*, the title of which recalls the innocence sacrificed in *Faust*, proves to be nearly unmarketable due to the glut and general downturn in the market for poetry, while he receives only poor offers for his historical novel *The Archer of Charles the Ninth*; even though it belongs to a popular genre, it is the work of a newcomer. The formula that Balzac forces upon his illusory poet in the novel was taken from an article he wrote in 1830 entitled "De l'état actuel de la librairie": "In fact the trade in books styled *livres de nouveauté* can be summed up in this commercial theorem: a ream of blank paper is worth fifteen francs; once printed it is worth five francs or three hundred francs according to the success it obtains."[230]

The publication history of Lucien's historical novel and the non-publication history of his *Marguerites* are emblematic of the general tendency that David Séchard had predicted in the provinces: the short-lived products of the periodical press were taking over from slow-burning books and starting to determine the laws of the literary market as a whole. Lucien meets publishers and book dealers who act solely in the interests of short-term profit.

The "Cénacle," a circle of poets and scholars around the incorruptible author Daniel d'Arthez, represents the solidity and permanence which is under threat, while the circle of journalists around the *petit journal* and its editor Étienne Lousteau represents the party of corruption and prostitution of the intellect which Lucien joins. The rapid rise in demand for journalistic texts caused the fees for essays and reviews to skyrocket, while newspaper criticism began to have a major influence on a book's sales potential. When Lucien (contrary to his own beliefs) publishes a scathing review of a friend's book in a newspaper, book publishers finally take an interest in him. There are so many episodes in *Illusions perdues* illustrating the entrenched division between literature and journalism that Karl Kraus was able to put together a collage of quotes from the novel as a philippic against the press in his journal *Die Fackel*.

But Balzac would not have been Balzac had he simply left it at that. The brilliant theater criticism penned by Lucien and the series of essays "In the Streets of Paris" which make him a pioneer in the successful union of the big city and the small format both undermine Balzac's general thesis that the hell of journalism would be the poet's ruin. As in Rousseau's paradoxical philosophy of history, the disease holds the key to its own cure for Balzac. With his *Societé d'abonnement général* of 1833, Balzac had hoped to reform the book trade for the benefit of novelists by adopting the subscription format and rhythmic publication cycle of the periodical press. The novels sold in this way were not to be seasonal, throwaway books but challenging, lasting literature. In its logical structure, this project resembled David Séchard's idea of harking back to an old tradition in order to create modern, lasting paper.

Both projects ultimately failed due to a lack of financing. Even in his articles about the book trade from the early 1830s, Balzac had noted that the common form of financing through credit was one of the main reasons for both the overproduction crisis and the large number of bankruptcies. In *Illusions perdues*, both strands of disillusionment—that of the poet and that of the paper inventor—are embedded in a tangle of credit financing and bill transactions. In Paris, Lucien plays the role of the unrestrained borrower, even forging bills of exchange issued in the name of his friend. David Séchard falls victim to financial intrigues which he is unable to see through. The final part of the trilogy, "An Inventor's Tribulations," is evidence of what Hugo von Hofmannsthal claimed was an affinity between the world of the *Comédie humaine* and Georg Simmel's *The Philosophy of Money*.[231] The Parisian paper merchant Métivier is a minor character who moves into a key position because he, like many paper dealers, carried on an unlicensed side business as a small-time banker and credit broker, an activity fiercely criticized by Balzac. In his role as a paper merchant and covert banker, he is a Parisian partner to the printing office of David Séchard as well as to that of David's competitors in Angoulême, the Cointet brothers. The more cunning Cointet brother is responsible for their paper business and financial transactions, while the stouter one runs the local print shop. The schemes that the Cointets carry out against the Séchard printing office and its philosophical inventor run through the entire trilogy, before Balzac ties the final knot in the end. This knot comes together as the activities of the periodical press of Paris become more entwined with the paper experiments in the provinces. Balzac supplements the Cointets' financial machinations with a technological scheme that is simple but highly symbolic. This scheme targets the core of David Séchard's idea—the search for modern, cheap, and durable paper— and exploits it with the intent of profiting from the boom in nondurable products.

Boniface Cointet is only able to devise this scheme because he owns a paper manufactory himself, one which produces paper in the provinces but has connections to the Parisian market and is aware of the different commercialization chains applicable to writing paper and printing paper. He is backed by the tradition of Angoulême, which owes its reputation as a long-standing center of papermaking to its fine writing paper. But in the provinces, he is an agent of technological modernization. He invests in the inventor's paper project so that he can profit from its success. When, after long experimentation, David Séchard finally manages to produce cheaper—though not high-quality—paper by adding plant matter to the traditional rag slurry, Cointet immediately recognizes the opportunities this opens up for him. He drives the inventor to conduct ever more dead-end experiments for creating paper which can compete with the fine, heavily sized writing paper for which Angoulême is known, the prized "postdemy." For this, the paper has to be sized while it is still in the vat. But Cointet is not really interested in the writing paper. He has recognized that the newspaper boom in Paris has opened up a lucrative new market for the mass production of unsized paper of a lesser quality. As David Séchard's contractual partner, he appropriates the inventor's knowledge of how to produce this paper, which is "diluted" with plant fiber. He installs paper machines in his factory, mass-produces the paper suitable for newsprint behind its inventor's back, and lucratively markets it through his connections with the paper merchant Métivier in Paris. In the end, thanks to the favorable terms of his contracts with David Séchard, he can easily secure the rights to Séchard's invention and reach a settlement with him which is negligible in light of the profits he is making in Paris. The inventor—thoroughly disillusioned, endowed only with his settlement and, soon, with the inheritance from his father—withdraws to his country home to lead a life with his wife and children which fits Jean Paul's description of an idyll: happiness within limits.

Balzac claimed that he wanted to put forward an argument in favor of family at the end of his trilogy, but it would take a very inexperienced reader indeed not to see that this idyll demands the death of the inventor, and that David Séchard only lives on as a ghost: "David Séchard has a loving wife, two sons and a daughter. He has had the good taste never to talk about his experiments. Eve has had the good sense to make him renounce the disastrous vocation of inventor, that of a Moses consumed in the burning bush of Horeb. He cultivates literature as a relaxation while living the happy, leisurely life of a landowner developing his estate. Having said good-bye once and for all to glory, he has sensibly taken his place in the class of dreamers and collectors. He is given to entomology and research into the as yet secret metamorphoses of insects only known to science in their final transformation."[232]

In the early 1820s in which Balzac's story is set, the technique developed by Moritz Friedrich Illig for sizing paper in the vat was already a good decade old. This does not minimize the symbolism of Cointet's technological scheme, however. Recent histories of the mechanization of French paper production have confirmed how important the periodical press was as a market for the machine-produced paper that could not initially compete with fine writing paper, and how much the formats and print runs of newspapers benefited from the availability and affordability of continuous paper.[233]

David Séchard had wanted to invent a durable writing and printing paper produced with modern technology, but his project shared the fate of his friend Lucien in Paris. The ambitions of both the poet and the philosophical inventor were subject to a new power, the periodical press. *Illusions perdues* reflects the dual emancipation of newsprint: It emancipated itself from literature as a medium for journalism, and it spun off technologically from writing paper and high-quality printing paper by absorbing the fast pace of journalism in its material structure. Because he has grasped this, the paper merchant Cointet appears on the last pages of *Illusions perdues* as a newly minted millionaire and respected citizen of the July Monarchy.

1.4. The Secrets of the Scriveners: Charles Dickens and Mr. Nemo

Paper underwent a massive double movement to become a fundamental motif in the self-interpretation of the nineteenth century. As in Balzac's *Illusions perdues*, literature reflected the rapid expansion of the sphere of printed paper, the periodical press, placards, and advertisements. It also addressed the advance of unprinted, unbound paper in everyday private correspondence and the exchange of legal documents. The circulation of paper in the big city became a motif in the nineteenth century which bound together every social sphere. Papers no longer contained only the secrets of young women from bourgeois households and the schemes of their aristocratic seducers; they contained the secrets of London and Paris themselves. Scribes, paper merchants, and rag sellers were products of the late Middle Ages and early modern period; we encounter them in folk songs, books of trades, and writers' satires. But as characters in the big city, they outgrew their traditional genres, found a new home in the world of serialized novels, and moved into the realm of the sinister.

In *Le Pére Goriot*, Balzac describes a boarding house owned by Madame Vauquer as a way of introducing the characters and plot, and at the start of *Le Colonel Chabert* he gives an account of the office of the lawyer Derville in much the same way. The titular hero, who has been declared dead following the Battle of Eylau, returns to Restoration Paris in order to officially confirm that he is still alive and married to a woman who has come into a considerable fortune. The heroism of the Napoleonic era is over, and a glimpse of the lawyer's office reveals to the brave solider that he will have to fight a paper war—one for which he is not equipped—in order to bring the dead back to life as in an old ghost story: "The office was decorated exclusively with those large yellow posters announcing real estate foreclosures, sales, settlements held in trust, final or interim judgments—the glory of a lawyer's office! Behind the head clerk the entire wall was covered from top to bottom with shelves and pigeon-holes. A seemingly infinite number of tickets hung from each crammed compartment, some with the red, taped ends that give legal dossiers a special appearance. The lower shelves were full of yellowed cardboard boxes rimmed with blue paper and labeled with the names of important clients whose juicy cases were stewing at that very moment."[234]

Balzac's own experience as an assistant in a law office informed this description. The depiction is embedded in a sketch of the profession of the clerk that could have been part of a newspaper article on "The Physiology of Copyists." Like recording equipment, the copyists write down everything that is said, even the name of the Devil when he sneaks into a dictation in the form of a curse. The speed, consistency, and thoughtlessness of the copyists intensify and accelerate the circulation of paper which funnels into an overflowing file cabinet.

In Carlyle's "Paper Age," paper had become associated with all that was illusionary, airy, and speculative. This breezy imagery still held sway in the mid-nineteenth century, but the literary diagnosis of paper's penetration of modern life had grown darker. In the literature of the nineteenth century, writers who were often paid by the piece were a complement to the journalists paid by the line, and in their role as living writing machines they contributed to the rising flood of paper which had its source in bureaucracy and the judiciary. In Balzac's *Le Colonel Chabert*, only a dim light filters through the dirty windowpanes into the clerks' office.

As literature mined the urban underworld and social misery for material resources, a shadow was cast over paper and the rooms through which it moved. This shadow was darkest in Charles Dickens's *Bleak House* (1853). No one who has read the Dickens novel can forget how, at the start, the narrator's gaze passes over a London shrouded in fog, grime, and November drizzle, until it comes to rest on the High Court of Chancery near Temple Bar, where the suits and countersuits, defense statements and rejoinders, injunctions and affidavits, decrees and petitions to higher authorities pile up in mountains of files. Legal clerks, recorders, shorthand writers, newspaper reporters, and copyists have buried the court in an avalanche of dirty paper. Even a small summary of a record amounts to "eighteen hundred sheets," and the endless case of Jarndyce versus Jarndyce has been documented by the copyists in the law office on "tens of thousands of Chancery folio-pages." The black flakes of soot that fall on London and the omnipresent dust mingle with and discolor the streams of paper flowing through the city in *Bleak House*.[235]

A dense network of characters and plot strands radiate far into the countryside from London, the dark center of nineteenth-century paper fantasies. For our purposes, it is best to view this sphere of action from the perspective of the tardy crow which, in the tenth chapter, after the gas lamps have been lit but before they have taken effect, flies westward over Cook's Court. The crow is spotted by Mr. Snagsby, a paper merchant and stationer who is standing outside the door to his shop. Foremost in the shop's range of goods is the chancery paper known as foolscap, followed by white and white-brown draft papers. The stationer deals in every legal form and every type of parchment and paper used by the chancery, along with sealing-wax and wafers, law lists, rubber erasers and pounce, penknives, pins, and goose quills, as well as modern steel nibs.

Mr. Snagsby is a switching point in the circulation of paper, not just on account of his range of goods. Records and documents can also be written out or copied in his shop. He has a number of piecework writers on hand for this purpose. The crow that flies across Chancery Lane in the direction of Lincoln's Inn Garden passes over the shop of a rag dealer named Krook in a side alley. There is a picture of a red paper mill in the front window of this "Rag and Bottle Warehouse." Bones, old iron, and discarded kitchen goods are bought here, and as the mass of wastepaper has grown, it has earned its own category in this emporium of rags. From the point of view of the middle-class merchant Mr. Snagsby, this is the lowest circle in which paper moves. This is where it sinks back into the world of rags from which it has come.

It is no coincidence that this place appears in Dickens's novel. Henry Mayhew had just published his three-volume work *London Labour and the London Poor* (1851–52), a compilation of articles documenting London's social topography which was a counterpart to the "physiologies" of Balzac's modern-day Paris.[236] The ragpickers who roamed the streets, the itinerant sellers of second-hand goods, and the established "rag and bones" shops were vividly depicted by Mayhew as part of the panorama of the lower classes. In *Bleak House*, the stationary rag collector emerges from the realm of social reportage and is transformed into an allegory of putrescent city life which descends into the realm of the dead. Krook's nickname is the "Lord Chancellor," and his neighbors call his shop the "Court of Chancery" because, like the judiciary, once he has something in his grasp he never lets it go again. Krook, a "disowned relation of the law," is a caricature of a hoarder who accumulates the refuse of the city and continually stows wastepaper in a kind of well under his shop. But Dickens took care not to portray him as an isolated troglodyte. He has legal clerks and copyists as lodgers, and he himself goes to the court nearly every day to watch the proceedings and see his fraternal counterpart, the noble and educated Lord Chancellor. Krook is no outsider; he is the Lord Chancellor of squalor.

The belated crow flies over Krook's rag emporium in the direction of Lincoln's Inn Fields, not far from the court building. It is here, in a large old house which has been turned into offices, that Mr. Tulkinghorn lives. Tulkinghorn is a lawyer who knows all the secrets of the aristocracy but commits very few of them paper, though the paper merchant Mr. Snagsby copies legal briefs for him. Tulkinghorn follows the crow's path in the opposite direction. He wants the paper merchant to tell him the name of the writer who recently copied an affidavit for him, because his client, the Lady Dedlock, had taken an obvious interest in the man's handwriting.

Whether Dickens succeeded in linking the two main strands of his story—the endless outgrowths of the case of Jarndyce and Jarndyce and all the characters involved in it, on the one hand, and the revelation of the secrets of Lady Dedlock, on the other—was a matter of much debate. The man whom Tulkinghorn tracks down through the stationer is the connecting link here. He was once a captain named Hawdon, but now he is a copyist of no means who lodges with Krook the rag dealer and calls himself Nemo. As a scrivener who can copy forty-two folio sheets in a single night, he plays a part in the circulation of the Chancery Court's case files; as the recipient of love letters in his former life as Captain Hawdon, he is the key to the secret of Lady Dedlock.

Mr. Nemo only appears in the novel as a dead man. When Tulkinghorn finds him, he is lying open-eyed on his bed next to a broken desk. Through Mr. Nemo, Krook's realm of rags becomes a realm of the dead, and London as a whole is shrouded in the mythology of the necropolis. A doctor is called in and determines that the cause of death was an opium overdose, remarking in passing that the writer was "as dead as Pharaoh."[237] And Mrs. Snagsby, the wife of the paper merchant, had consistently referred to the copyist as "Nimrod" while he was alive, giving him a Babylonian aura. In Victorian England and in America, rumors began circulating around 1850 that due to a shortage of rags, Egyptian mummy wrappings were being imported on a large scale and used to make paper. In *Bleak House*, the apparent alliance between the novel and big-city reportage gives rise to death allegories from the world of rags and paper at every turn. Many of the characters in the novel do not survive because they stand at the confluence of two deadly circulatory routes: the route taken by infectious diseases and the route taken by papers which conceal and reveal secrets, infiltrate and disintegrate life.

Bleak House features local reporters who are paid by the line and newspapers which publish notes on the inquest concerning Mr. Nemo. Articles are cut out of newspapers, aristocrats have libraries, and the middle class has an excessive culture of correspondence which, in the household of Mrs. Jellyby, a fanatical Africa activist, mutates into a type of philanthropic bureaucracy. After Krook's death, his rag shop is occupied by a relative, the moneylender Smallweed, who issues bills of exchange from it. But all of these paper worlds are overshadowed by the masses of paper sinking into the realm of rags and decay. The decisive version of the will pertaining to the never-ending Jarndyce case is found, after Krook's death, among singed piles of scraps, printer's waste, and spoiled writing paper. Paper's association with waste and infection in *Bleak House* is strengthened because unbound paper plays such a prominent role in the novel. When paper is trapped within a closed book in a library, there are fewer exposed areas that could be attacked by air, moisture, or light. But in Dickens's London, in the gloomy atmosphere choked with billowing fog and soot which is so vividly captured in the novel's opening paragraphs, there is plenty of room for attack. Unbound paper decomposes in this atmosphere; it gets dirty and displays all of the base and repulsive characteristics it has had at its disposal since the time of Rabelais and Grimmelshausen—more so than the dingiest book in a library ever could.

The death to which Dickens subjects the rag dealer Krook was also the subject of hefty debate. The notorious alcoholic spontaneously combusts, and all that remains of him is a slimy cinder in front of the fireplace. In death, he is consumed by the inexorable decomposition which governs his world of waste. Scientists quickly denied the plausibility of death by spontaneous combustion, which Dickens apparently believed in. This death was aesthetically necessary, however. When Dickens wrote *Bleak House*, he did so with a sideways glance at the "penny dreadfuls," popular horror stories printed on low-quality paper for a newly literate audience. The paper machine had contributed to the rise of penny dreadfuls, which were not tied to the standard three-volume format of a novel. Dickens may have disdained authors such as G.W.M. Reynolds, who featured body-snatchers in his serialized novel *The Mysteries of London* (1844–46) which was inspired by Eugene Sue, but he strayed into penny dreadful territory himself with the spectacularly horrific death of the ragman Krook. The stream of base, dirty paper flowing through *Bleak House* would ultimately lead to the pulp fiction of the early twentieth century.

In the second strand of the plot which runs through *Bleak House* and weaves together a detective story for a middle-class audience, paper attracts interest in its role as a witness and bearer of clues. The attention paid to newspaper clippings and the handwriting comparisons carried out by Inspector Bucket, who becomes responsible for solving all the mysteries in *Bleak House* after the lawyer Mr. Tulkinghorn is murdered, would later find its way into the virtuoso paper analyses of Sherlock Holmes. And finally, the third strand of the plot, which turns *Bleak House* into a source of paper mythology, transforms copyists into sinister allegories of modernity. The piece-work writer Nemo—who never sleeps, who is subject to the law of continuous working motion like a machine, and whom the novel embalms in an Egyptian cult of the dead—is a direct predecessor to Herman Melville's impenetrable scrivener Bartleby, who both embodies and disrupts the mechanical continuity of writing.

1.5. Foolscap and Factory Workers: Herman Melville and the Paper Machine

When Continental Army troops entered Philadelphia in June 1778, ads appeared in the newspapers which summoned residents to immediately deliver all their old paper, right down to the smallest scrap, to the army's camp. When the summons did not have the desired effect, soldiers fanned out to search private households and offices. In the garret of a house where Benjamin Franklin had recently set up his printing office, they struck it rich and seized 2,500 copies of a sermon on "Defensive War" by the Reverend Gilbert Tennent. The paper was used to make shell casings for the army's next battles.[238]

Paper shortages were a constant companion to the American Revolution. Though there were just over fifty paper mills in the colonies around 1765, mostly in Pennsylvania, they were utterly unable to keep up with rising demand. Paper was primarily an imported product and was therefore directly affected by the strife between the American colonies and England. The Stamp Act of 1765, a tax on all printed materials that the British had tried to impose on the colonies, was repealed after fierce protests. But the Townshend Acts of 1767, which introduced customs duties on imported everyday goods such as tea, glass, and paint from England, also covered paper. The boycotts and non-importation agreements that the colonists organized in response to this resulted in the rapid depletion of paper stocks. When the War of Independence began in 1775, paper was in drastically short supply and the support of domestic paper production became a patriotic task. The army needed shell casings, but the government also needed paper for printing dollars and for administrative purposes, and some newspapers ended up being published late or in a smaller format on account of the paper shortage. Men with paper-making skills were required to serve in paper mills instead of the army, and some imprisoned papermakers were even released. The shortage of rags also impeded increased paper production, so paper mills appealed to the colonists to send in used clothing with the promise of "cash given for rags." When the women at whom these ads were aimed were addressed as "fair Daughters of Liberty" in *The Massachusetts Spy* in March 1779, this honorary title placed them alongside the "Sons of Liberty" who had rebelled against the Townshend Acts. Sending in rags contributed to the fight for independence.[239]

The rhetorical coupling of paper and patriotism was matched by the affinity for paper found among the key players in the American Revolution. As Reverend Tennent's sermon was being turned into shell casings in Philadelphia, Benjamin Franklin—who had printed the sermon—was serving as an American commissioner in Paris, where he managed to secure a trade agreement and treaty of alliance between the United States and France just over a year after his arrival in December 1776. Franklin was a trained printer, and his many areas of experimentation included the study of electricity as well as paper technology. Even as a young man in Philadelphia he had run a paper business and published a pamphlet entitled *A Modest Enquiry into the Nature and Necessity of a Paper Currency* (1729), in which he advocated the colonial use of paper money which was independent of gold and silver and was instead secured by land. He also printed paper money for Pennsylvania from 1731 and began printing it for Delaware and New Jersey a short time later. In 1737, he invented a method of using copper plates to print images of leaves on the back of bank notes to prevent counterfeiting. While he was in Paris, he established a printing office in Passy and visited the Didot print shop, where he encouraged François Ambroise Didot and his grandson Firmin Didot to use the English method for creating velin paper which he had encountered during his stay in London between 1757 and 1762. Franklin participated in every debate on the advantages and disadvantages of paper money, and some of the banknotes issued by the Bank of North America, founded in 1782, were printed on marbled paper which Franklin had purchased in 1779 in France and brought back with him to America in 1785. In 1787, the *American Museum* magazine in Philadelphia published a humorous poem of several stanzas which bore the title *On Paper* and was "Ascribed to Dr. Franklin." In this poem, different types of paper are associated with different types of people; the hot-blooded gentleman who is always ready for a fight is compared to the quick-burning "touch paper" which was used for fireworks, for instance. The metaphor of "virgin paper" is poetically spelled out in the penultimate stanza:

Observe the maiden, innocently sweet,
She's fair white paper, an unsullied sheet;
On which the happy man, whom fate ordains,
May write his name, and take her for his pains.[240]

Benjamin Franklin could only have interpreted Carlyle's "Paper Age" as the title of a utopia. For him, paper was the medium of independence, freedom of thought and freedom of the press, economic prosperity, and the advance of civilization.

In late January 1851, Herman Melville set out with a horse and sleigh from Arrowhead, the farmhouse he had purchased in the summer of the year before in Berkshire County, Massachusetts, to visit a regional paper factory: Carson's Old Red Mill, about five miles from Pittsfield. The wave of new paper mills stemming from the era of the Revolution and War of Independence had reached Berkshire County in 1801. By the middle of the century there were already around forty paper mills in the area, and the paper machine had been making inroads there since the late 1820s. The proximity to New York—a market that was easy to reach via the Hudson—had helped the Berkshires become one of the most important centers of American paper production. When, around two weeks after his visit to the Old Red Mill, Melville wrote to Evert A. Duyckink that "a great neighborhood for authors, you see, is Pittsfield,"[241] he may have been thinking not only of Nathaniel Hawthorne, who lived in the area, but also of the paper mills.

The tale into which he wove his experiences at the paper mill is not a hymn of praise to an up-and-coming industry in modern America, however: it is the darkest allegory of white paper in nineteenth-century literature. Virgin paper is robbed entirely of its innocence here, the paper machine is a monster of Leviathan proportions, and the journey into modern America is a descent into hell. "The Paradise of Bachelors and the Tartarus of Maids" appeared in April 1855 in *Harper's New Monthly Magazine*. A month earlier, *Putnam's Monthly Magazine* had published the final installment of Melville's nine-part novel *Israel Potter*. In an episode set in Paris, Benjamin Franklin is sardonically portrayed as the eternally bustling and thoroughly unpoetic "type and genius of his land," and all the glory of the War of Independence has faded.

Melville had been inspired to experiment with a dual narrative structure after reading a book on the history of oil painting in 1848 and seeing religious diptychs in the National Gallery in London and among the ivory carvings in the Hôtel Cluny in Paris during a trip to Europe in 1849. "The Paradise of Bachelors and the Tartarus of Maids" is a diptych of sharply drawn contrasts, the two halves of which are connected only by the character of the narrator. In the first part of the story, he is invited to an opulent dinner at a club for bachelors near the hectic Fleet Street of the journalists and speculators. The club is in Elm Court, part of the complex of old buildings surrounding the Temple Church, where Samuel Johnson and later Charles Lamb had once lived. The modern bachelors have adopted the celibacy of the Templars whose residence they occupy, but only because it allows them greater freedom to travel and enjoy life. The religious warriors have been replaced by modern lawyers and jurists who take pleasure in the architecture of the Netherlands, the wines of Germany, and the treasures of the British Museum, and who tell each other jovial and suggestive anecdotes. This paradise of bachelors, a place of pure, uninhibited consumption, stands in contrast to the paper mill "not far from Woedolor Mountain," which features in the second section of the diptych the "Tartarus of Maids." The opposition between the Old and New Worlds, England and New England, consumption and production, is joined by the opposition between bachelors and maidens and between city and country. Unlike the textile factories that were an American counterpart to England's key sector of industrialization, paper factories were located not in cities but in the countryside. Melville had bought his farmhouse in the Berkshires largely on account of the beauty of the landscape. But the landscape that the narrator crosses in his horse-drawn sleigh is not a pastoral garden; it is a craggy, gloomy, windswept mountain landscape cut through with a gorge, where a dangerous, winding road leads to a "Dantean gateway." This part of the ravine is known as the Black Notch, and the hollow into which it opens is called the Devil's Dungeon. The hollow is funnel-shaped like Dante's Inferno, and the torrent that churns between the volcanic rocks is named Blood River. The mossy black ruins of an abandoned saw mill perch on a cliff above it. This depiction of the landscape is demonstratively allegorical, and it conspicuously alludes to the inscription above Dante's gate to hell: "Abandon all hope, ye who enter here."

Melville's narrator maps out a landscape which, like the page of a book, knows only two colors: black and white. The black is a deep black, and even the narrator's horse—named Black—contributes to it. The white is a deep white, too; it is the end of January, and the sleigh glides over crunchy, splintering snow. From afar, the snowy paper mill stands out against the dark background "like some great whited sepulcher," and by the time the visitor reaches it there can be no doubt that, even though it contrasts with the Dantean black, this white is also the color of death: "At first I could not discover the paper-mill. The whole hollow gleamed with the white, except, here and there, where a pinnacle of granite showed on wind-swept angle bare. The mountains stood pinned in shrouds—a pass of Alpine corpses. Where stands the mill? Suddenly a whirling, humming sound broke upon my ear. I looked, and there, like an arrested avalanche, lay the large whitewashed factory. It was subordinately surrounded by a cluster of other and smaller buildings, some of which, from their cheap, blank air, great length, gregarious windows, and comfortless expression, no doubt were boarding-houses of the operatives. A snow-white hamlet amidst the snows."[242]

In the chapter in *Moby Dick* entitled "The Whiteness of the Whale," Melville explored white as a demonic color: "There yet lurks an elusive something in the innermost idea of this hue, which strikes more of panic to the soul than that redness which afrights in blood. This elusive quality it is, which causes the thought of whiteness, when divorced from more kindly associations, and coupled with any object terrible in itself, to heighten that terror to the furthest bounds." In "The Paradise of Bachelors and the Tartarus of Maids," this inherently terrible object is the paper machine. In the context of Melville's dual narrative, which rivals the horror stories of Edgar Allan Poe, the machine is terrible because it embodies the utter subjugation of America's organic fertility to the laws of mechanical production. It produces white paper, but it also produces a deathly pallor on the faces of the girls who work at it. The allegorical nature of the machine is revealed to readers when they enter the paper mill in the company of the narrator, who runs a large-scale seed business and proudly announces at the start of the story that, as this business expanded, "my seeds were distributed through all the Eastern and Northern States, and even fell into the far soil of Missouri and the Carolinas." His seeds are sent to the northern and southern states in pieces of paper folded into squares, and he requires "several hundreds of thousands" of these envelopes each year. To free himself of reliance on wholesalers, he wants to satisfy his future paper requirements by dealing directly with the paper mill. Only a few sentences are dedicated to explaining this business. The economic transaction is merely a device by which the contrast between hellish black and papery white is extended into the factory itself. While Dante's route spiraled down through the circles of hell, the journey here leads from the periphery to the center of paper production. It is a journey like the one taken by Goussier for the *Encyclopédie* and by Lalande for the Académie Royale des Sciences. Melville's descriptions are no less precise than those found in the growing body of technological literature from the eighteenth century onward. But when Melville's narrator enters the room where the paper is folded and laid near the bright light of the windows, he is also stepping into the first circle of a white Tartarus: "Immediately I found myself standing in a spacious place, intolerably lighted by long rows of windows, focusing inward the snowy scene without. At rows of blank-looking counters sat rows of blank-looking girls, with blank, white folders in their blank hands, all blankly folding blank paper."[243]

The repeated adjective in this sentence echoes the monotonous rhythm of the huge, heavy iron machine in the background which is imprinting a decorative wreath of roses on quires of rose-colored writing paper. This machine, which produces the ideal note paper for young women in love, is operated by girls whose cheeks have been drained of all color. Nearby, an apparatus "strung with long, slender strings like any harp" is fed sheets of foolscap which are imprinted with lines, resembling the wrinkles that have been carved into the brow of an older worker. Foolscap, which had been brought to America from England, was older than the paper machine and took its name from the medieval watermark of a fool's cap and bells. It was frequently used for chancery paper, as immortalized in Dickens's *Bleak House*. In Franklin's paper poem, foolscap was associated with the schemes of politicians. American readers would have encountered it in the tales of Hawthorne, Washington Irving, and Edgar Allan Poe. The ruled foolscap in Melville's story is the bureaucratic antipole to the rosy paper used for love letters. Through the whitewashed factory comes a man named Cupid, who—as if in mockery of the pallid girls—is "dimpled and red-cheeked" like an actual cherub. In terms of his mythological role as a matchmaker, he has no work to do here. With a "not knowing heartlessness," he guides his visitor through the room where women cut up rags: "The air swam with the fine, poisonous particles, which from all sides darted, subtilely, as motes in sun-beams, into the lungs."[244]

Since the rags are sent from Leghorn and London, the narrator entertains the thought that there may be old shirts from the paradise of bachelors among them. It was no accident that Melville made his narrator a seed dealer. In passing, he repeatedly alludes to the connection between the bachelors in their London paradise and the maids in their Tartarus in New England—the connection being the voluntary or involuntary denial of organic reproduction. The celibacy of the urban bachelors, those modern successors to the Templars, may not have been so strict, but the American Cupid leads the narrator through a world where Eros has been entirely suspended. As the visitor finds out at the end of his trip, the paper mill exclusively employs "maids," never married women, to ensure that the continuity of the work—"twelve hours to the day, day after day, through the three hundred and sixty-five days, excepting Sundays, Thanksgiving, and Fast-days"—is not disrupted by pregnancy.

Melville expunged all male workers from his poetic paper mill, leaving behind only the young Cupid and the manager, a bachelor whose complexion is as dark as the girls are pale. Melville has often been accused of laying on the allegory of the demonic machine all too thickly. But this is not true when it comes to the center of his white Tartarus. Here, in front of the modern paper machine which was purchased by the owner for 12,000 dollars just a few months earlier, the allegorical description is perfectly balanced:

> Before me, rolled out like some long Eastern manuscript, lay stretched one continuous length of iron frame-work—multitudinous and mystical, with all sorts of rollers, wheels, and cylinders, in slowly-measured and unceasing motion. "Here first comes the pulp now," said Cupid, pointing to the nighest end of the machine. "See; first it pours out and spreads itself upon this wide, sloping board; and then—look—slides, thin and quivering, beneath the first roller there. Follow on now, and see it as it slides from under that to the next cylinder. There; see how it has become just a very little less pulpy now. One step more, and it

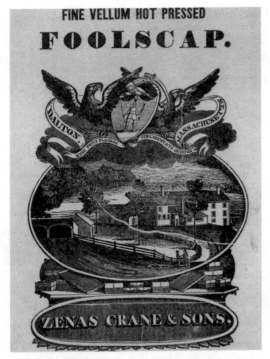

Packaging material depicting a pre-industrial paper mill in Berkshire County, 1840

grows still more to some slight consistence. Still another cylinder, and it is so knitted—though as yet mere dragon-fly wing—that it forms an air-bridge here, like a suspended cobweb, between two more separated rollers; and flowing over the last one, and under again, and doubling about there out of sight for a minute among all those mixed cylinders you indistinctly see, it reappears here, looking now at last a little less like pulp and more like paper, but still quite delicate and defective yet awhile. But—a little further onward, Sir, if you please—here now, at this further point, it puts on something of a real look, as if it might turn out to be something you might possibly handle in the end. But it's not yet done, Sir. Good way to travel yet, and plenty more of cylinders must roll it."[245]

Melville's description of the paper machine, which is deliberately interrupted here, is one of the great passages in which the literature of the industrial age took on the world of the factories, because it depicts the machine as it actually was. It appears not merely as the

Women sorting and cutting rags. This scene recalls Melville's description of a paper mill which was written just a few years earlier.

producer of a product but also as the producer of the continuity of movement. The precise repetition of the same movement over and over again is the decisive element of mechanical production, and Melville used it to skillfully make his point in his allegorical tale. After the interrupted description, Melville continues with an experiment in which Cupid invites the visitor to measure whether it takes exactly nine minutes for the pulp to pass from the wet to the dry end of the machine. The visitor writes the word "Cupid" on a slip of a paper, and the actual Cupid drops the slip into the suspension entering the machine. Watch in hand, the seed dealer times the production of an unfolded sheet of foolscap, upon which the half-faded word "Cupid" is visible. The machine has produced a surrogate Cupid. It is a self-sufficient bachelor machine, and maids are only allowed at its periphery—and then only as long as they remain maids whose cheeks are pale and whose blood is never stirred up, in contrast to the dirty reddish water of Blood River, which sets the huge waterwheel of the factory going. Jean Starobinski has rightly pointed out that in the context of Melville's allegory, which centers entirely on the opposition between mechanical and organic reproduction, the number nine cannot be a random number. Melville's nine minutes must be interpreted as a mechanically shortened counterpart to the nine months of pregnancy.[246]

The mill's production is oriented on its biggest market: foolscap paper. Cupid speaks the language of economic calculation instead of love: "Oh, sometimes, but not often, we turn out finer work—cream-laid and royal sheets, we call them. But foolscap being in chief demand, we turn out foolscap most." The fact that the Berkshire mill's main product is foolscap has to do with its proximity to New York, where foolscap, both unruled and ruled, was used in great quantities. The titular protagonist in Melville's *Bartleby the Scrivener*, for example, works for a Wall Street lawyer who uses foolscap. The paper on which Bartleby writes—for as long as he does write—comes from the whitewashed factory in Berkshire County. This factory is also the source of the mechanical principle that has turned the copyists into writing machines. Bartleby interrupts its continuity of movement with the phrase "I would prefer not to," which is repeated like a refrain parodying the mechanical regularity of production. Melville's pessimistic conclusion is that this mechanical regularity has long since expanded beyond the realm of industry. He hijacks the image of the white sheet of paper from philosophers and poets, who associated it with the mind and made it the setting for intellectual adventures. Foolscap paper, which was created to serve the purposes of legal and administrative institutions, could assimilate the course of an entire life as inevitably and irresistibly as the paper machine assimilates Cupid's scrap of paper: "It was very curious. Looking at that blank paper continually dropping, dropping, dropping, my mind ran on in wonderings of those strange uses to which those thousand sheets eventually would be put. All sorts of writings would be writ on those now vacant things—sermons, lawyers' briefs, physicians' prescriptions, love-letters, marriage certificates, bills of divorce, registers of births, death-warrants, and so on, without end. Then, recurring back to them as they here lay all blank, I could not but bethink me of that celebrated comparison of John Locke, who, in demonstration of his theory that man had no innate ideas, compared the human mind at birth to a sheet of blank paper; something destined to be scribbled on, but what sort of characters no soul might tell."[247] With this reference to John Locke's famous metaphor, Melville's narrative reaches a vertex where the description of the paper machine as a technical apparatus comes together with its allegorization as a demonic beast. Locke's metaphor was a fundamentally optimistic visualization of the process by which the empty human mind absorbs external impressions in order to flourish and acquire material for spinning ever more complicated webs of associations. In Melville's recasting of this meta-phor, blank paper is transformed into an indifferent sequence of birth, marriage, divorce, and death certificates in the mind's eye of the seed merchant as soon as the sheets leave the paper machine. Paper is where life is standardized in accordance with the principle that the visitor had noted in the room where the paper was folded, stamped, and ruled: "The girls did not so much seem accessory wheels to the general machinery as mere cogs to the wheels." Melville's critique of the assimilation of the labor force into the continuous rhythm of mechanical production had radical counterparts in Europe. In *Capital*, Karl Marx quoted a report on child labor from an English investiga-tive commission: "In the paper factories, where the paper is made by machinery, night-work is the rule for all processes, except rag-sorting. In some cases night-work is carried on incessantly through the whole week, by means of shifts, and thus continues from Sunday night until midnight of the following Saturday. ... Children under 13, young persons under 18, and women, work under this night system."

Marx's *Capital* bears a relation to Melville's entwining of the description and demonology of the paper machine. More than just a work of political economy, it embeds modern industry in old monster mythologies. Like Melville's story, the chapter on "Machinery and Large-Scale Industry" descends into a Dantean hell of mechanical torture. In this chapter, "huge masses of iron," "monster pair[s] of scissors," and "Cyclopean machines" which bear the names of gods—like the steam hammer named Thor—transform workers into "living appendages" who are drained of life by the vampiric nature of value production. While Melville turns the paper factory into an allegory of the industrialization of America, Marx holds up paper production as an example of the sequence of modes of production through dif-ferent cultures and ages: "In the paper industry generally, we may advantageously study in detail not only the distinctions between modes of production based on different means of production, but also the connection between the social relations of production and those modes of production. The old German paper-making trade provides an example of handicraft production; Holland in the seven-teenth century and France in the eighteenth century provide examples of manufacture proper; and modern England provides the example of automatic fabrication. Besides these, there still exist, in India and China, two distinct ancient Asiatic forms of the same industry."[248]

A sentence from *Capital* would not have been out of place above the gate to hell that Melville conjured up in Berkshire County: "As an example both of continuity of production and of the implementa-tion of the automatic principle, we may take a modern paper-mill."

This is the language of political economy. However, *Capital* deals not only with value production but with the percussions that are a result of the dimensions and rhythms of the giant machinery: "An organized system of machines to which motion is communicated by the transmitting mechanism from an automatic center is the most developed form of production by machinery. Here we have, in place of the isolated machine, a mechanical monster whose body fills whole factories, and whose demonic power, at first hidden by the slow and measured motions of its gigantic members, finally bursts forth in the fast and feverish whirl of its countless working organs."[249]

This Dionysian element has no counterpart in Melville's pallid paper factory, but Melville's story also draws an analogy between modern machines and mythical monsters, factory tours and descents into hell. In the face of the paper machine's inexorable advance, the visitor is overcome by a mixture of fear and reverence, horror and admiration, emotions such as those triggered by the white whale in *Moby Dick*: "Something of awe now stole over me, as I gazed upon this inflexible iron animal. Always, more or less, machinery of this ponderous, elaborate sort strikes, in some moods, strange dread into the human heart, as some living, panting Behemoth might. But what made the thing I saw so specially terrible to me was the metallic necessity, the unbudging fatality which governed it. Though, here and there, I could not follow the thin, gauzy vail of pulp in the course of its more mysterious or entirely invisible advance, yet it was indubitable that, at those points where it eluded me, it still marched on in unvarying docility to the automatic cunning of the machine. A fascination fastened on me. I stood spell-bound and wandering in my soul."[250]

This passage, which conjures up a white Behemoth as a companion to the Leviathan in *Moby Dick*, demonizes both the paper machine and the narrator. In his role as a seed merchant, he represents pastoral America. But the contract he signs with the paper mill contributes to the mill's workload, thus perpetuating the Tartarus of the workers and the might of the Behemoth.

2

Newsprint and the Emergence
of the Popular Press

᭶

2.1. The Boundless Resource Base

"Paper is the material medium for all of our intellectual dialogue, the conveyor of our ideas, the bearer of our thoughts, sensations and emotions, the trusty container for the fruits of human study. No other substance in the world goes through such a great series of transformations, no substance is ushered along such a strange route by the hand of industriousness from its original natural state to its ultimate consummation. A description of the fabrication of paper in these pages may be of value, as we are certain that the strange mechanism of the continuous paper machine is unlikely to leave any reader unsatisfied."[251] This is the opening line of "Die Maschine des end-losen Papiers" (The Continuous Paper Machine), the first of two articles which appeared in the autumn of 1834 in the *Pfennig-Magazin der Gesellschaft zur Verbreitung gemeinnütziger Kenntnisse*, a Leipzig-based magazine which devoted two sequential issues to introducing its readers, through text and images, first to the paper machine and then to the paper-cutting machine. The magazine was published every Saturday, and it modeled itself—right down to its subtitle—on the *Penny Magazine of the Society for the Diffusion of Useful Knowledge* which had been published in London since 1832. The *Pfennig-Magazin* was founded in 1833 at the same time as the Parisian *Magasin pittoresque*, and it had a circulation of 35,000 copies in its first year. Each issue consisted of eight pages with four to six illustrations, and it cost only eleven pfennigs (it was nearly twice as expensive to send a letter from Leipzig to Dresden) with an annual subscription rate of two thalers. The low price was made possible by large print runs. Just a few years after it had been founded, the *Pfennig-Magazin* reached a circulation of 100,000 copies. F.A. Brockhaus, the publisher who took it over in 1847, fitted its high-speed printing presses with steam engines to ensure the timely publication of the illustrated weekly. The magazine maintained a balance between entertainment and education in the tradition of eighteenth-century public enlightenment. In its descriptions of the paper machine and the paper-cutting machine, the magazine used the same reflexive movement that Balzac had employed in his novel to demonstrate to its readers the material makings of the very journal they held in their hands. The articles counter the assertion that the road to the modern popular press was a steep slope of intellectual and linguistic degeneration. They have something of the vivid precision with which natural phenomena, everyday things, and middle-class lifestyles were described in the prose of nineteenth-century narrative literature. In the *Pfennig-Magazin*, the description of the paper machine—which continually refers to the accompanying full-page illustration—is the culmination of a tour through a paper mill. It reinforces the notion that the machine should be interpreted as the realization of "the wondrous" by means of the human mind:

> Certainly, no other mechanism sparks the admiration of visitors as much as the paper machine. Just think, the substance that flows out of the vat at one end of this machine is wound in an endless sheet around a cylinder at the other end! Who would fail to be overcome by a sense of the wondrous, who would not marvel at the greatness of the human mind, which can tame the products of nature and put them to use by means of shrewd commands and calculations.—From vat A, an uninterrupted stream of pulp flows from a spigot into the large, rectangular tank B. The pulp flows over a small wire cylinder known as the 'sifter' which rises and falls with a sound like the clatter of cherry pits and is identified by the letter C. Once the substance has passed through the sifter, it flows against a slat and falls in an even stream, like a sheet of water, over a small dam. After this gentle plunge, it continues on along a five- to six-foot-long level section, identified by the letter E, where it takes on the appearance of a tablecloth spread smoothly over a table. As we focused on this surface, we became aware that it was moving forward slowly, that there was a continuous side-ways movement from right to left, and that it was an endless mesh of the finest filaments.

Progressing as slowly as the machine itself, the description moves on to the drying process and the point at which the paper arrives at the winding reel "around which it wraps itself like an endless, wide white band."[252]

In this context, where the machine stands on its own and does not seem to require any human operators, the endlessness that Melville associated with Dante's hellish punishments is a promise of limitless productivity. The English *Penny Magazine* showed that this type of newspaper was dependent on the combination of modern printing technology and the paper machine. The Stanhope press that Balzac mandated for the print shops in Angoulême was made of iron, but it was the last offshoot of Gutenberg's old printing technology. Its larger platen made it possible to print "in one go," but it still followed the old principle of flat surface against flat surface—platen against printing form. Friedrich Koenig's high-speed press heralded a transition to the principle of cylinder against flat surface. Koenig had taken this idea from the textile-printing technology of mechanized weaving mills. The cylinder was the element that would play a decisive role in revolutionizing printing technology in the nineteenth century.[253]

In the space of decades, the cylindrical high-speed press and machine-made paper replaced the combination of the manual press and handmade paper that had been stable for centuries—and this staccato pace of technological innovation was encouraged largely by the periodical press. Even Balzac realized that, in the modern newspaper, paper had found a partner with whom it could form an alliance as epochal as the one it had entered into with printing in the fifteenth century. But this alliance could only flourish as long as a balance was maintained between the capacity of the ever more powerful printing machines and the production output of the paper machines. We may recall that David Séchard's project was prompted by his awareness of the threat posed to this balance if paper machines were tied to a limited supply of raw materials. We can return to him for a moment in order to move closer to a solution to this problem. David is beset by debts that continue to accumulate through the bills of exchange forged by his friend Lucien in Paris. On his way to see the lawyer Petit-Claud, he absently chews on one of the nettle stalks he was steeping in water in his workshop. When he returns from his meeting with the lawyer, he feels a pellet of something between his teeth. Taking it out and flattening it in his hand, he finds "that it made a better pulp than any of the compounds he had produced hitherto; for the principle defect in pulps made from vegetable matter is that they lack adhesiveness. Straw for instance produces a brittle, half metallic and rustling paper. Chance discoveries like this are only made by bold researchers into natural causes. He told himself that he would use a machine and a chemical agent to carry out the operation which he had just accomplished automatically."[254]

While Balzac was writing the final part of *Illusions perdues*, the weaver and leaf-binder Friedrich Gottlob Keller in Saxony was keeping a notebook, which he had started in 1841, where he wrote down all of the technical projects he hoped would lead to lucrative inventions. One of his ideas was to "make paper from wood fibers generated by friction."[255] In his autobiography written years later, Keller described how, after a series of unsuccessful attempts to produce wood fibers by chemical means, he stumbled on the right method through one of those coincidences that Balzac celebrated as the reward of the tireless inventor. He recalled grinding down cherry pits in his youth to make chains out of them and how the ground-off filaments had formed small sheets after they dried. This memory gave him the idea to pulp wood by grinding it while adding water at the same time. Keller noted that in November of the year 1843 he made his first sheet of wood pulp paper using a regular grinding stone in his workshop. In the summer of that year, Balzac's "An Inventor's Tribulations" had been published in serial form in the newspapers *L'État* and *Le Parisien* in Paris.

Chance insights are a common motif in the invention anecdotes of the nineteenth century. For both David Séchard and Friedrich Gottlob Keller, there was a historical index to coincidence. Both inventors picked up on the thread that had run through the technological literature about paper since the second half of the eighteenth century, namely, the search for plant-based raw materials. Neither wood nor nettles had been overlooked; Jacob Christian Schaeffer had thoroughly investigated several different types of wood in his *Experiments and Examples of Making Paper Using No Rags or Only a Small Proportion of Them* (1765–72). As this reservoir of ideas became more of a priority in the nineteenth century, the move from an intuitive, tentative concept to an economically feasible implementation was abetted by several factors. First, ideas began to be explored with both scientific and procedural considerations in mind. Randomly chewing a stalk, a flash of childhood memories—this sounds like a narrow, individual horizon. But high-speed machinery of technological reflection was chugging away behind these intuitions. In Germany, this machinery took the form of publications such as the *Allgemeine Polytechnische Zeitung*, the *Polytechnische Centralblatt*, and the *Polytechnische Journal*. The academic knowledge of the Institute in Paris and the technological knowledge of the leading Didot print shop flowed into the development of David Séchard's idea. Keller's intuition was embedded in his extensive reading of polytechnic journals.

These journals were obsessed with the search for substitutes for costly luxuries and materials. This search was always tied to the goal of cheap mass production through the advance of mechanization and industrialization. Keller's basic procedural idea—to create pulp from wood fibers by grinding wood with water instead of merely using powdery wood shavings as an additive—fell within this remit.

Above all, however, the pressure to innovate had increased around Keller's invention. In the eighteenth century, the shortage of rags—which was just another way of saying the increased demand for paper—could be made less acute by easing the regulations and lordly privileges governing the rag trade. Not so in the nineteenth century, however. As the paper machine and printing machine made technological advances and the demand for paper grew among the press, the resource shortage intensified.[256]

Balzac himself had written for Émile de Girardin's newspapers around 1830, and after Girardin founded *La Presse* in 1836, Balzac was a contributor to that as well. *La Presse*, like the newspaper *Le Siècle* founded in the same year by Armand Dutacq, aimed for a low sales price and high circulation. As opposed to the usual French newspaper subscription rate of 80 francs, the two new newspapers cost just 40 francs. Their goal was to tap into a new audience, expand their market, and compensate for their lower price by a higher number of copies. They were also banking on advertising business and new strategies for building audience loyalty. Girardin's basic idea was to add value to information by combining novelty and narration—in other words, by handling news in a narrative fashion. He introduced literary, narrative, entertaining formats in place of the rhetorical and polemical opinion pieces which had traditionally dominated the politically oriented medium of the newspaper. His best-known innovation sprang from this concept: the institution of the *roman-feuilleton*, or serialized novel. This format quickly became a sensation, thanks not least to Balzac's novel *La Vieille Fille*, which appeared in *La Presse* in its first year of publication. But the short-form prose formats which reflected the readers' everyday lives were just as important. Both of the new newspapers were successful within the parameters of their time. *La Presse* quickly achieved a circulation of 10,000 copies, while 35,000 copies of *Le Siècle* were published in 1842. These were the parameters within which *Illusions perdues* appeared.[257]

Balzac had written that "all great achievements of industry and knowledge take place extraordinarily slowly through unremarkable accumulations, just like geological or other natural processes. In order to reach perfection, writing—and perhaps even language—had to undergo the same trials as the art of book printing and paper fabrication." This analogy between technological progress and natural history emerged from the realization that inventions were not events which could be precisely pinpointed but instead may have ranged over longer periods of time. One reason for this was that a procedural idea had to make its way through a web of contracts, patents, and other economic and cultural factors before it could be implemented. David Séchard and Friedrich Gottlob Keller were comparable in that both of them wanted to make an invention ready for production without having the necessary capital or an effective infrastructure to do so. As a consequence, the inventor was divorced from his invention—like Louis-Nicolas Robert and his paper machine. In Keller's case, the patent was taken over by the paper manufacturer Heinrich Voelter in Heidenheim. Voelter worked with a local engineer named Johann Matthäus Voith, and after some initial setbacks they developed an industrial-grade wood grinding machine with improved grinder presses as well as a "raffineur" for refining the milled wood. To begin with, groundwood pulp was an additive to be combined with rags, not a general substitute for rags. Around twenty-five years passed between Keller's idea and the implementation of the groundwood process. The 1867 World's Fair in Paris saw the final breakthrough for groundwood technology in international paper production.[258]

The first step had been taken, but paper's resource base had not yet been entirely revolutionized. This was because paper made solely from groundwood pulp quickly grew brittle and turned yellow when exposed to light. To make finer paper, rags still had to be used as a stabilizer in the production process. Rags were not relieved of this function until the 1880s when another newcomer appeared on the scene: cellulose, which was also derived from wood. Cellulose was a product of the chemistry boom which, since the late eighteenth century, had led to the expansion of paper's resource base when chlorine bleach was applied to rags. Chemistry also gave new impetus to the search for substitute raw materials. Balzac's imaginary inventor David Séchard was therefore in alignment with real history, since his plant experiments were first inspired by a chemist from the French Revolutionary era. The nettle anecdote, which prompted him to try to reproduce chemically what he had accidentally produced mechanically, reflected the fact that with the introduction of the paper machine, engineers and technicians were increasingly being joined by chemists. After the French chemist Anselme Payen identified cellulose in wood in 1838, magazines such as the *Polytechnisches Journal* began to document new experiments and processes for generating cellulose for paper production. From the 1880s, a rapidly growing chemical pulp industry joined the many wood grinding plants which had successfully crowded out straw as an alternative material. Handmade rag paper remained in circulation, but the combination of mechanical and chemical pulp and the use of steam—not so much as a source of power but as a source of heat—permanently changed the industrial mass production of paper. High-quality chemical pulp replaced the rags that had previously been added to the mechanical pulp in order to produce more high-quality paper.[259]

As rags grew less important, the paper industry distanced itself from both its old neighbor, weaving, and its successor, the textile industry. When excerpts from Anselme Payen's treatise "On the Structure and Chemical Composition of Wood Fiber" appeared in the *Polytechnisches Journal* in Germany in 1867, the year of the Paris World's Fair, his blueprint for the new chemical pulp production industry ended with the following observation: "From a forestry standpoint as well, the new branch of industry is very interesting in that it opens up new sales channels for the products of coniferous wood plantings."[260] And indeed, the forest took over from the rag trade as a supplier of raw materials. From a forestry perspective, the paper industry filled the vacuum that had been left behind by the retreat of traditional wood buyers. Coal deposed wood both in the smelting industry and generally as a fuel in the nineteenth century, and iron and steel were increasingly used in place of wood in the construction industry. The forest thus opened up to the paper industry as a source of raw materials at precisely the historical moment it was needed, and it helped the industry make the transition to industrial production. Increasingly powerful large-scale machinery could then be coupled with continually improved methods for producing raw materials chemically. The new scale of production escalated the demand for energy and capital, required sophisticated transportation logistics for the raw materials and finished products, and linked the profitability of an operation to its size on a higher level.[261] The redimensioning of paper production went hand in hand with a shift in its geographic centers. Rag paper came by its raw materials most easily in places with a high population density. But the move to mechanical and chemical wood pulp meant that the sparsely populated but heavily forested regions of North America and Northern Europe quickly grew in importance.[262] The traditional European paper regions in France, Holland, Germany, and England, which had led the way when the paper machine took off around 1800, slipped into second place on a global scale. This displacement was facilitated by a fundamental relationship that paper had maintained from its Chinese/Arab origins into the era of mechanization and industrialization: its relationship with water. Though water grew less important as a source of power, the availability of large quantities of water was essential to industrial production. The abundance of water found in the heavily wooded areas of northern Europe and North America contributed to the ascendency of these regions in the context of global paper production.[263] Even in pre-industrial times, papermaking had not been idyllic; mills reeked of old rags, and they polluted the water that they used. Water consumption and pollution intensified in the course of industrialization and the establishment of mechanical and chemical wood pulping. The residues from the chemicals used in paper factories were released into the environment through the factories' wastewater.

Traditional Arab- and Chinese-based European paper production was not comprehensively revolutionized until the latter third of the nineteenth century when it lost the constraints on its resource base. In terms of paper history, the era in which we live did not start with the paper machine and the high-speed press. It was only when the supply of raw materials became limitless that the mechanized sheet-formation process which had emerged in the late eighteenth century could finally realize its full potential, turning paper into a mass-produced, ubiquitous industrial product. The availability of paper continued to be restricted by economic and political factors, such as the economy of scarcity during and after wars, as had been the case in the Thirty Years' War. In principle, however, the cultivation of a renewable resource made it possible to continually adapt to the rising demand for paper in industrial society. The per capita consumption of paper in Germany around 1800 was just 0.5 kilograms. By 1873 it had risen to 2.5 kilograms, but this fivefold increase was just a prelude to the leap in consumption of 13 to 18 kilograms in the last quarter of the nineteenth century after the constraints had been lifted on paper's resource base.

Carlyle had skeptically branded the dawn of the industrial era as the "Paper Age," but this appellation echoed euphorically through the late nineteenth century as paper production expanded. The paper lobbyist Carl Hofmann, whose *Practical Manual of Paper Fabrication* (1875) became a standard work on the subject and who founded the *Papier-Zeitung* in 1876, said that the average per-capita consumption of paper was the gauge of a modern nation's state of civilization—a claim he made proudly because Germany led the field in paper statistics.

But ever since Thomas Carlyle's time, the paper industry's euphoric self-identification as a key industry of civilization had been tempered by skepticism toward both the periodical press and the machine-made paper upon which it was based. In an issue of *Gentleman's Magazine* from 1823, John Murray published a letter which was reprinted many times over, in which he presented multiple examples of paper's decline in quality as a result of its larger proportion of cotton compared to linen and the modern methods used to bleach it. Murray, who was a chemist, reiterated his criticisms in his book *Practical Remarks on Modern Paper* (1829), where his critique was embedded in a history of writing materials since antiquity. His investigation of how chlorine bleach weakened the fibers of modern paper culminated in a description of the deterioration of a Bible which had been printed on modern paper in Oxford in 1816. His diagnosis, printed in capital letters in the text, was CRUMBLING LITERALLY INTO DUST, and his chemical analysis of the paper's acid content and bleach residue explained the following alarming finding: "Almost the entire Book of Genesis has mouldered away, and left not a trace behind."

Murray was no Luddite; he wanted to strengthen the competitiveness of the British paper industry, particularly as compared to France, by pointing out the weaknesses apparent in English machine-made paper. Murray's early concerns regarding modern paper's lack of durability accompanied the shift from handmade to machine-made paper throughout Europe in the nineteenth century. Sometimes the sellers of machine-made paper avoided advertising it as such, and in some German states it was decreed that important documents were to be produced only on handmade paper; in response, quality assurance commissions were set up at the urging of paper manufacturers so that these restrictions would be lifted again.

It was a rule of thumb that paper faced more threats to its shelf life when mass-production technologies were introduced in the nineteenth century. This certainly applied to the resin size that Moritz Friedrich Illig used in place of animal size, which resulted in the alum, a salt of sulfuric acid, that John Murray had detected in paper. It also applied to the lignin that found its way into paper through groundwood pulp; when lignin breaks down, it releases acids which accelerate the degradation of paper unless they are neutralized by alkaline substances. Murray's vision of modern paper as an apparently durable, uniformly white material with a hidden tendency toward self-dissolution was vividly captured in a striking phrase: "Some of the most expensive works of modern times contain within themselves the seeds of destruction and the elements of decay."[264] This phrase encompassed all variants of the destabilization of paper's fiber structure. Dampness, external temperatures, UV rays, and air pollution such as that found in Dickens's London could all act as henchman of decay, of yellowing, and of fragility. Since the second half of the twentieth century, programs have been underway in libraries to restore the collections printed on wood-based paper.

2.2. The Newspaper, the Price of Paper, and the Patrioteer

At the start of the eleventh chapter of Theodor Fontane's novel *Effi Briest* (1895), which is set between 1878 and 1886–87, the protagonist and her husband, who have been living in Kessin on the Baltic coast of Pomerania since their wedding, stop off at the Prince Bismarck Inn. The inn is located at a point where the road to Kessin branches off from the road leading from the train station on the Berlin-Danzig line to Varzin. The inn bears its name for a reason: unlike the fictitious Baltic Sea resort of Kessin, Varzin is an actual village in Pomerania, with a manor house and park belonging to the Prince of Bismarck. As the conversation in the inn turns from casual to more serious topics, Varzin is mentioned. " 'Yes,' said Golchowski, 'just imagine the Prince running a paper-mill! It's all very odd; in actual fact he can't stand writing, and printed paper even less, and now he has acquired a paper-mill.' 'True enough, my dear Golchowski,' said Innstetten, 'but in life you can never get away from contradictions like that. And being a prince and achieving greatness doesn't help at all.' " Innstetten, a district administrator who represents the Imperial Chancellor in the province, picks up on the light mockery with which the innkeeper points out that Bismarck, who scorned journalism, had invested in a paper factory which would not exist were it not for the press. He defends the prince and his contradictions—which included availing himself of the despised press with virtuosity and worldly wisdom, in the case of the Ems Dispatch and other situations. Bismarck had acquired the manor in Varzin with all of its accompanying estates in 1867. From 1870, he ran the Hammermühle groundwood pulp and paper factory there, which he leased to the brothers Moritz and Georg Behrend. Although the factory constantly faced crises, Bismarck was proud of the modern facilities which used steam power to produce wood pulp. The paper factory had an exhibit at the World's Fair in Vienna in 1873, and a correspondent for a northern German newspaper sent a report from the hall of German industry on June 19, 1873, entitled "Letters from the World's Fair": "In a western wing of this southern section, visitors will find a few objects that are of interest, in part on account of their exhibitor and in part on account of the way they have been manufactured. It is an exhibition of types of paper made not from rags but from wood pulp, and the most important exhibitor in this field is Prince Bismarck, that is, the plant manager of the princely Bismarckian paper factories in Varzin. A simple wooden cabinet—which thousands of people pass without realizing who it is that has stepped into the industrial arena here—holds the respective paper samples, one of which is the invention of Mr. Behrend in Cöslin, director of the princely paper factory."[265]

The concept behind the facilities in Varzin was to combine paper production and wood pulp production. It was no surprise, then, that Bismarck's leaseholder Moritz Behrend became the driving force behind the initiative by German paper manufacturers to overturn German Imperial Patent No. 4179 in 1884. Five years earlier, the chemist Alexander Mitscherlich—grandfather of the psychologist of the same name—had been granted this patent for the sulfite process which improved the chemical separation of the cellulose found in wood, and which he had used in his own factory ever since. German paper manufacturers successfully argued before the Supreme Court of the German Reich that the American Benjamin Tilghman had patented this process back in 1867. The upswing in industrial chemical pulp production was given a vital boost by the revocation of Mitscherlich's patent. In Germany alone, a good sixty chemical pulp factories were established between 1884 and 1895.[266]

It was no coincidence that the Bible and documents played such a major role in nineteenth-century debates about machine-made paper and then wood pulp paper: the Bible embodied the demand for the perpetual transmission of printed literature, while documents embodied the same demand for unprinted literature. Industrially produced paper had to measure up to this standard.

Behind the project of Balzac's philosophical inventor David Séchard and the technological scheming of his antagonist Cointet, there was a dawning realization that, despite what John Murray believed, modern paper's lower resistance to ageing would not stand in the way of its triumphal march. In fact, new marketing opportunities opened up when modern paper embraced rapid, wide-scale, synchronous circulation and ceased trying to be a medium of long-term diachronic storage at the same time. In its epochal alliance with the periodical press, it was allowed to turn yellow and brittle more quickly than a Bible or a document as long as it fulfilled two other criteria: ample availability and low cost. Thanks to his low-price policy, Balzac's Cointet becomes the most important supplier of paper to the Parisian press. He is not harmed by the fact that his paper is not the modern "Chinese paper" that David Séchard was aiming for. If a medium is short-lived, its carrier medium can be short-lived as well. The difference between absolute and functional quality was the basis of the link between the modern press and the loss of constraints on paper production in the nineteenth century.

In the age of rag paper, newspapers had shared their carrier medium with books and general correspondence. But as the proportion of groundwood pulp quickly rose compared to the proportion of rags in newsprint, this type of paper spun off as a medium with its own rules. Newspaper historians report that, from the 1880s, most newsprint consisted of eighty percent mechanical pulp and twenty percent chemical pulp. Though rags were still occasionally used here and there, they had essentially ceased to be a raw material in the paper industry.[267]

In order to sell masses of newspapers, there had to be masses of people who could and wanted to read them and who were able to spend money on them. The advance of literacy alone was not enough; the relationship between work and leisure had to evolve as well in order to free up resources of time and energy for reading newspapers. Furthermore, economic and political restrictions on the production and distribution of newspapers had to be eliminated. In the first half of the nineteenth century, such restrictions included state intervention in the press in Germany and elsewhere. There was political censorship which restricted the content that could be published, there were deposits to be paid, and there were stamp duties on newspapers based on the Anglo-Saxon "knowledge taxes" which were not lifted in Germany until the establishment of the German Empire and the passage of the Imperial Press Law of March 1874. All of these factors influenced the development of the press. But without the industrialization of paper production, which depended on an unrestricted resource base, there would not have been a turning point in the second half of the nineteenth century which allowed the medium of the newspaper to achieve new dimensions. In Germany, most papers appeared no more than four times a week until 1820. It was not until the late nineteenth century that daily newspapers, in the literal sense, became a standard in all regions. Different papers also appeared at different times of day, inspiring Karl Kraus to write that "the day was divided into the evening edition and the morning edition."

The newspaper's increased circulation and frequency of publication went hand in hand with its evolution from a luxury item and medium for notabilities to an everyday consumer good. The removal of price barriers was essential to this. It was at this point that the technological elimination of limits on paper's raw materials became a factor in the social elimination of limits on the medium of the newspaper. While the fixed costs for editing and for a publisher's technical equipment—including expensive presses—became relatively less significant as circulation figures rose, this was not true for the cost of paper, which accounted for a greater proportion of total production costs as the number of copies grew. It was therefore not the mass availability of newsprint as a physical material as such that helped surmount the "price-publicity threshold" in the last quarter of the nineteenth century.[268] The decisive factor was the decline in price thanks to the elimination of resource constraints. After the shift to mechanical and chemical pulp, the price for 100 kilograms of newsprint fell continually from 73 marks in 1873 to 22.50 marks, or less than a third of the original price, in 1900. The price development for newsprint and the circulation development for newspapers thus ran counter to each other in the same period of time. Newspaper prices could remain steady or actually fall even if the circulation figures rose rapidly because the declining price of paper compensated for the increased consumption. In terms of its share of the annual earnings of an industrial worker, the effective price of a newspaper subscription sank in Germany in the second half of the nineteenth century. The technological elimination of resource constraints was not only instrumental in eliminating social constraints on the medium of the newspaper, it also played a role in the newspaper's physiognomic independence and differentiation. The general tendency in the nineteenth century was for formats to grow larger. Around 1800, newspapers were still being printed in quarto format, which gave the impression that they were associated with the world of books. But parallel to the technological differentiation of newsprint from book paper and writing paper, newspaper formats moved away from book formats in Germany between 1840 and 1900. Both rising circulation figures and the growing size of newspapers led to increased paper consumption. Because newsprint was cheap, however, this additional consumption did not initially result in a higher price for newspapers themselves.[269] Toward the end of the nineteenth century, they had reached the average size that they would continue to have through the twentieth century. The drawings, caricatures, and paintings showing newspapers and newspaper readers from the late nineteenth century reveal how the physiognomy of the newspaper and the newspaper reader began to acquire its own contours, and how newspaper formats made different demands on the arms, hands, and eyes of the reader as compared to books. In the nineteenth century, the foundations were laid for secret agents, murderers, and detectives in hotel lobbies to be able to keep a lookout behind an open newspaper in the films of the twentieth century.

Heinrich Mann's novel *The Patrioteer* (1914), which the author outlined in 1906 and largely completed in 1911–12, initially had a subtitle that was later dropped: "The History of the Public Soul under Wilhelm II." On October 31, 1906, Heinrich Mann wrote to the editor Ludwig Ewers about his planned novel: "The protagonist will be your average neo-German, someone who carries the spirit of Berlin into the provinces; above all, a Byzantine to the end. I plan for him to have a paper factory and to gradually start producing patriotic postcards depicting the Kaiser in battle scenes and apotheoses. As a paper producer, he has ties to the government paper in his region. I wanted to ask your advice about this. Can a semi-official county paper such as this have a large circulation? What kind of business figures would the paper producer be looking at? Which government officials would he be dealing with? Would there be a district administrator in the county?"[270]

In the finished novel, the production of patriotic postcards retreated into the background and the focus was placed on the close connections between the paper factory, the local press, and political intrigue. Even Diederich Hessling's father is a paper manufacturer in the fictitious town of Netzig, which was probably supposed to be in Brandenburg. He stood at the vat and made paper by hand before he was finally able to acquire a paper machine during the business boom after 1871. The main raw materials in his factory are still rags, which are shredded by a cutting machine after any buttons have been removed, then washed in chlorine bleach in a mechanical drum before being fed into a "large boiling machine." The factory also has ties to a chemical pulp manufacturer in Berlin. In accordance with this, Diederich Hessling studies chemistry in Berlin, and he has an affair with the daughter of the chemical pulp manufacturer which he brings to an end in despicable fashion. When he takes over the factory in his hometown after his father's death, he proves to be a loyalist and a strictly anti-Social Democratic modernizer. Technologically, his paper factory is just on the brink of leaving behind the age of rags, but Diederich Hessling is already moving in the modern world where newspapers and politics are in symbiosis.

Heinrich Mann was thinking of the booming paper business when he wrote *The Patrioteer*, and his protagonist occasionally dreams of moving into the Reichstag in Berlin as a lobbyist for the paper industry. But Diederich Hessling remains in the provinces, where he aligns paper production and the press with the interests of the emperor. When Mann outlined the novel in 1906, there were over 4,000 daily newspapers in Germany with an estimated circulation of 25.5 million copies. In both per capita paper consumption and newspaper consumption, Germany was ahead of all other European countries. When Theodor Fontane occasionally hinted in his novels that there was a dispatch editor at work in Bismarck, he was thinking of the growing overlap between the nation and the newspaper-reading public. In Wilhelmine Germany, the patrioteers were newspaper readers. This overlap delineates the space in which Diederich Hessling moves when he takes over the paper mill in Netzig. The Netzig-Berlin axis not only defines the protagonist's biography, it is also the background to the satirical parallels drawn between the emperor in Berlin and his loyal subject in the provinces. Hessling's assumption of power in the paper factory is modeled on the accession to power of Wilhelm II, whose striking turns of phrase ("My course is the right one, I am leading you to glorious days") and "personal regiment" are copied by the patrioteer, and whose association with technological progress is put into action when Hessling orders a "New Patent Cylinder Machine, Maier System" from the Büschli & Co. machinery manufacturers in Eschweiler. The novel starts in the early 1890s; the emperor is young, and so is his loyal subject. Diederich Hessling expresses his "full confession of the strongest and most strenuous opinions" regarding the young generation of blossoming nationalism and anti-liberalism and declares "that an end must be made, once and for all, in Netzig of the old liberal routine."

The Wilhelmine subject makes use of two media of patriotism and sovereign glorification in order to strike a final blow against the dying generation of 1848: the old medium of the monument and the new medium of the daily press, the latter in the form of the provincial newspaper that is characteristic of the newspaper landscape in Germany. The monument for which Diederich Hessling campaigns is to be erected for Wilhelm I on his 100th birthday in 1897. The patriotic daily press is the medium of tribute to Wilhelm II. The initial constellation becomes clear when, with an eye to the new Reichstag elections in a year and a half, the loyal subject meets with the "Jewish gentleman from the Public Prosecutor's Office" (who is unsurpassed in his antisemitism) and the mayor of Netzig to discuss the establishment of an election committee:

> Jadassohn explained that it was absolutely essential to get into touch with Governor von Wulckow. "In the strictest confidence," added the Mayor, winking. Diederich regretted that the "Netzig Journal," the chief newspaper in town, was tarred with the liberal brush. "A damned Semitic rag!" said Jadassohn. On the other hand, the loyal government county paper had practically no influence in the town. But old Klüsing in Gausenfeld supplied paper to both. As he had money in the "Netzig Journal," it did not seem improbable to Diederich that its attitude

might be influenced through him. They would have to frighten him into thinking that otherwise he would lose the county paper. "After all, there is another paper factory in Netzig," said the Mayor, grinning.[271]

This constellation is the source of the double movement in the novel which couples Diederich Hessling's attacks on the liberalism of the notabilities to his rise to become the leading paper manufacturer in the city. Through a speculative financial scheme, the loyal subject acquires a paper factory which has been turned into a stock company from his competitor Klüsing in Gausenfeld at a give-away price, and he brings his own cheaply sold paper factory into the new legal structure as fresh capital. In this new industrial-scale factory, certain machines produce a paper known as "World Power." This patriotic toilet paper is in keeping with the grotesque satirical register of the novel. But the book's author understood the affinity between Wilhelminism and the modern media so well that he depicted the paper industry, in all seriousness, as one of the key industries of the German Empire. The maxim that the loyal subject takes from his ruler—"German spirit, supported by German workmanship"—refers not to the conquering of world power in the novel, but to the conquering of the public. The public is the battlefield upon which Diederich Hessling serves the emperor.[272] The satirical side of the novel can be seen in the fact that Hessling evades military service by calling on his connections in the Neo-Teuton student corps. The energy with which the patrioteer strengthens his own affective ties to the emperor through the paper-based medium of the newspaper is rooted in the apocalyptic stratum underlying the novel. This becomes apparent when a demonstration by the unemployed which was put down in Berlin in 1892—and which Diederich Hessling witnessed, along with a dashing appearance by the emperor—is subsequently echoed in the town of Netzig when a worker from Hessling's factory is shot. The patrioteer fakes a telegram of congratulations from the emperor to the regiment command praising the sentry who fired the killing shot "for his bravery in the face of the domestic enemy" and promoting him to the rank of lance-corporal, and he publishes it in the *Netzig Journal*. When the Berlin press gets hold of it, there is no denial but rather a note of confirmation in the Berlin *Lokal-Anzeiger*: "It is well known that yesterday the Emperor telegraphed, promoting the brave soldier to the rank of lance-corporal." Heinrich Mann turns this telegraph scheme in the provinces into a counterpart to the actual encounter between the patrioteer and the face of power at the demonstration on Unter den Linden in Berlin. At the sight of his telegram in the newspaper, the patrioteer experiences a mystical union with the emperor which is brought about by the modern medium: "He could hardly contain himself with sheer joy. Was it possible? Had he really anticipated what the Emperor would say? Was his ear so acute? Did his brain work in unison with ...? He was overpowered by a sense of mystic relationship. ... There! not a denial but a confirmation! He had adopted Diederich's own words and had taken action in the sense Diederich had indicated! ... Diederich spread out the newspaper, and gazed into its mirrored reflection of himself draped in royal ermine."[273]

Without having the term at his disposal, Heinrich Mann portrayed Wilhelminism as a media-supported monarchy. At the novel's apocalyptic end, when a storm breaks out over the festive gathering for the unveiling of the monument and old Buck in his deathbed thinks he has seen the Devil in Diederich Hessling, we must imagine the patrioteer in ermine made of newsprint.

2.3. Émile Zola, the *Petit Journal*, and the Dreyfus Affair

In the second volume of *Illusions perdues* published in 1839, the journalist Lousteau refers to the imaginary newspaper in which Lucien de Rubempré causes a furor with his feuilletons as "*notre petit journal.*" After Balzac's death, this title was given to the newspaper that represented the transition to the popular press in France: *Le Petit Journal*. The paper was founded in 1863 and—in part to evade the taxes applied to political newspapers—it billed itself explicitly as a "*quotidien non-politique.*" The *Petit Journal* differentiated itself from the "big," challenging press even in its name, with its "small" trademark referring to both its low price and its halved page format. The newspaper cost just five centimes, or one sou, and it was the model for "*la presse à un sou,*" the French counterpart to the English Penny Press.[274]

The *faits divers* played a prominent role in the *Petit Journal*. As in Dickens's London, the reporters who wrote these pieces roamed the big city in search of accidents, suicides, unexplained deaths, and crimes. Even in *La peau de chagrin*, Balzac had described the world of the *faits divers* as a challenge to literature: "Where can you find in the great ocean of literature, a book still afloat which can compete in genius with a newspaper item like this one: *Yesterday at four o'clock a young woman threw herself into the Seine from the parapet of the Pont des Arts*. Everything pales before this laconic Parisian notice: dramas, novels. ..."[275] The ongoing coverage of the murder of a family of eight, until the perpetrator was arrested and executed, caused the circulation of the *Petit Journal* to jump from 357,000 to 594,000 copies in the space of just a few months from September 1869 to mid-January 1870.[276] Considering the production conditions for the daily press, circulation figures such as these were only possible because the alliance of the printing press and paper had reached a new technological level. Émile de Girardin, with whom Balzac worked, was one of the key figures on the side of French journalism, from the July Monarchy through the Second Empire until the Third Republic, who drove this technological process forward. The increased speed of printing played to his concept of high circulation and low newspaper costs.

His partner on the side of French engineering was Hippolyte Auguste Marinoni, who supplied a printing machine which offered a fourfold increase in daily output for Girardin's *La Presse* in 1848. Not long after this, Marinoni saw Jacob Worms, a German immigrant, build one of the first rotary presses in the Parisian print shop for *La Presse*, though this press was not used on a large scale at the time due to political restrictions. Drawing on suggestions from Worms and English mechanical engineering—which he strove to emulate—Marinoni developed a French counterpart to the rotary press in 1866–67 for the *Petit Journal* which was fully automated in the United States by William Bullock. While Gutenberg's platen press had followed the principle of flat surface against flat surface and Koenig's high-speed press had followed the principle of cylinder against flat surface, this development reached a vanishing point with the principle of cylinder against cylinder. The triumphal march of the cylinder depended on one fundamental characteristic of paper: its pliability. This applied not only to where the rolls of the "endless paper" produced by the paper machine met the printing machine, but also to the printing process itself. As rotary printing presses became more widespread, stereotypes of printing forms began to be made from paper instead of plaster. The mechanisms for feeding in paper and cutting the printed pages were both integrated into printing machines around the counterrotating cylinders. In 1894, the Brockhaus encyclopedia described the self-contained continuity of movement in these new machines as follows: "Each sheet must be placed individually in a typical high-speed press, so after highly complicated four- and eightfold high-speed presses requiring many operators had been built and used for a long time, the idea arose to feed endless paper into the machine automatically, so after each sheet was printed on both sides by means of cylindrically curved printing forms (stereoplates), it would be cut into the respective format in the machine itself by a cutting apparatus and then folded or left unfolded, achieving an extraordinarily large output (up to 20,000 copies in one hour)."[277]

As had been the case with Koenig's high-speed press in 1810, the fact that the English *Times* was the first customer to take advantage of the rotary press in 1856 accentuated the close relationship between the periodical press and innovations in printing and paper technology. The rotary press was the ideal companion to paper production which had been freed of resource constraints—and this union was the ideal companion to the expanding newspaper industry.

The revolutionized alliance between paper and the printing press benefited all four elements constituting the medium of the newspaper according to the science of journalism: periodicity, or the reliability and frequency of rhythmic publication; topicality, which relied not only on the speed with which messages were sent by telegraph offices but also on the speed of printing; universality, or the non-specific coverage of a variety of subjects through the erosion of boundaries and internal differentiation of formats; and publicity, or public, non-exclusive accessibility which was encouraged by wide circulation. The daily newspaper rose to become the central mass medium of industrial modernity—one which still faced no competition from radio or television in the late nineteenth and early twentieth century—and it owed this position above all to its combination of low price and high circulation.[278] Without the resulting social expansion of newspaper consumption, the effects of topicality, periodicity, and universality would have remained limited.

What emerged, compared to the newspapers of the seventeenth and eighteenth centuries, was a new medium. With the industrialization of paper production and elimination of resource constraints, the newspaper industry exponentially increased the synchronous circulation of unbound papers. These papers massively saturated society on a daily basis and then sank into the realm of non-transmission, just like the paper-based dispatches from telegraph offices which disappeared in their material form as soon as they had been reformatted into newspaper reports by editors. As a popular nineteenth-century joke had it, the morning's newspaper was the evening's toilet paper. At the heart of this joke was the realization that, of the masses of paper that were fed to the public, the proportion of paper that would not survive was growing exponentially. The newspapers bound into annual volumes and stored in libraries and archives did not mitigate this mass disappearance. The continual disappearance of newsprint was the flip side to its intermittent impact. The omnipresence of newsprint in nineteenth-century caricatures, the hordes of newspaper

readers and journalists in nineteenth-century novels, and the inform-
ers' reports in police archives regarding the sentiments of newspaper
readers concerning the *faits divers* as well as political notices and
editorials, were the traces left behind by the newsprint which was fed
to the social organism on a daily basis.

The *Petit Journal* was representative of the triangle formed by the
paper industry, printing technology, and the periodical press. It initially shared the four-page format of the "big" newspapers, but
instead of the normal size of 43 × 60 cm, the pages were halved to
43 × 30 cm. But the concept of "small," light tabloid journalism was
not bound to a physically small format. In 1873, Émile de Girardin
assumed the presidency of the newspaper's management company, a
position he held until his death in 1881. In 1882, this key journalistic
figure was succeeded as president by a key technological figure:
Hippolyte Auguste Marinoni.[279] At the Paris World's Fair in 1889,
he presented his new rotary press, which printed rolls of paper in
various formats on both sides, cut them, and folded them into newspapers. Since 1890 the *Petit Journal* had appeared in a larger format,
a move supported by both the abolishment of the paper tax in 1886
and the elimination of constraints on paper's resource base. In 1890
the newspaper's circulation crossed the one-million threshold, and at
the same time the *Petit Journal* began to publish a weekly eight-page
Supplement illustré which cost five centimes, just like the normal
edition of the paper. The inclusion of color pictures turned the *Petit
Journal* into a leading specimen of the European popular press. It
became one of the greatest sounding boxes for technical and civilizational progress in the French Third Republic, a propagandist for
the telegraph, phonograph, telephone, car, and Tour de France, and
an amplifier of nationalism. It may have started as a "*quotidien non-
politique*," but from the late nineteenth century it was undoubtedly
a political force.

It cultivated the new raw materials of journalism: scandal and
sensation. It published pictures of bomb attacks and train wrecks, of
everyday life in the colonies, portraits of high-ranking generals, of
guests and hosts during state visits, of circus viewers being devoured
by lions. But first and foremost, the *Petit Journal* became the mouth-
piece of the anti-Dreyfusards after Émile Zola published "J'accuse!"
on the front page of *L'Aurore* on January 13, 1898, his open letter
to President of the Republic Félix Faure. The Dreyfus Affair was not
just an affair of state, it was also—and above all—one of the first
modern media battles. This media battle was encouraged by the personal animosity between Hippolyte Auguste Marinoni and Georges
Clemenceau, the editor of *L'Aurore* who had been responsible for the

spectacular headline to Zola's letter. *L'Aurore*'s normal circulation of 20,000 to 30,000 copies may have skyrocketed to more than 300,000 thanks to Zola's article, but it was up against the millions of copies of the *Petit Journal*—and the second large popular paper with a circulation in the millions, *Le Petit Parisien*, also fueled the fire of the anti-Dreyfusards.

A long series of images relating to the Dreyfus Affair could be taken from the *Supplement illustré* of the *Petit Journal*, starting not with the famous cover of January 13, 1895, which shows the captain being degraded by having his saber broken, but with the trial that had preceded it. The anti-Dreyfusism of the *Petit Journal* manifested itself in antisemitic attacks on Dreyfus as well as a campaign against Émile Zola, the "protagonist of anti-patriotic scandals," and his literary output. *Le Petit Journal* reported on the libel suit brought against Zola by the military in February 1898 in an article entitled "l'Affaire Zola." In the spring of 1898 it became part of the affair itself when on May 23—the day that Émile Zola was to appear before the court in Versailles—the editor-in-chief Ernest Judet published a defamatory biographical profile of François Zola, Émile Zola's father, depicting him as a thief and freeloader. This attempt to counter Zola's political intervention by making a scandal out of an element of his personal biography not only led Zola to bring a case against the *Petit Journal*, Marinoni, and Judet, but also prompted him to write a series of articles about his father in *L'Aurore* under the title of "François Zola." In novels such as *Thérèse Raquin*, Zola had taken up Balzac's challenge to bring the world of the *faits divers* into the world of the novel. Now he wrote newspaper articles in defense of his father's honor which simultaneously settled scores with the *Petit Journal* and its smear campaign. He explicitly told the public that he had not read this newspaper since July 18, 1898, when he left France following the trial in Versailles, and that he would never read it again: "Je ne le lis jamais."[280]

3

Illuminated Inner Worlds

3.1. Wilhelm Dilthey, Historism, and Literary Estates

Wilhelm Dilthey knew precisely when modern historical scholarship began in Germany: after the revolutionary wars, the end of the Old Empire, and the turbulence of the Napoleonic Era, when a growing number of formerly fragmented sources from monastic, episcopal, and royal archives were transferred to "the great modern state archives," which were opened up to scholars, "letting air and sunlight into these scrupulously guarded chambers full of paper and secrets, state secrets and family secrets."[281] Modern historical scholarship only emerged when the corpus of unprinted sources was consolidated and made accessible. Political state archives were a central motif in the lecture that Dilthey gave on January 16, 1889, at the first meeting of the Association for German Literary History, which had been founded the year before. In this lecture, he made a case for "archives of literature." He said that since the attainment of political unity, the German nation had turned to the question of "what its literature, this prime expression of the German spirit, this unifying band in the dark days of political turmoil and military impotence, means to it." Dilthey's lecture was published in the popular magazine *Deutsche Rundschau* (1889) and was flanked by an essay on "Archives of Literature and Their Importance to the Study of the History of Philosophy" in *Archiv für Geschichte der Philosophie* (1889).[282] This parallel approach was in keeping with the broad understanding of literature that formed the basis of Dilthey's argument. For Dilthey, literature included "all of a people's linguistic expressions of life which are of lasting value, that is, literature as well as philosophy, history and science."[283]

The literature archives he had in mind were of a material scope that tended to surpass the collections held in secret state archives. Standing in the way of this, however, was Dilthey's distressing realization that the world of unprinted sources relating to literary and intellectual history lay in ruins. In his lecture and his essay, Dilthey explored these ruins of fragmentary literary estates, manuscripts which had been carelessly lost or burned, letters which ended up in boxes and attics where they were forgotten, and the marginal notes of important philosophers concerning their own works which had wound up as maculature in publishing houses. His argument for archives of literature was formulated as a great rescue operation for the "helpless masses of paper," a call to safeguard, consolidate, systematically organize, and open up the manuscripts of German authors since the age of humanism. Dilthey adopted this dramatic tone not only because he had discovered that literature was being transmitted inadequately, but because he attributed a prominent status to manuscripts. Since he viewed manuscripts as a key to understanding printed texts, and since he suspected that unprinted papers held hidden truths that were not revealed in printed works, their loss was deemed especially significant: "The greater someone's life's work is, the deeper the roots of this intellectual work will reach into the soil of the economy, conventions and law of his time, and the more this work will breathe and grow in a diverse and lively interaction with the air and light around it. In such a delicate, deep and tangled context, each apparently trivial piece of paper may be an element of causal insight. The completed book says little about the secret of its genesis. Plans, outlines, drafts, letters—this is where the breath of a person's vitality is to be found, just as sketches reveal more of this than finished pictures."[284] With this upward revaluation of outlines and drafts as compared to completed works, Dilthey took up the mantle of the "found among the papers" trope in his concept of literary history. The "apparently trivial piece of paper" thus gained importance not only when it was found among the papers of Leibniz, Kant, Schiller, or Goethe; in the realm of consequent historism, the undoubtedly trivial piece of lettered paper took on fantastic dimensions. This was due both to the broad understanding of what literature was and the programmatic inclusion of the literary remains of second- and third-rate authors in archives of literature. These authors would be included not only as the possible recipients of letters from more important authors, but because without them it would be impossible to study the internal connections within intellectual movements. The ideal of gapless transmission was therefore accompanied by the expansion of what was expected to be transmitted. Anything that was printed constituted an object of literary history. But such objects could only be fathomed by looking at all of the manuscripts that had preceded the printed work, not just the fair copies.

Concern for manuscripts was institutionalized by the historism of the nineteenth century. The growing synchronous circulation of printed newspapers was joined by an energetic exploration of unprinted papers from the past. Just as ancient manuscripts had been hunted down in libraries during the age of humanism, this brand of historism turned the entire realm of transmission since that age, both inside and outside of libraries, into its hunting ground. Historism was a diachronic paper machine which continuously passed new manuscripts to philologists for examination and interpretation before feeding them into historical-critical editions; it thrived on the ongoing exchange between the archives of literature and the printed collections in libraries, and it worked on the perpetual transformation of unprinted paper into printed paper.

"People will say: paper and more paper! Is this not a new a form of Alexandrinism?" Dilthey repeatedly invoked the frightening vision of a culture that had become unproductive under the pressure of masses of paper from the past. His counterargument was always that these masses of paper would be tamed by the methods for achieving causal insight which were illustrated by the intellectual movements documented in the papers. The material compilation of sources was the prerequisite for gaining such a causal insight. This is why the "literary estate" was the key category in Dilthey's argument for archives of literature and the perspectival fixed point for their internal organization. Literary estates were collections based not on paper formats but on an author's name, and within them letters were associated not with the name of the recipient but with the name of the writer.

In a witty passage from his description of William Hogarth's copperplate engravings, Georg Christoph Lichtenberg proposed a "Pantheon on signboards" for Germany: "Would it be any worse to lodge in the 'Herr von Leibniz' than in the 'King of Prussia'?" The purpose of this thought experiment is to compare the transmission media of marble and paper, which converge at the inn signboard:

A few more words about the German Pantheon in general. I would not advise a marble one: one can foresee that eventually it would become a stony company of Germans which would not be of much more value than our papery one; even less, for it seems to me it is quite a question whether there are any other monuments at all in the world except papery ones, since tradition has ceded all her privileges to the printing presses, and now in its second childhood carries on a not quite honest traffic on the principle that one hand washes the other. I think the question must be answered in the negative. Even the eternal monuments which our fellow men have erected to themselves upon the rocks of the moon and the borders of the universe through new planets with new satellites, and on the path of the planets and comets, would be nothing without their paper certificates attached. ... On the road to the temple of eternal fame, a man may help himself along to the first few post-stations by means of gold and silver, etc., but whoever would continue his journey cannot do so without genuine paper money. Now let us keep in mind what paper signifies! A field of flax, what a prospect! What is not latent here, as a physicist would say! Oh! whoever goes past such a field, be it on horseback or on foot, he should doff his hat and ponder, not only on latent cuffs for his shirts, but on immortality too. If one wants to do something more, then I should advise signboards, for besides the publicity of marble, they possess all the imperishableness of paper.[285]

Lichtenberg was counting on his readers to be familiar with the clothing-based relationship between flax and paper as well as the bad reputation of paper money. His observation that monuments were made of paper in modern culture put ironic quotation marks around paper's guarantee of immortality. And yet it highlighted a viewpoint that rivaled the philologist's interest in unbroken chains of transmission—namely, the author's concern for posthumous fame. In 1889, when Dilthey published his plea for literature archives, Schiller's literary estate was incorporated into the Goethe Archive that had been founded in 1885, turning it into the Goethe and Schiller Archive. The noun *Nachlass*, or "estate," was not included in Volume 13 of the Grimms' German dictionary, which appeared in 1889. But the concept of a literary estate had formed even before the term itself was legally and philologically codified. Goethe was a prominent example of this. What he left behind (and what he did not) was not merely a legacy; it was the estate of an author who knew that the posthumous publication of unprinted letters, diaries, and fragments erased the boundaries of a work and could have a lasting influence on the overall perception of it. Goethe had what one might call "estate awareness." When he said that he himself would become historic, he was looking at his own work from the anticipated perspective of posterity. His minor writings testify to how he wanted his estate to be dealt with. In 1823, an essay on the "Archive of the Poet and Author" appeared in his journal *Über Kunst und Alterthum* (On Art and Antiquity), and the next year he published a follow-up, "Securing My Literary Estate and Preparations for a True, Complete Edition of My Works."[286] The first essay starts by looking at the thirty-volume edition of Lessing's writings and the role of Lessing's brother Karl, who "was himself a literator and tirelessly collected the surviving works, writings, and even more minor output and whatever else was suited to entirely preserving the memory of that unique man, and continually published them." Here, as always, Goethe's estate awareness revolved not around the immediate survivors but around distant posterity. Goethe undoubtedly emphasized the important role that Karl Lessing had played in publishing his brother's writings in order to provide an example of careful estate management to the people around Goethe himself. But as he began to become "historic" himself, he acted as his own literary executor and thought constantly about the relationship between his unprinted papers and his printed writings. In a note relating to his essay on the author's archive, he wrote under the heading "Preparations for publishing my works": "In the years left to him, the author will turn his attention to editing, refining and securing the accumulated mass of papers."[287] There could be no clearer expression of the equal status given to working on one's literary output and working on one's literary estate.

Goethe did not wait until he was an old man to start gathering and organizing his papers. Ernst Robert Curtius wrote an essay on "Goethe's File Management" describing Goethe's archiving techniques. These were a product of Goethe's employment as an administrator, but they also accompanied his literary works from the moment of their inception. During his third trip to Switzerland in August 1797, Goethe wrote to Schiller that in order to counter the danger all travelers face of passing judgment too quickly, he "had a blank book made, into which I stitch all kinds of public papers that just now fall in my way, newspapers (daily and weekly), extracts from sermons, ordinances, play-bills, price-currents."[288] It is worth keeping this variety of multifariously categorized papers in mind when reading Goethe's 1823 essay concerning the organization of his own literary estate. One of his notes on the "Archive of the Poet and Author" reads: "Surrounded by piles of papers which are organized yet all but useless to anyone save myself." When it comes to managing a literary estate, the perspective needs to be shifted to that of posterity. It was for posterity that Goethe strove for "a neat and orderly collection of all papers, especially those relating to my life as a writer, with nothing neglected or regarded as unworthy."[289] This makes it sound as though Goethe had already organized his papers in accordance with the legacy concept underlying Dilthey's literature archive. But Goethe did not assume the viewpoint of the future philologist when he looked through his published and unpublished writings. The collection he assembled arose from the perspective he had as the author of the works, a perspective he wanted to make binding for the public. The work he put into his literary estate served to verify the unity of his published works. This verification was necessary because, at first glance, the works could have been accused of being the product of "scattered and fragmentary activity," and only the author knew the thinking behind important acts that had been intended but never carried out: "I refrained from doing some things because I had hoped to achieve something better with greater learning; I did not use some of what I collected because I had hoped for a more complete collection; and I drew no conclusions from that which I had in my possession because I feared making an overhasty judgment."[290]

In his remarks "In fraternal remembrance of Wieland," Goethe hinted at the standard upon which he modeled the management of his own literary estate. Wieland's "careful handling of his writings" had started as soon as "the impatience of creation subsided somewhat and the desire to offer up something complete to the community became more forceful and active."[291] For Goethe, creating something complete meant presenting a complete, cohesive body of work by influencing the perception of the work. His work on his own literary estate therefore comprised not only organization, selection, and transmission, but also sealing and destruction. Ernst Robert Curtius pointed out that the large envelopes Goethe liked to use to store his papers were referred to as both "cases" and "bags." Goethe described this method of storage in a letter to Schiller dated January 10, 1798: "I have, namely, kept notes from the beginning, and thus preserved an account of the false as well as of the right steps I had taken, but especially of all my experiments, experiences and ideas; I have now separated the pile, had paper bags made, classed these according to a certain system, and put the different papers into them."[292]

Straight lines lead directly from these classified paper bags to the most spectacular decisions that Goethe made concerning his literary estate: to seal his manuscript of *Faust II* and move the second part of the Walpurgis Night scene from *Faust I* to his "Walpurgis bag." In both cases, important parts of his work were denied publication. Goethe was aware of the time-bomb effect this would have. This is apparent in his comment that the Germans would not be quick to forgive him "if, after my death, my Walpurgis bag should be reopened, and all the Stygian sprites, which I have shut up therein, should break forth to teaze them as they have been teazing me."

By preparing their own literary estates, authors can extend their control over their work beyond their own death. Some of this control is lost whenever an author wants papers to remain unpublished but these papers survive after the author's death. The only way to guarantee that something will remain permanently unpublished is to destroy it and ensure there are no copies. If Goethe had followed Dilthey's rules, he should have saved the letters written to him by other authors with an eye to the integrity of their own literary estates. In Goethe's great auto-da-fé of 1797, when he burned letters that had been sent to him, a contemporary reported that he hesitated for two days over the letters from Johann Heinrich Merck "on account of their intellectual content."[293] In the end, however, this content did not stop him from destroying the correspondence. With this act, he blocked posterity's access to the full correspondence between himself and Merck, even while he initiated and promoted the publication of his correspondence with Schiller while he was still alive. Goethe laid the groundwork for Dilthey's proposed "archives of literature" when he promised that nothing should be "neglected or regarded as unworthy" when his papers were collected. But he put limits on the philologists' interest in unfiltered transmission with the innocuous relative clause which specified that the papers most in need of collection were "those relating to my life as a writer." He defined the dimensions of his authorship through a mixture of transmission and destruction. Merck's letters may well have related to Goethe's "life as a writer," yet his literary estate preserved not this collection of letters but rather the act of destruction to which it fell victim. Despite his respect for the author, Dilthey would have had to restrain Goethe. His plea for archives of literature was a plea for the development of stronger inhibitions toward destroying "helpless masses of paper."

3.2. Henry James, Edith Wharton, and the Autograph Hunt

When a young woman asked Thomas Carlyle in 1873 to write something in her album, he granted her request. But what he wrote to the supplicant—in a carelessly penciled scrawl which could not be attributed to his age alone—was a warning: "Quit that of 'Autographs,' dear young lady; that is a weak pursuit which can lead you to nothing considerable!"[294] The nineteenth century saw a large number of autographs created solely so that they could be added to a collection, in Victorian England and elsewhere. Carlyle knew that whatever he wrote would be an "autograph," even though the handwriting in question scorned the very act of collecting autographs and placed distancing quotation marks around the word itself.

In 1836, the year that Émile de Girardin founded the high-circulation newspaper *La Presse* in Paris, Pierre-Jules Fontaine published his *Manuel de l'amateur d'autographes*, the first manual for fans of autographs. Its list of subscribers; its indices of old and contemporary autographs that were sold at auctions, including the prices they fetched; its bibliographies of works containing facsimiles of the handwriting of famous people—all of these indicated that the book merely ratified a movement that had begun long ago. It ended with the draft of a statute for a future "Societé des Autographofiles." As the market for mass-printed current newspapers grew during the nineteenth century, so too did the market for unprinted paper which was written on by hand, from the past and present.[295]

Autograph collections had existed in France since the late sixteenth century; these were collections of documents, memoirs, emissary's reports, certificates and letters from famous historical figures. But the autograph trade was a more recent development. The first auctions had taken place around 1800, the first autograph catalog had appeared in Paris in 1822, and the number of auctions rose rapidly in the decade that followed. In June 1830, Goethe—who owned an autograph collection himself—wrote to his grandson Wolfgang Maximilian: "Distribute the accompanying pages to sympathetic friends, I wrote them myself and did not write them myself; a riddle that you, such a clever boy, are sure to solve."[296] Not long after, he wrote to Marianne von Willemer and her husband: "Many a time a handwritten note is demanded of me, but I find it increasingly impossible to write some little saying which anyone and no one could take to heart. For this reason I have turned to the panacea of lithography. Then the thing is done once and for all, and one thing or the other can be given to the right person depending on the circumstances. I have enclosed a few; if you would like more of them, I will be happy to send them."[297]

These predecessors to the modern autograph revolved around the center of elaborate autograph collections. Just as the antiquities collectors of the Society of Dilettanti antedated public museums and art history as an academic discipline, manuscript enthusiasts established their collections even before Dilthey called for public "archives of literature" which would preserve such manuscripts in the interests of literary history. These private collections and private libraries did not adjoin political state archives; they adjoined the interior spaces of the private sphere. Within this sphere, autographs took their place alongside bibliophilic treasures, portfolios of drawings, portraits, statues, and jewelry collections.

Dilthey's essays described how the chance that a scholar's literary remains would be passed on in the seventeenth century depended on the author's proximity to academies and libraries. They also revealed how fragmentary were the estates of literary authors even into the eighteenth century. Dilthey thought that the more the "helpless masses of paper" remained tied to the private sphere, the more their chance of survival decreased. Families appeared to him to be potential black holes of non-transmission, and he only mentioned the autograph trade in passing. He identified two types of fragmentation here: With the first type, a literary estate was divided up into different batches held in different locations, while with the second type, individual components continually split off from a large corpus of literary remains. It was by this route that individual manuscripts wound up in autograph collections. The goal was usually not to assemble a complete literary estate but to collect many autographs from many authors, with some authors being represented by several different pieces or even entire bundles of works. The *Handbuch für Autographensammler* (1856) by Johann Günther and Otto August Schulz categorized the "hobby" of autograph collecting as one of the most "noble and ingenious" because it "takes on the estimable task of collecting and organizing the visible relics of thought, the emanations of the intellect, the most expressive daguerreotypes of the psyche of famous, thoroughly distinguished people, in the form of their own writings—within which a single line often characterizes them more accurately than an extensive biography—and preserves them for posterity as monuments which speak for themselves."[298]

Manuals for autograph collectors show how the physiognomic view of the ensemble of a manuscript and the medium on which it was written took on an existence independent from the philological orientation on a cohesive body of work. The term "autograph" emphasizes the connection to the originator even more strongly than the term "manuscript." The fact that an important person had touched the paper, contemplated it, and written on it with his or her own hand became an independent motive for collecting autographs, alongside the goal of creating an appealing contextual relationship between the collected autographs. Dilthey wrote: "The vital conditions which arise for the history of intellectual movements from the fundamental notions of the individual, the period of life and the generation always demand recourse to intimate expressions of life."[299] Dilthey explicitly uses the word "intimate" here in relation to the "devotion to the insignificant" found in the philology of Jacob Grimm.

Philology objectifies relics and collects sources. Philologists do not own the sources they study in archives. Autograph collectors—as the manual says—collect relics. They own the objects of their consideration. They are amateurs, hobbyists, but even they must objectify their hobby and give it scientific traits in order to build up a collection. *"La science des autographes est une science nouvelle,"* Fontaine wrote on the first page of his *Manuel de l'amateur des autographes*, which he considered to be an introduction to this young discipline. Paper knowledge accumulated in the world of autograph collectors, just as it had in the world of watermark research in the nineteenth century. Manuals for autograph collectors included detailed information on the types of paper Schiller used, as well as on wove paper, paper formats, manual and mechanical folds, and the combinations of different inks and papers. They featured extensive sections on paper-based organizational systems and storage techniques for a well-managed collection. In their manual of 1856, Günther and Schulz published long excerpts from the expert reports relating to a case that had been tried that same year concerning forged Schiller manuscripts circulated by the architect Victor von Gerstenbergk.[300] Autograph collectors had to be handwriting and paper experts to protect themselves against such forgeries. On a material level, autograph collectors were related to both archivists and philologists—but they were in competition with public archives.

Nineteenth-century historical novels frequently claimed to base their content on old manuscripts and chronicles, which they quoted in the strange diction of the times as a form of verification. Alessandro Manzoni does this at the start of his novel *The Betrothed*. Relics of a family's or a region's past which reflected the fate of a nation were joined by the peculiar hybrid of the autograph in the literature of the nineteenth century. Like historical novels themselves, autographs were the object of a modern passion for evidence of the past and the vanishing present. In printed historical novels, readers were carried back into the past by means of their imagination. But in the case of autographs, collectors had the past right before their eyes—in unique specimens whose authenticity grew more important as reproduction technologies began to penetrate the world of writing, images, and three-dimensional artworks. Obscure manuscripts which had never before been published became the focus of a passion for a hidden truth which grew in intensity as the public sphere evolved.

In his novella *The Aspern Papers* (1888), Henry James illuminates the inner life of an autograph hunter who hopes to coax an old woman in Venice to give him the letters she received in her youth from the famous romantic poet Jeffrey Aspern. James drew on real events which had taken place in Florence in 1879, when an admirer of Percy Bysshe Shelley had lodged with the old Lady Clairmont, a former lover of Lord Byron and half-sister to Shelley's wife, because he suspected that she had papers from the romantic poet in her possession. The tale that James fabricated from this material owes its dense atmosphere to the irresolvable ambiguity that permeates it. This ambiguity results from the internal self-deception of the first-person narrator, who claims that even his most unscrupulous attempts to find the autographs hidden in the Florentine palazzo where the old woman lives with her niece have been made solely on account of the inestimable significance of the papers for the historical understanding of Jeffrey Aspern. It also results from the understated yet unmissable analogy that Henry James sets up behind his narrator's back: the romantic "Aspern papers" are the object of a desire which is related to sexual desire and which will stop at nothing to achieve satisfaction. From the actual Florentine story, James took the idea that a path to the hidden papers could open up for the autograph hunter if he responded to the ill-concealed intimations of the relatively unattractive niece with a promise of marriage. Like a dragon in an old fairy tale, a threat stands in the way of the treasure hidden in the palazzo and hangs over the narrative—namely, that the hunter will himself become the prey. The goal of the story is not to disclose the secret of the titular papers but to make it unassailable. The upward revaluation of unprinted works which accompanied the "found among the papers" trope reached its zenith and turning point in James's story. Instead of editorial fiction, which surrounded stories with the illusion of a higher truth stemming from the realm of secrecy, we have the fictionalization of the editor. The Florentine palazzo thus stood side by side with the eerie castles of Gothic literature which cast an unbreakable spell over their visitors. In the end, it is not clear whether the Aspern papers ever actually existed, and the narrative snaps shut around them like a clamshell that can never be opened again.[301]

The autographs in *The Aspern Papers* were not affiliated with archives and philology; they were affiliated with the newspapers and journals of the late nineteenth century. They were also affiliated with literary salons, where the liveliness of the discussion about a book based on a spectacular trove of autographs would be in direct proportion to the intimacy of the secrets revealed in it. Henry James was familiar with the debates about "New Journalism" that had been kicked off by the English critic Matthew Arnold. These revolved around the personalization of political reporting, the prevalence of interviews and revelations, and the use of investigative research not just in the political sphere or large commercial enterprises but in the private sphere.[302] The autograph hunter in *The Aspern Papers*, who has tracked down the last untapped source of information about the life of the romantic poet in Florence, thus appears to be a relative to the investigative journalist who does not want to admit to their similarities. He seeks the romantic author's letters not so that he can add them to an autograph collection but so that he can include the sensational love story he hopes to find in them in his biography of his idol. News and sensations come not only from current events in the present but from updates to the past. The previously unknown writings of a prominent author were ideal material for electrifying the high-tension lines between privacy and publicity.

Two years after the publication of *The Aspern Papers*, an essay by Samuel D. Warren and Louis D. Brandeis entitled "The Right to Privacy" appeared in the *Harvard Law Review*. Prompted by unease with the American daily press, this article was an attempt to hinder the undesired publication of "personal writings" by invoking not property rights but the right to one's own "personality."[303] Texts would thus be viewed not as physical property but as a component of personality. Echoing this construction, the autographs in Henry James' story become the object of desire not solely as a body of text but as the "living" manifestation of the physical and intellectual existence of a long-dead author. Like Warren and Brandeis, Henry James argued for stronger fortifications between the spheres of privacy and publicity, and his literary criticism addressed the increasingly frequent publication and upward revaluation of "literary remains" as compared to works published during an author's lifetime. At the same time, however, he knew that the type of privacy he was defending had only crystallized as a counterpart to publicity. He did not give his readers so much as a glance at Jeffrey Aspern's literary remains, but, equally, his narrative was not just a critique of its protagonist's investigations. Instead, its insinuations also fed the reader's "insurmountable desire to know." It kept the romantic author's secret safe while at the same time acknowledging the inescapable need to reveal it.[304]

The American writer Edith Wharton, who was friends with Henry James, picked up on James's theme of autographs caught in the contemporary tension between privacy and publicity and carried it further in her novella *The Touchstone* (1900). *The Touchstone* opens with a newspaper announcement placed by a literature professor looking for letters from the deceased author Margaret Aubyn, whose biography he plans to write. The professor promises to "promptly return any documents entrusted to him." The young man who reads the announcement in a club on Fifth Avenue in New York has a large number of the author's letters in his possession, as for years he had been the recalcitrant object of her futile love. Now he wants to marry, but he fears that his precarious financial situation will prevent it. The back room of the club is not a study, and the young Stephen Glennard is neither a scholar nor someone with a literary education, but the novella in which he plays the main role follows the old motif of the pact with the devil. After reading the announcement, he begins to ponder the idea of capitalizing on the packets of letters by entrusting them not to a literary archive, in the form of the professor, but to the book market. The role of the seducer is played by one of his friends, who has just added an autograph collection to his exquisite library, in which the bindings of books play just as great a role as their content. The dandy presents to him a "queer little collection," which was Wharton's nod in the direction of James's *Aspern Papers*: " 'half a dozen of Shelley's letters to Harriet Westbrook. I had a devil of a time getting them—a lot of collectors were after them.' Glennard, taking the volume from his hand, glanced with a kind of repugnance at the interleaving of yellow crisscrossed sheets. 'She was the one who drowned herself, wasn't she?' Flamel nodded. 'I suppose that little episode adds about fifty per cent to their value,' he said meditatively." Edith Wharton's protagonist enters into a pact with the devil which is really a pact with the market: "He sat a long time staring at the scattered pages on his desk; and in the sudden realization of what they meant he could almost fancy some alchemistic process changing them to gold as he stared."[305]

He quickly finds an interested publisher, and the two-volume edition of letters to an unnamed recipient from the famous Mrs. Aubyn—who had always tried to separate her private life from her work—becomes a bestseller. In the literary salons, it causes an uproar both as a book of revelations and an object of speculation as to whether the owner's publication of the letters, which are of obvious literary value, was legitimate. With every devil's pact there is a price to pay, and that price is always the life of the person who entered into the pact. In this case, the young man who established the economic foundations of his marriage by selling the letters becomes a public mystery himself by revealing the mysteries of his deceased friend. The price of transmuting paper into gold is that, as both the recipient and anonymous seller of the letters, he is forced to drift through his own house and his marriage like an uncanny doppelgänger. The ironic thrust of the story is that this internal disintegration makes him much more interesting than the banal young man to whom the famous author had written her letters. Like Henry

James, Edith Wharton does not quote a single word from these letters, even though her entire novella revolves around their publication. She was also on the side of the "right to privacy," and she also concealed the "personal writings" in her narrative as if in a clamshell.

By enclosing them within this shell, the "literary remains" and "personal writings" that were of most interest to the public were symbolically denied to the public while being exploited as a literary motif at the same time. The shell was filled with the unmistakable rustle of scandal and sensation, the echo of the printing presses that turned unpublished papers into gold. The professor to whom Stephen Glennard could have sent the autographs did not want to buy them, he only wanted to evaluate them for his biography. It would have helped him had the letters been preserved in one of Dilthey's "archives of literature." Wharton's novella thus illustrates the tension between the autograph trade and public archives, entities which were in competition with each other even when the stakes were not life secrets but merely the secret behind the creation of texts. Modern edition philology was interested in the materiality of the writing surface and thus became a paper expert—not in order to peer into the souls of authors, but to study the genesis of texts and the production techniques to which they owed their existence.[306] Philologists usually studied the manuscripts in an archive in terms of works that had been published long before, and when they themselves published correspondence or fragments from an author's literary estate, it was as a complement to the previously published works. An autograph, by contrast, often owed its market value not to the fact that it harbored unknown texts or even secrets but rather—like Kafka's novels and diaries—to its most elemental feature: it was a one-of-a-kind original. Even as it became easier to make facsimiles, an autograph's uniqueness enabled it to elude reproduction, because its authenticity was the thing that could not be reproduced. This is why the autograph trade moved closer and closer to the art trade to which it had always been related. It was always possible to transfer a literary estate directly to a public archive or library, avoiding public auctions altogether. But as literary remains from the Paper Age took on the role of "valuable manuscripts"—a role largely played by medieval documents on parchment in Dilthey's era—the rivalry between private collectors and public archives for their shared objects of desire grew more spectacular.

The scarcity of literary remains from authors such as Friedrich Schiller, who tended to destroy the fair copies and drafts of his work after publication, is one example of this. When a previously unknown fair copy of the last five chorale verses of Schiller's "Ode to Joy" was suddenly discovered and auctioned in October 2011, it fetched 500,000 Swiss francs from a private collector. Despite launching its own donation campaign to finance the purchase, the Weimar Classics Foundation was shut out.

3.3. Laterna Magica: Paper and Interiors

Before the narrator in Adalbert Stifter's *Die Mappe meines Urgroßvaters* (My Great-Grandfather's Portfolio [1847]) comes across the old "leather book" with parchment pages which contains the story he will tell, he has to sift through the "jumble of plunder" between the granary and attic in his parents' house—"bundles of papers, scripts, packages, rolls, various hand tools, binding equipment and other flotsam." A tangle of papers plays the main role in this mess of relics from the past life of the house and its occupants: "With the faint golden shimmer of the statue next to me and the light patter of the rain above me I started my investigation, and after an hour I was up to my knees in paper. What curious, peculiar things! There were completely useless pages, then others with only a few words on them, or a saying—others with cut-out hearts and drawings of flames—my own copybooks, a paper hand mirror with glass that had just fallen out—invoices, receipts, a yellowing document concerning a common pasture—then countless pages with long-faded songs, letters of long-extinguished love, only the prettily drawn shepherds still posed at the edges—then there were patterns for clothing that no one wears anymore, rolls of packing paper in which nothing is wrapped anymore—even our schoolbooks were kept there, and the inside covers still bore the names of all my siblings; each had inherited them from the other and, just as if they had been the last and eternal owner, they would cross out the name of their predecessor with a heavy line and write their own name beneath it in the large handwriting of a child. Next to them were the dates in yellow ink, black ink and then yellow again."[307]

Papers flowed into houses from educational institutions, businesses, and private and official correspondence, only to disappear again or wind up trapped in drawers, cabinets and attics. Compulsory schooling, the bureaucracy of the growing state administrative apparatus, the armies of civil servants, the offices of trade and industry— all of them were ravenous consumers of paper who were responsible for using up the lion's share of writing paper. But they were also paper distribution machines who pumped their printed and unprinted output into the social organism as steadily as the expanding periodical press pumped out newsprint every day.

The bundles of paper described by Stifter harked back to the early nineteenth century. The long-faded songs would have been noted down on handmade paper. But at the time Stifter was writing, the proliferation of paper machines in paper factories had been joined by mechanization processes in the paper processing industry. We have already looked at one of the oldest products of the paper processing industry: playing cards made from layers of paper pasted together. By the eighteenth century, these cards were being produced in special factories, and graphic designs found their way onto their previously blank backs. The nineteenth century saw a transition from woodcut to copperplate engraving, steel engraving, and modern lithography; cutting machines spread out from England, to be joined later by high-speed presses which accelerated the speed of printing many times over. Bookbinding workshops were the source of one main strand of the paper processing industry. The connection between writing materials and stationery was exemplified by the rise of envelopes or "covers," which had played only a minor role in the eighteenth century when letters would be folded and sealed. Envelopes were produced on an industrial scale from the early nineteenth century, and the envelope machines that began to emerge in the 1840s were among the innovations displayed at the Great Exhibition in London in 1851.[308]

At the same time, the number of paper objects in the world of things began to far exceed the world of books, newspapers, letters, forms, files, certificates, and copybooks. Newcomers appeared on the scene, like cigarette paper, which had first been made by machine in France in 1830 and was produced in special factories from the 1860s. Meanwhile, packaging materials such as cardboard boxes, bags, and sacks—which, like playing cards, reached back to the earliest days of European paper production—became mass-produced items for one-time use. These humble characters were counterparts to the "luxury papers" which, since the mid-nineteenth century, had comprised a wide range of machine-made paper flowers, garlands, greeting cards, pictures of saints, and collectors' cards. These papers were not aimed exclusively at the higher classes or the wealthy middle class; some of them found their way into petit-bourgeois and proletarian households as well.[309]

It is hard to overstate how important the short- and long-lived, preserved and exploited products of the paper-processing industry were to the historical profile of the imagination in the nineteenth century and its reservoir of metaphors and symbols. The deep-rooted mutual relations between packaging paper and writing paper found their way into one of the most famous quotes of the nineteenth century, namely, Heinrich Heine's heavy sigh of dismay in view of the prospect of Communism, which he did not want to reject outright: "the nightingales, those useless singers, will be chased away, and alas! my 'Book of Songs' will be used by the grocer to make paper cornets with in which he will pour coffee or tobacco for the old wives of the future."[310] Poetry's descent into an existence as an egalitarian paper bag echoed a topos from the times in which paper was not yet a mass product and grocers often had to meet their requirements by turning to abandoned archives and libraries, the printed and handwritten maculature from publishing houses, or used notebooks. Against this backdrop, the "herring papers" and "coffee sacks" in Jean Paul's *Life of Fibel* became important figures. In the late nineteenth century, shortly before Dilthey bemoaned the loss of Kant's autographs to this old grocers' channel, hygiene regulations put a stop to the reuse of written paper as a bag or pouch for comestibles.[311]

Luxury papers made a dazzling entrance at the Vienna World's Fair in 1873 and were described in the fair's official report as follows:

> Not satisfied with the role assigned to it by the prosaic business and utility industry, paper is crossing the boundaries of everyday life and entering the realm of luxury and fantasy in the shape of flowers and leaves, of richly decorated love letters, cards, chocolate boxes and cartons. It takes the form of glossy labels, badges, candle holders, fans and bouquet holders, paper plates and napkins, and today thousands of human hands in all civilized countries are busy conjuring up the most magnificent flowers and buds from paper, which nearly surpass the natural ones in their luster and color, and creating lace and fringe, silver and gold borders, glossy and varnished papers—in brief, the many luxury goods made from paper which make so many common objects into decorations and ornaments and which are pleasing to the eye of the beholder.[312]

Luxury paper was created when raw paper was printed in color, stamped or punched to create a relief surface, embellished with different materials, shaped into a three-dimensional object by means of gluing, folding, or wrinkling, or turned into crêpe paper by crinkling together a damp sheet of machine-made continuous paper. From around 1860, paper was associated with a concept of luxury that did not revolve around decadence, unrestrained extravagance, or lavish wealth but was instead, at heart, concerned with decoration, with beautifying an otherwise mundane everyday life through accessories and festive adornments. In the eighteenth century, this type of luxury was embodied by Friedrich Justin Bertuch, a publicist, businessman, and propagandist for industriousness who founded the *Journal des Luxus und der Moden* in Weimar in 1786, followed by his "Landes-Industrie-Comptoir" enterprise in 1791. He had previously acquired an old grinding mill which he converted into a paper and pigment mill, and his wife ran his "flower factory" which produced artificial flowers made from silk and fine fabrics with great success. When he spoke of "typographical luxury" he meant special editions printed on good paper, such as Goethe's essay "Das römische Karneval." Moving between English gardens and the everyday side of Classicism, his projects encouraged the cultivation of taste.[313] The works of the classicist Karl August Böttiger, which were published for several years in the *Journal des Luxus und der Moden* starting in 1797, bridged the gap between the exploration of the decorative arts in everyday life in the ancient world and contemporary classical fashions. When Böttiger described the Roman wreaths and artificial flowers made of "papyrus bast" in *Sabina oder Morgenszenen im Putzzimmer einer reichen Römerin* (Sabina, or Morning Scenes in the Dressing Room of a Wealthy Roman Woman [1803]), he depicted them as predecessors to modern artificial flowers.[314] The fabric flowers produced in the factories of the eighteenth century had a great future ahead of them as machine-made products of the nineteenth-century paper processing industry. They had been incorporated into everyday middle-class life, and their stylistic metamorphoses through the age of art nouveau and beyond meant that they could adapt easily to the tastes of the times.

Just as newspapers evolved from luxury items into consumer goods in the nineteenth century, luxury papers also reached a zenith as a consumer product. Their development—into garlands for party decorations, for example—was abetted by the paper machine and ground-wood paper. Their golden age was the time between 1860 and 1930. With the exception of companies such as Hagelberg in Berlin—the world's largest luxury paper factory, which had over one thousand employees in 1900—most luxury papers were produced by small and medium-sized enterprises. Luxury papers were further removed from machine shops than they were from household interiors, where they took the form of tear-off calendars and wall calendars, illustrated notebook covers, devotional images, embroidered house blessings, and genre cards. In private households, consumers were often also the producers and archivists of paper objects. Since the late eighteenth century, pens, scissors, and needles, often in the company of glue, had repeatedly been put to use in the production of paper-based written and visual media. Friedrich Justin Bertuch's *Bilderbuch für*

Kinder (Picturebook for Children [1790]) was addressed not only to the eye but to the hand: "Children must have full control over it, like a toy; they must be able to look at the pictures at any time, they must illuminate it; and with their tutor's permission, they must even be allowed to cut out the pictures and glue them onto pasteboard. A father must not treat a children's picturebook like a good library book that does not belong in a child's hands, he must not protect it or only occasionally relinquish it to be viewed."[315]

It was not only in Classical- and Romantic-era Weimar that the interplay of the eye, the hand, and paper moved to the center of literary socializing. This interplay was relevant to the act of leafing through books and manuscripts, folding and unfolding letters, and reading, but it was also relevant to the production of the pictures surrounding the text. The fashion for silhouettes and papercutting which influenced the correspondence, magazines, and novels of the late eighteenth and early nineteenth centuries was encouraged by Classicism, which placed great value in outlines and contours. Classical treatises on the origin of painting always cited an anecdote found in Pliny concerning the daughter of a potter who drew the outline of her departing love on a wall in order to have a memento of him.[316] The physiognomic theories of Johann Christoph Lavater played a part in making an attraction out of black "shadow paper" and the "shadow profiles" cut from it, because it was thought that a person's inner qualities were revealed not only through the facial features but the shape of the head, which could be copied by using the cut-out negative as a stencil. This reproducibility, along with the speed and ease of creating shadow profiles and even full-body portraits in characteristic clothing and positions, contributed to the popularity of the silhouette. A silhouetting chair was invented which made it possible to copy a profile in a single sitting, like sitting for a painted portrait. But anyone who knew how to skillfully and inconspicuously handle scissors freehand could produce "snapshots" of their contemporaries without the portrayed person ever noticing. The paper silhouettes made of famous artists passing through a town were thus a counterpart to the autographs requested of them. Within social networks of friendships and correspondence, the traits of familiar and unknown individuals which were reflected in their writing could be supplemented with quickly produced images created using scissors—predecessors to the camera. Like letters, papercut images were gifts that were exchanged and sent back and forth. Furthermore, papercuttings were not restricted to portraits; virtuosos such as Luise Duttenhofer, who was surrounded by Swabian Classicism and the educated Stuttgart bourgeoisie, experimented with subjects ranging from puppetry, dance, and carnivals to figures and scenes from ancient mythology and Christian legend.

The punched-out hearts, painted flames, and shepherds that Adalbert Stifter described as random relics in the bundles of papers in the attic could be stored in a special place in the nineteenth century, just like books in a library or painted portraits in a collection—namely, in an album.[317] Albums themselves were products of the aspect of luxury paper that could be traced back to bookbinding workshops, and the wide range of albums that became available indicated how important they were as a medium for the continual archiving of everyday life. Albums were attractive because they could be used for storage, protection, and collection, but unlike an archive, there were practically no rules governing the collection strategy or organizational structure. The scrapbooks that became popular in the early nineteenth century in England—which showed their reverence for cuttings and snippets even in their name—could be used to hold anything at all, and it was up to users to decide whether they would

Court lady, stork, and dancer. Folded and cut design by Hans Christian Andersen, 1860

allow random, chronologically based juxtapositions or opt for a fixed order. In the 1830s and 1840s, there was a good chance that the wood engravings from the *Penny Magazine* in England, the *Magasin pittoresque* in France, and the *Pfennig-Magazin* in Germany would be added to a scrapbook. The papers that were cut from various sources and pasted into an album may have originally served decorative, educational, or pragmatic purposes, but once assembled, they led a second life as objects of contemplation or remembrance. Verses snipped from a magazine, a ticket for the theater or for a train ride, a visiting card, or images cut from an illustrated consumer catalog could be turned into a homemade picture book. And when the paper cutting obsession gripped an author such as Hans Christian Andersen, it could give rise to a whole universe of images made from glossy paper, paper flowers, and newspaper clippings, like real-world counterparts to the tin solider in the fairy tale who sails down the gutter in a boat made from newspaper and falls in love with a paper ballerina.[318]

There had always been something theatrical about the interplay of the eye and the hand when handling printed, illustrated, or blank paper. The frivolous leaflets of the early seventeenth century featured paper flaps which a narrator could lift to reveal a scene of infidelity, for example, and he would create a feeling of suspense by choosing the moment at which to lift the flap—or not.[319] The risqué lithographs or *"Images dites à portes et à fenêtres"* produced in Paris around 1830, which hid their erotic scenes from the prying eyes of voyeurs behind sliding doors and windows, applied the same principle to a modern pictorial medium.[320] But a paper dancer also had the advantage of three-dimensionality. Cutting, folding, and pasting were in league with this three-dimensionality—and with miniaturization. While scenes from the *Iliad* or the *Odyssey* were depicted by history painters on a large scale on canvas (and later on the film screen), they found their way into the everyday surroundings of readers by way of book illustrations and sketches, or through paper dolls. In the first volume of his novel *Anton Reiser* (1785), Karl Philipp Moritz describes how the protagonist reproduces the copperplate engravings from an illustrated edition of *The Adventures of Telemachus* by Fénelon in the form of three-dimensional figures: "When he returned home from Pyrmont he cut out paper figures of all the heroes of *Telemachus*, painted them from the engravings with helmet and breastplate, and set them up for some days in battle array, till at last he decided their fate and raged among them with cruel strokes of his knife, cut open one hero's helmet and another's skull, and saw nothing but death and destruction around him."[321]

Had Anton Reiser been a middle-class child in the nineteenth century, he might have received one of the paper theaters for his birthday which, with the help of translucent paper, elaborate scenery (complete with a starry sky), and printed scripts, fed the theatromania and actors' craze of the time. After the revolutionary wars and battles of the Napoleonic era, ancient heroes were joined in the nineteenth century by whole armies of paper soldiers who reflected the history of nineteenth-century European wars in miniature. They emerged from cut-out sheets and were clothed in uniforms, just like paper jumping jacks and dolls with their fool's costumes and dresses. The descendants of Anton Reiser are depicted in a long passage in *An Old Man's Reminiscences of His Youth* by the painter Wilhelm von Kügelgen, which is dedicated to the papercraft encouraged by a tutor named Senff:

> By varying the colors and by making slight changes in the folds we were able to represent all the component parts of an army, for Senff had made the discovery that the soldiers, by a clever and final manipulation, could be so changed and stretched out as to do duty as horses quite as successfully as men. Nothing was needed but to mount the foot soldiers on the horses. Finally, out of quills and pieces of whalebone small shooting toys were made which did duty as cannon, and which darted the shot with vehemence across the room. I scarcely remember anything that gave me more delight than the equipment of this small paper army and our games therewith. By degrees we each of us augmented the number of our troops to eight hundred or a thousand men: and when putting our battalions in order we drew outlines and maps on the floor with chalk. Whoever after ten shots counted the greatest number of dead had to part with a portion of his territory, so that hourly the geographical boundaries were changing in our room as in the wide world beyond us.[322]

Like the collecting impulse and the keepsake craze, which resulted in luxury papers and various cuttings being added to albums, paper's suitability as an assistive medium for two- and three-dimensional miniaturization and reproduction influenced nineteenth-century culture as whole, not just the world of childhood. The technologies for reproducing objects from nature, art, and industry were so closely allied with paper that, even before the invention of photography, paper was suspected of playing the role of a confederate to epigonism and stylistic eclecticism. In the preface to his treatise "Preliminary Remarks on Polychrome Architecture and Sculpture in Antiquity" (1834), the architect Gottfried Semper attacked the Frenchman Jean-Nicolas-Louis Durand, whose *Précis des leçons d'architecture* (1802), which was based on lectures for engineers at the École Polytechnique in Paris and was reprinted many times, had become the most influential work on architecture in the early nineteenth century. Based on a ruthless Classicism and the basic forms of the square and the right angle, Durand had developed a system for combining standardized building elements whose anti-decorative functionalism was a forerunner to the Crystal Palace of the Great Exhibition in London in 1851. His drawings never featured a perspective projection. Semper called Durand's collection of patterns a counterpart to the assignats of the French Revolution and an expression of paper's dominance over an architecture conceived on the basis of structure:

> Conscious of its guilt and pressured by its creditors, an almost bankrupt architecture seeks relief and recovery by introducing into circulation two kinds of paper currencies. The first are Durand's assignats, which this chancellor of the exchequer of failed ideas has put into circulation. They consist of blank sheets that are divided into many squares in the manner of a knitting pattern or chessboard, on which the plans of buildings arrange themselves quite mechanically. ... Who still doubts their sterling value?—since without a second thought we can gather the most heterogeneous things under one umbrella, everything the ancients threw together so higgledy-piggledy. With them, the first-year polytechnic student in Paris becomes a complete architect within six months: riding schools, baths, theaters, dance salons, and concert halls almost spontaneously assemble themselves on his grids into one plan and carry off the great academic prize. Following such rigid principles, entire cities like Mannheim and Karlsruhe are laid out.[323]

Semper combined this criticism of paper-based standardization—and thus made his attack into a criticism of architectural historism *avant la lettre*—with a diatribe against tracing paper which he claimed led architects to collect past styles as options for their own buildings instead of developing the architecture of the present based on the needs of the present. Tracing papers, oil papers, and "copying papers" in general were constant topics of discussion in the polytechnic journals of the nineteenth century. Semper's early objection to them shows how well suited paper was to becoming a symbol of the aesthetic disposition which led to the production of stylistic copies:

> Through this magical expedient we become absolute masters of ancient, medieval, and modern times. The young artist traverses the world, crams his notebooks full of pasted-on tracings of every kind, then returns home with the cheerful expectation (taking care to show his specimens to the right connoisseur) that soon he will receive the

commission for a Walhalla à la Parthénon, a basilica à la Monréale, a boudoir à la Pompeii, a palace à la Pitti, a Byzantine church, or even a bazaar in the Turkish taste! What miracles result from this invention! Thanks to it our major cities blossom forth as true extraits de mille fleurs, as the quintessence of all lands and centuries, so that in our pleasant delusion we forget in the end to which century we belong![324]

Semper's warning contained a realization that was not tied to the image of the present day being overrun with styles from the past. The abandon with which paper was used as a medium for creating two- and three-dimensional replicas of the external world was not bound to the scrapbook of historical architectural styles. Instead, the reproduction of the world in paper encompassed the buildings of the present as well as the recent achievements of machines and heavy industry. Paper construction kits could adorn the inner worlds of aesthetic historism, but they could also help accommodate one to the continually changing present by providing models which might be called the media of "ensoulment" in the industrial age, to use the words of the art historian Aby Warburg. Right at the start of the nineteenth century, Heinrich Rockstroh's "Instructions for Modeling with Paper: A Useful Pastime for Children" (1802) had been published in Weimar to great acclaim from Friedrich Justin Bertuch. After this, paper models left behind many traces in the literature of memory from the nineteenth century. The painter Kügelgen, for example, gave an account of the Christmas attraction created by his tutor Senff in 1809:

Senff had built up on the floor the city of Constantinople, with houses, palaces, and mosques made of paper. Nothing could be more elegant than this paper city. Thickly strewn white sand indicated the land; blue sand the sea, which was alive with ships. After Senff had given a rapid description of the most striking points, he remarked that Constantinople had often been burned, and therefore he set fire to the first house in the Pera suburb. Soon the flame broke forth, seized the nearest building, then the whole street, rushed toward the other streets, sprang into the wells which were filled with spirits, and spread over the whole city. At last the blaze caught the seraglio, whose numerous towers sparkled up as miniature fireworks, thus concluding the entertainment with the due amount and kind of noisy explosion. In such fashion as this, our teacher knew how to furnish us with subjects and suggestions continuously; for naturally, we were eager to imitate everything—from the small nutshell lamps up to the small ships and paper buildings. The fortifications and cities, which previously we had merely traced in outline for our warlike sports, now rose to all the dimensions of space, and we acquired in many ways knowledge and skill.[325]

Paper model kits known as "Le Petit Architect" in France and "Der kleine Baumeister" in Germany emerged in the 1860s and made it possible to reconstruct not only distant lands and cities, but also the attractions of the immediate present: the palace of the International Exhibition in Paris in 1867, locomotives and steam engines, the Statue of Liberty in New York, the newly constructed Eiffel Tower. The paper objects, figures, and replicas of the nineteenth century found their way into the literature of the early twentieth century as materials from the interior world. One example of this is the passage about the Victory Column in Walter Benjamin's *Berlin Childhood Around 1900*: "On many days, people would be standing there up above. Against the sky they appeared to me outlined in black, like the little figures in paste-on picture sheets. Once I had the buildings in place, didn't I take up scissors and glue-pot to distribute mannikins like these at doorways, niches, and window-sills?"[326] And in Marcel Proust's *In Search of Lost Time*, the unfolding of memories—which is also, and above all, the unfolding of the perceptions contained within them—is tied to the taste of the madeleine, but also to Japanese paper:

And as in the game wherein the Japanese amuse themselves by filling a porcelain bowl with water and steeping in it little pieces of paper which until then are without character or form, but, the moment they become wet, stretch and twist and take on colour and distinctive shape, become flowers or houses or people, solid and recognisable, so in that moment all the flowers in our garden and in M. Swann's park, and the waterlilies on the Vivonne and the good folk of the village and their little dwellings and the parish church and the whole of Combray and its surroundings, taking shape and solidity, sprang into being, town and gardens alike, from my cup of tea.[327]

4

The Inventory of Modernity

4.1. Typewriter Paper, Deckle Edges, and White Space

Iron and steel—as embodied in big machines, locomotives, and networks of railroad tracks—formed the hard skeleton of industrialization. But this skeleton was wrapped in paper, the pliable medium of technical and civilizational modernization, on the street and in the home, at school and in administration, in the office and the warehouse. World War I was accompanied by a paper shortage, but it was also a catalyst for the expansion of paper. The Treaty of Versailles was written on parchment, but through tons of leaflets and newsprint it was forged into an ideological weapon. Like the assignats of the French Revolution, the inflation of the year 1923 was a challenge to paper production in Germany. The Giesecke & Devrient printing company in Leipzig developed a special, very thin banknote paper which it fed into twelve printing machines running simultaneously.

The usage statistics of the German Pulp and Paper Association for the year 1928 divided paper into different types depending on its use: 32 percent packaging; 26 percent newspapers; 20 percent magazines, books, pictures, printed materials; 14 percent writing and drawing paper; and 8 percent miscellaneous, including toilet tissue, for example. This range of uses had developed by the end of the nineteenth century. The high percentage of packaging paper reflected the intensive circulation of goods and consumption, while the high percentage of newsprint reflected the evolution of the daily newspaper into a mass medium.[328]

In the nineteenth century, steam power had supported the industrialization of paper production. The rising consumption rates of the twentieth century were a product of electrification combined with complete automation. Webs of paper grew wider and moved forward faster, and the rollers for mechanical dry pressing were improved, as were the steam-heated cylinders for thermally expelling the water in the paper as well as the calenders that the paper snaked through in the smoothing phase. Like mechanization, electrification was a universal principle. It affected the production sector as well as everyday life as a whole; it brought electric lights, telephones, radios and new household appliances into private homes. From the late nineteenth century, this ever-expanding electrification took its place alongside the mass saturation of the social organism with paper-based media and daily routines. Like paper, it offered a growing number of options for storing and circulating words, images, and data. Substitution, competition, symbiosis, and parallelism are models which describe the overlap and mutual penetration of electrification and paper expansion in the twentieth century.

The telegraph had been allied with paper machines and rotary presses in the nineteenth century; many newspapers, such as the *Daily Telegraph* founded in London in 1855, bore its name in their title as a promise of topicality, just as newspapers included "messenger" and "post" in their names to pay tribute to the older partners of the periodical press. When experiments proved the existence of electromagnetic waves in the late nineteenth century, the telegraph went "wireless"—but, above all, a door opened up to the development of radio. The dissociation of wireless telegraphy and newspapers claimed a victim in the long term, a paper-based medium in which the atmosphere of topicality generated by the periodical press had coalesced: the "extra edition." Originally a quantitative supplement to a newspaper, it acquired a temporal accent in the Napoleonic era when it served the purposes of rapidly spreading news from the battlefields. Like telegrams in private long-distance communication, extra editions were reserved for events of striking importance. It was only thanks to the combination of the paper machine and the rotary press that they became a mass medium for the intensified experience of the present as a "historic moment." They were the key medium of topicality during the July Crisis of 1914 and the outbreak of the Second World War. Karl Kraus's play *The Last Days of Mankind* captures this in the very first scene and elsewhere: "NEWSPAPER HAWKER: Extra edition! Heir to the throne murdered! Culprit arrested!"[329] By the start of World War II, radio had already taken over as the key medium of topicality. The extra edition survived World War II, but its function as a medium for breaking news had been lost to television and radio.

These substitutions of electric media for paper-based media were countered by a wealth of short- and long-term symbioses in the twentieth century. The railway had resulted in timetables, and now the telephone was joined by the telephone book, and the paper tentacles of a range of special periodicals encircled the gramophone, radio, and television. In private homes, trade, and industry alike, mechanization and electrification went hand in hand. In this new constellation, paper and electric media mutually shaped the environment. This is also why Paul Valéry was able to metaphorically pass electrical currents through paper in 1932. Paper did not have to be electrified itself in order to enter into a relationship with this new environment.

The mechanization of writing and the diffusion of cinema and then radio were parallel processes in the early twentieth century. Huge anthologies could be filled with excerpts from the books, diaries, and letters of authors, journalists, and philosophers from the late nine-

Extra supplement to the *Frankfurter Oberpostamtszeitung*, April 7, 1814

teenth to the late twentieth century in which the typewriter is welcomed and scorned, cursed and embraced as an indispensable companion. And there are just as many subtle observations on the dissolution of the unit of the hand, paper, and pen—which had become a steel nib by the nineteenth century—and complaints about the typewriter's deindividualization of writing. But the arguments from the authors' perspective concerning the relationship between handwriting and typewriting were just background noise drowned out by the swelling staccato of type bars pounding letters into typing paper. This is because the office was the typewriter's headquarters. It was in the office that the typewriter's assets came into their own: it could match the speed of writing to the speed of dictation when used professionally, and it could be turned into a copying machine by inserting several sheets separated by carbon paper. The male scriveners we met in the form of Balzac's legal assistants, Dickens's Mr. Nemo and Melville's Bartleby, morphed into an army of female stenotypists, a permanent fixture in movies, on the radio, and in illustrated magazines.[330]

Typewriter paper showed a tendency for plurality and standardization. In the world of the office, the single sheet wound into a typewriter was associated with the stack of paper from which it was taken, and the stack, in turn, was formed of paper of a standard format and quality that could withstand the type bars. The DIN 476 paper size standard established in Germany in 1922 by the German Institute for Standardization, following negotiations between public authorities, industry, paper producers, paper sellers, and book printers, was based on an aspect ratio of $1 : \sqrt{2}$, enabling the size to be scaled up or down by doubling or halving a page. The old lines of tradition relating to standardization were thus adopted and systematized under the conditions of industrial paper production. We have seen how even Arab papermakers established formats which were coordinated with one other, and a standardization ratio of $1 : \sqrt{2}$ was proposed during the French Revolution shortly before the invention of the paper machine. In a letter to Johann Beckmann, originator of the word "technology," from October 1786, Georg Christoph Lichtenberg wrote that he had asked an Englishman to find a sheet of paper with formats that were all similar to one another, and he enclosed an uncut sheet of small folio paper which he had discovered was already the size he wanted. In an essay in the *Göttinger Taschenkalender* of 1796 entitled "About Book Formats," Lichtenberg discussed this issue and explicitly acknowledged the anonymous originator of the format, which was postulated by algebra and pleasing to both the writing hand and the reading eye. Lichtenberg rightly suspected that it was no coincidence his normal writing paper happened to be in the calculated format. The "reçute" format of around 31.5 × 44.5 found on the Bologna stone from the late fourteenth century—the early record of European paper standardization we encountered earlier—was a forerunner to "chancery" paper and had an aspect ratio close to $1 : \sqrt{2}$. Algebraic calculations "discovered" a format that had been circulating in Europe for centuries. Jean-Baptiste-Moise de Jollivet, a delegate to the National Assembly in Paris, presented his suggestions for establishing paper formats in the Republic on August 21, 1792, the same day that a proposal for defining the meter as a unit of measurement was submitted to the Assembly. Jollivet's reasoning was not based on history; the goal, as he saw it, was to implement the unrealized reforms of the Ancien Régime for reducing the costs of paper production and storage and simplifying the system of officially stamped papers. He had reached the same conclusion as Lichtenberg, but while the stamped paper act that was passed in November 1798—in which five of the six defined formats followed the $1 : \sqrt{2}$ ratio—allowed for the use of centimeters as a unit of measurement, it was less successful than the motion for a prototype meter that was adopted in July 1796. Mathematically exact implementation would have been beyond his reach in any case. Each sheet of paper scooped out of a vat was still a one-off that was not entirely identical to its neighbor, and neither the paper machine nor the paper cutting machine had been invented yet. It was the mechanization and industrialization of paper production that led to a dramatic rise in the pressure to standardize while simultaneously guaranteeing that the adopted formats could be produced on a mass scale. In particular, the A series of paper formats based on the DIN 476 standard, with its base size of 0.841×1.189 ($=1 \, \mathrm{m}^2$), left a lasting impression on the physiognomy of industrial society, influencing everything from address books, calendars, and files to newspapers and magazines. A few years ago, the French mathematician Benoît Rittaud investigated the square root of 2 as a "universal constant," from the Babylonians through the Egyptians and ancient Greeks and Romans to the Renaissance and the present day.[331] From this perspective, the paper formats of the twentieth century stand shoulder to shoulder with the architectural treatises of the Renaissance as building blocks of the modern world. Within the world of things—in Europe, though not in the USA—A4 paper ($210 \times 297 \, \mathrm{mm}$) is a ubiquitous universal. Jan Tschichold's *The New Typography: A Handbook for Modern Designers* (1928) shows the extent to which this standard was perceived as a sign of modernity after it was introduced. In both word and image, right down to the reproduction and detailed explanation of the DIN 476 standard, this book portrays the new typography as being in alliance with the new paper formats, especially the A4 sheet. Tschichold, like Lichtenberg, found it to be "a practical and pleasant size" and encouraged its use in private correspondence as well as business letters. Throughout the book, typography is treated as a lesson in both type design and paper technology. The rationalization and simplification of paper formats took up position alongside Tschichold's criticism of ornament in contemporary architecture, his criticism of blackletter script, and his arguments in favor of roman typefaces for modern daily newspapers and the radicalized "skeleton letters" of sans-serif roman type. Tschichold's new typography is as concerned with the design of leaflets, advertisements, daily newspapers, magazines, postcards, and posters as it is with books. It places the typewriter on a level with the airplane and the automobile. This was not a random juxtaposition. Tschichold embraced standardized paper formats as tools for saving materials and time: less common formats would not need to be stockpiled in large quantities; the divisibility of the initial format would minimize material losses; the repetition of sheet sizes would benefit bookbinders; it would be possible to simultaneously print materials of different sizes; calculations and price lists would be simplified; and customers could be dealt with more quickly.[332] Like the typewriter, the DIN 476 paper standardization system—with its base A series and the B, C, and D series derived from it for related paper products such as envelopes, binders, and folders—led not only to standardization but to the intensification and acceleration of written correspondence.

With a certain degree of deviation tolerance, even handmade writing paper and envelopes can be aligned with DIN standards. But their deviation from machine-made paper is never gradational, no matter how closely they adhere to the standards. It is paper of a different type. In the second volume of the Grimm brothers' dictionary, published in 1860, "handmade paper" is tersely defined as "paper scooped from a vat, as opposed to machine-made paper." Unfortunately, no usage example is given which could indicate when the term first appeared. It can only have arisen with the spread of paper machines. Prior to this, handmade paper did not need to be a compound word—it was just paper. As "vat paper," it became a special item in the inventory of paper and stayed true to its old resource base, rags. Its mark of authenticity is the irregular deckle edge on all four sides of the sheet, a product of the dipping process which cannot be created after the fact. There is a DIN standard (6730) that protects handmade paper from imitations; such paper has its own market and its own price. Anyone buying it today would never cut off the deckle edge, as was usual when handmade paper was the only paper.

The paper machine did not do away with handmade paper; it turned it into an option which—like wove paper in the eighteenth century—was attractive for the way it signaled a deviation from the norm. In the age of cheap, mass-produced paper, handmade paper is an island of remembrance harking back to a time when paper was scarce and relatively expensive. It would be easy to define it in terms of the kind of passion for retro design, anti-modern nostalgia, or snobbery that places value in social distinction as expressed through handmade letter paper and the calling cards that go with it.

But falling back on unnecessary pre-modern traditions is a typically modern gesture, no different than the use of packing paper or of newspapers and posters saturated with the spirit of disposability in the collages of avant-garde artists. These gestures always involved more than just playing with deviation or invoking symbolic stimuli, however; the empirical, physical materiality of paper had to be accommodated in their manifestos when it was integrated into a framework of aesthetic standards which was often no less strict that the system of DIN standards. William Morris, the leading figure in the fine printing movement in late nineteenth-century England, was a student of John Ruskin and critic of Victorian factories and mass production. A socialist who wanted to liberate labor through a return to craftsmanship, he dedicated the last years of his life to a "typographical adventure." With his Kelmscott Press which was founded in 1891, he turned his attention to the production of the "Ideal Book" and, in the process, became a historian of printing, typefaces, and paper. These books were exclusive, not because of any elitist artificial scarcity but because of the great effort that had to go into their creation. They were printed with a hand-press on handmade linen paper, or occasionally on fine parchment. Morris, who despised the roman Bodoni typeface of the late eighteenth century, developed his own neo-Gothic typefaces with an eye to works from the early days of the printing press in the fifteenth century and pages from medieval books.[333] All of this was free quotation, an appropriation of older forms out of an aesthetic opposition to modern works and mass printing on poor paper. But it was also an attempt to create a stage for modern poetry on paper in which every material element was in harmony. The gloomy grey that had settled over paper in *Bleak House* was to be driven off in favor of striking black-and-white contrasts; the relief of the letters was to come to the fore again; and the compact typeface with tight word and line spacing was to appear to readers as a strong and clear bodily presence. The contrast between individual design and mass production was not the only genuinely modern aspect of the Arts and Crafts Movement. This secession movement from the world of the rotary press and groundwood paper also encompassed the contemporary dramatization of gender tensions and debates about the decadence and feminization of modern civilization. In 1892, the American printer Theodore Low De Vinne published his "Masculine Printing" manifesto, in which he praised handmade paper not on account of its rarity or costliness, but as a tool of simplicity, clarity, directness, and masculinity in the fight against the feminization of the world of books. In opposition to rotary presses and fonts with sharp serifs which only fleetingly touched the repellent groundwood paper during the high-speed printing process, De Vinne advocated strong, manly printing which melded organically with handmade paper.[334] He said the combination of the rotary press and modern paper brought about a weakened, feminine form of text, while the old combination of linen paper and the handpress brought about a stronger, masculine form. He felt that the weaker gender was embodied in the standard typography of Victorian novels, which were aimed at a growing female audience. In De Vinne's view, such type wavered above the grey-white empty space on a page, its letters seeming to resist adhering to the paper. The relationship between the printing press and paper therefore reflected contemporary gender mythology. However, the polemic against the "emasculation" of the industrial book and the argument for handmade paper as a source of vitality did more than just express a sense of unease with anemic women who withered at the slightest touch; for both De Vinne and William Morris, the arguments for robustness, strength, and clarity, for a virile modern age, were also heralds of the criticism of ornamentation. Morris countered the light typography of Victorian novels by producing a massive edition of Chaucer's *Canterbury Tales*. The American partisans of "masculine printing" moved Walt Whitman's work into position against "feminine printing." With the limited edition of *Leaves of Grass* published by Random House in 1930, the printers Edwin and Robert Grabhorn fought back against the playfully decorative elements that had appealed to Victorian taste with a resoluteness that both De Vinne and Morris would have admired: large folio sheets of handmade linen paper with letters printed with such pressure that they were nearly sculptural.

The first edition of *Leaves of Grass* had been published anonymously in 1855, though with a frontispiece portrait of the author as a casual young man, a steel engraving based on a daguerreotype: his left hand in his pocket, his right hand on his hip, his collar open to reveal his undershirt, his black hat at an angle on his head. The title page of this first edition was as simple as it was challenging: oversized Scotch Roman type, with the word "Leaves" in 72 point and the word "Grass" in 108 point.[335] This title page bothered many readers because it recalled commercial rather than literary type, and its cool, hard aura stood in calculated contrast to the vital, sexual aura of the author's portrait. On the cover, however, the letters were floriated almost to the point of illegibility, as though the words had been sown or were growing out of the book. In the latest German translation of Whitman's book, Jürgen Brôcan has rendered the title as *Grasblätter* (Leaves of Grass) for the first time instead of the usual *Grashalme* (Blades of Grass), in part because the word "leaves" is encircled by associations which encompass both the organic/vital and the technical/cool side of the title: "In the printer's jargon of the time, 'grass' was an experimental page that had been typeset in one's free time, while 'leaves' was a stack of paper. In the work of Justus Liebig, Whitman had read that 'leaves' was the scientifically correct term for the green parts of all plants, including grass."[336] Few readers would have understood the reference to book printing, and just as few would have appreciated the biological basis of the title. Nonetheless, *Leaves of Grass* was a well-chosen name. Even in common parlance, "leaves"—unlike "blades"—were hybrids of nature and culture, something found not only in fields but also in books. They were associated with the unbound leaves on which the author had written. Furthermore, deviating from the commonly expected "blades" drew more attention to the "leaves." Over the four decades in which his main work grew and evolved, Whitman frequently made compromises in the design of the editions in keeping with the tastes of the times. But he remains a key figure in the adoption of the leaf and the page by the aesthetic modern world.

The book historian Jean-Henri Martin once remarked that the typographic innovations of the mid-seventeenth and early eighteenth centuries had contributed to the "triumph of white space over black type."[337] Marginal notes began to disappear, and footnotes lost ground as well. From the seventeenth century, poems—at least short-form ones—developed a closer relationship with white space. The ragged margins of free verse and Mallarmé's "Coup des Dés" laid the groundwork for the aesthetic use of the contrast between black and white. However, the prominence of white space was not tied to the exclusive realm of Symbolist poetry any more than it was to bibliophilic editions of books on handmade paper. In its rejection of a central axis and its arguments for asymmetry as a design principle, Tschichold's New Typography made the emphasis on white space a priority for advertisements and business letters on DIN paper as well: "In asymmetric design, the white background plays an active part in the design. The typical main display of the old typography, the title-page, showed its black type on a white background that played no part in the design. ... In asymmetric typography, on the other hand, the paper background contributes to a greater or lesser degree to the effect of the whole. ... The New Typography uses the effectiveness of the former 'background' quite deliberately, and considers the blank white spaces on the paper as formal elements just as much as the areas of black type. In this way the New Typography has enriched the art of printing by giving it a new medium of expression. The powerful effect in many examples of the New Typography depends directly on the use of large areas of white: white is always stronger than grey or black."[338] Anyone familiar with the garlands, roses, glasses, bottles, and columns of smoke made of letters which are found in Baroque poetry, or with the ancient tradition of pattern poetry, may question whether playing with white space was an exclusively modern development, or whether the paper background played only a passive role in the visual poetry of earlier times.[339] But if we look beyond the world of books into the space in which it was embedded, then Tschichold's emphasis makes sense, as it reflects how white advanced to become the color that signaled modernity. The management of white space in the New Typography is related to white gallery walls, the emphasis on light and transparency in architecture, and the social utopian mythology of light and air. In view of this, it is worth remembering that in his later years, Jan Tschichold rejected the naïve idea that paper contributed most to modernity by physically getting whiter and whiter. In fact, he felt so uncomfortably dazzled by offset paper that he protested against it: "What catches the untrained eye in a collection of printing papers is of course the detergent-white offset paper. ... Perhaps because the people in the offices of print shops fall victim to the allure that emanates from a sheet of stark white blank paper; perhaps also because some feel it's more 'modern'—does it not remind one of refrigerators, modern sanitary appliances and the dentist's office?—or perhaps because white offset works best for art prints and no one makes toned art paper; because one wants the finished product to be 'brilliant'; and perhaps also because inexperienced lay persons had a say in the matter, we have too terribly many pure white books today."[340]

This mistrust of "clinical" white may recall the potential for horror that literature and films of the nineteenth and twentieth centuries found in the color white, from Adalbert Stifter and Herman Melville through Georg Wilhelm Pabst's *The White Hell of Piz Palu* (1929) to the snowed-in hotel in Stanley Kubrick's *The Shining* (1980). At the same time, however, the skepticism toward too-white paper also harked back to early criticisms of machine-made paper. Ever since John Murray's *Practical Remarks on Modern Paper* (1829), bleached paper had been suspected of having gained extra whiteness at the expense of durability. Tschichold's warning against using offset paper for printing books was therefore accompanied by an elegiac bow in the direction of handmade paper and its pre-modern white hue:

> Raw material used for making paper has to be bleached chemically before it attains a stark white color. But unbleached paper is not only more durable, it is also more beautiful. Today it is very rare and shows up only in the form of handmade paper. The wonderful tone of our oldest printed books and—older yet—paper manuscripts has stood the test of time and remains as beautiful as ever, provided the books have not suffered from water damage or decay. When one praised 'pure white' paper in days gone by, what was meant was the slightly ecru tone that unbleached paper took on from the linen and the sheep's wool, the original material from which paper was made. Even today this tone is the most beautiful of all.[341]

4.2. James Joyce, Newsprint, and Shears

When Leopold Bloom attends the funeral of Patrick Dignam in James Joyce's *Ulysses*, the thought crosses his mind that even if you live alone for your whole life, you still need someone at the end to put you in the ground. With subtle logical consistence, this thought reminds Bloom—who here and elsewhere is revealed to be a reader of Defoe—of the most famous example of long-term solitary living: "Say Robinson Crusoe was true to life. Well then Friday buried him. Every Friday buries a Thursday if you come to look at it."[342] This dry observation has a double meaning if one takes into account that this thought is sparked in the mind of an ad canvasser. In the following chapter, Bloom will be busy placing an ad with patriotic keys for a Mr. Keyes. And in the editorial office of the *Freeman's Journal* for which he works, he will have a thought that is like an echo of his realization in the cemetery: "One story good till you hear the next."[343] Every Friday buries a Thursday—especially in the world of newspapers: the Friday edition buries the Thursday edition.

In the Aeolus chapter, Leopold Bloom dives deep into a world in which the preceding day is continually buried. This episode is subject to the god of the winds, in part because journalists, editors, and proofreaders were closely associated with the old windbag imagery and were accused of blowing hot air. From the start, it is set in a sphere of ceaseless physical movement and the acoustic surge of shouts, machinery, and traffic. As would be expected from the old alliance between newspapers and transportation, the glimpse we receive of the editorial office is preceded by a glimpse of the general post office and its mail carts. A telegram boy bursts into the newspaper office that Leopold Bloom has entered, throws an envelope on the counter, and shouts one word before rushing off again: *Freeman*, the name of one of the newspapers represented in the office. Newspaper boys call out the headlines, and Bloom steps over packing paper on his way to the reading closet. In passing, Leopold Bloom reveals the secret of the business: "It's the ad and side features sell a weekly, not the stale news in the official gazette."[344] The growing importance of ads had influenced more than just the weekly press since the mid-nineteenth century; some newspaper theorists in the first third of the twentieth century viewed the editorial part of the paper merely as a tool for creating ad space. Bloom's newspaper theory is a theory pro domo. It reveals not only the secret of the newspaper but also why it is Bloom who is the novel's protagonist, not an editor or author. Bloom is the one who just drops into the editorial office; he sees how the newspaper is technically produced, the "obedient reels feeding in huge webs of paper" in the printworks; he is the ideal observer. He knows that a newspaper not only contains news, not only continually buries the day before, but is also a medium for the return of the same old elements, that ads are only effective if they are placed repeatedly. He negotiates with the newspaper's foreman concerning the number of months that Mr. Keyes' patriotic ad should run.

Prior to this, he had visited the man with the shears—Red Murray, who is responsible for newspaper clippings in the office—and gotten a mockup ad to take to the *Telegraph* later: "Red Murray's long shears sliced out the advertisement from the newspaper in four clean strokes. Scissors and paste."[345] With the "cut square" in hand, Bloom makes his way through the editorial office and printing works. The clipping is an unassuming yet important requisite of his work. In her enlightening study of the newspaper clipping as a "modern paper object," Anke te Heesen has shown how this mini-medium emerged from the industrialization of the periodical press in the nineteenth century.[346] Her book explains how, from the 1880s, newspaper clipping offices joined telegraph offices in European cities, and how their customers were individuals as well as institutions. Newspaper clippings were attractive for their feedback effects; collections of clippings served as a medium of self-observation and evaluation for

editorial offices, as a source of information for the young academic
disciplines of sociology and history, as research tools for individual
academics, as a reflection of fame for celebrities, and as evidence of
their insignificance for unsuccessful artists.

Newspaper clipping collections did not duplicate newspaper
archives. They were produced when assistants, most of whom were
female, scanned newspaper pages for specific terms, marked them,
and then handed them to other assistants, most of whom were male,
to be cut out. The collections were assembled not according to an
ongoing chronological registry but by regrouping data according to
keywords. This resulted in a second-order paper medium which
lengthened the circulation of the short-lived daily newspaper by
taking individual elements from it, integrating them into a new system
and feeding them back into the social organism. But the rise of the
newspaper clipping was not tied exclusively to professional clipping
offices. Every newspaper reader—and every author—was a potential
producer of newspaper clippings. We have seen how private archival
formats for readers emerged in the households of the nineteenth
century through scrapbooks and albums. The industrialization of the
press and the albums of the nineteenth century became sources for
the avant-garde artists who established the collage as a permanent
fixture in modern art.

Leopold Bloom is a professional user of this small paper medium.
He has old ads cut out of a newspaper so that new ones can take
their place. He is more closely connected to the newspaper's smaller
formats than to its headline articles. This becomes apparent when he
walks through the case room and passes an old, bowed, bespectacled
man, the "dayfather," who is responsible for miscellanea. Bloom is
familiar with the section in which he wants to place the key ad from
Mr. Keyes: "Queer lot of stuff he must have put through his hands
in his time: obituary notices, pubs' ads, speeches, divorce suits, found
drowned."[347] This last notice is a classic—we encountered it in
Balzac's *La peau de chagrin*. But a lot changed between Balzac and
Joyce. The *faits divers* had become a small-scale superpower. No
longer an incidental addition to a paper, they were now a narrative
mini-genre with its own rules, a setting for the clash of coincidence
and causality. Just as the serial novel relied on tension, the *faits divers*
relied on surprise.

Hanns Zischler and Sara Danius traced the rise of the *faits divers*
and their literarization, taking James Joyce at his word when he wrote
to the composer George Antheil in 1931: "I am quite content to go
down to posterity as a scissors and paste man."[348] According to
Zischler and Danius, Joyce—like Leopold Bloom—was an expert

utilizer (and collector) of newspaper clippings, and his main area of interest was the *faits divers*. He divided up the Aeolus chapter using perplexing, ironic captions which play a rhetorical game with newspaper headlines ("How a great daily organ is turned out") and make parts of the novel appear to be newspaper articles. He recognized and appreciated that newspapers not only report events but are events themselves, and he adopted the newspaper's strategy of depicting everyday life in order to tell his "little story" of a single day. But the little story is not a *fait divers*; it is a great novel. It marks the vanishing point in a long series of negotiations between the European novel and the newspaper. In Joyce's work, the newspaper's development into a mass medium is both content for the novel as well as a formative force behind it. The novel takes on the challenge and absorbs the energies circulating through the newsprint. Its goal is self-assertion, not adaptation to the other medium.

For a long time, this self-assertion was supported by a strong authority figure: the narrator. When the press first began to flourish in England and negotiations between the novel and the newspaper were well underway, Henry Fielding—in one of the narrator's asides to the audience typically found at the start of chapters in his book *Tom Jones*—made fun of the historians who felt "obliged to fill up as much paper with the detail of months and years in which nothing remarkable happened, as [they employed] upon those notable eras when the greatest scenes have been transacted on the human stage. Such histories as these do, in reality, very much resemble a newspaper, which consists of just the same number of words, whether there be any news in it or not. They may likewise be compared to a stage coach, which performs constantly the same course, empty as well as full."[349] Because it is not subject to the harsh law of periodicity, the novel can teasingly proclaim its sovereign power to adapt the narrative rhythm and distribution of content to the course of events—without mentioning, of course, that it determines the course of events itself as it sees fit. In Joyce's work, the empty stage coach is the weekly paper *Titbits*, which Leopold Bloom reads in the outhouse, the realm of Aeolus, god of the baser winds, flatulence. It is in keeping with Joyce's love/hate relationship with the baser products of the press that the cheap weekly should make an appearance in the toilet. *Titbits* was cobbled together from books, magazines, and other newspapers, a raw counterpart to a newspaper clipping collection. Bloom's expert eye does not fail to see that, in mid-June, it is an empty stage coach. "Print anything now. Silly season."[350]

Unlike Fielding, however, Joyce shows us what is inside the empty coach. His novel digests even the indigestible and absorbs the aroma of *Titbits*. The novel's sovereignty is apparent in how it does away with the traditional narrator and invents a new form so that its narration of the little stories of day-to-day life can compete with the daily and weekly press. But what are we saying when we say that *Ulysses* assimilated the world of newsprint, its makers and readers alike? Hadn't that happened on a wider scale back in the nineteenth century? Wasn't a serialized novel—which actually appeared in a newspaper and was subject to its periodical publication—closer to the modern press than Joyce's book? And hadn't Balzac, in his tale of the printer David Séchard, dedicated an entire novel to telling the story of the birth of modern newsprint? All of this was true, but it did not mean that Fielding had to resign his post. The narrator never withdrew, not even in newsprint, and when he had Lucien de Rubempré produce a complete little feuilleton, he was unmistakably the figure with authority over the course of events and the rhythm of the narrative.

Marshall McLuhan dedicated his first book, *The Mechanical Bride* (1951), to the business in which Leopold Bloom tries to earn a living: advertising. The book starts with a comparison of the front pages of the "quiet" *New York Times* and the "more sensational" *Journal-American*, which was part of the Hearst empire. The central perspective, linearity, and continuity which gave rise to "typographic man" are even missing from the comparatively quiet *New York Times*. Instead, we have the world of the "mosaic" which anticipates the electronic undermining of printing in McLuhan's media theory; here, the simultaneity and discontinuity of the newspaper page corresponds to the visual technique of Picasso and the literary technique of James Joyce. And we have a hidden homage to Stephane Mallarmé who, in the late nineteenth century, not only wanted to capture the entire world in a book but also realized that in the modern press—and not least in the *faits divers*—aesthetic forces were at work which could not simply be dismissed. Mallarmé had wondered whether the newspaper was perhaps a modern counterpart to the popular *One Thousand and One Nights*. Like Mallarmé's idea, Joyce's *Ulysses* presupposes the existence of the fully developed newspaper page which is independent of the book, with its sections and columns, its intermingled articles and advertisements, the physical juxtaposition of contextually unrelated material. In Joyce's case, the novel takes on not only the *faits divers* as a genre but the entire newspaper page on which these stories appear. But the novel does not want to become like this page. Like the epistolary novel of the eighteenth century which, after over a century of increasingly stable postal service and decades of rapid development in private correspondence, made use of all the formal elements of the letter, *Ulysses* adopts the aesthetic strategies that had been created by the modern press in the nineteenth century. But unlike the epistolary novel, which used typography to create the illusion that it was merely a proxy for the manuscripts it conveyed, *Ulysses* did not resemble the newspaper in its format. It is the "little story" of a single day, but it is not an oversized daily newspaper. It brings non-linearity to the page like Laurence Sterne, to whom tribute is paid in the Aeolus chapter in the caption "Uncle Toby's page for tiny tots." The narrator has invisibly cloaked himself in his techniques, not to remove himself from the novel but to remain undisturbed while he devours and digests the newspaper. His field of action is determined not by the layout of a newspaper page but by the page of a book. This page may contain notes, newspaper-like captions, dialogue, and question-and-answer games, but it remains a book page with a clever paragraph structure,[351] the site of a paradoxical superimposition of simultaneity and non-linearity. It drags newspaper clippings into an encyclopedic novel that is just as much at home in the National Library as it is on the streets of the city.

For this reason, you need to be more than just an experienced newspaper reader if you want to take on *Ulysses*, because the habits of the newspaper reader—skipping articles, ignoring entire pages— will not serve you well. The rhetorical tricks and erudite references, the paragraphs, the allusions and reminiscences that flash into existence and immediately disappear again—none of this is captured by the type of cursory glance that takes in a *fait divers* here, an obituary there, and an ad for potted meat right underneath it. *Ulysses* needs to be read more like the Bible: carefully, repeatedly, and with a willingness to uncover the multiple meanings in the *fait divers*.

Because of this, there is a counterpart to the newspaper clipping with the Keyes ad that Leopold Bloom hopes will help him secure another Keyes ad. "What becomes of it after?" Bloom asks as he watches (and hears) the great printing machines in the newspaper building and imagines that if no one were there to shut them off, they would run on endlessly. The answer: "O, wrap up meat, parcels: various uses, thousand and one things."[352] The oriental fairy tale number has become an assuming adjective heralding the further adventures of waste paper. Ever since buying pig offal from the butcher Dlugacz that morning, Leopold Bloom has been carrying around a piece of cut wrapping paper which hints at the Orient: It features an illustrated ad from a Zionist newspaper. It will not help him in his canvassing. Agendath Netaim, a company on Bleibtreustrasse in Berlin, is advertising for investors in agricultural operations in Palestine. One large theme of the novel is introduced in a small

format here, namely, Leopold Bloom's dual affiliation and non-affil-
iation with the Jewish people and the Irish. By following this ad
through *Ulysses* and taking note of when Leopold Bloom reaches for
it whenever he remembers it, you are rewarded with a novel within
the novel, the story of a newspaper clipping that could never be told
by a newspaper.[353] The ad is an invisible presence when, in the Aeolus
chapter, Moses and the Holy Land appear as rhetorical figures in Irish
politics. It entices with its promises of "orangegroves and immense
melon fields north of Jaffa," with olives, almond trees and lemons,
but in a split second it can turn into a prospectus for a wasteland,
an Old Testament desert landscape with the Dead Sea, Sodom,
Gomorrah, and Edom. The web of references that spread from this
ad throughout the novel grows from scene to scene. It encompasses
the lemony smell of the piece of soap that Leopold Bloom is also
carrying in his trouser pocket. It pops up as a witness for the defense
during the phantasmagorical court scene concerning Mary Driscoll
with which Leopold Bloom is confronted. The scents it evokes also
surround Molly Bloom, her breasts are also melons, and when it
comes to the Holy Land and home, she can vie with Jaffa because
she uses orange blossom water. In a late-night ceremony, shortly
before the end of the novel, Leopold Bloom rolls up the piece of paper
into a thin cylinder and burns it, and from the crater of the resulting
tiny volcano there arises "a vertical and serpentine fume redolent of
aromatic oriental incense."[354] The aroma comes from the Irish soap.
In all of twentieth-century literature, no other piece of newsprint
would have been so swallowed up without a trace in a novel.

4.3. William Gaddis, the Paperwork Crisis, and Punch Cards

In Leopold Bloom's Dublin of 1904, it is impossible not to hear the
voices of the newsboys as they persistently shout out the extra editions with the results of the horse races. They are banking on a
special, feverish type of curiosity. No one hoping for a small win by
betting on a favorite would be indifferent to the news of an outsider's
victory. In the Circe episode, the swaggering Bello is a link between
horse betting and the stock exchange: "Bytheby Guinness's preference
shares are at sixteen three quarters. Curse me for a fool that I didn't
buy that lot Craig and Gardner told me about. Just my infernal luck,
curse it. And that Goddamned outsider *Throwaway* at twenty to
one."[355] Bello bet on the wrong horse, and he ignored an insider tip.
In the first case, he had bad luck. In the second case, he lacked the

skill to act on the knowledge circulating about the stock exchange. In an insider tip, knowledge takes the form of a forecast, but in its raw state it is a stock market bulletin. Stock market news benefited directly from the alliance of the telegraph and the daily newspaper, and stock market dispatches were the main business of the telegraph offices that sprang up from the mid-nineteenth century. They were the hot core of economic topicality. The distribution of handwritten bulletins from the financial markets grew up as a separate business around the stock exchanges. The media of economic topicality not only supplied information to newspapers; they also led to the creation of newspapers: "Charles H. Dow went to New York as a young man in 1879 and worked as a reporter for the *Kiernan News Agency*. For some time, this financial news agency had specialized in compiling stock market bulletins for banks and brokerages. Just five years later Dow went independent and, together with Edward D. Jones and Charles M. Bergstresser, founded his own news agency named *Dow Jones & Company*. The company dealt in financial news—handwritten bulletins for brokers which were distributed around Wall Street by couriers. These bulletins were known as 'flimsies': thin slips of very light paper which were duplicated using carbon paper. This news medium gave rise to the *Wall Street Journal* on July 8, 1889, with Dow as its first editor."[356] Securities transactions and the communication media that carried news of them converged in the course of the industrialization of time and space. Communication media not only mapped the movement of money and blocks of shares, they also influenced the direction of this movement. The transatlantic telegraph cable that was laid in 1866, the stock tickers that came into use the following year, and the telephone—all technologies of long-distance communication—made it possible to transmit daily stock prices between Europe and America and connected stock exchanges that were far removed from one another to form a synchronous space of action.[357] But data not only had to circulate quickly, it had to be stored, archived, and managed quickly as well. The asymmetry between the tempo of synchronous circulation and dramatic growth in the number of financial transactions on the one hand and the slower tempo of data storage and management on the other led to a "paperwork crisis" at the end of the 1960s. It took place in the "nerve center of American capitalism," on Wall Street, and its principal theater of action was the "back office" of the securities traders. Computer technology had barely made inroads here on account of the investment costs, so paper was the recording medium still used to process stock transactions and the legal transfer of ownership in the back offices, even as the speed of the market accelerated thanks to upgraded telephone exchanges.[358] A study commissioned by the New York Stock Exchange in 1965 had predicted a rise in daily turnover from five million shares per day to ten million in 1975. In fact, ten million shares per day were already being traded by 1967, and twelve million by 1968. But the speed of data processing lagged far behind the speed and scope of data transmission. In the back offices, the tide of paper was rising. Employees had to work up to twelve hours a day and up to seven days a week, because the key players in the securities industry shared the fate of journalists in print media: they had a deadline. A stock certificate had to be signed and notarized within five days after the completion of a transaction in order for the transaction to be legally valid. As a result, "fails" were commonplace. Anyone who had not caught the computerization wave in the late autumn of 1968 faced bad times ahead. Between 1968 and 1970, around one hundred New York Stock Exchange brokerage firms disappeared from the market.[359]

The electronification of the back offices was a way out of the crisis. It was a dramatic crash course in computer technology involving a number of adaptive challenges for the employees and their bosses alike. One problem was overadaptation: many employees had so much faith in their new electronic colleagues that they stopped manually recording data altogether. Around 1970, the best computers were connected to teleprinters via telephone lines. Streams of data could thus circulate automatically between the trading floor and the back offices: "Commands and user programs were usually found on punch cards consisting of stiff paper with eighty columns which had to be submitted to operators in a stack and, crucially, in the correct sequence."[360]

Punch cards are an unassuming yet enlightening example of how electronic media emerged from the paper age. A modern descendent of Rabelais would describe them as an offshoot of pantagruelion. In the history of the punch card, the city of Lyon plays a major role as a European center of both printing and the textile industry. When Joseph Marie Jacquard looked to the automata and calculating machines of the eighteenth century to perfect punch card technology as a control mechanism for weaving looms around 1800, he used the technology of the first industry for the further development of the second. His mechanism involved a press which resembled a printing press or wine press, and he did not stamp the blank cards individually but instead punched holes in the cards using a galley, like printers used to press type into paper. After all, in his youth he had been apprenticed to the printer and bookseller Jean-Marie Barret, as Birgit Schneider explains in her informative study of the media history of punch card weaving.[361] Of course, the cards were not cheap because their raw material, paper, was not cheap. They only became cost-effective in the 1820s with the appearance of the paper machine. As they spread, they triggered a boom in punch card weaving. In Manchester, the center of the English textile industry, the mechanical engineer Charles Babbage would have encountered the mechanism as well. Babbage liked to place his "analytical engine," which he worked on from 1833 to 1846, on a par with its eighteenth-century neighbors: the automata, the androids, and the technologies of silk weaving. The punch card, which was a control mechanism and storage medium in one, internalized this history when it made a name for itself with automated musical instruments. Herman Hollerith turned it into a tool for censuses and modern bureaucracy, while Alan Turing made it a part of the electronic computer. The punch card could handle both things: it could trigger electrical impulses or the mechanical movement of making a small check mark.

The American author William Gaddis was a private historian of punch cards. He must have had an obsessive relationship with perforated paper cards and tapes, for they are a conspicuous presence in his literary work in their two most important functions: as triggers for music and triggers for calculations. In Gaddis's last, posthumously published novel, *Agapē Agape* (2002), an old man nearing death bends over the punched holes in which the music is in danger of disappearing. His monologue is a reverberation of the enormous tapestry of voices that Gaddis unfurled in his 1975 novel *JR*. This tapestry of voices—in which the dialogue breaks are indicated not by quotation marks but by dashes—captures that historical moment of the twentieth century in which paper-based, electrical, and electronic media began to interact with each other at a frequency never seen before. Computers had already become a familiar figure in technological debates, though they had not yet found their way into private households on a large scale. But after the paperwork crisis had been overcome, they ensured that the acceleration and expansion of the circulation of securities was no linger hindered by the asymmetry between data transmission and data processing. The dollar was untethered from the gold standard in 1971, and not long after the Bretton Woods agreement of 1944 was formally dissolved: "With the end of Bretton Woods, unsecured paper money or money of account was no longer considered a stopgap measure in times of crisis but rather a prerequisite, functional component and inevitable fate in the international movement of capital."[362]

In *JR*, the eleven-year-old title character, still a child but already on the road to cocky adolescence, is gripped and infected by the dynamics of Wall Street. Or rather, he charges into them with all flags flying, like a knight riding out into the world in a medieval epic. He lives in Massapequa on Long Island, his school has been equipped with audio-visual media, some of his teachers have become stars of the school television broadcasts, and the electrification of teaching goes hand in hand with the introduction of punch cards for assessment tests which are meant to weed out potential school dropouts. The school modernization program includes an introduction to the economic system of the United States, and the students are expected to do more than just learn the theory of how to "buy stock from a broker." The class takes a field trip with the goal of purchasing actual stock on Wall Street. The device on the desk of the broker, Mr. Crawley, is mistaken for a television by the students. They are not yet computer kids. "This, this is called a Quotron. Just by pressing a button or two I can ask it for the latest information on any stock, number of shares traded, latest bid and asked prices."[363] Quotron Systems had been a leader in the electronification of the stock exchange since the 1950s. It was one of the winners in the paperwork crisis. The computer on Crawley's desk underscores the statement he has just given over the phone to a press officer concerning "the long overdue technical readjustments taking place in our present dynamic market situation." And it gives a modern meaning to the hackneyed maxim that the broker slips into his little speech: "Time is money, isn't it. I guess you've, we've all heard that haven't we."[364] Mr. Crawley does not need to quote Benjamin Franklin's "Advice to a Young Tradesman" (1748) and explain the consequence of the time-is-money formula, namely, acceleration; his computer appends this consequence to the central formula of the American Dream through its presence alone. Gaddis's satire, to the extent that it is a financial satire, just needs an accelerant to bring all of its material together. This accelerant enters the picture in the form of a voice. As is often the case with Gaddis, it is not clear to whom the voice belongs—but JR is the likely option. The question is, "What are futures?" It is a question about a recent financial product with a bright future ahead of it. Futures entail an obligation to buy or sell an asset at a predetermined date in the future for a price agreed in the present.

JR receives no answer to his question, so he looks into it himself. In a nutshell, this sums up the actions of the title character in this monumental novel. Several hundred pages later, he suggests to his teacher that futures should be covered in class and the class should repeat its first Wall Street foray, but instead of purchasing a people's share—"our share of America"—it would be a risky commodity futures transaction. From a newsletter, JR has learned that you can "increase the turnover in a firm's capital with the leverage provided through bank loans."[365] By this point he is already heavily involved in financial deals and is building his own business empire with nearly Mephistophelian innocuousness and ease. But there is one thing he is not: demonic. He is just a child who has taken the lessons of Mr. Crawley and Mr. Franklin to heart and who annoys the adults with his endless questions; he is a model student without an unfathomable inner life; he is getting a D in math but solving very complex problems in the real world.

The tapestry of voices in which he is embedded has not been woven according to a naturalistic pattern. Satire and mythology both watch over JR in rare harmony, right from the novel's opening scene, right from its first sentence:

- Money ...? in a voice that rustled.
- Paper, yes.
- And we'd never seen it. Paper money.
- We never saw paper money till we came east.
- It looked so strange the first time we saw it. Lifeless.
- You couldn't believe it was worth a thing.
- Not after Father jingling his change.
- Those were silver dollars.[366]

The speakers are old women thinking back to the good old days when the gold and silver standards were still inviolate. In the banks where they are forced to deal with matters of inheritance after their brother's death, paper money is no longer a newcomer: it is a discontinued model. This is the stuff of satire. The mythology is brought into play through music, which is the family's intangible inheritance, and the reference to a nephew, Mr. Edward Bast, who rehearses Wagner with his students in a synagogue, of all places, because the cafeteria of the modern school has been taken over for something considered more important: driver training. Wagner's music swells unmistakably in the novel's sound track as the teacher tries to coax from his Rhinemaidens not a howl but a cry of triumph and joy: "Rhine ... GOLD!" This invokes the old opposition between gold and paper money which, during the Wall Street field trip a short time later, is updated to become an opposition between gold and shares. To the sound of Wagner's German music in a Jewish temple, JR is transformed into the mythological figure who will invisibly guide him in his financial transactions throughout the rest of the novel: he is the dwarf Alberich. He is utterly miscast in this role because he is not musical and he is anything but a guardian of gold. But the magic cap that gives the dwarf the strength of twelve men is transferred to him. In a market in which invisible hands are at work, he is an invisible market participant. No one can see how young he is because he handles all of his transactions over the phone. He talks through a handkerchief to bring his child's voice down to an adult frequency, and he opens his accounts in Nevada, where nobody checks whether he is at least twenty-one. And when the music teacher Mr. Bast loses his job at the school, JR uses him as a mask and a straw man, without Bast ever really realizing what he has gotten into.

The media constellation in which JR operates is critical to the substance of the financial satire and its permeation with the mythological motifs of magic and treasure-hoarding. JR sees the "wonders of the computer"[367] as if in a window display, but he cannot access them. The age of paper still holds sway in his school life as well as all around him: telephones have cables, carbon paper has to be wound into a typewriter to make copies, and you need scissors to cut out the most interesting securities offers and hottest tips from the newsletters and newspapers.

Alan Turing introduced his computing machine by making a man/machine comparison: "It is possible to produce the effect of a computing machine by writing down a set of rules of procedure and asking a man to carry them out. Such a combination of a man with written instructions will be called a 'Paper Machine.' A man provided with paper, pencil, and rubber, and subject to strict discipline, is in effect a universal machine."[368] If you add a telephone to this definition, then it applies fairly well to JR. His rules of procedure are found in the papers, brochures, and newspapers that are his constant companions, and his elementary control command comes from Benjamin Franklin. William Gaddis construed JR as the perfect machine for casting a negative light on the American Dream by eagerly and radically fulfilling it. Gaddis creates a sense of claustrophobia and an atmosphere of expansive decay by flooding the space of his novel with masses of unbound paper. There is no "rag and bones" shop here like in Dickens's London. But there is the law of entropy, a word the students are asked to spell at the start of the book, and there is the continual shift between order and disorder, between communication and interruptions, people talking into telephones with no one listening at the other end. The arts are inexorably slipping away; all that remains of lofty book ambitions are yellowing manuscripts and old newspaper clippings which are no longer legible, and what was meant to be a great oratorio shrinks in the end to a wispy piece for an unaccompanied cello. The music of Johann Sebastian Bach falls on deaf ears. Before JR's empire falls apart, it will swallow up a paper factory with an associated publishing house: "The magazine's being acquired to round out this whole vertical integration picture wood pulp source through paper manufacture with the Triangle deal into this field growing faster than defense getting the publishing end under one roof."[369] By the end of the novel, a few volumes of a big encyclopedia for children have been published—and they are full of errors. With satirical energy, Gaddis counters this with his own encyclopedic novel, along with mythological company names which recall the monsters that populated the great industrial machine halls in the works of Karl Marx and Herman Melville. In the nineteenth century, Laocoön was often entangled in telephone wires. Gaddis cannot get away with just a few snakes, however. The most powerful company in his novel is called Typhon, named after the giant with one hundred snake heads, born of the union of Gaia and Tartarus.

4.4. Rainald Goetz, the Mystic Writing Pad, and the Smell of Paper

Sigmund Freud wrote his "Note Upon the 'Mystic Writing-Pad'" in October 1924 to illustrate his understanding of the mind's perceptual and memory apparatus. His short text starts with a comparison between a sheet of paper that has been written on with ink and a piece of slate that has been written on with chalk. The advantage of the paper is that it will indefinitely preserve the note written upon it as a "permanent memory-trace." The disadvantage is that the writing space is limited, and to discard the note you have to discard the writing surface as well. The advantage of the slate is that notes can be erased easily without having to destroy the writing surface itself. On the contrary, the surface remains receptive for an unlimited time. The disadvantage is that this unlimited receptivity comes at the expense of the inability to permanently preserve memory traces. The "Mystic Pad" approximates Freud's image of the human perceptual apparatus because it offers both advantages at once: "an ever-ready receptive surface and permanent traces of the notes that have been made upon it." In the interaction between the celluloid sheet which protects against tearing and the wax slab which preserves the traces that would seem to have been lost through repeated erasure, Freud sees an image of the "unconscious" which "stretches out feelers" into the external world and "hastily withdraws them as soon as they have sampled the excitations coming from it."[370]

If we set aside Freud's interest in finding an image to represent the mental perceptual apparatus, then what remains of the mystic writing pad is a recording apparatus which combines the two basic models that have governed the relationship between writing and writing surfaces since antiquity: wax tablets and textiles. The wax tablet is represented in Ovid's *Metamorphoses* by the figure of Byblis, who writes a letter to her brother declaring her love for him. She is the ideal user of a stylus and wax tablet because the incest taboo hampers her writing and prompts her to repeatedly erase what she has written. The counterpart to Byblis is Philomela, whose rapist Tereus cuts out her tongue so that she cannot speak of the terrible deed. She weaves the story of the crime into a tapestry which she sends to her sister. In this case, the symbols are irrevocably bound to the medium that bears them, and the medium itself points to the misdeed by the very fact that it must stand in as a substitute for the silenced tongue. This polarity of permanent and loose connections between symbols and the materials that carry them permeates the history of recording media. The monitor of a computer upon which the white page of a text editing program appears is a mystic writing pad enabling both the continual deletion and permanent storage of characters. In the forgotten, overwritten, yet reconstructable data on a hard drive, Freud might see a representation of the unconscious. But when a computer is connected to the internet, the polarity between storage and deletion which was the focus of Freud's "Note on the Mystic Writing-Pad" is joined by a circulation option.

At the end of the twentieth century, from February 1998 to January 1999, the Freud-denigrator Rainald Goetz kept a public online journal which was eventually published as a book with the title *Abfall für alle. Roman eines Jahres* (Garbage for Everyone: A Novel of a Year). In this journal, the technological infrastructure still has something fragile about it, and the author speaks ironically of the "Stone Age of the electronic world" and makes the best of it by turning glitches into punchlines and insights: "Thomas sends me a nice email, and the gods of the Stone Age of the electronic world decide that it should sit in my mail program in a single long line of words, like a necklace of word beads, unprintable. So I write it out by hand. I can understand words better when I read them on paper than on a screen. Still, it is precisely the fluidity of the computerized text form that makes garbage speak and able to speak."[371] This note makes it clear that the electrification of writing has preceded that of reading. At the same time, the Byblis aspect of writing on a computer and the unstable status of what has been written encourages the creation of texts that can be viewed as optional, provisional, revisable. In looking at modern authorship and its ties to the printed book, we have seen how the polarity between printed and unprinted material is linked to the polarity between what is optional and what is definitive. Since publication was identical with printing, what was unpublished was optional and what was published was definitive. But Goetz, the internet author, ventured into a type of publication associated with optionality: "The internet's special form of publicity—which consists of an almost groundless, abstract availability, where a text exists more as a possibility than as a real object, something which is only realized when someone registers their interest and clicks on the address—accommodates a type of expression and way of writing that is probing, tentative, but also impulsively explosive and able to be corrected or revoked the next day if need be. ... But despite all of this, a form of PUBLICITY is realized nonetheless, and we seek the binding nature of the published text."[372]

During the "Stone Age of the electronic world," Rainald Goetz was viewed primarily as a pioneering writer on the internet. But he wrote *Abfall für alle* as a dual authorial figure. Inside the writer of the electronic journal was the book author whose concept of what was binding and definitive was determined by books printed on paper, the intellectual and material production of which was documented by the journal. When he occasionally cried, "There's no PAPER SHORTAGE, man!" he was referring to more than just the endless writing surface supplied by a computer monitor. Unlike Jack Kerouac, he did not have to tape paper together in a long roll so that he could type continuously without stopping and winding in a new sheet. But even Goetz's notes paint a portrait of a workplace which could justifiably be described as that of a paper worker. In his very first online journal entry, he receives a courier letter from his publisher with the proofs of his new book *Rave* and the corrected cover layout. The galley proofs of this book and others pop up continually from that point on. He constantly receives faxes; the copy shop, mailbox, newspaper stand, and bookstores are his permanent ports of call; notes are pinned to the walls; and the printer—an important interface between the computer and paperwork—is often in need of repair: "drowning / in the madness of my papers / nice feeling." "Snowed under with papers."[373] The internet author's everyday life is made up of printer paper, newspapers, coated paper from the glossy magazines that he reads and occasionally considers working on projects for; the extended triad of "letters, books, office, mail" reverberates through him. In his correspondence with the publisher, printed paper's old connections to the pole of the definitive repeatedly takes its toll: "Call from Hans-Ulrich. Discussed the written clarifications concerning typesetting. Correct, clarify further, reject, weigh up, pin down."[374] The author's concerns regarding his printed books do not end with the correction of the galley proofs. They extend to the production process and the paper used for the text and cover. The author, it turns out, is sensitive to smells, so he calls the publisher: "Well, the paper is held in vats, and there's a lot of water involved, and if they don't stir the vats for a while in their paper factory, you would get some—well: DECOMPOSITION, and then it would—me STINK—him: yes, smell a bit. But in our paper factory, we make sure to stir the vats. Thank you, paper factory."[375]

Even more than the fact that you can touch paper and it rustles, it is paper's smell that, with the advance of digitization, has become a sign of the authenticity of the "old" materiality of paper. It leads the internet author to the modern paper factory, where the production lines have reached an unsurpassable width of up to eleven meters and a belt speed of thirty-three meters per second. The printer paper used in such copious amounts by the internet author is made largely of recycled paper, as the utilization rate for recycled paper has reached nearly seventy percent in Germany.

The author's material connection to the world of paper is accompanied in the "Stone Age of the electronic world" by a connection to the symbolic form of the book. The authorial figure has not yet been freed of the concept of a book printed on paper. The internet journal could only be included among the works of Rainald Goetz in the form of a book. At the end of *Abfall für alle* in early January 1999, shortly before taking leave of his readers, Goetz views the literary estate of Heiner Müller in the Archive of the Academy of Arts in Berlin. The space once occupied by the manuscript could easily be confused with the space now occupied by electronic writing and its wealth of optionality. But Goetz the author ends his internet journal by fortifying the border between books—the world of definitiveness—and unprinted papers: "The old papers, the spirit that was there, where now there are scribbles, notes, typescripts and revisions, vestiges of intellectual activity, of an energy that is no longer there, that is dead, gone. The author is the work in the completed guise of the book. ... The word written on a trial basis is not really an early form of the text, it is, even in the flash of life in which the note comes into being, the MEMORY of a moment of experimentation. You should not approach these experimental materials, you should push yourself away from them in order to translate them back into their true function. Then you end up at the person who was everything there, all of the anecdotes, the photos, the imago that was generated, on the one hand—and, above all, at these intellectual objects directly, at the BOOKS. Last stop, everybody off. Right there is what it's all about. The way into the work leads over the work, through the work, and the way to the author leads to books."[376]

Epilogue

The Analog and the Digital

᯽

In his essay "La conquête de l'ubiquité" (The Conquest of Ubiquity) from 1928, Paul Valéry wondered whether a philosopher had ever "dreamed of a company engaged in the home delivery of Sensory Reality." By founding such a company, he would fulfill the prognostications concerning the future of the arts that Valéry had developed in his essay: "For the last twenty years neither matter nor space nor time has been what it was from time immemorial. We must expect great innovations to transform the entire technique of the arts, thereby affecting artistic invention itself and perhaps even bringing about an amazing change in our very notion of art. ... Works of art will acquire a kind of ubiquity. We shall only have to summon them and there they will be, either in their living actuality or restored from the past. They will not merely exist in themselves but will exist wherever someone with a certain apparatus happens to be. A work of art will cease to be anything more than a kind of source or point of origin whose benefits will be available—and quite fully so—wherever we wish. Just as water, gas, and electricity are brought into our houses from far off to satisfy our needs in response to a minimal effort, so we shall be supplied with visual or auditory images, which will appear and disappear at a simple movement of the hand, hardly more than a sign."[377] Valéry's vision appeared in a collection of texts about music which had been inspired by the gramophone and the young medium of radio. Because he viewed music as the art "most involved in social existence," music seemed to be the natural protagonist for entering an age in which spatiotemporal constraints on the arts were lifted. He took it for granted that forms rooted in the sphere of the visible, be they works of art or natural beauty—"a sunset on the Pacific, a Titian in Madrid"—would then follow.

The company founded by Valéry's imaginary philosopher would have been a large stock corporation along the lines of the large energy companies which, together with the iron and steel industry, had come to shape everyday life since the late nineteenth century. Its business model would have entailed aligning aesthetic convenience with technical and civilizational convenience through the distribution of sounds and images. In Valéry's vision, the delivery address was a home address; the philosopher himself would have had to track down the smart-phone users circulating through the city. When he emphasized the minimal gestures that would be required to call up sounds and images and dismiss them again, Valéry was clearly thinking about flipping a light switch or turning on a faucet. He could have thought about picking up a telephone receiver as well. His thought experiment was conditional on the progressive electrification of everyday life as well as on the everyday mechanization of factories and households described by Siegfried Giedion a good decade later in *Mechanization Takes Command* (1948).

At the start, we saw how Valéry metaphorically electrified paper in his microbe experiment in order to accentuate its capacities as a storage and circulation medium. How does his diagnosis of paper's indispensability to modern civilization relate to his prediction of the "conquest of ubiquity," which inevitably makes us think of television and the internet?

At the time Valéry formulated these ideas, they complemented one another. Radio may have overpowered the extra edition in the long run, but it was unthinkable that the paper age would come to an end, especially when paper was viewed the way Valéry envisaged it, as a protean substance occupying a variety of aggregate states and functions. Like money, it was indifferent to every use to which it was put—in war and peace, revolution and counterrevolution, administration and private correspondence. This contributed to its assortment of guises, much like the malleability which enabled it to appear in the form of a loose DIN A4 sheet here, an extravagantly large book page there, a punch card somewhere else.

Now, however, at the start of the twenty-first century, electronic media threaten to surpass the catastrophic scenario that paper was subjected to in Valéry's microbe experiment. "The virus," the author Botho Strauss wrote some time ago, "which, in a single blow, erases all of the electronic memory upon which life on earth currently depends, and Valéry's microbe, which will destroy all paper on earth before long, differ monumentally in their speed of attack. We switched media at the right time, from paper to paperless storage, before the appearance of the microbe. But how will we protect our collections from the threat of the electronically ubiquitous virus?"[378] This anxious question has been deferred in favor of the observation that, in both this scenario and in Valéry's, the vision of destruction functions as proof of universality. But if electronic storage is indispensable, does it really follow that paper is dispensable? Have we really already made the move "from paper to paperless storage"?

Young disciplines tend to present their findings as sensationally as possible in order to seem important. Perhaps this is why the media theories of the nineteenth century were so fond of talking about "media revolutions" that shaped entire epochs, changed mentalities, resulted in religious schisms, or even brought forth modern nation-states. Paper—which insinuates itself into existing routines and encourages them to stabilize and develop instead of spawning new routines, and which tends to support rather than compel the storage and circulation of data—is not the ideal hero of a media revolution. It has played the role of a silent partner in a variety of cultural technologies in the modern media world, and it has usually realized its full potential in combination with other media, maintaining close relations with both the unspectacular "small tools" of scholars, merchants, and chanceries and with the great innovations of the times.

Embedding the paper age in the "Gutenberg era" has served a dual purpose here. It aims to relieve the "from script to print" formula of its sole responsibility for interpreting our world of origin while also preventing the formula's overly hasty translation into "from the analog to the digital age." Yes, the telegram has disappeared as has the railroad timetable, the stock markets are unlikely to experience another paperwork crisis, and navigation systems are sometimes more convenient than maps. But the term proposed at the beginning to summarize such phenomena—*la retraite*, the retreat of paper—does not explain what else happens in the transitional period in which we currently find ourselves. It gives the impression of an uneven movement, dramatic in one area yet minimal in another, and says nothing about how stable each position is in the field. Retreat from an expansive position of hegemony does not necessarily have to be irreversible across the board, and it can even involve temporary advances. We do not know what role the printed paper book will play in the distant future, across continents and cultures, or what will happen to paper money or periodical print media. We tend to quickly place each phenomenon on a diachronic temporal axis, with an index of the past and an expiration date. But just as the printing press brought the synchronous tension between printed and unprinted materials into the world, the synchronous tension between the analog and the digital has been brought into the world as a binary opposition of the type that the ethnologist Claude Lévi-Strauss researched in the form of "the raw and the cooked."

With this in mind, questioning the relationship between paper and e-paper brings into play the entire host of paper's manifestations: bound and unbound, printed and unprinted. Does every analog format have a digital counterpart? What corresponds to a newspaper clipping, or to a slip of paper where both sides are written on but at different times? Do an e-book and an electronic daily newspaper relate to each other like an analog book and a printed newspaper? How do the individual pages compare, and what is the exact digital counterpart to the fundamental unit of analog paper, the sheet?

We have seen that in the synchronous tension between printed and unprinted materials, the printed book has a high affinity with the pole of definitiveness, while the handwritten manuscript has a high affinity with optionality. Are there correspondences to this in the new opposition? A novel's text is the same in an e-book as in a hardcover printed book. But an e-book file integrates supplemental material differently than a printed book. The latent space of optionality that surrounds the e-book and gives it room to develop is larger than the space of the printed, self-contained book. If you view both types of book primarily as reading devices, this is, above all, a material optionality. But the electronic book's openness to bonus material accentuates its fundamental material and physical difference to the analog book: regardless of what is included in an e-book, it remains unchanged as a reading device. Its easy access to ubiquity comes at the expense of limited individualization options. When two hundred physiognomically different hardcovers are placed on a reading device in the form of e-books, they lose weight and gain the opportunity to travel together. But their dissimilarity also becomes less weighty in e-book mode. The analog book, on the other hand, cannot become any lighter than it already is. But its materiality and associated physiognomic individuality are features that it can play up. Walter Benjamin preceded his essay "The Work of Art in the Age of Mechanical Reproduction" with an excerpt from Valéry's article. But in his own essay, Valéry himself was not terribly interested in either reproductions or their complementary concepts, originals. The Titian hanging in Madrid, which he sees as being on its way to ubiquity, cannot circulate through the homes of art lovers around the world as an original. Its authenticity is tied to the singularity of its material and physical form. No printed book has this unique character, but in its contrast to an electronic book it might acquire the aura of being the original *format*. However, this only becomes apparent when we cease to compare the electronic book to "the printed book" as a general concept and compare it instead to the abundance of physical formats into which this general concept breaks down upon closer inspection. Not all of these formats are equally similar or dissimilar to an electronic book, and not all of them are equally easy or difficult to replace with an electronic book. The paperback version of a novel or travel guide can be transformed into an electronic book with much less resistance than an elaborately designed art book about the Italian Renaissance or a large-format coffee table book. It may be no coincidence that, for some time now, bookstores have displayed more and more small-format, physically compact books which seem to call out to potential buyers: You can stick me in your pocket but I am not a pocket book, I am a small hardcover, so you can also give me as a gift. This is an effect of the fact that as electronic books have come to be taken for granted, the physical design of hardcovers has grown more important. Many publishers are attaching greater value to the design of original editions, experimenting with formats, and placing an emphasis on the physical format itself—the distinguishing feature of a hardback should be that it is a hardback.

The electronic book, in turn, is seen as a commodity and pays an additional price for its lightness and speed: It offers more targets for unauthorized access. And because it technologically radicalizes the nature of the printed book, which circulates not as an original but as a "copy," the electronic book is also subject to restrictions that limit the ability to make copies of it. Anyone who buys an electronic book should not be able to resell it as a "used book." This is why readers do not acquire ownership of such a book: they acquire a usage right, a license to read. When libraries procure e-books, they are usually granted a time-limited right of use which has to be renewed, generally after one year. Complicated agreements stipulate how many people may use an electronic book in a certain period of time, and there are license fees for long-term archiving as well. Electronic books no longer exist in a rigid format, like printed books; this is part of their appeal and an aspect of the options available to them. They appear in a variety of technical standards and are not bound to a fixed layout. In principle, they are dynamic objects that can be continually updated, revised, and enhanced. When e-books are enhanced with links to audio and video sequences, their boundaries with objects outside of themselves are blurred and they can move in the direction of websites or databases, in the case of academic non-fiction books, or computer games, in the case of children's books. As we have seen, paper's non-specific openness to a variety of uses has always gone hand in hand with standardization processes, through which physical formats have acquired social and cultural significance. When it comes to electronic books, the interplay between the exhausting of options and standardization has only just begun.

The affinity between the digital and the optional is even more apparent when we look at the periodical press instead of books. Most newspapers are produced once a day and updated multiple times in the evening, usually with the exception of Saturday. This day-and-night rhythm has, until now, also largely applied to the digital editions of daily newspapers. But while the paper version of a newspaper only appears one time a day—at least eight to twelve hours later than the events it covers—the online edition can be updated at intervals of two or three hours, if not continuously. The printed daily newspaper increasingly finds itself echoing the live stream of advancing topicality. It stretches, extends, and concentrates the reflective impulses emanating from core events in the staccato rhythm of its publication intervals over the course of days and sometimes weeks. The temporal climate in which it operates is a patchwork of varying degrees of topicality. One of its tasks, therefore, is to compensate for its own belatedness—as compared to electronic media—through its formats and writing styles. The sports sections of major daily newspapers in particular have become virtuosos in the journalistic management of belatedness. On Mondays, they address readers who have already heard about all the important events in major-league sports. For this reason, they are moving away from event reporting and instead developing formats and writing styles for physiognomically characterizing the activities on the fields and around them.

However, it would be a mistake to believe that the online edition of a daily newspaper is always more up to date than the printed version. Every online edition (and this applies to all newspapers) contains articles that are much older than those found in yesterday's newspaper. "Online" not only means more topicality, it also means more of an archive. Instead of thinking of print and online media solely as opposites, it would be more accurate to speak of different mixing ratios, especially when it comes to longer articles. While a newspaper article on the internet is subject to a diffuse temporal structure, a printed newspaper is clear on this point: Even though printed newspapers have long been suffused with, and benefited from, digital technologies in their entire production process, these newspapers appear only once a day in just one identical edition, though not necessarily everywhere they are distributed; front page pictures can be changed, articles switched, reports updated—but the framework, the physical format, remains the same.

One of the many jokes attributed to Count Bobby, a character invented in Vienna in the 1950s, was his mock astonishment that every single day, precisely enough things happened around the world to fit into the next day's newspaper. This joke harbors an insight into the foundations of a newspaper. You can write about anything, and the subjects and styles are virtually endless, but you have to do it in a limited space for a specific point in time. These two elements—temporal and material self-containment—are among the fundamentals of every copy of a printed newspaper. For a long time, these limitations were so self-evident and seemed so trivial that hardly anyone gave them a second thought. But now this self-containment stands in striking contrast to the seemingly limitless ability of digital media to absorb the flow of events and circulate it worldwide, so further reflection is needed. "The medium is the message"—this also means that the physical design of a newspaper is part of its message.

A printed newspaper is an internally structured ensemble of pages which can be separated because they are divided into different sections—known as *Bücher* or "books" in German newspaper jargon—so that one person can read the business section at the breakfast table while another reads the sports and a third reads the politics pages or the feuilleton. But each person can only read as much as is printed on the page or look at as many pictures as the newspaper contains. And these pictures don't move. A newspaper comprises a certain number of pages; each of its sections has a first and last page which have no opposing pages, but within each section the recto/verso principle of the book world holds sway, with right-hand pages which catch the eye first and left-hand pages opposite them. Each of these pages is either a front or back side, and each follows the layout of a newspaper, not that of a book: in its division into columns (which are usually separated from one another with vertical lines), in its headlines and subheadings—in brief, in all of the elements involved in the technical production and graphical planning of a newspaper. This physical organization is what makes it possible to leaf through a newspaper, and it exists before the first line is ever written. If a newspaper's first and foremost task is to select and weight the news, the counterpart to this task in the newspaper's technical and graphical apparatus is a physical structure which supports such an arrangement and weighting. The newspaper obeys an artificial order which turns a potentially endless number of events and subjects into the order of a day. In the way it manages the space on the page within the scope of topicality delineated by its production and distribution conditions, a newspaper gains its "reputation" and its authority to determine the order of a day and to decide what should be included and what should not.

Of all the qualities a newspaper may possess, this authority is the most difficult to attain. But it is of such fundamental importance that there is a special term for this kind of paper in both English (a "newspaper of record") and French (a *"presse de référence"*). Such authority can only be acquired over long periods of time. It accrues through long, continually renewed, intermittent accompaniments to everyday life in the form of comprehensible justifications in political analyses; global reportage; and commentary and glosses which assess events, thwart them, and question the conditions that make them possible. It takes years and decades to build up this kind of authority. This also means that while original ideas or even "scoops" may support a newspaper's authority, they cannot guarantee it.

The print edition of a daily newspaper is updated many times over, but every proof is self-contained. The version for tablet computers, however, offers technological options that can—and must—be used or rejected. This applies to both the diachronic temporal axis, or the opportunities for updates, and to the synchronous linking of every single article, or the addition of supplemental material. Providers have to weigh up how often they want to take advantage of the options available under the breaking news threshold. This decision determines what exactly constitutes a newspaper page in electronic format. This space has not yet been clearly defined. An electronic newspaper page only has fixed, immediately visible limits when it imitates the printed newspaper page in the form of e-paper. In online newspaper portals, where scrolling recalls a scroll of paper, the boundaries are drawn differently, the divisions between sections and the borders of individual articles are emphasized, and there does not have to be an exact equivalent to the ensemble of articles on a printed newspaper page. An individual article can open up to a wealth of reader comments which are directly attached to it. One symptom of the revision of the limits that were associated with self-contained newsprint can be seen in mixed forms and hybrids such as direct links between printed newspapers and digital content. In some printed daily newspapers—including *Die Welt* in Germany since September 2013—certain articles now include QR codes which allow readers to access additional material, such as the extended video version of a printed interview or the interactive version of an image, via an app on a smart phone or reading device. As a result, the newspaper page loses its material self-containment, and paper gains windows that readers can open to integrate digital content into their reading experience. This strategy of electronically expanding a printed newspaper clearly interrupts the newspaper reading experience as much as it enhances it. By following the model of the hyperlink and opening a window in the printed page, another medium is brought into play which also addresses both the eye and the hand of the reader. While the eye and ear are occupied with the bonus material, the act of reading the printed newspaper page is suspended. Apps therefore not only give readers more news and entertainment content for their money—as the name "bonus material" would suggest—they also give readers more to do. Readers have always consumed newspapers in a much more selective and less linear way than books; they leaf through them, skip some things, get absorbed in this or that, stop reading for a bit and then start again later. But the virtual timeframe in which this took place was determined by the physical finiteness of the newspaper page, so in principle it could be calculated. With the introduction of digital windows in newsprint, reading has entered a new, more open, less easy to calculate time frame. Readers must respond to this by developing new forms of time management.

Just as the printed newspaper has, for four centuries, explored and defined the formats, internal structures, departmental structures, rhetorical strategies, and techniques for managing topicality which are possible within the limits set for it, online journalism will have to develop its own formats and, in doing so, distance itself more and more from the paradigm of the printed newspaper that iPad versions still follow. Online journalism has to accommodate both the live stream of topicality and the options that allow it to integrate audio and video files into the text of a large investigative report. Like the electronic book, electronic newspapers will have to balance the wealth of options available to them through a differentiation of formats. And printed newspapers will have to find their own place in the era of "post-digital print"[379] by reflecting on themselves in their contrast to electronic formats.

It can also be helpful to look back at the history of paper because paper was never on its own; it always sought a symbiosis with other media. When examining the relationship between different media— such as film and television, printing and electronic media—twentieth-century media theories typically emphasized the elements of competition and crowding out. But media history also encompasses effects of resonance amplification and the symbiosis and feedback between media which have not become technologically integrated but instead react to and cooperate with one another as distinct, separate spheres. Both the gramophone record and radio brought their own special journals to the market, and radio still does press reviews; on television we find press discussions where newspaper journalists sit around a table; ad-financed online magazines link the content found in newspapers and transform material from printed newspapers into synoptically organized extracts. Some magazines which appear weekly as a supplement to a daily newspaper instead of being displayed at a kiosk owe their successful economic existence not only to their symbiosis with the daily newspaper but to their carrier medium, which stands well apart from conventional newsprint—namely, the high-gloss paper that is attractive to certain advertisers in the jewelry, cosmetics, and fashion industries. Bonus content in digital formats accumulates around this high-gloss nucleus. An example from the audio-visual world illustrates how many forces influence the use of these options: the combination of remote controls and the establishment and expansion of private channels set a high level of optionality for television consumption. The resultant effects were not limited to the sofa, however—they reached all the way to the cinema. One emergent quality of the cinema was that it became a place where you could not change the channel; you could only leave. The physical finiteness of a paper-based newspaper not only represents a lack of options, it also eases the burden posed by the ever-growing abundance of options that are still far from being exhausted within digital media.

Paul Valéry's vision tacitly assumes that the ubiquity of works encompasses both their synchronous circulation in space and their long-term storage along a diachronic temporal axis. This ubiquity maintains the balance that Harold Innis wanted to see preserved between space- and time-biased media. Valéry was thinking both of the live global transmission of music and the broadcasting of recorded concerts (or studio recordings). Right now, many collections in our libraries and archives are being digitized, including entire corpora of medieval manuscripts, series of encyclopedias, extensive correspondence, and whole libraries of older magazines. This process is not following the logic of substitution which replaced the analog timetable with a digital one, however. The goal, for manuscripts and the other materials, is usually to create parallel archives of digitized and analog collections. This is because analog paper, and especially older rag paper, has a fundamental advantage on a diachronic temporal axis: it is amenable to restoration but not to innovation. Electronic paper, by contrast, must face continual reformatting on a long timeline. It is a rule of thumb that newcomers mimic the older media to which they attach themselves. Our electronic wastepaper basket rustles when we delete a file, and the icon for cutting marked text is a pair of scissors. The printer icon on the computer screen has a partner in the analog world: DIN A4 paper. It still rustles. As opposed to what was often said early on, electronic paper does not lack a haptic quality. We swipe open old manuscripts in exhibitions and museums. We search through enormous digital files, and from time to time we may stop to look for a scrap of paper where we jotted down an important note during a telephone call. Printing and publishing are no longer the same thing. They have diverged in the age of digital publishing. The printout now stands side by side with the printed page. We read and write on analog paper, and we read and write on electronic paper. We live in a world where the analog and the digital reciprocally permeate each other; we are hybrids, and so are our media.

Valéry's microbe would still have a lot to do. The Paper Age is not yet finished.

Notes

1   Valéry 1963, 107.
2   Derrida 2005, 42.
3   Valéry 1963, 107f.
4   Tschudin 2002, 69ff.
5   Schmidt 1994b, 77.
6   Ibid., 78.
7   Loveday 2001, 19f.
8   Karabacek 1887, 87ff.; Karabacek 2001.
9   Hunter 1978, 22.
10 Sporhan-Krempel 1952, 8f.
11 Loveday 2001, 23ff.; Pedersen 1984, 54ff.
12 Daiber/Junod 2010, 149; Axworthy 2008, 78ff.; Al-Khalili 2011, 67ff.
13 Karabacek 2001, 27.
14 von Kremer 1920, 373ff.
15 Bloom 2001, 8ff.
16 Bloom 2006, 301f.
17 Daiber/Junod 2010, 31.
18 Gruendler/Marx 2011.
19 Goitein 1999, Volumes 1–6.
20 Scholem 2012, 158.
21 Goitein 1999, 10.
22 Goitein 2006, 83ff.
23 Loveday 2001, 1.
24 Allen/Richards 2006, 245ff.
25 Al-Khalili 2011, 90f.; Irwin 2004, 198f.
26 *The Arabian Nights* 2008, 5.
27 Ibid., 257.
28 Ibid., 128.

29 Ibid., 222.
30 Goitein 1999, 240ff.
31 *The Arabian Nights* 2008, 223.
32 Ibid., 138.
33 Goethe 2010, 95.
34 Ibid., 95f.
35 Ibid., 229ff.
36 Goethe 1985–98, Vol. 11.1.2, 615; Köpnick 1992, 362f.
37 Goethe 2010, 273.
38 Goethe 1985–98, Vol. 11.1.2, 438.
39 Goethe 2010, 3.
40 Bayerl/Pichol 1986, 38ff.
41 Franzke/von Stromer 1990, 15ff.
42 Loveday 2001, 25ff.
43 Febvre/Martin 1997, 30ff.
44 Neddermeyer 1998, 265.
45 Rouse/Rouse 1994, 69ff.
46 Zaar-Görgens 2004, 204.
47 Franzke/von Stromer 1990, 26; Hoffmann 1973.
48 Breitkopf 1784/1985.
49 Lessing 1994, 280.
50 Breitkopf 1784/1985, 38.
51 Ibid., 39.
52 Ibid., 44.
53 Rosenfeld 1990, 327ff.
54 Ibid., 335.
55 Landfester 2009, 13.
56 Goethe 1860, 342.
57 Ibid., 347.
58 Ibid., 355.
59 Brendecke 2006a.
60 Schmitt 2008, 22f.
61 Brendecke 2009a, 11ff.
62 Ibid., 14.
63 Brendecke 2009b, 88ff.; Patze 1970, 10.
64 Vismann 2008, 81.
65 Patze 1970, 39.
66 Franzke/von Stromer 1990, 28f.
67 Braudel 1996, Vol. 1, 501.
68 Peri 1707, Vol. 3, 44ff.; Fahy 2003/04.
69 Patze 1970, 62.
70 Braudel 1996, Vol. 1, 508ff.
71 Grasshoff 1899, 28.
72 Meynen 2003, 206.
73 Ibid., 205f.
74 Ibid., 215.
75 Peri 1707, Vol. 3, 9ff.

76   Sombart 1916, 120; Baecker 1993, 259ff.
77   Arlinghaus 2000.
78   Ibid., 325ff.
79   Ramazzini 1705, 199.
80   Brentano 1976, 7f.
81   Grimm 1893, Vol. 14, 306.
82   Brentano 1976, 8.
83   Wienker-Piepho 2000, 355.
84   Brentano 1976, 397.
85   Weigel 1698/1977, 154f.
86   Ibid.
87   Rabelais 2006, 251.
88   Ibid., 47.
89   Kline 1963, 18ff.; Rommel 1997, 51ff.
90   Rommel 1997, 51ff.
91   Auerbach 2003, 278.
92   McLuhan 1962, 149.
93   McLuhan 2001, 188.
94   Ibid., 101ff., 117ff.
95   McLuhan 1962, 147.
96   Ibid.
97   McLuhan 1962, 138.
98   Giesecke 2006, 134.
99   Hunter 1978, 62.
100 Giesecke 2006, 107.
101 Tschudin 1997, 23.
102 Rabelais 2006, 601f.
103 Pliny 1991, 177.
104 Rabelais 2006, 602.
105 Ibid., 607f.
106 Tin 2000, 130ff.
107 Kline 1963, 6.
108 McLuhan 2001, 90.
109 Innis 1999, 34.
110 Ibid., 19.
111 Innis 1997, 14ff.
112 McLuhan 2001, 110.
113 Behringer 2003, 50ff.
114 Ibid.
115 Caspary 2006, 47.
116 Beyrer/Dallmeier 1994, 15ff.; Schröder 1995, 10ff.
117 Needham 1994, 138.
118 Assmann 1995, 29; Müller 1994, 32ff.
119 Trithemius 1974; Müller 1994, 36.
120 Assmann 1995, 22ff.
121 Goethe 1860, 51f.
122 Weiss 1962, 80ff.

123   Karabacek 2001, 56.
124   Needham 1994.
125   Weiss 1962, 45ff.
126   Beetz 1990, 200ff.
127   Karabacek 2001, 47ff.; Loveday 2001, 52f.
128   Weiss 1962, 63.
129   Ibid., 45.
130   Chaytor 1945, 1; McLuhan 1962, 86f.
131   Mentzel-Reuters 2010, 434; Flachmann 2003, 128ff.
132   Luhmann 1995, 64.
133   Lebrave/Grésillon 2000, 32.
134   Brandis 1997, 38.
135   Goethe-Wörterbuch 1989, 749.
136   Locke 1975, 104f.
137   Brendecke 2005, 55ff.
138   Eckermann 1850, 341.
139   Jean Paul 2012, excerpt V-BVA-04-1787-1789-0036.
140   Lichtenberg 1968, Vol. 1, 432.
141   Ibid., 803.
142   Jean Paul 1975, Vol. 11, 428.
143   Goethe 1992, 479.
144   Plachta 1997, 46ff.
145   Lessing 1989, 115–134, 173–350.
146   Voltaire 1786, 170.
147   Cervantes 2003, 45ff.; Theison 2009, 172ff.
148   Cervantes 2003, 55.
149   Ibid., 59.
150   Ibid., 67.
151   Ibid., 68f.; Wirth 2008, 193ff.
152   Cervantes 2008, Afterword, 736ff.
153   Rommel 1997, 50.
154   Ibid., 53.
155   Cervantes 2003, 874f.
156   Ibid., 939.
157   Foucault 1994, 46.
158   Grimmelshausen 1986, 546.
159   Ibid., 486.
160   Garzoni 1588, 238ff.
161   Kremer 2007, 96.
162   Grimmelshausen 1986, 497.
163   Ibid., 497f.; Jessing 2009.
164   Grimmelshausen 1986, 536f.
165   Defoe 1995, 48.
166   Ibid., 102.
167   Ibid.
168   Strobel 2010, 65.
169   Joost 1990, 65ff.

170 Zedler 1731/54, Vol. 4, 1359f.; How 2003.
171 Strobel 2006, 7ff.
172 Richardson 1985, 130; Price 2001, 117ff.
173 Richardson 1985, 1472.
174 Sterne 2009, 32.
175 Ibid., 180.
176 Sterne 2006, afterword by Wolfgang Hörner, 839.
177 Ibid.
178 Keymer 2002, 81.
179 Jean Paul 1975, Vol. 11, 374.
180 Carlyle 1841, 243.
181 Lichtenberg 1968, Vol. 2, 166.
182 Lichtenberg 1968, Vol. 1, 813f.
183 Zedler 1731/54, Vol. 8, 2321f.
184 Décultot 2004, 179ff.
185 Lichtenberg 2000, 62; supplemental translation in brackets.
186 Krajewski 2011, 17ff; Heesen, te 2006, 28ff.
187 Krajewski 2011, 65ff.
188 Ibid., 34ff.
189 Jean Paul 2004, 114.
190 Jean Paul 2002, 2ff.; Krajewski 2011, 44.
191 Jean Paul 2002, 3.
192 Blaze de Bury 1850, 171.
193 Selg/Wieland 2001, 470.
194 Diderot/D'Alembert 1751/1780, Vol. 11, 836ff., 846ff.
195 Lalande 1984, 144.
196 Ibid., 22ff.
197 Rosenband 2000b, 33ff., 41ff.
198 Darnton 1993, 132ff.
199 Claproth 1947b, 2f.; Lichtenberg 1968, Vol. 1, 673.
200 Rosenband 2000b, 147f.
201 Rosenband 2004, 170ff.; Coleman 1958, 80ff.
202 Coleman 1958, 179ff.
203 Ibid., 201ff.
204 Erickson 1996, 19ff., 170ff.
205 Ibid., 21.
206 Carlyle 1858, 100, 114.
207 Carlyle 1999, 44.
208 Jean Paul 2012, fascicle IIa-11-1787-0286; Carlyle 1841, 249f.
209 Carlyle 1999, 35.
210 Carlyle 2002, 25f.
211 Ibid., 268.
212 Jean Paul 2012, fascicle IIa-13-1788-0593.
213 Mercier 1994b, 532.
214 Ibid., 752.
215 Benjamin 1999, 178.
216 Carlyle 2002, 253.

217 Burke 2009, 242; Goethe 2009, 48.
218 Nicholson 1994, 46.
219 Ibid., 147.
220 Goethe 2009, 50.
221 Vogl 2004, 45.
222 Chollet 1983, 18ff.
223 Balzac 2012, 22.
224 Ibid., 35.
225 Ibid., 33.
226 Balzac 1976, 3.
227 André 1996, 266f.
228 Balzac 1976, 110; André 1996, 421ff.
229 Balzac 1976, 111f.
230 Balzac 1976, 365; Chollet 1983, 40.
231 Hofmannsthal 2009, 173f.
232 Balzac 1976, 681f.
233 André 1996, 259ff.
234 Balzac 1997, 5.
235 Dickens 1853, 4.
236 Mayhew 2008, 200f.
237 Dickens 1853, 112; Baker 2002, 59ff.; Stauffer 2007, 1ff.
238 Leonard 1950, 498f.
239 Ibid., 495f.
240 Hunter 1978, 238ff.
241 Melville 1987, 710.
242 Melville 2009, 85; Fisher 1971.
243 Melville 2009, 88.
244 Ibid., 90.
245 Ibid., 92.
246 Starobinski 1997, 563.
247 Melville 2009, 94.
248 Marx 1990, 503.
249 Ibid.
250 Melville 2009, 94f.
251 Anonymous 1834b, 581.
252 Ibid., 584; Oligmüller 1997, 75ff.
253 Stöber 2005, 118ff.
254 Balzac 1976, 537.
255 Schlieder 1994, 2.
256 Ibid., 1f.
257 André 1996, 259.
258 Friebel 2001, 141.
259 Ibid., 143f.
260 Payen 1867, 315.
261 Schmidt 1994a.
262 Bayerl/Pichol 1986, 153ff.
263 Ibid.

264 Murray 1829, 82.
265 Anonymous 1873.
266 Schmidt 1993.
267 Friebel 2001.
268 Meyer 1967, 339ff.
269 Ibid., 224ff.
270 Mann 1980, 423.
271 Mann 1921, 113.
272 Ibid., 356.
273 Ibid., 155f.
274 Palmer 1983.
275 Balzac 2012, 9f.
276 Palmer 1983, 30.
277 Brockhaus 1894, Vol. 14, 564.
278 Meyer 1967, 345.
279 Le Ray 2004, 452ff.
280 Zola 1900; Le Ray 2004, 650ff.
281 Dilthey 1921.
282 Dilthey 1889; Kopp-Oberstebrink 2010.
283 Dilthey 1921, 555.
284 Ibid., 561ff.
285 Lichtenberg 1966, 290f.
286 Goethe 1987, Div. 1, Vol. 41.2, 25–28, 75f.
287 Ibid., 402.
288 Goethe 1845, 310f.
289 Goethe 1987, Div. 1, Vol. 41.2, 27.
290 Ibid., 26.
291 Goethe 1985–98, Vol. 9, 948f.
292 Goethe 1890, 9f.
293 Merck 2007, Vol. 5, 17.
294 Corrêa do Lago 2005, 9.
295 Ibid., 7.
296 Goethe 1987, Div. 4, Vol. 47, 110; Hentschel 2010.
297 Goethe, ibid., 145.
298 Günther/Schulz 1856, Foreword, III.
299 Dilthey 1921, 564.
300 Günther/Schulz 1856, 31ff.
301 James 2003, 182f., 185ff.
302 Salmon 1997, 117ff.
303 Bulman 2004, 41ff.
304 Salmon 1997, 77ff.
305 Wharton 1900, 26.
306 Bockelkamp 1982; Schubert 2010.
307 Stifter 2006, 19.
308 Schmidt-Bachem 2011, 370ff.
309 Pieske 1983, 10ff.
310 Stigand 1875, 360.

311 Schmidt-Bachem 2001, 42ff.
312 Pieske 1983, 10.
313 Middell 2002.
314 Böttiger 1806, Vol. 1, 204ff., 228ff.
315 Bertuch 1790, 12.
316 Neumann/Oesterle 1999, 163ff.
317 Metken 1978, 301ff.; Schlaffer 1986, 7–19.
318 Metken 1978, 302.
319 Münkner 2009, 50ff.
320 Benjamin 1999, 214.
321 Moritz 1926, 21.
322 Kügelgen 1870, 115.
323 Semper 2010, 46.
324 Ibid., 46f.
325 Kügelgen 1870, 119f.
326 Benjamin 2006, 47.
327 Proust 2003, 64.
328 Oligmüller 1997, 14.
329 Kraus 1978, 21.
330 Kittler 1999, 183ff.
331 Rittaud 2006, 188ff.
332 Tschichold 1998, 97.
333 McGann 1993, 45ff.
334 Benton 2001, 71ff.
335 Miller 2010, 185.
336 Whitman 2009, notes to the German edition, 779.
337 Martin 1994, 329.
338 Tschichold 1998, 72.
339 Adler/Ernst 1987.
340 Tschichold 1991, 169f.
341 Ibid., 169.
342 Joyce 2010, 98.
343 Ibid., 112.
344 Ibid., 106.
345 Ibid., 105.
346 Heesen, te 2006.
347 Joyce 2010, 109.
348 Zischler/Danius 2008, 93.
349 Fielding 2005, 73.
350 Joyce 2010, 61.
351 Zischler/Danius 2008, 129ff.
352 Joyce 2010, 107.
353 Ibid., 53.
354 Ibid., 612.
355 Ibid., 466.
356 Reichert 2009, 28.
357 Ibid., 58f.

358 Wells 2000.
359 Reichert 2009, 111.
360 Ibid., 99.
361 Schneider 2007, 290f.
362 Vogl 2010, 87.
363 Gaddis 1993, 85.
364 Ibid.
365 Ibid., 473.
366 Ibid., 3.
367 Ibid., 168.
368 Ince 1992, 113.
369 Gaddis 1993, 513.
370 Freud 1997, 207ff.
371 Goetz 1999, 315.
372 Ibid., 357f.
373 Ibid., 17ff.
374 Ibid., 463.
375 Ibid., 377.
376 Ibid., 838.
377 Valéry 1964, 225f.
378 Strauss 2009, 154.
379 Cf. Ludovico 2012.

Bibliography

Adler, Jeremy, and Ulrich Ernst (1987) *Text als Figur: Visuelle Poesie von der Antike bis zur Moderne*. Weinheim: VCH.

Al-Khalili, Jim (2011) *The House of Wisdom. How Arabic Science Saved Ancient Knowledge and Gave Us the Renaissance*. New York: Penguin Press.

Allen, Roger, and Donald S. Richards (eds.) (2006) *Arabic Literature in the Post-Classical Period*. Cambridge: Cambridge University Press.

Amann, Jost (1930) *A True Description of All Trades*. [Translator not named.] Brooklyn: Mergenthaler Linotype Co. [*Eygentliche Beschreibung aller Stände auff Erden*, 1568.]

André, Louis (1996) *Machines à papier: Innovation et transformations de l'industrie papetière en France, 1798–1860*. Paris: Éditions de l'École des hautes études en sciences sociales.

Anonymous (1834a) "Über Stereotypie und Polytypie." In *Pfennig-Magazin der Gesellschaft zur Verbreitung gemeinnütziger Kenntnisse*, No. 72. Leipzig, pp. 572–574.

Anonymous (1834b) "Die Maschine des endlosen Papiers." In *Pfennig-Magazin der Gesellschaft zur Verbreitung gemeinnütziger Kenntnisse*, No. 73. Leipzig, pp. 581–584.

Anonymous (1834c) "Die Papierschneidemaschine." In *Pfennig-Magazin der Gesellschaft zur Verbreitung gemeinnütziger Kenntnisse*, No. 74. Leipzig, pp. 585f.

Anonymous (1873) "Briefe von der Weltausstellung." In *Wöchentliche Anzeigen für das Fürstenthum Ratzeburg*, Vol. 53, No. 50, 27 June.

The Arabian Nights (2008) Translated by Husain Haddawy, edited by Muhsin Mahdi. New York: W.W. Norton & Company.

Arlinghaus, Franz-Josef (2000) *Zwischen Notiz und Bilanz. Zur Eigendynamik des Schriftgebrauchs in der kaufmännischen Buchführung am Beispiel der Datini/di Berto-Handelsgesellschaft in Avignon (1367–1373)*. Frankfurt am Main: Peter Lang.

Assmann, Jan (1995) *Stein und Zeit. Mensch und Gesellschaft im alten Ägypten.* Munich: Wilhelm Fink.

Auerbach, Erich (2003) *Mimesis: The Representation of Reality in Western Literature.* Translated by Willard R. Trask. Princeton: Princeton University Press. [*Mimesis. Dargestellte Wirklichkeit in der abendländischen Literatur,* 1946.]

Axworthy, Michael (2008) *A History of Iran: Empire of the Mind.* New York: Basic Books.

Baecker, Dirk (1993) "Die Schrift des Kapitals." In Gumbrecht, Hans Ulrich, and K. Ludwig Pfeiffer (eds.), *Schrift.* Munich: Wilhelm Fink, pp. 257–272.

Baker, Nicholson (2002) *Double Fold: Libraries and the Assault on Paper.* London: Vintage.

Balzac, Honoré de (1976) *Lost Illusions.* Translated by Herbert J. Hunt. London: Penguin Books. [*Illusions perdues,* 1837–43.]

Balzac, Honoré de (1997) *Colonel Chabert.* Translated by Carol Cosman. New York: New Directions Publishing Corp. [*Le Colonel Chabert,* 1832.]

Balzac, Honoré de (2012) *The Wild Ass's Skin.* Translated by Helen Constantine. Oxford: Oxford University Press. [*Le peau de chagrin,* 1831.]

Bange, Evamarie (2009) "Wirtschaft und Kompetenz—Wasserzeichen als Quelle zu Handel und Organisation in mittelalterlichen Schreibstuben." In Embach, Michael, and Andrea Rapp (eds.), *Zur Erforschung mittelalterlicher Bibliotheken. Chancen—Entwicklungen—Perspektiven.* Frankfurt am Main: Klostermann, pp. 11–31.

Bayerl, Günter, and Karl Pichol (1986) *Papier. Produkt aus Lumpen, Holz und Wasser.* Reinbek/Hamburg: Rowohlt.

Becker, Peter (2000) " 'Kaiser Josephs Schreibmaschine': Ansätze zur Rationalisierung der Verwaltung im aufgeklärten Absolutismus." In *Jahrbuch für europäische Verwaltungsgeschichte* 12, pp. 223–256.

Beckmann, Johann (1787) *Anleitung zur Technologie, oder zur Kenntnis der Handwerke, Fabriken und Manufacturen, vornehmlich derer, die mit der Landwirthschaft, Polizey und Cameralwissenschaft in nächster Verbdinung stehn, Nebst Beyträgen zur Kunstgeschichte. Dritte, verbesserte und vermehrte Ausgabe.* Göttingen: Vandenhoeck & Ruprecht.

Beetz, Manfred (1990) *Frühmoderne Höflichkeit. Komplimentierkunst und Gesellschaftsrituale im altdeutschen Sprachraum.* Stuttgart: J. B. Metzlersche Verlagsbuchhandlung.

Behringer, Wolfgang (2003) *Im Zeichen des Merkur. Reichspost und Kommunikationsrevolution in der Frühen Neuzeit.* Göttingen: Vandenhoeck & Ruprecht.

Benjamin, Walter (1999) *The Arcades Project.* Edited by Rolf Tiedemann, translated by Howard Eiland and Kevin McLaughlin. Cambridge, MA: Harvard University Press. [*Gesammelte Schriften,* Vol. 5: *Das Passagen-Werk,* 1982.]

Benjamin, Walter (2006) *Berlin Childhood around 1900.* Translated by Howard Eiland. Cambridge, MA: Harvard University Press. [*Berliner Kindheit um 1900,* 1950.]

Benton, Megan L. (2001) "Typography and Gender: Remasculating the Modern Book." In Benton, Megan L., and Paul C. Gutjahr (eds.), *Illuminating Letters: Typography and Literary Interpretation.* Amherst: University of Massachusetts Press, pp. 71–93.

Bertuch, Friedrich Justin (1790) *Bilderbuch für Kinder*. Vol. 1: *Plan, Ankündigung und Vorbericht des Werks*. Weimar: Verlag des Industrie-Comptoirs.

Beyrer, Klaus, and Martin Dallmeier (eds.) (1994) *Als die Post noch Zeitung machte. Eine Pressegeschichte*. Giessen: Anabas.

Blaze de Bury, Marie Pauline Rose (1850) *Germania: Its Courts, Camps, and People*. Vol. 1. London: Henry Colburn.

Blechschmidt, Jürgen (ed.) (2010) *Taschenbuch der Papiertechnik*. Munich: Hanser Verlag.

Blechschmidt, Jürgen, and Alf-Mathias Strunz (1996) "Der Beginn eines neuen Zeitalters der Papierfaserstoff-Erzeugung—die Erfindung des Holzschliff-Verfahrens durch Friedrich Gottlob Keller." In Schmidt, Frieder (ed.), *Papiergeschichte(n). Papierhistorische Beiträge. Wolfgang Schlieder zum 70. Geburtstag*. Wiesbaden: Harrassowitz, pp. 137–150.

Bloom, Jonathan M. (2001) *Paper before Print: The History and Impact of Paper in the Islamic World*. New Haven: Yale University Press.

Bloom, Jonathan M. (2006) "Paper: The Transformative Medium in Ilkhanid Art." In Komaroff, Linda (ed.), *Beyond the Legacy of Genghis Khan*. Leiden: Brill, pp. 289–302.

Blum, André (2003–4) "Paper Making in Seventeenth-Century Genoa: The Account of Giovanni Domenico Peri (1651)." In *Studies in Bibliography*, Vol. 56, pp. 243–259.

Bockelkamp, Marianne (1982) *Analytische Forschungen zu Handschriften des 19. Jahrhunderts. Am Beispiel der Heine-Handschriften der Bibliothèque Nationale Paris*. Hamburg: Hauswedell.

Boehncke, Heiner, and Hans Sarkowicz (2011) *Grimmelshausen. Leben und Schreiben. Vom Musketier zum Weltautor*. Frankfurt am Main: Eichborn.

Bohnenkamp, Anne, and Waltraud Wiethölter (2010a) *Der Brief—Ereignis & Objekt. Frankfurter Tagung*. Frankfurt am Main: Stroemfeld.

Bohnenkamp, Anne, and Waltraud Wiethölter (2010b) *Der Brief—Ereignis & Objekt*. Catalog of the exhibition in the Freies Deutsches Hochstift. Frankfurt am Main: Stroemfeld.

Bösch, Frank (2004) "Zeitungsberichte im Alltagsgespräch. Mediennutzung, Medienwirkung und Kommunikation im Kaiserreich." In *Publizistik*, Vol. 49, pp. 319–336.

Bosse, Heinrich (1981) *Autorschaft ist Werkherrschaft. Über die Entstehung des Urheberrechts aus dem Geist der Goethezeit*. Paderborn: Schöningh.

Böttiger, Karl August (1806) *Sabina oder Morgenszenen im Putzzimmer einer reichen Römerin: Ein Beytrag zur richtigen Beurtheilung des Privatlebens der Römer und zum bessern Verständniss der römischen Schriftsteller*. Leipzig: G. J. Göschen.

Brandis, Tilo (1997) "Die Handschrift zwischen Mittelalter und Neuzeit. Versuch einer Typologie." In *Gutenberg-Jahrbuch* 72, pp. 27–57.

Braudel, Fernand (1996) *The Mediterranean and the Mediterranean World in the Age of Philip II*. Two volumes. Translated by Siân Reynolds. Berkeley: University of California Press. [*La Méditerranée et la Monde Méditerranéen à l'Époque de Philippe II*, 1949.]

Breitkopf, Johann Gottlob Immanuel (1779) *Über die Geschichte der Erfindung der Buchdruckerkunst. Bey Gelegenheit einiger neuern darüber geäußerten besondern Meynungen*. Leipzig: J.G.I. Breitkopf.

Breitkopf, Johann Gottlob Immanuel (1815) *Inquiry into the Origin of Playing Cards, Paper Made of Linen, and Wood Engravings.* Translated by I. W. May. Gravesend.

Breitkopf, Johann Gottlob Immanuel (1985) *Versuch, den Ursprung der Spielkarten, die Einführung des Leinenpapiers, und den Anfang der Holzschneidekunst in Europa zu erforschen. Erster Theil, welcher die Spielkarten und das Leinenpapier enthält.* Munich: K. G. Saur. [Reproduction, original published 1784.]

Brendecke, Arndt (2005) " 'Durchschossene Exemplare'. Über eine Schnittstelle zwischen Handschrift und Druck." In *Archiv für Geschichte des Buchwesens,* Volume 59, pp. 50–64.

Brendecke, Arndt (2006a) " 'Diese teufel, meine Papiere. ...' Philipp II. von Spanien und das Anwachsen administrativer Schriftlichkeit." In *aventinus nova Nr. 5* (Winter 2006). http://www.aventinus-online.de/no_cache/persist ent/artikel/7785/ accessed October 28, 2013.

Brendecke, Arndt (2006b) "Papierfluten. Anwachsende Schriftlichkeit als Pluralisierungsfaktor in der Frühen Neuzeit." In *Mitteilungen des Sonderforschungsbereiches 573.* Munich: Ludwig-Maximilians-Universität.

Brendecke, Arndt (2009a) "Papierbarrieren. Über Ambivalenzen des Mediengebrauchs in der Vormoderne." In *Mitteilungen des Sonderforschungsbereiches 573 "Pluralisierung und Autorität in der Frühen Neuzeit"* 2. Munich, pp. 7–15.

Brendecke, Arndt (2009b) *Imperium und Empirie. Funktionen des Wissens in der spanischen Kolonialherrschaft.* Cologne: Böhlau Verlag.

Brentano, Clemens von (1976) *Sämtliche Werke und Briefe 7: Des Knaben Wunderhorn. Alte Deutsche Lieder Teil II.* Stuttgart: Kohlhammer.

Brockhaus' Konversations-Lexikon (1894) *Vierzehnte vollständig neubearbeitete Auflage. In sechzehn Bänden.* Leipzig/Berlin/Vienna: F. A. Brockhaus.

Bruns, Alfred (ed.) (1984) *Die Kunst Papier zu machen. Nach dem Text von Joseph Jérôme le François de Lalande übersetzt und kommentiert von Johann Heinrich Gottlob von Justi 1762.* Münster: Landschaftsverband Westfalen-Lippe.

Bulman, Jessica (2004) "Edith Wharton, Privacy and Publicity." In *Yale Journal of Law and Feminism,* Vol. 16, No. 1, pp. 41–82.

Burke, Edmund (2009 [1790]) *Reflections on the Revolution in France.* Oxford: Oxford University Press.

Busch, Werner (1993) *Das sentimentalische Bild: Die Krise der Kunst im 18. Jahrhundert und die Geburt der Moderne.* Munich: Beck.

Carlyle, Thomas (1841) *German Romance: Specimens of its Chief Authors; With Biographical and Critical Notices.* Vol. 2. Boston: James Munroe and Company.

Carlyle, Thomas (1858) "Signs of the Times." In *Collected Works.* Vol. 3. London: Chapman and Hall, pp. 98–118.

Carlyle, Thomas (1999 [1836]) *Sartor Resartus.* Oxford: Oxford University Press.

Carlyle, Thomas (2002) *The French Revolution: A History.* New York: Modern Library.

Caspary, Gundula (2006) *Späthumanismus und Reichspatriotismus. Melchior Goldast und seine Editionen zur Reichsverfassungsgeschichte.* Göttingen: Vandenhoeck & Ruprecht.

Castagnari, Giancarlo (ed.) (2007) *L'impiego delle tecniche e dell'opera dei cartai fabrianesi in Italia e in Europa*. Fabriano: Cartiere Miliani.

Cervantes Saavedra, Miguel de (2003) *Don Quixote*. Translated by Edith Grossman. New York: Ecco. [*El ingenioso hidalgo don Quijote de la Mancha*, 1605/1615.]

Cervantes Saavedra, Miguel de (2008) *Don Quijote von der Mancha*. Translated by Susanne Lange. Munich: Hanser Verlag.

Chaytor, Henry John (1945) *From Script to Print: An Introduction to Medieval Literature*. Cambridge: Cambridge University Press.

Chollet, Roland (1975) "Balzac et sa 'Grande Affaire' de librairie. L'Acte de societé de 1833." In *L'Année Balzacienne*, pp. 145–175.

Chollet, Roland (1983) *Balzac Journaliste: Le tournant de 1830*. Paris: Klincksieck.

Claproth, Justus (1947a [1774]) *Abhandlung von 1774 über die Verwendung von Makulatur zur Papierherstellung*. Hagen-Kabel: Papierfabrik Kabel.

Claproth, Justus (1947b [1774]) *Eine Erfindung aus gedrucktem Papier wiederum neues Papier zu machen, und die Druckerfarbe völlig heraus zu waschen*. Hagen-Kabel: Papierfabrik Kabel.

Coleman, Donald C. (1958) *The British Paper Industry 1495–1860: A Study in Industrial Growth*. Oxford: Clarendon Press.

Corrêa do Lago, Pedro (2005) *Schriftstücke. Autographen aus sieben Jahrhunderten*. Translated by Eva Plorin and Ilse Strasmann. Hildesheim: Gerstenberg.

Crick, Julia, and Alexandra Walsham (2004) *The Uses of Script and Print, 1300–1700*. Cambridge: Cambridge University Press.

Curtius, Ernst Robert (1951) "Goethes Aktenführung." In *Neue Rundschau*, Vol. 62, pp. 110–121.

Daiber, Verena, and Benôit Junod (eds.) (2010) *Treasures of the Aga Khan Museum. Masterpieces of Islamic Art*. Exhibition catalogue. Berlin: Nicolai Verlag.

Darnton, Robert (1993) *Glänzende Geschäfte. Die Verbreitung von Diderots Encyclopédie. Oder: Wie verkauft man Wissen mit Gewinn?* Abridged and translated from English into German by Horst Günther. Berlin: Wagenbach. [*The Business of Enlightenment: A Publishing History of the* Encyclopédie, *1775–1800*, 1979.]

Décultot, Élisabeth (2004) *Untersuchungen zu Winckelmanns Exzerptheften. Ein Beitrag zur Genealogie der Kunstgeschichte im 18. Jahrhundert*. Translated by Wolfgang von Wangenheim and René Mathias Hofter. Ruhpolding: Verlag Franz Philipp Rutzen. [*Johann Joachim Winckelmann. Enquête sur la genèse de l'histoire de l'art*, 2000.]

Defoe, Daniel (1995) *Robinson Crusoe*. Ware, Hertfordshire: Wordsworth Editions Limited. [*The Life and Strange Surprizing Adventures of Robinson Crusoe, Of York, Mariner: Who lived Eight and Twenty Years, all alone in an un-inhabited Island on the Coast of America, near the Mouth of the Great River of Oroonoque; Having been cast on Shore by Shipwreck, wherein all the Men perished but himself. With An Account how he was at last as strangely deliver'd by Pyrates. Written by Himself*, 1719.]

Delbanco, Andrew (2005) *Melville. His World and Work*. New York: Knopf.

Derrida, Jacques (2005) *Paper Machine.* Translated by Rachel Bowlby. Stanford: Stanford University Press. [*Papier machine,* 2001.]

Dickens, Charles (1853) *Bleak House.* London: Chapman and Hall Ltd.

Diderot, Denis, and Jean le Rond d'Alembert (eds.) (1751/1780) *Encyclopédie, ou dictionnaire raisonné des sciences, des arts et des métiers, par une société de gens de lettres.* Paris: Briasson, David, Le Breton, Durand.

Dilthey, Wilhelm (1889) "Archive für Literatur." In *Deutsche Rundschau,* Vol. 58, pp. 360–375.

Dilthey, Wilhelm (1921) *Die Jugendgeschichte Hegels und andere Abhandlungen zur Geschichte des Deutschen Idealismus.* Leipzig/Berlin: Teubner.

Dotzler, Bernhard J. (1996) *Papiermaschinen. Versuch über Communication & Control in Literatur und Technik.* Berlin: Akademie Verlag.

Dulken, Stephen van (2002) *Inventing the 20th Century: 100 Inventions That Shaped the World.* New York: New York University Press.

Eckermann, Johann Peter (1850) *Conversations of Goethe with Eckermann and Soret.* Volume II. Translated by John Oxenford. London: Smith, Elder & Co. [*Gespräche mit Goethe,* 1836.]

Eisenstein, Elizabeth L. (2005) *The Printing Revolution in Early Modern Europe.* Cambridge: Cambridge University Press.

Eisermann, Falk (2004) *Verzeichnis der typographischen Einblattdrucke des 15. Jahrhunderts im Heiligen Römischen Reich Deutscher Nation.* Wiesbaden: Reichert.

Erickson, Lee (1996) *The Economy of Literary Form: English Literature and the Industrialization of Publishing, 1800–1850.* Baltimore: Johns Hopkins University Press.

Fahy, Conor (2003/04) "Paper Making in Seventeenth-Century Genoa: The Account of Giovanni Domenico Peri (1651)." In *Studies in Bibliography,* Vol. 56. Charlottesville: Bibliographical Society of the University of Virginia, pp. 243–259.

Faulstich, Werner (ed.) (2008) *Das Alltagsmedium Blatt.* Munich: Wilhelm Fink.

Febvre, Lucien, and Henri-Jean Martin (1997) *The Coming of the Book.* Translated by David Gerard. London: Verso. [*L'Apparition du livre,* 1958.]

Fielding, Henry (2005 [1749]) *The History of Tom Jones, A Foundling.* London: Penguin Books.

Fisher, Marvin (1971) "Melville's 'Tartarus': The Deflowering of New England." In *American Quarterly,* Vol. 23, No. 1, pp. 79–100.

Flachmann, Holger (2003) "Handschrift und Buchdruck bei Martin Luther." In Gerd Dicke and Klaus Grubmüller (eds.), *Die Gleichzeitigkeit von Handschrift und Druck.* Wiesbaden: Harrassowitz, pp. 121–140.

Fontaine, Pierre-Jules (1836) *Manuel de l'amateur d'autographes.* Paris: Paul Morta.

Fontane, Theodor (1998) *Effi Briest.* Edited by Christine Hehle. Berlin: Aufbau.

Fontius, Martin (1988) "Post und Brief." In Gumbrecht, Hans Ulrich, and K. Ludwig Pfeiffer (eds.), *Materialität der Kommunikation.* Frankfurt am Main: Suhrkamp, pp. 267–279.

Foucault, Michel (1994) *The Order of Things: An Archaeology of the Human Sciences.* Translated by Alan Sheridan. New York: Vintage. [*Les mots et les choses,* 1966.]

Franzke, Jürgen, and Wolfgang von Stromer (1990) *Zauberstoff Papier. Sechs Jahrhunderte Papier*. Munich: Hugendubel Heinrich GmbH.

Freud, Sigmund (1997) "A Note upon the 'Mystic Writing-Pad.'" In *General Psychological Theory: Papers on Metapsychology*. Translated by James Strachey. New York: Touchstone, pp. 207–212. [*Notiz über den Wunderblock*, 1925.]

Friebel, Alexander (2001) "Ohne Papier keine Zeitung: Die Erfindung des Holzschliffpapiers als Meilenstein in der Entwicklung des deutschen Pressewesens." In *Jahrbuch für Kommunikationsgeschichte*, Vol. 3. Stuttgart: Franz Steiner Verlag, pp. 132–156.

Gaddis, William (1993) *JR*. New York: Penguin Books.

Garzoni, Tommaso (1588) *La piazza universale di tutte le professioni del mondo, nuovamente ristampata e posta in luce da Thomaso Garzoni da Bagnacauallo. Con l'aggionta d'alcune bellissime annotationi a discorso per discorso*. Venice: Giovanni Battista Somasco.

Gastgeber, Christian, and Gabriele Mauthe (1999) *Die Direktion der Hofbibliothek zur Jahrhundertwende*. Vienna: Österreichische Nationalbibliothek.

Giedion, Siegfried (1948) *Mechanization Takes Command: A Contribution to Anonymous History*. Oxford: Oxford University Press.

Giesecke, Michael (2006) *Der Buchdruck in der frühen Neuzeit. Eine historische Fallstudie über die Durchsetzung neuer Informations- und Kommunikationstechnologien*. Frankfurt am Main: Suhrkamp.

Goethe, Johann Wolfgang von (1845) *Correspondence Between Goethe and Schiller, from 1794 to 1805*. Vol. 1. Translated by George H. Calvert. New York and London: Wiley and Putnam.

Goethe, Johann Wolfgang von (1860) *Dramatic Works of Goethe: Comprising Faust, Iphigenia in Taurus, Torquato Tasso, Egmont and Goetz von Berlichingen*. Translated by Anna Swanwick and Sir Walter Scott. London: Henry G. Bohn.

Goethe, Johann Wolfgang von (1890) *Correspondence Between Schiller and Goethe, from 1794 to 1805*. Vol. 2. Translated by L. Dora Schmitz. London: George Bell and Sons.

Goethe, Johann Wolfgang von (1985–98) *Sämtliche Werke nach Epochen seines Schaffens*. Munich edition, 21 volumes, edited by Karl Richter in cooperation with Herbert G. Göpfert, Norbert Miller, Gerhard Sauder, and Edith Zehm. Munich: Hanser Verlag.

Goethe, Johann Wolfgang von (1987) *Werke*. Edited on behalf of the Grand Duchess Sophie of Saxony. 4 divisions, 143 volumes. Weimar, 1887–1919. Reprinted in Munich: dtv.

Goethe, Johann Wolfgang von (1992) *Italian Journey*. Translated by W.H. Auden and Elizabeth Mayer. London: Penguin Books. [*Italienische Reise*, 1816–17.]

Goethe, Johann Wolfgang von (2009) *Faust: Part 2*. Translated by David Constantine. London: Penguin Books. [*Faust. Der Tragödie zweiter Teil*, 1832.]

Goethe, Johann Wolfgang von (2010) *West-East Divan. The Poems, with "Notes and Essays": Goethe's Intercultural Dialogues*. Translated by Martin Bidney and Peter Anton von Arnim. Albany: State University of New York Press.

Goethe-Wörterbuch (1989) Volume 2: *B—einweisen*. Stuttgart: Kohlhammer.

Goetz, Rainald (1999) *Abfall für alle. Roman eines Jahres*. Frankfurt am Main: Suhrkamp.

Goitein, S.D. (1999) *A Mediterranean Society: The Jewish Communities of the Arab World as Portrayed in the Documents of the Cairo Geniza. Volume I: Economic Foundations*. Berkeley: University of California Press.

Goitein, S.D. (2006) "The Oldest Documentary Evidence for the Title *Alf Laila wa-Laila*" [originally published in 1958]. In Ulrich Marzolph (ed.), *The Arabian Nights Reader*. Detroit: Wayne State University Press, pp. 83–86.

Grasshoff, Richard (1899) *Das Wechselrecht der Araber. Eine rechtsvergleichende Studie über die Herkunft des Wechsels*. Berlin: Otto Liebmann.

Grimm, Jacob, and Wilhelm Grimm (1893) *Deutsches Wörterbuch*. Vol. 14. Leipzig: Hirzel.

Grimmelshausen, Hans Jakob Christoffel von (1986) *An Unabridged Translation of Simplicius Simplicissimus*. Translated by Monte Adair. Lanham, MD: University Press of America. [*Der abenteuerliche Simplicissimus Teutsch*, 1668.]

Gröger, Claus (1990) "Papier—Vom Aufstieg des Handgeschöpften zum unentbehrlichen Massenprodukt." In *Internationales Archiv für Sozialgeschichte der deutschen Literatur*, Vol. 15, pp. 184–206.

Groth, Otto (1928) *Die Zeitung. Ein System der Zeitungskunde*. Vol. 1. Mannheim: J. Bensheimer.

Grove, Lee E. (1966) "John Murray and Paper Deterioration." In *Libri. International Library Review and IFLA-Communications-FIAB*, Vol. 16, No. 3, pp. 194–204.

Gruendler, Beatrice, and Michael Marx (2011) "Papyrus-Pergament-Papier. Über den medialen Wandel der arabischen Buchkultur." Lecture at the Wissenschaftskolleg zu Berlin.

Günther, Johannes, and Otto August Schulz (1856) *Handbuch für Autographensammler*. Leipzig: Verlag von Otto August Schulz.

Heesen, Anke te (2006) *Der Zeitungsausschnitt. Ein Papierobjekt der Moderne*. Frankfurt am Main: Fischer Verlag.

Hentschel, Uwe (2010) "Faszinosum Handschrift oder: Warum Goethe Autographen sammelte." In Remmel, Andreas, and Paul Remmel (eds.), *Liber Amicorum. Katharina Mommsen zum 85. Geburtstag*. Bonn: Bernstein Verlag, pp. 185–199.

Hoffmann, Detlef (1973) *The Playing Card: An Illustrated History*. Translated by Christopher Salt. Leipzig: Edition Leipzig. [*Die Welt der Spielkarte. Eine Kulturgeschichte*, 1972.]

Hofmannsthal, Hugo von (2009 [1908]) Introduction to the new Balzac edition. *Sämtliche Werke XXXIII. Reden und Aufsätze 2*. Edited by Konrad Heumann and Ellen Ritter. Frankfurt am Main: S. Fischer Verlag, pp. 166–178.

How, James (2003) *Epistolary Spaces: English Letter Writing from the Foundation of the Post Office to Richardson's Clarissa*. Aldershot: Ashgate.

Hoyer, Fritz (1941) *Einführung in die Papierkunde*. Leipzig: Karl Hiersemann Verlag.

Hunter, Dard (1978) *Papermaking. The History and Technique of an Ancient Craft*. New York: Dover Publications.

Ince, D.C. (ed.) (1992) *The Collected Works of A. M. Turing: Mechanical Intelligence*. Amsterdam: North Holland.

Innis, Harold A. (1997) *Kreuzwege der Kommunikation. Ausgewählte Texte.* Edited by Karlheinz Barck, translated by Friederike von Schwerin-High. New York: Springer.

Innis, Harold A. (1999) *The Bias of Communication.* Toronto: University of Toronto Press.

Innis, Harold A. (2007) *Empire and Communications.* Toronto: Dundurn Press.

Innis, Harold A. (2011) "The Coming of Paper." In *Intermédialités: historie et théorie des arts, des lettres et des techniques / Intermediality: History and Theory of the Arts, Literature and Technologies,* No. 17, pp. 232–255.

Irwin, Robert (2004) *The Arabian Nights. A Companion.* London: Tauris Parke Paperbacks.

James, Henry (2003) *Die Aspern-Schriften.* Translated from English into German and with an afterword by Bettina Blumenberg. Munich: dtv. [*The Aspern Papers,* 1888.]

Jean Paul [pseudonym of Johann Paul Friedrich Richter] (1975) *Werke in zwölf Bänden.* Edited by Norbert Miller, with an afterword by Walter Höllerer. Munich: Hanser Verlag.

Jean Paul (2002) " 'Schreiben Abzeichnen Eingraben'—Aus den unveröffentlichten Exzerptheften (1782–1800)." In *Jahrbuch der Jean-Paul-Gesellschaft* 37, pp. 2–13.

Jean Paul (2004) *Lebenserschreibung. Veröffentlichte und nachgelassene autobiographische Schriften.* Edited by Helmut Pfotenhauer. Munich: Hanser Verlag.

Jean Paul (2012) *Exzerpte.* Digital edition, published online by the Universität Würzburg, Arbeitsstelle Jean-Paul-Edition. [http://www.jp-exzerpte.uni-wuerzburg.de, accessed December 9, 2013; from a fascicle of 1787–88.]

Jessing, Benedikt (2009) "Doppelte Buchführung und literarisches Erzählen in der frühen Neuzeit." In Judith Klinger and Gerhard Wolf (eds.), *Gedächtnis und kultureller Wandel. Erinnerndes Schreiben—Perspektiven und Kontroversen.* Tübingen: Max Niemeyer, pp. 187–200.

Joost, Ulrich (1984) *Der Briefwechsel zwischen Johann Christian Dieterich und Ludwig Christian Lichtenberg.* Göttingen: Vandenhoeck & Ruprecht.

Joost, Ulrich (1990) *Lichtenberg—der Briefschreiber.* Göttingen: Wallstein Verlag.

Joyce, James (2010) *Ulysses.* Ware: Wordsworth Editions Limited.

Justi, Johann Heinrich Gottlieb von (1762) *Schauplatz der Künste und Handwerke, oder vollständige Beschreibung derselben, verfertiget oder gebilligt von denen Herren der Academie der Wissenschaften zu Paris.* Berlin.

Karabacek, Joseph von (1887) *Das arabische Papier. Eine historisch-antiquarische Untersuchung. Sonderabdruck aus dem II. und III. Bande der "Mittheilungen aus der Sammlung der Papyrus Erzherzog Rainer."* Vienna: Verlag der kaiserlich-königlichen Hof- und Staatsdruckerei, pp. 87–178.

Karabacek, Joseph von (1888) *Neue Quellen zur Papiergeschichte. Mittheilungen aus der Sammlung der Papyrus Erzherzog Rainer.* Vol. 4. Vienna: Verlag der kaiserlich-königlichen Hof- und Staatsdruckerei.

Karabacek, Joseph von (1894) *Papyrus Erzherzog Rainer. Führer durch die Ausstellung.* Vienna: A. Hölder.

Karabacek, Joseph von (2001) *Arab Paper.* Translated by Don Baker and Suzy Dittmar. London: Archetype Publications.

Keymer, Thomas (2002) *Sterne, the Moderns, and the Novel*. Oxford: Oxford University Press.

Keymer, Thomas (2006) *Laurence Sterne's* Tristram Shandy. *A Casebook*. Oxford: Oxford University Press.

Keymer, Thomas, and Peter Sabor (2005) Pamela *in the Marketplace: Literary Controversy and Print Culture in Eighteenth-Century Britain and Ireland*. Cambridge: Cambridge University Press.

Kittler, Friedrich A. (1999) *Gramophone, Film, Typewriter*. Translated by Geoffrey Winthrop-Young and Michael Wutz. Stanford: Stanford University Press. [*Grammophon Film Typewriter*, 1986.]

Kline, Michael B. (1963) *Rabelais and the Age of Printing*. Geneva: Droz.

Köpnick, Lutz (1992) "Goethes Ikonisierung der Poesie. Zur Schriftmagie des West-Östlichen Divans." In *Deutsche Vierteljahresschrift für Literaturwissenschaft und Geistesgeschichte*, Vol. 66, pp. 361–389.

Kopp-Oberstebrink, Herbert (2010) "'Archive für Literatur!' Wilhelm Dilthey und die Anfänge der Literaturarchiv-Gesellschaft in Berlin." In *Trajekte*, Vol. 10, No. 20, Berlin, pp. 37–45.

Krajewski, Markus (2011) *Paper Machines: About Cards & Catalogs, 1548–1912*. Translated by Peter Krapp. Cambridge, MA: MIT Press. [*Zettel Wirtschaft. Die Geburt der Kartei aus dem Geiste der Bibliothek*, 2002.]

Kraus, Karl (1978) *Die letzten Tage der Menschheit. Teil 1*. Munich: dtv.

Kremer, Alfred von (1920) *The Orient under the Caliphs*. Translated by Salahuddin Khuda Bukhsh. Calcutta: University of Calcutta. [*Culturgeschichte des Orients unter den Chalifen*, 1875–77.]

Kremer, Detlef (2007) "Groteske Polyphonie: Zur poetologischen Funktion der Kleinformen im *Simplicissimus Teutsch* am Beispiel der Schermesser-Episode." In *Simpliciana. Schriften der Grimmelshausen-Gesellschaft*, Vol. 29, pp. 89–99.

Küffner, Georg (ed.) (2007) *Von der Rolle des Papiers*. Munich: Deutsche Verlags-Anstalt.

Kügelgen, Wilhelm von (1870) *Bygone Days or, An Old Man's Reminiscences of His Youth*. Vol. 1. [Translator not named.] London: Chapman and Hall. [*Jugenderinnerungen eines alten Mannes*, 1870.]

Lalande, Joseph-Jerôme (1984 [1762]) *Die Kunst Papier zu machen*. Translated by Heinrich Gottlob von Justi, edited by Alfred Bruns. Münster: Landschaftsverband Westfalen-Lippe. [*Art de faire de la papier*, 1761.]

Landfester, Ulrike (2009) "Schöner lesen. Buch und Gestalt." In Dora, Cornel (ed.), *Buchgestaltung: Ein interdisziplinäres Forum*. Wiesbaden: Harrassowitz, pp. 11- 23.

Lebrave, Jean-Louis, and Almuth Grésillon (eds.) (2000) *Écrire aux XVIIe et XVIIIe siècles. Genèses de textes littéraires et philosophiques*. Paris: CNRS Éditions.

Leonard, Eugenie Andruss (1950) "Paper as a Critical Commodity during the American Revolution." In *The Pennsylvania Magazine of History and Biography*, Vol. 74, No. 4, pp. 488–499.

Le Ray, Eric (2004) *Un des fondateurs de la presse moderne: Hippolyte Auguste Marinoni (1823–1904), entrepreneur, innovateur, constructeur de machines à imprimer, patron de presse et homme d'influence*. Paris: Ecole pratique des hautes etudes.

Lessing, Gotthold Ephraim (1989) *Werke und Briefe, Band 8: Werke 1774–1778.* Edited by Arno Schilson. Frankfurt am Main: Deutscher Klassiker-Verlag.

Lessing, Gotthold Ephraim (1994) *Briefe von und an Lessing 1776–1781.* Edited by Helmuth Kiesel. Frankfurt am Main: Deutscher Klassiker Verlag.

Levine, Michael (1998) "Screenwriting: William Gaddis' JR." *Journal of Narrative Techniques*, Vol. 28, No. 1.

Lichtenberg, Georg Christoph (1966) *Lichtenberg's Commentaries on Hogarth's Engravings.* Translated by Innes and Gustav Herdan. London: Cresset Press.

Lichtenberg, Georg Christoph (1968) *Schriften und Briefe.* Edited by Wolfgang Promies. Munich: Hanser Verlag.

Lichtenberg, Georg Christoph (1990) *Briefwechsel. Band III (1785–1792).* Munich: C.H. Beck.

Lichtenberg, Georg Christoph (2000) *The Waste Books.* Translated by Reginald John Hollingdale. New York: New York Review of Books. [*Sudelbücher*, 1765–99.]

Locke, John (1975 [1689]) *An Essay Concerning Human Understanding.* Edited by Peter Nidditch. Oxford: Oxford University Press.

Loveday, Helen (2001) *Islamic Paper. A Study of the Ancient Craft.* London: Archetype Publications.

Ludovico, Alessandro (2012) *Post-digital Print: The Mutation of Publishing Since 1894.* Eindhoven: Onomatopee.

Luhmann, Niklas (1995) *Gesellschaftsstruktur und Semantik. Studien zur Wissenschaftssoziologie der modernen Gesellschaft.* Vol. 4. Frankfurt am Main: Suhrkamp.

Mann, Heinrich (1921) *The Patrioteer.* Translated by Ernest Boyd. New York: Harcourt, Brace and Company. [*Der Untertan*, 1914.]

Mann, Heinrich (1980) *Briefe an Ludwig Ewers. 1889–1913.* Berlin: Aufbau-Verlag.

Martin, Henri-Jean (1994) *The History and Power of Writing.* Translated by Lydia G. Cochrane. Chicago: University of Chicago Press. [*L'histoire et pouvoirs de l'écrit*, 1988.]

Marx, Karl (1990) *Capital: A Critique of Political Economy.* Vol. 1. Translated by Ben Fowkes. London: Penguin Books. [*Das Kapital*, 1867.]

Marx, Leo (1964) *The Machine in the Garden: Technology and the Pastoral Ideal in America.* Oxford: Oxford University Press.

Marzolph, Ulrich (ed.) (2006) *The Arabian Nights Reader.* Detroit: Wayne State University Press.

Maxwell, Richard (1992) *The Mysteries of Paris and London.* Charlottesville: University of Virginia Press.

Mayhew, Henry (2008 [1851]) *London Labour and the London Poor.* A Selection by Rosemary O'Day and David Englander. Ware: Wordsworth Editions Limited.

McGann, Jerome (1993) *Black Riders: The Visible Language of Modernism.* Princeton: Princeton University Press.

McGaw, Judith (1987) *Most Wonderful Machine: Mechanization and Social Change in Berkshire Paper Making, 1801–1885.* Princeton: Princeton University Press, pp. 47 and 339.

McLaughlin, Kevin (2005) *Paperwork: Fiction and Mass Mediacy in the Paper Age.* Philadelphia: University of Pennsylvania Press.

McLuhan, Marshall (1954) "Joyce, Mallarmé, and the Press." In *The Sewanee Review*, Vol. 62, No. 1, pp. 38–55.

McLuhan, Marshall (1962) *The Gutenberg Galaxy: The Making of Typographic Man*. Toronto: University of Toronto Press.

McLuhan, Marshall (2001) *Understanding Media: The Extensions of Man*. London: Routledge.

McLuhan, Marshall (2002 [1951]) *The Mechanical Bride: Folklore of Industrial Man*. Berkeley: Gingko Press.

Melville, Herman (1987) *The Piazza Tales and Other Prose Pieces, 1839–1860*. Evanston, IL: Northwestern University Press.

Melville, Herman (2002 [1851]) *Moby Dick*. Ware: Wordsworth Editions Limited.

Melville, Herman (2009) *Billy Budd, Sailor and Selected Tales*. Oxford: Oxford University Press.

Mentzel-Reuters, Arno (2010) "Das Nebeneinander von Handschrift und Buchdruck im 15. und 16. Jahrhundert." In Ursula Rautenberg (ed.), *Buchwissenschaft in Deutschland. Ein Handbuch*. Volume 1. Berlin/New York: Walter de Gruyter, pp. 411–442.

Mercier, Louis-Sébastien (1994a) *Tableau de Paris. 1781–1788*. Edited by Jean-Claude Bonnet. 2 volumes. Paris: Mercure de France.

Mercier, Louis-Sébastien (1994b) *Le Nouveau Paris. 1799*. Edited by Jean-Claude Bonnet. Paris: Mercure de France.

Merck, Johann Heinrich (2007) *Briefwechsel*. Edited by Ulrike Leuschner in cooperation with Julia Bohnengel, Yvonne Hoffmann, and Amélie Krebs. Five volumes. Göttingen: Wallstein Verlag.

Metken, Sigrid (1978) *Geschnittenes Papier. Eine Geschichte des Ausschneidens in Europa von 1500 bis heute*. Munich: Callwey.

Meyer, Hans-Friedrich (1967) "Zeitungspreise in Deutschland im 19. Jahrhundert und ihre gesellschaftliche Bedeutung." Inaugural dissertation. Münster: Institut für Publizistik der Universität Münster.

Meynen, Gloria (2003) "Routen und Routinen." In Siegert, Bernhard, and Joseph Vogl (eds.), *Europa: Kultur der Sekretäre*. Zurich: diaphanes, pp. 195–219.

Middell, Katharina (2002) *Die Bertuchs müssen doch in dieser Welt überall Glück haben. Der Verleger Friedrich Justin Bertuch und sein Landes-Industrie-Comptoir um 1800*. Leipzig: Leipziger Universitäts-Verlag.

Miller, Matt (2010) *Collage of Myself: Walt Whitman and the Making of Leaves of Grass*. Lincoln, NE: University of Nebraska Press.

Moritz, Karl Philipp (1926) *Anton Reiser: A Psychological Novel*. Translated by Percy Ewing Matheson. Oxford: Oxford University Press. [*Anton Reiser: Ein psychologischer Roman*, 1785–90.]

Müller, Jan-Dirk (1994) "The Body of the Book: The Media Transition from Manuscript to Print." In Gumbrecht, Hans Ulrich, and K. Ludwig Pfeiffer (eds.), *Materialities of Communication*. Translated by William Whobrey. Stanford: Stanford University Press, pp. 32–44.

Müller, Lothar (1991) "Herzblut und Maskenspiel. Über die empfindsame Seele, den Briefroman und das Papier." In Jüttemann, Gerd, Michael Sonntag, and Christoph Wulf (eds.), *Die Seele. Ihre Geschichte im Abendland*. Weinheim: Psychologie Verlags Union, pp. 267–292.

Müller, Lothar (2006) " 'Don Quijote im Sortenlager.' Der Pakt des Archivs mit dem Papier." Essay. In: Marbachkatalog.

Müller, Lothar (2011a) "Das Ungedruckte autorisieren. Wie die Wahrheit zu Papier kommt." In *Zeitschrift für Ideengeschichte*, Vol. 4, pp. 14–22.

Müller, Lothar (2011b) "L'imprimé et le non-imprimé: Théorie des médias et poétique du papier." In *Intermédialités: histoire et théorie des arts, des lettres et des techniques / Intermediality: History and Theory of the Arts, Literature and Technologies*, No. 17, pp. 19–29.

Münkner, Jörn (2009) "Handgreifliches—Flugblätter bewegen ihre Betrachter." In Brückner, Wolfgang (ed.), *Arbeitskreis Bild Druck Papier. Tagungsband Hagenow 2008*. Münster: Waxmann, pp. 45–55.

Murray, John (1829) *Practical Remarks on Modern Paper, with an Introductory Account of Its Former Substitutes*. Edinburgh: William Blackwood.

Muser, Gerhard (1918) *Statistische Untersuchung über die Zeitungen Deutschlands 1885–1914*. Leipzig: Emmanuel Reinicke.

Neddermeyer, Uwe (1998) *Von der Handschrift zum gedruckten Buch. Schriftlichkeit und Leseinteresse im Mittelalter und in der frühen Neuzeit. Quantitative und qualitative Aspekte*. Volume 1: *Text*. Wiesbaden: Harrassowitz.

Needham, Paul (1994) "Res papirea: Sizes and Formats of the Late Medieval Book." In Rück, Peter (ed.), *Rationalisierung der Buchherstellung im Mittelalter und in der frühen Neuzeit*. Marburg: Philipps-Universität Marburg/Institut für Historische Hilfswissenschaften, pp. 123–145.

Neumann, Gerhard, and Günter Oesterle (eds.) (1999) *Bild und Schrift in der Romantik*. Würzburg: Königshausen & Neumann.

Nicholson, Colin (1994) *Writing and the Rise of Finance. Capital Satires of the Early Eighteenth Century*. Cambridge: Cambridge University Press.

Oligmüller, Johannes Georg (1997) *Papierzeit*. Exhibition catalog. Essen: Klartext-Verlag.

Palmer, Michael B. (1983) *Des petits journaux aux grands agences*. Paris: Aubier.

Parshall, Peter, and Rainer Schoch (eds.) (2005) *Die Anfänge der europäischen Druckgraphik. Holzschnitte des 15. Jahrhunderts und ihr Gebrauch*. Nuremberg: Germanisches Nationalmuseum.

Patze, Hans (1970) "Neue Typen des Geschäftsschriftgutes im 14. Jahrhundert." In Patze, Hans (ed.), *Der deutsche Territorialstaat im 14. Jahrhundert*. Sigmaringen: Jan Thorbecke, pp. 9–64.

Payen, Anselme (1867) "Über die Structur und die chemische Constitution der Holzfaser." In *Polytechnisches Journal*, Vol. 185, pp. 308–315.

Pedersen, Johannes (1984) *The Arabic Book*. Translated by Geoffrey French. Princeton: Princeton University Press. [*Den Arabiske Bog*, 1946.]

Pepys, Samuel (2010) *The Diary of Samuel Pepys*. Eleven volumes. Edited by Robert Latham and William Matthews. London: HarperCollins.

Peri, Giovanni Domenico (1707) *Il Negotiante*. Three volumes. Venice: Giovanni Giacomo Hertz.

Pieske, Christa (1983) *Das ABC des Luxuspapiers. Herstellung, Verarbeitung und Gebrauch 1860 bis 1930*. Berlin: Dietrich Reimer Verlag.

Plachta, Bodo (1997) *Editionswissenschaft. Eine Einführung in Methode und Praxis der Edition neuerer Texte*. Stuttgart: Reclam.

Pliny the Elder (1991) *Natural History: A Selection*. Translated by John F. Healy. London: Penguin Books. [*Naturalis Historia*, 77–79 AD.]

Price, Steven R. (2001) "The Autograph Manuscript in Print: Samuel Richardson's Type Font Manipulation in *Clarissa*." In Benton Megan L., and Paul C. Gutjahr (eds.), *Illuminating Letters: Typography and Literary Interpretation*. Amherst: University of Massachusetts Press, pp. 117–136.

Proust, Marcel (2003) *In Search of Lost Time*. Vol. 1: *Swann's Way*. Translated by C.K. Scott Moncrieff and Terence Kilmartin. New York: Random House. [*À la recherché du temps perdu*, 1913–27.]

Rabelais, François (2006) *Gargantua and Pantagruel*. Translated by Michael A. Screech. London: Penguin Books. [*La vie de Gargantua et de Pantagruel*, 1532–64.]

Ramazzini, Bernardino (1705) *A Treatise of the Diseases of Tradesmen*. Translator not named. London: Andrew Bell [*De Morbis Artificum Diatriba*, 1700.]

Rautenberg, Ursula (ed.) (2003) *Buch und Bibliothek als Wissensräume in der frühen Neuzeit. Symposion des Wolfenbütteler Arbeitskreises fuer Bibliotheks-, Buch- und Mediengeschichte*. Wiesbaden.

Reichert, Ramón (2009) *Das Wissen der Börse. Medien und Praktiken des Finanzmarktes*. Bielefeld: Transcript Verlag.

Renker, Armin (1950) *Das Buch vom Papier*. Wiesbaden: Insel-Verlag.

Requate, Jörg (ed.) (2009) *Das 19. Jahrhundert als Mediengesellschaft*. Munich: Oldenbourg Verlag.

Richardson, Samuel (1985 [1747–8]) *Clarissa, or, The History of a Young Lady*. London: Penguin.

Richter, Jean Paul Friedrich (2000) *Ideen-Gewimmel. Texte und Aufzeichnungen aus dem unveröffentlichten Nachlaß*. Edited by Thomas Wirtz and Kurt Wölfel. Munich: dtv.

Rittaud, Benoît (2006) *Le fabuleux destin de $\sqrt{2}$*. Paris: Le Pommier.

Rommel, Bettina (1997) *Rabelais zwischen Mündlichkeit und Schriftlichkeit*. Tübingen: Niemeyer.

Rosenband, Leonard N. (1997) "Jean-Baptiste Réveillon: A Man on the Make in Old Regime France." In *French Historical Studies*, Vol. 20, No. 3, pp. 481–510.

Rosenband, Leonard N. (2000a) "The Competitive Cosmopolitanism of an Old Regime Craft." In *French Historical Studies*, Vol. 23, No. 3, pp. 455–476.

Rosenband, Leonard N. (2000b) *Papermaking in Eighteenth-Century France: Management, Labor, and Revolution at the Mongolfier Mill, 1761–1805*. Baltimore: Johns Hopkins University Press.

Rosenband, Leonard N. (2004) "Comparing Combination Acts: French and English Papermaking in the Age of Revolution." In *Social History*, Vol. 29, No. 2, pp. 165–185.

Rosenfeld, Hellmut (1990) "Wann und wo wurde die Holzschnittkunst erfunden? Papier-Zugänglichkeit, Zeugdruck-Kenntnis und Kartenspiel-Invasion als Voraussetzungen." In *Archiv für Geschichte des Buchwesens*, Volume 34, pp. 327–342.

Rouse, Richard H., and Mary A. Rouse (1994) "The Dissemination of Texts in Pecia at Bologna and Paris." In Rück, Peter (ed.), *Rationalisierung der Buchherstellung im Mittelalter und in der frühen Neuzeit*. Marburg: Institut für Historische Hilfswissenschaften, pp. 69–77.

Rudin, Bo (1990) *Making Paper. A Look into the History of an Ancient Craft.* Translated by Roger G. Tanner. Vällingby, Sweden: Rudins, p. 127.

Salmon, Richard (1997) *Henry James and the Culture of Publicity.* Cambridge: Cambridge University Press.

Sandermann, Wilhelm (1988) *Die Kulturgeschichte des Papiers.* Berlin: Springer Verlag.

Saulnier, V.L. (1956) "L'Énigme du Pantagruelion ou: Du tiers au Quart livre." In *Études Rabelaisienne.* Volume 1. Geneva.

Scherer, Jacques (1957) *Le 'livre' de Mallarmé.* Paris: Gallimard.

Schlaffer, Hannelore (1986) *Die Scherenschnitte der Luise Duttenhofer.* Frankfurt am Main: Insel-Verlag.

Schlieder, Wolfgang (1994) "Zur Erfindung des Holzschliffs durch Friedrich Gottlob Keller vor 150 Jahren." In *IPH*, Vol. 4, Issue 1, pp. 1–5.

Schmidt-Bachem, Heinz (2001) *Tüten, Beutel, Tragetaschen. Zur Geschichte der Papier, Pappe und Folien verarbeitenden Industrie in Deutschland.* Münster: Waxmann.

Schmidt-Bachem, Heinz (2011) *Aus Papier: Eine Kultur- und Wirtschaftsgeschichte der Papier verarbeitenden Industrie in Deutschland.* Berlin: De Gruyter.

Schmidt, Frieder (1993) "Tilghman, Mitscherlich und der Fall des Reichspatents 4179." In *Das Papier.* 47, pp. 192–199.

Schmidt, Frieder (1994a) *Von der Mühle zur Fabrik. Die Geschichte der Papierherstellung in der württembergischen und badischen Frühindustrialisierung.* Ubstadt-Weiher: Verlag Regionalkultur.

Schmidt, Frieder (1994b) "Papier. Zur Geschichte eines Materials, ohne das es keine Zeitung gäbe,." In Klaus Beyrer and Martin Dallmeier (eds.), *Als die Post noch Zeitung machte.* Giessen: Anabas, pp. 77–84

Schmidt, Frieder (2000) "Die internationale Papierversorgung der Buchproduktion im deutschsprachigen Gebiet vornehmlich während des 18. Jahrhunderts: in: *Paper History*, Vol. 10, Issue 1, pp. 2–24.

Schmitt, Carl (2008) *Gespräch über die Macht und den Zugang zum Machthaber.* Stuttgart: Klett-Cotta.

Schneider, Birgit (2007) *Textiles Prozessieren. Eine Mediengeschichte der Lochkartenweberei.* Berlin/Zurich: Diaphanes Verlag.

Scholem, Gershom (2012) *From Berlin to Jerusalem. Memories of my Youth.* Translated by Harry Zohn. Philadelphia: Paul Dry Books. [*Von Berlin nach Jerusalem. Jugenderinnerungen*, 1977.]

Schröder, Thomas (1995) *Die ersten Zeitungen. Textgestaltung und Nachrichtenauswahl.* Tübingen: Gunter Narr Verlag.

Schubert, Martin (ed.) (2010) *Materialität in der Editionswissenschaft.* Berlin/New York: De Gruyter.

Sedillot, René (1992) *Muscheln, Münzen und Papier. Die Geschichte des Geldes.* Translated by Lind Gränz. Frankfurt/New York: Campus. [*Histoire morale et immorale de la monnaie*, 1989.]

Selg, Anette, and Rainer Wieland (eds.) (2001) *Die Welt der Encyclopédie.* Translated from French into German by Holger Fock, Theodor Lücke, Eva Moldenhauer, and Sabine Müller. Frankfurt am Main: Eichborn Verlag.

Semper, Gottfried (2010) "Preliminary Remarks on Polychrome Architecture and Sculpture in Antiquity." In *The Four Elements of Architecture and Other Writings.* Translated by Harry Francis Mallgrave and Wolfgang Herrmann.

Cambridge: Cambridge University Press, pp. 45–73. [*Vorläufige Bemerkungen über die bemalte Architektur und Plastik bei den Alten*, 1834.]

Shavers, Rhona, and Joseph Tabbi (2007) *Paper Empire: William Gaddis and the World System*. Tuscaloosa: University of Alabama Press.

Sick, Birgit (2002) "Bücher-Vampyr und Schreibmensch. Jean Paul zum 175. Todestag. Jahresgabe für die Mitglieder der Jean-Paul-Gesellschaft," © Birgit Sick 2002, p. 17.

Siegert, Bernhard (1993) *Relais. Geschicke der Literatur als Epoche der Post 1751–1913*. Berlin: Brinkmann & Bose.

Siegert, Bernhard, and Joseph Vogl (eds.) (2003) *Europa: Kultur der Sekretäre*. Zurich/Berlin: diaphanes.

Sombart, Werner (1916) *Der moderne Kapitalismus*. Volume I: *Die vorkapitalistische Wirtschaft*. Munich and Leipzig: Duncker & Humblot.

Sporhan-Krempel, Lore (1952) *Ochsenkopf und Doppelturm. Die Geschichte der Papiermacherei in Ravensburg*. Stuttgart: Self-published.

Starobinski, Jean (1997) "Water-Wheels: The Factory on the River," translated from the French by Richard Pevear, in: *The Hudson Review*, Vol. 49, No. 4, pp. 553–568.

Stauffer, Andrew M. (2007) "Ruins of Paper: Dickens and the Necropolitan Library." In *Romanticism and Victorianism on the Net*, Number 47. [URL http://www.erudit.org/revue/ravon/2007/v/n47/016700ar.html accessed February 11, 2014.]

Sterne, Laurence (2006) *Leben und Ansichten von Tristram Shandy. Gentleman*. Translated into German and annotated by Michael Walter. Frankfurt am Main: Eichborn.

Sterne, Laurence (2009 [1759–67]) *The Life and Opinions of Tristram Shandy, Gentleman*. Edited by Ian Campbell Ross. Oxford: Oxford University Press.

Stifter, Adalbert (2006) *Die Mappe meines Urgroßvaters*. Stuttgart: Reclam.

Stigand, William (1875) *The Life, Work, and Opinions of Heinrich Heine*, Vol. 2. London: Longmans, Green, and Co.

Stöber, Rudolf (2005) *Deutsche Pressegeschichte: Von den Anfängen bis zur Gegenwart*. Constance: UVK Verlagsgesellschaft mbH.

Strauss, Botho (2009) *Vom Aufenthalt*. Munich: Hanser Verlag.

Strobel, Jochen (ed.) (2006) *Vom Verkehr mit Dichtern und Gespenstern. Figuren der Autorschaft in der Briefkultur*. Heidelberg: Universitätsverlag Winter, pp. 7–32.

Strobel, Jochen (2010) "Zur Ökonomie des Briefs—und ihren materialen Spuren." In Martin Schubert (ed.), *Materialität in der Editionswissenschaft*. Berlin/New York: Walter de Gruyter, pp. 63–78.

Stromer, Ulman (1990) *Püchel von mein geslecht und von abentewr*. Facsimile. Bonn: Verband Deutscher Papierfabriken.

Tammaro, Belinda (2006) "Die Papierherstellung im Spiegel der 'Encyclopédie'." In *Schweizer Papier-Historiker*, No. 84.

Theisohn, Philipp (2009) *Plagiat. Eine unoriginelle Literaturgeschichte*. Stuttgart: Kröner.

Tin, Louis-George (2000) "Qu'est-ce que le Pantagruelion?." In *Études Rabelaisiennes*, Vol. 39, pp. 125–135.

Trithemius, Johannes (1974) *In Praise of Scribes: De laude scriptorum*. Edited by Klaus Arnold, translated by Roland Behrendt. Lawrence, Kansas: Coronado Press. [*De laude scriptorum*, 1494.]

290 *Bibliography*

Tschichold, Jan (1991) "Printing Paper: White or Tinted?." In *The Form of the Book: Essays on the Morality of Good Design*. Translated by Hajo Hadeler. London: Lund Humphries, pp. 169–173. [*Ausgewählte Aufsätze über Fragen der Gestalt des Buches und der Typographie*, 1975.]

Tschichold, Jan (1998) *The New Typography: A Handbook for Modern Designers*. Translated by Ruari McLean. Berkeley: University of California Press. [*Die neue Typographie. Ein Handbuch für zeitgemäss Schaffende*, 1928.]

Tschudin, Peter F. (1997) "Die Symbiose von Druckern und Papiermachern in der Zeit des Frühdrucks." In *International Paper History*, Vol. 7, Issue 2, pp. 23–28.

Tschudin, Peter F. (2002) *Grundzüge der Papiergeschichte*. Stuttgart: Hiersemann.

Unverfehrt, Gerd, Liselotte Krausser, and Wulf Pförtner (eds.) (2001) *Die ganze Welt ist aus Papier. Graphiken und Objekte zu allen Gelegenheiten 1800–1930*. Göttingen: Vandenhoeck & Ruprecht.

Valéry, Paul (1963) "Politics of the Mind,." In *The Outlook for Intelligence*, edited by Jackson Mathews, translated by Denise Folliot and Jackson Mathews. New York: Harper & Row, pp. 89–113. [*La politique de l'esprit*, 1932.]

Valéry, Paul (1964) "The Conquest of Ubiquity." In *The Collected Works of Paul Valéry: Aesthetics*. Translated by Ralph Manheim. Princeton: Princeton University Press. [*La conquête de l'ubiquité*, 1928.]

Vismann, Cornelia (2008) *Files: Law and Media Technology*. Translated by Geoffrey Winthrop-Young. Stanford: Stanford University Press. [*Akten. Medientechnik und Recht*, 2000.]

Vogl, Joseph (2004) "1797—die Bank von England." In Barkhoff, Jürgen, Hartmut Böhme, and Jeanne Riou (eds.) *Netzwerke. Eine Kulturtechnik der Moderne*. Cologne: Böhlau Verlag, pp. 37–51.

Vogl, Joseph (2010) *Das Gespenst des Kapitals*. Zurich: diaphanes.

Voltaire (1786) "Ungedrucktes Schreiben des Herrn von Voltaire." In *Journal aller Journale*. 1786–1788. Vol. 4. Hamburg: Chaidron und Comp, pp. 170–173.

Watt, Ian (2000) *The Rise of the Novel: Studies in Defoe, Richardson and Fielding*. London: Pimlico.

Weber, Therese (2004) *Die Sprache des Papiers. Eine 2000-jährige Geschichte*. Bern: Haupt Verlag, p. 101.

Wegmann, Thomas (2011) "Wertpapiere und Zettelwirtschaften: Zur Poiesis und Mediologie gehandelter Drucksachen." In Drügh, Heinz, Christian Metz, and Björn Weyand (eds.) *Warenästhetik. Neue Perspektiven auf Konsum, Kultur und Kunst*. Berlin: Suhrkamp, pp. 296–327.

Weigel, Christoph (1977 [1698]) *Abbildung der Gemein-Nützlichen Haupt-Stände Von denen Regenten Und ihren So in Friedens- als Kriegs-Zeiten zugeordneten Bedienten an, biß auf alle Künstler und Handwercker*. Dortmund: Harenberg.

Weiss, Karl Theodor (1962) *Handbuch der Wasserzeichenkunde*. Leipzig: Fachbuchverlag.

Wells, Wyatt (2000) "Certificates and Computers: The Remaking of Wall Street, 1967–1971." In *The Business History Review*, Vol. 74, No. 2, pp. 193–235.

Wharton, Edith (1900) *The Touchstone*. New York: Charles Scribner's Sons.

Whitman, Walt (2009) *Grasblätter*. Translated into German by Jürgen Brocan. Munich: Hanser Verlag. [*Leaves of Grass*, 1855.]

Wienker-Piepho, Sabine (2000) *"Je gelehrter, desto verkehrter"? Volkskundlich-Kulturgeschichtliches zur Schriftbeherrschung.* Munster: Waxmann.

Wiesner, Julius (1886) *Mikroskopische Untersuchungen der Papiere von El-Faijûm. Mittheilungen aus der Sammlung der Papyrus Erzherzog Rainer.* Vol. 1. Vienna: Verlag der kaiserlich-königlichen Hof- und Staatsdruckerei.

Wilke, Jürgen (2004) "Die telegraphischen Depeschen des Wolff'schen telegraphischen Büros (WtB)." In *Publizistik*, Vol. 49, pp. 125–151.

Wirth, Uwe (2008) *Die Geburt des Autors aus dem Geist der Herausgeberfiktion. Editoriale Rahmung im Roman um 1800: Wieland, Goethe, Brentano, Jean Paul und E.T.A. Hoffmann.* Munich: Wilhelm Fink.

Zaar-Görgens, Maria (2004) *Champagne—Bar—Lothringen. Papierproduktion und Papierabsatz vom 14. bis zum Ende des 16. Jahrhunderts.* Trier: Porta Alba.

Zedler, Johann Heinrich (1731/54) *Großes vollständiges Universal-Lexicon aller Wissenschaften und Künste, welche bißhero durch menschlichen Verstand und Witz erfunden und verbessert worden.* Leipzig/Halle: Johann Heinrich Zedler.

Zischler, Hanns, and Sara Danius (2008) *Nase für Neuigkeiten. Vermischte Nachrichten von James Joyce.* Vienna: Zsolnay Verlag.

Zola, Émile (1900) "Francois Zola." In *L'Aurore*. January 23. Paris.

Image Credits

Index

Note: page numbers in *italic* refer to figures